Elizabeth I
in Film and Television

Elizabeth I
in Film and Television

A Study of the Major Portrayals

BETHANY LATHAM

McFarland & Company, Inc., Publishers
Jefferson, North Carolina, and London

Library of Congress Cataloguing-in-Publication Data

Latham, Bethany, 1979–
Elizabeth I in film and television : a study of the major
portrayals / Bethany Latham.
p.   cm.

ISBN 978-0-7864-3718-4
softcover : 50# alkaline paper ∞

1. Elizabeth I, Queen of England, 1533–1603 — In motion pictures.
2. Elizabeth I, Queen of England, 1533–1603 — On television.
3. Historical films — History and criticism.
I. Title.
PN1995.9.E42L38   2011   791.43'658 — dc22   2011005069

British Library cataloguing data are available

Front cover images: © 2010 Shutterstock; Dame Judi Dench
as Queen Elizabeth (© Miramax Home Entertainment).

Manufactured in the United States of America

*McFarland & Company, Inc., Publishers
Box 611, Jefferson, North Carolina 28640
www.mcfarlandpub.com*

To my parents,
who give so much and ask so little.

Table of Contents

Acknowledgments

I had this odd idea that I could watch a few films on Elizabeth I (something I'd be doing anyway since, as a student of history, she's always been a figure of intense interest to me) and then bash out a book in no time flat, holding eloquently forth on what I'd seen. It's not the most insane idea I've ever had, but I'd class it in the new heights of idiocy category. This book, as I'm hoping will be apparent lest all that hard work count for naught, ultimately required a great deal of time spent in research.

Fortunately, I wasn't alone in my quest — colleagues and friends were kind enough to help me. Some dug through distant library stacks for me or forwarded unsolicited bits and pieces my way, others did a little proofing and provided helpful hints here and there, one allowed me to plague her heart out with Interlibrary-Loan requests. For all the ways in which they helped me, I'd like to express my gratitude. Special thanks to Mary Bevis, Debra Deering-Barrett, John-Bauer Graham, Sarah Johnson, Carley Knight, Harry Nuttall, and all my colleagues at the Houston Cole Library.

Lastly, I acknowledge an overwhelming burden of gratitude to William Thornton, the tireless encourager, who, in addition to everything else, thought I could actually get a book out of this in the first place.

Preface

The research for this work and subsequent writing occurred over an approximately three-year period. During that time, not only were the 18 Elizabethan offerings included in this book examined, but also various other Tudor-related film and television (e.g., *The Private Life of Henry VIII, A Man for All Seasons, Anne of the Thousand Days, Lady Jane, The Other Boleyn Girl, The Tudors,* etc.). These additional offerings were viewed in order to develop an understanding of the popularity of the Tudor period with filmmakers, and also the overarching themes to be found in these period adaptations of notable Tudor lives.

With regard to the Elizabethan films examined in this book (with the exception of *The Virgin Queen* [1923], which is no longer extant), each film was viewed at least three times — once to garner a first impression, once to closely examine and annotate the film scene by scene, and a final time as an overview. Once this watching and re-watching had been done, screenplays were consulted where available, as well as the source material upon which these cinematic adaptations were based (e.g., Maxwell Anderson's plays, which formed the basis for the films *The Private Lives of Elizabeth and Essex* and *Mary of Scotland;* A.E.W. Mason's novel from which *Fire Over England* was adapted; Margaret Irwin's *Young Bess,* etc.).

In addition to my own thoughts and appraisals, I also consulted all major criticism and scholarly works that could be discovered with regard to these films and miniseries. The bibliography for this work is not intended to be an all-inclusive list of everything written about these films and miniseries; rather, it is an attempt to include, within reason, previous scholarship which could provide significant or original elucidation on these offerings. This scholarship takes many forms, from book chapters to scholarly articles in a variety of fields, but primarily from history, women's studies, and film studies. Due to the fact that a major element of the examination of these films was their impact on audience perception of Elizabeth and her times, popular, non-scholarly sources were also consulted. In addition to this, I read a great number of reviews, both contemporary to the films and with the modern benefit of hindsight, and have attempted to include at least a few contemporary reviewer comments for each film in order to provide a context for original audience reaction to these offerings.

My approach in analyzing these films has been to familiarize myself with the period in which they were made, as well as the historical period they purport to represent. In this way, they can be evaluated as to how they were shaped by current events, as well as how they fare with an eye to historicity for the Tudor period. Though it is the favorite of scholars, an adherence to historical truth is not the only criterion for evaluation utilized in this work — these offerings are also examined in terms of their value as entertainment, as well as expressions of cinematic art. In addition, each actress or actor portraying Elizabeth is considered, and these portrayals and films are compared with one another in order to illuminate recurring themes and document how they differ — the original elements each offering brings to the canon of film Elizabeths.

At their most fundamental, these films and miniseries are all representations of one woman, so a thorough understanding of that woman's life and character was essential to an informed examination of these offerings. This, necessarily, required consulting a number of historical and biographical sources about the Queen and her contemporaries, including the speeches and writings of Elizabeth herself. Accordingly, I read every biography of Elizabeth I, both popular and scholarly, that I could lay hands on. *Elizabeth I: Collected Works* was particularly enlightening since it provides a portrait of Elizabeth in her own words — it includes everything from Elizabeth's correspondence to translated prayers to her poetry. As this work neared completion, *Royal Portraits in Hollywood: Filming the Lives of Queens* by Elizabeth A. Ford and Deborah C. Mitchell was published, and this proved to be one of the most inclusive works, not with regard to depth, but in light of the sheer number of Elizabeth films it briefly examines in one of its chapters. Accordingly, it was a particularly valuable source for overview with regard to several of the offerings covered in this book.

Various article-length studies, essays, and book chapters have been produced which focus on a single film or briefly examine a handful of films relating to Queen Elizabeth I. However, no monograph has examined all major representations of Elizabeth I on film and in television miniseries. This work attempts to fill that gap and also to consolidate previous scholarship on Elizabethan film studies into a single work. Representations of Elizabeth I in film and television are so numerous that it would take several volumes to include each one and provide sufficient coverage for it. Thus, this volume focuses on key English-language film and miniseries representations of Elizabeth I, the historical context of the period in which they were made, the extent of these portrayals, and how these representations have informed the characterization of Elizabeth I in film, as well as popular understanding of the historical woman.

CHAPTER 1

Why Elizabeth I?
A Look at the Life and Times
of the Historical Elizabeth

No English monarch has been portrayed in film more often than Queen Elizabeth I (1533–1603, reigned 1558–1603). There are at least a dozen feature films about her life, with yet another planned as a sequel to the last glittering historical film, *Elizabeth: The Golden Age*, starring Cate Blanchett, which was released in 2007. Elizabeth has been portrayed by some of the most celebrated actresses ever to appear on stage or screen — the divine Sarah Bernhardt and the immortal Bette Davis, amongst many others, have brought Gloriana to life. Add to the notable feature films a number of miniseries and television appearances, not to mention countless books, both novels and nonfiction, and the rabid popular interest in one of England's most famous monarchs is readily apparent. But what is it about this woman, this queen, which inspires such fascination? There are other monarchs, including female ones, who led equally absorbing lives, but they are not the subject of a bevy of film treatments and innumerable books. In short, why Elizabeth?

It's doubtful that there is one solitary reason which can be singled out as *the* cause of Elizabeth's lasting celebrity. Rather, Elizabeth's popular status is attributable to a number of factors which ultimately coalesced in her favor to ensure that her life was not only fascinating and enduring in the collective imagination, but also continually relevant. Elizabeth is famous for a reason: she was a unique personality and there was much of great significance that occurred during her lifetime; this, naturally, makes for interesting drama on the screen. Also integral to any drama are distinctive characters who provoke an emotional response, either positively or negatively, and with whom the audience can connect in some way — and audiences connect with Elizabeth. The persona of Elizabeth that has been popularized to the point of being familiar to the public at large is at once the quintessential Elizabeth and not Elizabeth at all. Some modern historians, as well as historical novelists, posit that the existence of absolute historical truth is a myth, espousing the view that each person views history and historical "fact" through the lens of his or her own subjective perception, a perception colored by personal and societal experiences. Whether the person is a modern filmmaker examining Elizabeth's behavior from a feminist viewpoint or an Elizabethan courtier writing about Elizabeth's "female fault" of indecisiveness, the perception is different, and the picture which emerges of Elizabeth differs accordingly. Views of Elizabeth as a queen, as a politician, and as a woman vary, and scholars, novelists, biographers, and especially filmmakers enjoy coming up with their own "version" of Elizabeth — choosing to portray her in a multitude of ways based on their own vision. Each film and television adaptation brings something new to the historical perception of Elizabeth, and each new actress who portrays her adds a fresh interpretation to the ever-expanding canon.

One of the most prominent features which makes Elizabeth attractive to filmmakers is her distinctive image. Elizabeth is more than merely a person or even a queen — she is a brand. Elizabeth's image — the red hair studded with jewels, the stark-white face makeup, the Elizabethan mode of dress — is one which inspires instant recognition and, depending on the viewer, can engender a variety of associations. The era named after her conjures all the glory of the Elizabethan Age, as well as the Golden Age of English literature — everything from William Shakespeare's plays to the flowering of English Protestantism is associated with Elizabeth. Like all branding, however, this is deceptive; some of Shakespeare's most famous works were first performed during the reign of Elizabeth's successor, King James I, and Elizabeth's reign was rife with religious unrest. However, as with modern political figures and so much else in life, it is not the fact but the *perception* that is key. As one author noted, "Perhaps the truth is that the persistence of Elizabeth's iconic status is a testament to the power of the myth, the extent to which we, historians and filmmakers, are still under her spell."[1]

Though the myth of Elizabeth did not end with the historical woman, it certainly began with her. During her lifetime, Elizabeth and her administration were careful curators of her image and the associations it conjured. Elizabeth was a masterful manipulator of the English people's public opinion, as well as what amounted to the mass media of her time; the result was such a triumph of image building and mythmaking that a fascination with her endures even today, more than 400 years after her death. As with any brand, a distinctive vision is essential, and Elizabeth turned situations and circumstances that would have been considered detrimental into assets for her image. Most sixteenth-century rulers and policymakers considered it political (and sometimes literal) suicide for a woman to attempt to rule alone without a male consort, but Elizabeth used this to her advantage. She pitted the male rulers of Europe against one another by dangling the prize of her hand in marriage (and England along with it) before them, for many years keeping any of them from forming a serious design against England. When it became obvious that Elizabeth would never have a consort, her failure to marry and resulting virginity would have been considered a definite setback for a queen whose duty was to produce legitimate heirs to succeed her on the throne, but Elizabeth put a positive spin on this as well by instituting the cult of Gloriana. Rather than portray her unmarried state as the result of her own desires (which would have been considered "unnatural"), Elizabeth presented it as a sacrifice she made for her kingdom, going so far as to tell Parliament that she would never take a husband prejudicial to its interests and that she was "married to England."

Thus, she transformed her image into that of the glorious virgin, worthy of veneration, who had sacrificed and saved herself for her one true love: her country.

The time period in which she lived also ensures that Elizabeth is a fashionable subject for filmmakers, as the Tudor epoch encapsulated a series of extraordinary events that makes for compelling period drama. As one author noted, the Tudor period allows filmmakers to delight "in the unrestrained passions of the early modern period rather than the genteel reserve of Austen's drawing-rooms or the bourgeois respectability of Forster's."[2] This attitude by filmmakers and screenwriters concerning the mores of Elizabeth's time, though not necessarily an accurate perception of them or the future periods with which the Tudor era is compared, goes some length towards explaining why it is Elizabeth, rather than a monarch such as Queen Victoria, whose representation most often graces the screen. In addition to the perception of Elizabethan social mores as being less inhibited than later eras, there are also the actual historical events of the Tudor period which filmmakers can use for readymade dramatic plotlines. When Elizabeth ascended the throne in 1558, the England she ruled over had seen a sea change since the reign of her grandfather, Henry VII. Henry VII was not only the patriarch of the Tudor dynasty, but also, along with his wife, Elizabeth of York, the main impetus for the end of England's devastating War of the Roses. Elizabeth's father, Henry VIII, is famous (or perhaps infamous) enough in his own right to warrant multiple film and book treatments. Henry's divorce of both his wife, Catherine of Aragon, and the Roman Catholic Church, completely changed traditional alliances and the power dynamic of sixteenth-century Europe.

It is against this historical backdrop that Elizabeth was born and grew to adulthood, and her lineage is yet another factor that makes her attractive to filmmakers. Elizabeth is perhaps the principal personality of the Tudor era, but her family was peopled by a number of compelling historical personalities who figure largely into Elizabeth's story: her father, Henry VIII; her mother, Anne Boleyn; her sister, Mary; and her cousins, Mary, Queen of Scots and Lady Jane Grey, amongst others. These people, by turns commanding, dynamic, glorious, sexy, pitiful, and tragic, add gripping back-story to Elizabeth's life, which filmmakers are in an excellent position to exploit for dramatic effect. Filmmakers have been more than happy to take advantage of this opportunity without Elizabeth; the 2000s has seen a bevy of Tudor-related films and television focusing on her relatives.[3] As will be seen in later chapters on modern film adaptations of Elizabeth's life, filmmakers have a penchant for making the most of history (and, in the process, often rewriting it) in order to render it relevant to today's audiences. Take, for example, an article in *Time* magazine from 2007 entitled "When Royals Became Rock Stars" concerning Hollywood's engineering of a Tudor revival.[4] Of Henry VIII, it is observed, "Unlike the corpulent old Henry VIII many of us remember from our history textbooks, young Henry VIII lived a life that was positively high-def-TV-ready, one that could have spiced up 16th-century newsstands, had tabloid editors been around instead of Erasmus." The article goes on to describe the Tudor monarch as Hollywood's "hunk du jour" and "hubba hubba" Henry. As ridiculous as language like this may sound from a scholarly point of view, it reflects the appeal which Tudor monarchs and the period in which they lived holds for modern audiences, and how screenwriters skew their personalities and the events of their lives to keep them continually relevant. Screenwriter Michael Hirst, who also wrote the screenplay for *Elizabeth: The Golden Age*, about Elizabeth's middle years, had this to say about the period's appeal: "It was a sexy time. It was a dangerous time. You can't exaggerate the violence and the beauty." This statement is blatantly untrue; of course filmmakers can, and often do, exaggerate the violence and the beauty, as well as various other aspects of the Tudor era, for dramatic effect. The author of the article encapsulated the modern fascination with all things Tudor thus, "For audiences who like their history juicy, relatable and full of comforting moral certainties — which is to say pretty much everybody without a Ph.D — there may be no better subject."

In the case of the real Elizabeth, what is the historical fact behind this "juicy" history full of "moral certainties"? Elizabeth's childhood was a time of extreme positional instability for her, and her birth was an intense disappointment to both her parents, who had confidently expected the long-awaited male heir to the throne. Though there is evidence that she was treated well in her infancy, when her mother, Anne Boleyn, fell from favor, Elizabeth also shared in the disgrace. Filmmakers are not the only ones who enjoy psychoanalyzing the motives behind Elizabeth's actions — post–Freudian psychologists have had a heyday theorizing about the effect Anne Boleyn's execution, orchestrated as it was by Elizabeth's father, and Elizabeth's unstable childhood, would have had on the precocious little girl and the queen she was to become. But Elizabeth's uncertain status had only begun with her mother's death. During the short reign of Henry's long hoped for and elaborately welcomed heir, Edward, Elizabeth knew relative security. A Protestant like herself (though more radical) and sharing some of the same tutors, Edward had much in common with Elizabeth and they got along relatively well; affectionate letters from Elizabeth to her half-brother are extant. Edward, however, was not destined to live past his sixteenth year, leaving the country in turmoil after his death in 1553. A plot by the Duke of Northumberland to put his son, Guildford Dudley, and the Protestant Lady Jane Grey on the throne failed, leaving Elizabeth's Catholic half-sister, Mary (known to history as Bloody Mary for her persecution of Protestant Christians), as the undisputed Queen of England. This put Elizabeth's position again in jeopardy.

Scholars have examined Mary's reign and her relationship with Elizabeth in detail,[5] and for filmmakers, who often enjoy treating the subject of sibling rivalries, Elizabeth's relationship with Mary provides fodder for rivalry on a grand scale. These were not sisters trivially vying for the affections of a parent or a male love interest (though Mary's husband, Philip II of Spain, did tentatively seek Elizabeth's hand after Mary's death, if not before). Rather, these were sisters struggling for the rule of an entire nation. Accordingly, Elizabeth and Mary's relationship was a complicated one. On the one hand, each was the only close kin the other had and they were, after all, half-sisters. Both had experienced extreme uncertainty during their formative years, including being declared illegitimate, and both lived under the shadow of a father at once awe-inspiring and terrifying. In personality, theology, and viewpoint, however, the two were universes apart. When she came to the throne, Mary was already 37 years old, and she had been shaped for years by the anguish of having her mother waste away, abandoned, and seeing her own life pass her by. Biographers love to theorize, but whether Mary held her father responsible as the greater guilty party for Catherine of Aragon's abandonment and neglect as well as the fall of the "true religion" in England, or chose to direct most of her ire at "the great whore" Anne Boleyn, is uncertain. Though it would be a misleading oversimplification to state that, because Mary hated Anne Boleyn, she held her daughter responsible as well, there was an element of taint by association that Mary sometimes displayed towards Elizabeth. This was tempered by the fact that Mary had spent a good deal of time with Elizabeth when she was a child, and she had shown marked affection towards the little girl. Mary faced the agonizing conflict of reconciling her feelings about the child she had loved with the young woman that child had become — a woman whom Mary and her Catholic councilors viewed as a threat.

Mary's devotion to the Roman Catholic religion was both sincere and passionate, and while it might not be accurate to label her a fanatic, she was willing to go to extreme measures to reinstitute and safeguard Roman Catholicism in England because she truly believed she was preserving the immortal souls of her subjects. The irony that this preservation of soul came at the cost of burning their bodies alive seems to have been lost on her. It's sometimes difficult for modern film audiences to truly understand the fundamental role religion played in the lives of the sixteenth-century English, despite screenwriters' attempts to relate it to current religious conflict and fanaticism. Like today, it was a polarizing force, but because there was no separation of church and state and it was believed that rulers held their position by divine right, if one was vocal in differing religiously from the reigning monarch, it was akin to promoting treason. Elizabeth understood this, and had seen it graphically illustrated in the tragic fate of her cousin, Lady Jane Grey (who has had her own film treatments), which is why Elizabeth did her best to keep a low profile. Despite this, Elizabeth was a rallying point for English Protestants, so much so that it put her own life in danger. Mary even went so far as to imprison her in the Tower of London due to a rebellion led by Sir Thomas Wyatt on Elizabeth's behalf, if not with her knowledge. Elizabeth was later released, but the ill-fated Lady Jane and her husband paid for this Protestant uprising with their lives.

Mary, desperate to produce an heir, married the Catholic prince Philip of Spain. The xenophobic English, both Catholic and Protestant, feared being subject to Spain and bled dry to finance its wars and empire building. The marriage was extremely unpopular, and Philip, who had made a political alliance rather than an attempt at domestic felicity, soon returned to Spain, leaving Mary alone with her growing governmental difficulties. As it became increasingly apparent that there would be no heir, support for Elizabeth became more vocal, making her position with Mary more and more precarious. With Mary's death in 1558, however, Elizabeth finally came to the throne and into her own. She was 25 years old.

After spending so much of her life in fear and uncertainty, Elizabeth reveled in her newfound power and freedom. She loved to dance, ride, and play the game of courtly love. She was young, healthy, handsome, and fiercely intelligent, and the mood in England was one of jubilation and hope. Unlike her sister, Mary, Elizabeth had her political priorities in order, and it is easy to see in her subsequent behavior that she learned from her sister's mistakes, both political and personal. Elizabeth had inherited a kingdom that was nearly bankrupt, torn by religious strife, and at the mercy of the two world superpowers of the time, Spain and France. Elizabeth understood the power dynamics at play, and with the help of skillful councilors, she expertly manipulated them to England's advantage, transforming the isolated island nation into a powerful force. Elizabeth's tale is one of success, and filmmakers have always found it difficult to resist a story containing various setbacks and tragedies, but resolving into an eventual, in this case majestically happy ending — at least for England.

The multitude of significant events that happened in Elizabeth's life and history's interpretation of their effect has been the subject of numerous works of nonfiction;[6] it is not within the province of this work to scrutinize all these events in detail. There are, however, some events and personalities which, for various reasons, appear again and again in film adaptations of Elizabeth's life and, as such, warrant examination. When a novel is adapted for the screen, one of the first steps filmmakers and screenwriters take is to read and re-read the novel in order to extract events, characters, and settings to be included in the film. With the exception sometimes occasioned by the miniseries format, no film or television media provide enough screen time to cover every significant event in any given novel. Consequently, those attempting to adapt a book must pick and choose which events and characters merit inclusion, and which settings can be convincingly replicated within the constraints of time, technology, and budget. So it is when attempting to adapt a historical person's life, or pieces of it, for the screen. As popular Tudor biographer Alison Weir has stated, "The Elizabethan Age is a vast canvas, and there are so many aspects to Elizabeth and her reign that a writer's hardest task is choosing what to include and what to leave out."[7] Like writers, filmmakers must pick and choose which events and personalities in Elizabeth's life they consider important or dramatic enough to be included in their filmed fictional biography. Which events are chosen and how they are manipulated or, in some cases, completely rewritten, often depends on the filmmaker's particular vision not only of Elizabeth, but of the agenda of his or her film. Some films are produced with the sole motive of entertaining the audience and raking in box-office profits, but depending upon whom the filmmakers and producers believe the audience will be, different aspects of Elizabeth's times and personality are emphasized in order to provide the most appeal to this target demographic of viewers. Others seek to intentionally slant history in a certain way so that it appears more relevant to current events or to further a political or personal agenda. It's stating the obvious to note that movies are not documentaries; they are entertainment, and therefore, many filmmakers argue, should not be held to any rigorous standards of historicity. This parallels similar arguments regarding fidelity to source material made by those examining films adapted from novels. As one commentator put it, "For decades, the study of film adaptation has been troubled by questions of veracity. Too often, adaptation studies have merely compared films to their literary sources, a 'tiresome' endeavor ... that inevitably privileges the literary work over what comes to be seen as its inferior film derivation."[8] Novels, however, are a separate animal from the historical record; as works of fiction, fabrication, they are inherently "untrue." The historical record, by contrast, represents what is accepted as fact. As Robert Toplin notes in his preface to *History by Hollywood*, "Critics of historical movies have recognized that Hollywood's version of the past can make a significant impact on the viewers. Dramatic motion pictures that feature famous stars in the roles of historical characters and present vivid scenes of yesteryear through sophisticated cinematography can make strong impressions. Historical films help to shape the thinking of millions."[9] It would not be far off the mark to note that, in an age where television has entirely replaced reading as a pastime for many, especially in the younger demographic, films are sometimes the only version of "history" with which the viewer may be familiar. A filmmaker's interpretation of a historical period or person has great influence; most filmmakers realize this and use it to further their own particular vision of Elizabeth and her times. This causes great divergences in the way historical events in Elizabeth's life and Elizabeth's personality are portrayed in these films and miniseries, but it is interesting to note that, regardless of interpretation or slant, from this vast panorama, filmmakers usually choose to include roughly the same small group of events and people. The main events in Elizabeth's life which are most often dramatized are: Elizabeth's romantic relationships, her various marriage prospects and negotiations, the religious conflict and Elizabeth's treatment of it, court intrigues, the defeat of the Spanish Armada, and the executions of Mary, Queen of Scots and Robert Devereaux, Earl of Essex. It is instructive to examine these events with an eye to their historical sources to determine where the two diverge in film adaptations, and thus understand why filmmakers have chosen to interpret them as they do, and how this interpretation fits in temporal and cultural context.

As James Chapman noted in his essay on representations of Elizabeth in film, before making any examination of these offerings, it is important to distinguish between the "historical" drama and the "costume" drama. A historical drama is based on actual historical events and persons, whereas a costume drama has a historical setting, but its plotting and characters may be partly historical or entirely fictional. Of the film offerings covered in this book, some lean more towards one category than another, but as Chapman notes, Elizabethan films often "straddle the boundary between the historical film and the costume film: historical in the sense that they focus on an actual historical personage, but costume in the sense that they often include fictional elements within their narratives."[10]

Since Elizabeth is known as the Virgin Queen, it's unsurprising that the aspect of her virginity figures heavily in film adaptations, often even appearing in the films' titles. As Susan Doran noted in an essay examining why Elizabeth never married, "Elizabeth I's virginity has been her most famous attribute since the late sixteenth century. This is understandable, not least because her chastity was celebrated from the 1580s onwards in art, poetry, and drama."[11] Elizabeth's own reasoning behind why she chose not to marry will probably never be definitively established. Many psychological theories involving her father and the unenviable fate of the female figures in her life who did their "duty" and married (e.g., her mother, Anne Boleyn, and stepmothers Jane Seymour, Catherine Howard, and Catherine Parr) are often put forth. Some historians disagree with these psychological theories, instead positing that it was a deliberate decision Elizabeth made in order to retain her full power and authority rather than be forced to subordinate herself to a male consort. Still others speculate that Elizabeth did not look upon the married state with complete disfavor, and would have married had both she and her councilors, in addition to the suitor in question, been able to agree on the myriad aspects of policy and personal preference surrounding any one marriage suit — and Elizabeth had a significant number of suits during her long lifetime. Thus, it's not surprising that many of the film adaptations of her life focus on Elizabeth's romantic relationships. Different filmmakers tend to dramatize Elizabeth's romances in various ways; as will be seen, some adaptations, predominantly the more modern, revisionist offerings, regularly opt to portray Elizabeth's loves as physical rather than courtly and/or unconsummated, despite historical evidence to the contrary, in order to play up the "juicy" angle to the utmost. The one thing the adaptations do have in common is the identity of the male love interest in the relationship, and very seldom is it an officially sanctioned political suitor. Elizabeth's relationship with Robert Dudley, Earl of Leicester, is most often treated, and her May–December romance with Robert Devereaux, Earl of Essex, is another perennial favorite. Elizabeth's pubescent romantic relationship with Lord High Admiral Thomas Seymour has also appeared on screen, as has the relationship of Elizabeth and Sir Walter Raleigh, amongst other court favorites. The portrayal of these romantic relationships is often used to further a popular theme that appears in most, if not all, of the films about Elizabeth: the binary opposition of duty versus womanhood, public role versus private inclination (i.e., love for "unsuitable" suitors), and denial versus desire.[12]

Elizabeth's myriad marriage prospects and negotiations, from the aforementioned Lord High Admiral to the Duke of Anjou, have received more than their fair share of screen time, but they are often forced to share the limelight with the court intrigues they engendered. Court intrigue, whether motivated by these marriage prospects, religious conflict between Roman Catholics and Protestants, personal plays for power, or other reasons, often appear in film adaptations of Elizabeth's life. However, as will be seen in the later examination of these films and miniseries offerings, power, politics, and almost everything else takes a backseat to romantic drama — political machinations and power play are used as a backdrop to further interpersonal relationships, usually romantic ones, rather than being the focus themselves.

These interpersonal relationships, romantic and otherwise, involve a number of historical personages converted into characters, the most popular being Robert Dudley, Earl of Leicester; William Cecil, Lord Burghley; Sir Francis Walsingham; Sir Walter Raleigh; Lord High Admiral Thomas Seymour, and Robert Devereaux, Earl of Essex. As is readily apparent from this list, the focus is almost always on Elizabeth's relationships with males, either in their capacity as romantic interests or as councilors. Elizabeth's female interpersonal relationships are less apparent in adaptations. Though Elizabeth is often portrayed as surrounded by a bevy of ladies-in-waiting and female courtiers, with few exceptions, she is not truly interacting with them on any personal or emotional level; they serve more as set dressing or plot furtherance, often by having an affair with one of Elizabeth's romantic interests. The one female relationship that does receive significant screen time is that of Elizabeth and Mary, Queen of Scots. This is particularly notable since, in historical fact, Elizabeth and the Scottish Queen never met in person. For filmmakers concerned with historicity, the interaction must be portrayed through scenes where intermediaries relay information, or where correspondence is read in voice-over while the camera focuses on one of the women. For those less concerned with historical accuracy, dramatic face-to-face confrontations are often staged.

Filmmakers usually prefer to have a protagonist that is relatively attractive or, barring that, exceptional-looking in some way, and Elizabeth fits the bill in both cases. When she was young, Elizabeth was most probably handsome in appearance rather than beautiful, though naturally she was addressed as such by her courtiers, even when she was well past the age when she had ceased to be physically attractive. Elizabeth and her council strictly regulated the representation in portraiture of her royal person during her reign, and so the majority of the portraits of her that survive follow a stylized pattern. These portraits, of which there are a significant number extant, conveniently provide filmmakers and their make-up and wardrobe artists with detailed visual documentation from which to work. Whether these portraits depict what Elizabeth truly looked like is less certain, since it was traditional to portray her as eternally youthful and attractive according to the contemporary perception of beauty, and later in the reign, much of her portraiture was allegorical in nature, modeling her physical attributes after various symbolic figures (e.g., Diana, Cynthia, Phoebe). Portraits of her as a child and her coronation portrait, however, provide the viewer with a closer facsimile of her actual appearance. Scholars estimate her height to have been between 5'3" and 5'5", making her relatively tall for the time period in which she lived, and she kept herself in shape by dancing, riding, and other athletic pursuits. She has been described as having both a ruddy and a fair complexion, which in later years she enhanced by the use of lead-white face paint, which she may have also used to hide smallpox scars. Elizabeth's most readily recognizable feature was the Tudor red hair she inherited from her father, which was probably closest to a vibrant strawberry blond when she was young. In later years she adopted red wigs, curled, frizzed, and styled elaborately. This is not necessarily, as some assert, because she was bald; many noblewomen of the era wore wigs since it was easier than styling their own hair. It was also fashionable to pluck the hairline in order to provide the illusion of a high forehead. Much has been made of Elizabeth's vanity, and she considered her hands, which boasted long, slender fingers, to be her best feature; accordingly, she had them prominently displayed in her portraiture.

Along with these features, Elizabeth is easily recognizable by her mode of dress. Though she dressed in a relatively conservative manner when she was younger, as Elizabeth aged, her clothing, and by extension Elizabethan women's fashions in general, became more elaborate and ornate. Tudor fashions provide filmmakers and their costume designers (as well as the actors who have to actually wear them) with a challenge, but also with a multitude of fabulous costuming possibilities that appear to great advantage on screen. The popularity of visually stimulating historical dress has even given rise to what one reviewer dubbed a subgenre of royal costume drama: textile porn.[13] Elizabethan fashions, for both men and women, were involved, and made up of a number of garments and pieces. Since many of these pieces are not visible when the person is completely dressed, designers have a range of costuming options depending on how historically accurate and detailed they wish to be.

A woman's clothing began with her chemise, a tunic-like undergarment usually made of white linen, which could be simple or elaborately embroidered depending on the wearer's status. A woman wore knee-high stockings held up with simple garters, and could wear knee-length drawers for warmth. Over the chemise went multiple petticoats and the "pair of bodies" or corset. Elizabethan corsets did not sport the whalebone of later eras; they were usually made with caning, bundles of rushes, or stiffened buckram, though some surviving examples are also made of iron and leather. Waistlines were long and came to a v-point, and the Elizabethan woman also wore a cone-shaped farthingale, padding around the hips, a bum roll or, later in the era, a drum-shaped farthingale to shape the drape of the skirt, which fell to the floor at the beginning of the era and stopped near the ankles towards the end. Over all this, the Elizabethan woman would wear a gown, which could be made up of a number of pieces. Some had separate bodices and skirts (sometimes with a short train), others had a split skirt which allowed a decorative petticoat or "fore-part" to show through. Elizabethan women were either pinned or sewn into their dresses, or the different parts of the gown could be tied together with "points," weighted strings threaded through eyelets. Sleeves were often separate from bodices, and were tied or pinned on at the shoulder. Necklines came with or without lapels, and could be modest or very low cut, with low necklines usually being square-shaped. A partlet, an undergar-ment which covered from the neckline of the gown to a band gathered at the wearer's actual neck, could be worn for modesty, though Elizabeth seldom chose to adopt one and most at court followed suit. One of the most easily recognizable of all Elizabethan cos-tuming items, the starched ruff, was worn around the neck, often with matching wrist cuffs, and came in a variety of sizes and trims. Later in the period, the ruff flattened out and attached to the points of the collar, riding high in the back, often with an attached veil, which was wired to give it shape and could be floor length. There were a variety of styles for caps, hoods, and veils which women used to cover their hair. Hairstyles usually involved putting the hair up in a simple bun at the back which was covered with a cap or hood, and the front was either curled, frizzed, or pinned around "rats"—wads of hair, shaped roughly like a rat's body, which were used to provide shape and fullness. The aris-tocracy, Elizabeth included, would often wear jewels in their hair and on their headdresses, as well as on their gowns and persons. Elizabeth's wardrobe in later years was truly mon-umental, and though she possessed thousands of gowns in addition to a multitude of other items, very few of these survive.[14]

A man's clothing consisted of fewer pieces, beginning with an undershirt similar to a woman's chemise, but shorter. Over this he would wear a padded doublet, which, as with women's clothing, could be pinked or slashed to have a decorative under-layer pulled through. Men wore hose consisting of two parts: the upper hose, which could be knee-length, paned, and bell-shaped, and the nether hose, which are the modern equivalent of tights or stockings. The nether hose were usually held up by garters, which could be simple or very elaborate. The codpiece, so prominent during Henry VIII's reign, had generally fallen out of fashion by the Elizabethan era. Over all this, an Elizabethan man would wear a cloak and a hat, which came in a variety of styles. Hairstyles were relatively short, and the beard was almost universal. Male courtiers also wore garments and adorn-ments specifically related to their positions, such as Lord Burghley's distinctive bonnet and carcanet, both marks of his office. Aristocratic men, like women, often wore jewels—on their doublets, hats, and person.

Though these detailed costuming possibilities offered by the Tudor period provide much in the way of visual cues for the audience, an attractive tableau is usually not enough to make a film—filmmakers need at least some fodder from which to fashion a plot. One factor that the Elizabethan era offers in abundance for filmmakers, as well as historical novelists, in the way of plot device is court intrigue. Courtiers conspiring in dark hallways, machinations to bring about the favorite's fall from grace, assassination plots, jockeying for power and prestige — these elements of court life make for gripping cinema. Elizabeth's life and reign provide a multitude of opportunities for dramatizing such events. Even before Elizabeth came to the throne, there were schemes to overthrow her sister, Mary, such as the aforementioned Wyatt rebellion, which endangered Elizabeth's life and even landed her in the Tower. During Elizabeth's reign, there were various conspiracies, some painstakingly detailed and others almost laughably imbecilic. This has given rise to emphasizing one figure that often appears in film characterization and is currently a popular topic in Elizabethan nonfiction,[15] Elizabeth's "spymaster," Sir Francis Walsingham. Arguably the father of modern intelligence, though Walsingham served in a variety of positions during Elizabeth's reign, he is most noted for his espionage-related activities and the unveiling of plots against the Queen's life, such as the Ridolfi, Throckmorton, and Babington conspiracies. Despite the amount of historical documentation on the real Walsingham, filmmakers' representations run the gamut — portraying his role in administering Elizabeth's intelligence community as the embodiment of everything from fanatical religious conviction to extreme Machiavellian amorality. Regardless of the characterization, Walsingham's main purpose in films is usually to further plotlines by ferreting out conspiracies against his queen. The real plots these dramatizations represent revolved around different individuals at different levels of power, and sometimes resulted in the malefactor's execution. Filmmakers also have a penchant for dramatic death scenes, and the execution of major players, such as Mary, Queen of Scots, the Duke of Norfolk, the Earl of Essex, and others provide a number of options for impressive final exits. The impression this gives can be misleading, as Elizabeth was usually most reluctant to carry out sentences of death, and relatively few executions occurred during her reign, especially as compared with that of her father and sister.

While all these gorgeously costumed characters and their interplay of love and intrigue engage the viewer, Gloriana is the one the audience pays to see, and she wins the most points with filmmakers for sheer force of personality. The historical Elizabeth possessed a personality that was complicated and sometimes contradictory, but always compelling. She has been psychoanalyzed, examined, revised, and re-examined by psychologists and scholars of every ilk, and it is doubtful at this point that there will ever be a truly definitive psychological portrait accepted by all as the "real" Elizabeth. True to the red-headed stereotype, her character is often described as mercurial. She could respond to situations with detached logical reasoning in some cases and passionate emotional outbursts in others. She was adept at studied indecision, procrastination and avoidance, often using these tools until solutions to thorny problems presented themselves, or the problem went away of its own accord. She was also known to make important decisions, reconsider, and then immediately rescind them. This often drove her councilors insane with frustration, but in many cases, worked out to Elizabeth's advantage. Elizabeth displayed loyalty and touching compassion towards those she loved, but she could fragment or even shift responsibility for controversial decisions to the point of irrationally blaming and punishing others for her own actions. She was highly intelligent and erudite, as well as eloquent, gifts she used in equal measure to inspire loyalty and love or deliver a devastating tongue-lashing. Elizabeth is frequently her own screenwriter — her speeches were brilliant, and she was known for pithy outbursts and one-liners, especially when angry. This provides filmmakers with witty lines and convenient imagery all at the same time. For example, Elizabeth screaming with red-headed fury at Robert Dudley, "I will have here but one mistress and no master!" is a scene readymade for staging, with dynamic dialogue already included. Elizabeth had become such a powerful cultural symbol that her writings and speeches were already being freely adapted and transformed to meet current occasions as early as the mid–seventeenth century.[16] Modern filmmakers have followed suit, including in their dialogue not only quotes whose provenance can be traced to the historical Elizabeth, but also apocryphal statements attributed to her.

In her address, Elizabeth could be careful and courteous with those around her, but she was also known to spit and swear like a sailor. Though her emotions had weight and she often gave vent to them, unlike her misguided cousin Mary, Queen of Scots, Elizabeth seldom fell into the trap of letting her emotions completely overrule her intellect when important decisions hung in the balance. This invites comparison between Elizabeth and the aforementioned Mary, Queen of Scots, as well as Elizabeth's predecessor on the throne, Mary Tudor. Filmmakers find much dramatic fodder in contrasting characters and portraying rivalries, and Elizabeth provides a variety of opportunities for this. Filmmakers also like to pursue the angle of religion in films, either to promote it, contrast past morality with current social mores, or highlight the dangers of intolerance. Accordingly, the inclusion of brief glimpses of the reign of Elizabeth's sister, Mary Tudor, not only offers filmmakers a chance to portray sibling rivalry and contrast the two queens, but it also gives them powerful imagery they can use to convey the dangers of intolerance; they often take advantage of this to draw parallels with current world events or to contrast Elizabeth's stance on religion with Mary's. Though of strong religious conviction herself, Elizabeth was private about her faith, and wished to leave others to practice theirs in peace, thus her famous statement about having no desire "to make windows into men's souls." At the same time, she could blast clerics out of the water for pronouncing views from the pulpit with which she did not agree, even threatening them with the Tower.

Though she invites comparison with other contemporary queens, Elizabeth has a seemingly contradictory attribute that also makes excellent film fodder — she can be portrayed as a woman alone and apart. Obviously Elizabeth was not the first woman to rule, nor even the first queen to rule for a significant period without a male consort in a world controlled by men, but she was the most successful. The loneliness of the person in power is a topic often treated by filmmakers and, in Elizabeth's case, her femininity is an added attraction for those who espouse a postmodern feminist viewpoint. The motivation of appealing to politically concerned, feminist audience members has led modern filmmakers to highlight what they perceive as Elizabeth's lone struggle against her male-dominated world. Elizabeth herself might find this amusing, since she was fond of pointing out, not without some irony, that she was "but a weak and feeble woman," and often portrayed herself as being able to rule in spite of the weaknesses and vices occasioned by her femininity.

As can be seen, the answer to the question of why Elizabeth is such a popular subject for screen treatment is not a simple one, nor does it have a single, easy answer. It's a combination of several factors, among them her image; her virginity; her lineage; her varied romantic interests and marriage prospects; the conflicts, crises, and personality clashes of her reign and the intrigue this engendered; and the time period in which she lived, which evokes all the glory and "juiciness" of the Tudor and Elizabethan ages. But among all these factors, one shines forth — Elizabeth herself. At the heart of the drama and intrigue, the religious and political machinations, is one extraordinary woman who encapsulates a host of aspects which filmmakers and audiences find irresistible: ruler, virgin, scholar, religious leader, lover, cinematic icon ... Gloriana.

CHAPTER 2

The Silent Era:
Divas and Aristocrats

LES AMOURS DE LA REINE ÉLISABETH (1912)

Portrayals of Elizabeth in film date back almost as far as the origins of cinema itself, with her first onscreen appearance, in 1912's *Les Amours de la Reine Élisabeth,*[1] occurring while cinema was still in its infancy. In order to comprehend this film and the singular impact it had on the budding American film industry, it is important to understand the historical background against which *Les Amours* was produced. By the time *Les Amours* was made, rudimentary motion pictures in various forms had existed for approximately two decades; George Eastman's invention of celluloid roll film in 1888 led inventor Thomas Edison and others to attempt to apply this technology to zoopraxiscopes and kinetoscopes. These technologies were clumsy, however, and had to be accessed by looking into a box to view the strips of running film, limiting the number of people who could view the moving picture. When Edison and others took this technology a step further and combined it with projection devices, the moving picture available for viewing by a large audience was born. These moving pictures were shown not only in small nickelodeon theaters, but also at arcades, fairs, bazaars, and carnivals.[2]

The motion picture's popularity with the masses quickly skyrocketed, and short films were made portraying everything from a man sneezing to the beheading of Mary, Queen of Scots. Due to the type of venues in which motion pictures appeared and their sometimes sensational subject matter, they attracted the same type of audience as vaudeville — the working classes. The motion picture industry was profit-driven from the very beginning, and it was thought that the profit margin could be increased exponentially if a different (i.e., wealthier) clientele could be enticed to partake of the developing movie mania. Adolph Zukor, a Hungarian immigrant who was later to found the company which would become Paramount Pictures Corporation, felt that one method which could be employed to draw the social upper classes to moving pictures would be to produce "legitimate" films. In his view, these would be feature-length films starring respected actors/actresses of the stage, and their narrative plotlines would be similar to those familiar to theatergoers.

Unlike today when actors often cross the divide between stage and film, in the beginning of the twentieth century this was a novel concept, making Zukor's importation of the French film, *Les Amours de la Reine Élisabeth,* an entrepreneurial venture which involved some risk.[3]

Les Amours was the child of a French film school which had the stated intention of creating cinema that was both serious and artistic. Similarly to Zukor, though with a less capitalistic motivation, those interested in artistic cinema felt it would be imperative to employ not only important, respected actors and actresses, but also significant directors, playwrights, composers, and painters. The subject matter, unlike the short films produced for distribution to nickelodeons, would be substantive and edifying. The principal French film company which espoused this viewpoint was the Film d'Art, which produced its first film, *The Assassination of the Duke of Guise,* in 1908. Though leaps and bounds had been made in the nascent science of cinematography by directors such as Edwin S. Porter (e.g., *The Great Train Robbery* [1903]), the Film d'Art considered the stage play to be the artistic archetype which cinema should emulate, and therefore eschewed the innovative shots and blocking which were coming into common usage in favor of the traditional focus on the carefully staged "scene." Thus, while *The Assassination of the Duke of Guise* was praised by many for bringing the dignity of the theater to the new medium of film, at the same time, the motion pictures made by Film d'Art lost significant ground in the area of cinematography due to their artificially composed scenes, lack of editing, and painted drop-cloth sets.[4]

Les Amours certainly fits into this category; though some choose to view *Les Amours*'s photographed stage play composition as an artistic choice, with the benefit of hindsight most modern critics now agree that it represents an unfortunate regression in both cinematography and acting. In essence, it was already an anachronism by the time it was made. Charles Ford wrote of the film, "Although *Queen Elizabeth* had little enough to recommend it and deserves attention only because of its influence on the American motion picture industry, it provoked a veritable sensation when Adolph Zukor opened it at New York's Lyceum Theater in July of 1912."[5] Zukor was after status, not innovation, and *Les Amours* certainly had cachet. In the title role the film starred a highly respected French stage actress who was already a legend in her own time: Sarah Bernhardt (1844–1923), dubbed "the divine" by playwright and novelist Oscar Wilde. Wilde was only one of a multitude of famous men, from Russian tsars to the Prince of Wales, who knew (sometimes in the biblical sense, though obviously not in Wilde's case) and greatly admired Bernhardt. Bernhardt meticulously cultivated a distinct public persona, designed to be at once eccentric (she let it be known that she sometimes slept in a coffin) and enchanting. Her theatrical behavior and numerous high-profile affairs ensured her a reputation of being, in modern parlance, one of the first superdivas, a fitting personality for an actress who would portray Elizabeth. Along with the rest of the world, Americans of all stripes came to revere the divine Sarah. Mark Twain, with characteristic verve, remarked that there were five types of actresses: bad, fair, good, great—"and then there is Sarah Bernhardt."[6]

Though Bernhardt was not considered beautiful when measured against the ideal of her time (she was viewed as too thin and her hair was too unruly), this was no impediment whatsoever to her acting career. She more than made up for this perceived lack of beauty with her signature acting style and distinctive, musical voice. Dubbed "golden" by Victor Hugo, who had written plays specifically for Bernhardt, the divine's voice was considered to be one of her greatest theatrical assets. Bernhardt favored melodrama, which played to her acting strengths; she was an accomplished tragedienne who could play passionate love scenes and heartrending sorrow with equal fervor. Her distinctive acting style was considered to be less stylized and more truthful than that practiced by her contemporaries; however, this is relative as Victorian and Edwardian acting could be highly stylized, with formalized and overstated facial expressions and gesturing as the norm. Bernhardt's signature style was considered to be so important that she authored a book about her life and, in particular, acting and the theater in order to give "friendly advice" to young people about the "dramatic art ... and guide them by [her] experience." It's particularly interesting to note what Bernhardt has to say regarding naturalism, given how her acting style in *Les Amours* is perceived by modern audiences. In an entire chapter devoted to the subject, Bernhardt states,

> Great actors have always been judged by the naturalism they exhibit in their acting. Fidelity to the truth does not always distinguish in our present-day art, and the public will not tolerate a glossing over of reality. The conventions and affected behaviour that might have been admissible at certain periods would certainly not be acceptable at the present time. In this respect, dramatic art has made remarkable progress in the course of the last century.[7]

This book was first published in 1924, after Bernhardt's death, so her perception of acting at the time she wrote it in the early 1920s had matured somewhat since she starred in *Les Amours,* and must be viewed against the "course of the last century." During this time, Bernhardt's style at its most naturalistic was still a far cry from what modern theater and moviegoers are accustomed to seeing. Her performance in *Les Amours* in particular suffers by comparison when viewed in light of the realism of the Stanislavsky method which was emerging from the Moscow Art Theatre, and also the evolution of style occurring in contemporary silent films. As Robert Horville has noted:

> Admiration always tends to have a purifying effect. Posthumous fame scours those whom it touches of the imperfections which ordinary life showed up in broad daylight. The image of Sarah Bernhardt which has gradually emerged has been especially subject to this rather mystifying kind of distortion. Crowned with the halo of her legend, she has become a veritable myth. Hidden under eulogy, often of a retrospective nature, her stage technique is represented as perfect, proclaimed as incomparable, and is seen only as a part of this general myth.[8]

This general myth often results in a disinclination to impartially criticize Bernhardt's technique, especially in the area of naturalism. Bernhardt herself admits, perhaps not without irony, "If you would be natural, you must avoid the persistent mannerisms that actors frequently adopt, believing they please the public.... You must avoid stiff and chronic poses" for "it is never by employing mannerisms that [an actor] can plunge an audience into emotion."[9]

Since she preferred melodrama and had always been unconventional, it would seem to be no surprise that Bernhardt was willing to venture into the title role in *Les Amours* for her most enduring appearance on film. In actuality, however, it took a good bit of cajoling to secure Bernhardt's participation. As film historian David Menefee has noted,

"Bernhardt began by despising the cinema. This was ironical, because by appearing on the screen, she did more than anyone to dignify it."

Noted British film historian Kevin Brownlow had the rare opportunity in 1964 to sit down with Adolph Zukor to discuss his part in bringing *Les Amours* to the American screen, and in particular Sarah Bernhardt's feelings about appearing in the film. Zukor had this to say:

> I had financed a picture, *Queen Elizabeth*, which was made in Paris in 1912. I had obtained the American rights for that picture ... they had approached Sarah Bernhardt before her season closed in the spring of 1911. It required quite a bit of convincing Sarah Bernhardt that this was something that would remain in existence for posterity. So if you want to perpetuate yourself for future generations, in addition to the compensation, I told her, you will have great satisfaction. So while she could always use money, she wasn't anxious enough to take money if she felt it would bring her down instead of lifting her up. And I paid her. The amount that she received was $40,000 in American money. That was an awful lot of money in those days, even in America, for a motion picture. After the launch of that picture was successful, we decided to form the Famous Players Company and use famous names and famous personalities in established plays and produce them for the screen.[10]

Like its Film d'Art predecessor, *The Assassination of the Duke of Guise*, the cast for *Les Amours* was made up of performers (Bernhardt among them) from the Comédie Française, France's prestigious national theater, which had put on the stage play. The film was directed by Louis Mercanton, which added even more to the film's reputation, and it took a grand total of three months to film. The making of a moving picture starring such an exalted cast was unheard of, and an excerpt from *The Literary Digest* for August 1912 illustrates contemporary attitudes and why Bernhardt and others approached the project with some trepidation:

> Much has been heard of the moving-picture machine as the ignoble but dangerous rival of legitimate drama, crowding the players off the boards and debasing the public taste with its crude and tawdry substitute for dramatic art.... But to many it will doubtless be a surprise to learn that no less an artist than Sarah Bernhardt has entrusted her art to the films, and that she will be seen this season in the United States in a historical photo-play.[11]

As a "photo-play," *Les Amours* was a filmed adaptation of a stage play of the same name by Emile Moreau.[12] Bernhardt had played the titular role in the theater production, and it was a natural progression to cast her in the starring role for the film. Having a celebrated stage actress appear in a film was a relatively new phenomenon and therefore, as illustrated by the comments of the anonymous *Literary Digest* writer, engendered a degree of uncertainty as to reception, but Bernhardt finally agreed to take on the part, though not without serious consideration and persuasion. She is said to have remarked that she assented to being in films, in part, because she felt that motion pictures would be her one chance at "immortality."[13] Her other motive was probably to recoup some of the losses she had sustained from the theatrical version of *Les Amours* which, by most accounts, had a respectable, but less than robust run. At the time *Les Amours* was imported into the American cinema market, it represented a paradigm shift not only in subject matter and star power, but also in terms of length. The working-class audiences Zukor hoped to supplement were accustomed to paying a small sum (originally a nickel, hence the term "nickelodeon") to watch short films, usually "one-reelers." American producers felt that working-class audiences had neither the time nor the inclination to attend longer, feature-length films.[14] At four reels and just under an hour in length, *Les Amours* was three times as long as most American films, and the American film industry's view at the time was comparable to what a modern studio executive would probably feel upon being presented with a six-hour long feature film for release.

Sources differ on how much Zukor actually paid for the rights to *Les Amours,* with the figure ranging from $18,000[15] to as much as $35,000.[16] Regardless, anything in this range was considered an almost astronomical sum for the rights of a rather obscure film which had made a respectable, but less than phenomenal showing in the European market. The film was marketed by selling the rights to screen it on a state by state basis. Advertisements in trade publications, such as that in *Moving Picture World,* billed the film as "the only feature film that has all the qualities that make it worthy of the name," and these qualifications included "prestige, drawing power, the greatest actress at her best, and perfect production." If the potential buyer was left in any doubt of the film's worthiness, Zukor summed up the list with, "Everything pertaining to this production spells success."[17] It would certainly spell success for Zukor, who made approximately $80,000 on his investment, a sum which he used to help found what would become Paramount Pictures Corporation.

As will be seen in later film portrayals of Elizabeth's life, *Les Amours* takes enormous liberty with historical fact, but there are some attempts at historical accuracy, such as a plausible reproduction of the real Elizabeth's signature on the warrant for Essex's execution, and an attempt to include correct historical dates. Audiences of the day, whether working class or otherwise, were not adamant about historical accuracy, but they did expect high drama and romance from their entertainment, as well as witty dialogue, which playwrights such as Oscar Wilde provided. Since the technology of the day was not advanced enough to provide sound to sync with a moving picture, dialogue, witty or otherwise, for *Les Amours* was clearly not an option. This put the divine Sarah at an immediate disadvantage because she could not utilize her greatest asset — her golden voice. This robbed her of (in her own words) "the dramatic artist's most necessary instrument."[18] Due to the lack of sound, the story in *Les Amours* is told by scenes interspersed with explanatory title cards. The title cards appear before each scene takes place, informing the viewer of exactly what is to occur in the subsequent scene. The actual arrangement of the 23 scenes in *Les Amours* was tailored to Bernhardt's specifications. Though the stage play version could relate its story primarily by its dialogue, plotting in the motion picture was much more complicated because it could not be presented in this way — it was forced to rely on visuals rather than speech. While a play is about composition *and* dialogue, a silent film is *exclusively* about composition and visualization; the audience must be led to understanding solely by the meaning they infer from what they see. Bernhardt's solution to this problem was to adapt the play by turning it into a pantomime of action scenes which were augmented only when absolutely necessary by the explanatory title cards.[19] Though the film itself was silent, films were always accompanied by live music when shown in the theater. This was usually accomplished through either a pianist or an organist placed near the screen. Unlike modern films, most early silent offerings did not have a dedicated score as such — producers would provide theater owners with a list of popular favorites which they felt fit the mood of particular scenes, and theater owners could then choose which music to include with the film. *Les Amours* was unique in that, in another attempt to set it apart from its contemporaries, it was one of the first films to have a dedicated score, composed by Joseph Carl Breil.

Bernhardt was in her late sixties at the time she filmed *Les Amours,* allowing her to be convincing as an aging but glorious Elizabeth in love with a younger man. The man in question in this film, Robert Devereaux, Earl of Essex, is portrayed by Dutch stage actor Lou Tellegen (1883–1934). Tellegen owed much of his stage experience to Bernhardt, who saw the circus performer turned actor, recognized his potential, and offered him employment. Tellegen was a handsome man with a tall, graceful physique (he even modeled for the sculptor Auguste Rodin), and he was over 30 years Bernhardt's junior, which ensured that his age also fit in well with the timeline of Elizabeth and Essex in *Les Amours.* Despite the age difference, Tellegen remarked that Bernhardt looked no more than 20, and the two were rumored to be romantically involved. The romantic relationship between Tellegen, an admitted and voracious womanizer, and Bernhardt, who was old enough to be his grandmother, was not of great length. However, the two remained working colleagues and appeared in various films together. After the reception of *Les Amours,* Tellegen would eventually leave Bernhardt to attempt to make a career for himself in Hollywood's silent films. In his recollection, he was one of the main factors which persuaded Bernhardt to appear in *Les Amours.* Though at first Bernhardt thought he was "mad" for begging her to star in the film, eventually "after weeks of swearing 'Never!' ... she finally gave in and we went to work."[20]

Les Amours is essentially a melodrama, and though the historical personages portrayed by the main players are exalted, the plotline is less so. Love and betrayal take center stage in this Peyton Place in Tudor-cum-Edwardian clothing. Events and characterization are radically streamlined; the historical personages one would expect to see characterized and which so often appear in other adaptations are not present due to a necessarily small cast. The basic plot of the film revolves around only four main characters: Elizabeth (Sarah Bernhardt); Robert (or James, according to some cast billings) Devereaux, Earl of Essex (Lou Tellegen); the Countess of Nottingham (Mademoiselle Romaine); and her husband, the Earl of Nottingham (Monsieur Maxudian). Queen Elizabeth is in love with the Earl of Essex, a man much younger than she. In typical star-crossed fashion, a fortune-teller warns that Essex will meet his doom on the scaffold, and Elizabeth will lead a life of unhappiness. In order to forestall this, Elizabeth gives Essex a ring, informing him that he can return it to her and, come what may, be delivered from the scaffold. Essex goes on to have an affair with the Countess of Nottingham, and the two are discovered when the Earl of Nottingham interrupts their tryst. Vowing revenge, Nottingham, with the help of Sir Francis Bacon, frames Essex by writing a letter to Elizabeth accusing the Earl of treason. Elizabeth, who has happened upon Essex with the Countess, believes him capable of anything and issues his death warrant, intending to pardon him when he sends her the ring. Though she is in disgrace, the Countess of Nottingham is sent for and Elizabeth asks her to persuade the proud Essex to accept clemency. The Countess succeeds in her task, but on her way back to Elizabeth, the villainous Earl of Nottingham intercepts her and wrests the ring from her, throwing it out the window into the Thames. Elizabeth, believing Essex too proud to ask for forgiveness, allows the execution to go forward. Essex is beheaded, and when Elizabeth views the body, she discovers the ring is missing, demonstrating that he had attempted to beg for salvation. Elizabeth is forever despondent, eventually dying, and both the fortune-teller's prophecies are fulfilled.

The film begins with a title card that boldly states "Adolph Zukor presents," making his role in the production of the film unmistakable to the audience, an early form of the branding which is familiar to modern moviegoers. Rather than have a single title card listing all the players and their parts, *Les Amours* provides a separate title card for each of the main actors, then shows a short snippet of the actor in costume. All other actors are uncredited. The title card announcing the first scene reads: "The Queen, anxiously awaiting news of the Spanish Armada, is struck by the enthusiasm and noble bearing of Earl Essex [*sic*], who alone is confident of success. Drake arrives and announces the total defeat of the Spaniards."

The actual historical event on which this scene is based concerns the Armada of ships sent in 1588 by the Catholic monarch Philip II of Spain, formerly Elizabeth's brother-in-law, in a vain attempt to invade and subdue the heretical English, depose Elizabeth, and bring England under Spain's domination and back into the fold of the Catholic Church. What befell the over-confident Spanish Armada is now the stuff of legend. Between engagements with England's navy under the command of Admiral Lord Howard of Effingham and Sir Francis Drake, miscommunication, incompetence, and extremely unfavorable weather, the much larger and better-equipped Spanish Armada suffered one of the worst defeats in naval history. Elizabeth was at Tilbury, where she delivered what is accounted by many to be the most famous and brilliant speech of her reign, addressing and rallying the troops assembled in preparation to repel the expected Spanish invasion.

As can be seen by the film's title and by this first title card, though the scene is ostensibly about the defeat of the Spanish Armada, a watershed event, it's used only to further the romantic plotline surrounding Elizabeth and Essex. The world may be falling down around her ears, but Elizabeth is "struck by the enthusiasm and noble bearing of Earl Essex [*sic*]" and his "confidence." This is a theme which is repeated again and again — a focus on Elizabeth's personal, romantic relationships over her political acumen. Tellegen goes out of his way to display this supposed enthusiasm and noble bearing, with grand sweeping gestures, flourishing of and then tossing away his hat, impressively brandishing his sword, and even laying down his cloak for the Queen to walk across, a (probably apocryphal) gesture attributed to Sir Walter Raleigh. Bernhardt, for her part, shows Elizabeth taking a vested interest by smiling broadly and often, clasping her hands together at her cheek, and generally mooning about like a teenage girl in the throes of puppy love. Perhaps in an attempt to contrast this or show that this is not the typical reaction Elizabeth has towards men, Sir Francis Drake enters with news of the Armada's defeat and steps towards the Queen as if to embrace her, but she stops this familiarity firmly in its tracks and then kisses him chastely on the top of the head and sends him on his way.

The convention of the establishing shot — showing a location and conveniently labeling it (e.g., an exterior shot of a palace with the caption "England, 1588") to anchor the viewer in the historical place and time period of a film before moving on to the scene at hand was an approach that would have been unknown in cinematography at the time *Les Amours* was produced; accordingly, the film does not provide any clue as to what the setting or time period might be. Though obviously filmed indoors against painted-drop cloth sets, the opening scene represents an outdoor setting, most probably the camp at Tilbury. Multiple courtiers as well as guards armed with pikes mill about in the background, and Essex can be seen in the foreground at stage left, pointing to a map which sits on a table. His costuming is grand: he sports a doublet, belt with sword, upper hose with thigh-high boots, a cloak, and, as one might expect from a man with such a large ... opinion of himself, a hat with a very prominent plume. Elizabeth enters from stage left, and Essex grandly sweeps down on one knee, spreading his cloak for the Queen to walk upon. The viewer then receives the first glimpse of Bernhardt in the first portrayal of Elizabeth on screen as she, rather awkwardly, walks across from stage left. Bernhardt's costuming is idiosyncratic, a strange mixture of Tudor and Edwardian. Though she wears a small ruff and a floor-length gown with a sleeved overdress, a style Elizabeth has been pictured wearing, the waistline is low and the unfitted bodice overhangs it to create the distinctively Edwardian, pigeon-breast profile; there is also no evidence whatsoever of a farthingale, much less the exaggerated drum-shaped style of farthingale that Elizabeth would have been wearing in 1588. This is even more curious given the fact that the female courtiers surrounding Bernhardt do have Tudor-like silhouettes, though they more closely resemble the styles from earlier in the period. Bernhardt also wears a large, flat-brimmed hat which would not have been out of place on an Edwardian lady out for an afternoon stroll. Though this hat mostly obscures her hair, in other indoor scenes Elizabeth and her ladies are shown with Edwardian hairstyles: they are pulled back and up but loosened around the face, with the back sometimes enclosed in a snood or cap, but most often in a "Gibson Girl" up-do, ornamented with ribbons.

The way in which the actors are made up is conspicuously that of the theater, and due to the remoteness of the camera angles for much of this film, is not inappropriate. Though different actors had different styles of make-up depending on parts being played and personal preference, almost all (men and women) included heavy penciling around the eyes, prominently rouged cheeks and lips, and an overall powdering of the face. White grease paint was often employed to de-emphasize lines when actresses wished to appear younger than their years or hide defects, and to combat the effect of mime-like white face this sometimes occasioned, the inside of the nostrils could be rouged to give them contrast and the face a more natural appearance. Overall in *Les Amours*, the effect of the makeup on the various actors is perhaps more subtle than would be the case for a stage play, though not by much.

Bernhardt makes her way to the chair next to the table, sits, and begins to examine the map. Throughout the scene, Bernhardt never moves without a courtier literally at her elbow. This blocking seems strange, unless the viewer is aware of Bernhardt's physical condition. Due to a theater-related accident in 1905, Bernhardt suffered from a chronic and worsening leg injury that made it difficult for her to walk without support, hence the blocking which provided for her to be surrounded by actors who could be leant upon or come to her aid quickly should she need them.[21] Bernhardt's injury would eventually result in the amputation of her leg, though during the filming of *Les Amours*, this was still some way off. Still, she's seldom seen walking for any great distance, and never without support. She's even carried out at the end of the first scene on a litter, after much rejoicing at the defeat of the Spanish.

The following scene provides the first glimpse of the set which represents the inside of the palace, probably Whitehall, as Elizabeth, Essex, and the court attend a performance of Shakespeare's *The Merry Wives of Windsor*. The choice of this play is interesting in that it was not published until 1602, and probably not performed before 1597 at the earliest. Thus, though no date or estimate of time elapsed are provided by the title card accompanying this scene (the viewer learns only that "Essex has become the Queen's favorite"), the scene can be set at approximately a decade after the defeat of the Armada. The other motive for the inclusion of this scene may be the gratuitous introduction of Shakespeare in his first meeting with Elizabeth (facilitated by Essex) in order to include a glimpse of the Bard in the film; otherwise this scene seems oddly out of place, as it does not further the plot in any way. After the play, Elizabeth and Essex are shown, heads together in cozy conversation, when the film's foreshadowing is literally dragged into the room in the form of the fortune-teller. The fortune-teller pores over Elizabeth's palm, and throughout the palm-reading Bernhardt reacts to what the fortune-teller is relating, and motions to her bystanding courtiers, who then mimic her reactions, responding as one. Essex also has his palm read, and when the fortune-teller attempts to flee, he roughly seizes her and makes her relate his fortune. The viewer can assume his fate to be less than favorable given that, unless she is pantomiming the universal sign for choking assistance, the fortune-teller predicts it by grabbing her throat with both hands and staggering out. Though Elizabeth and Essex seem relatively undisturbed by the fact that, respectively, an "unhappy future" and death "on the scaffold" have been predicted for them, the Countess of Nottingham, who stands to the side, is less sanguine. She's visibly distressed, standing apart from the chamber full of courtiers with her hand to her face. Her husband notices, and he confronts her. The viewer is told by title cards that, regardless of appearances, Elizabeth *is* greatly upset, and she gives Essex her ring, telling him that he may return it and she will save him "however great his fault may be."

It's interesting to note that, in this first appearance of Elizabeth on screen, the myth that she gave Essex a ring that he could return in exchange for his own salvation, no matter what his crime, is perpetuated. This legend of the ring is often repeated, and figures in other film adaptations of Elizabeth's life. Perhaps filmmakers are unable to resist the romance and tragedy the insertion of the ring myth brings to their films. Certainly several elements from this legendary tale are used for dramatic effect in *Les Amours*, and it's obvious that Moreau centered the majority of his play around it. It's illuminating to examine the legend, for in this myth lies an explanation for some of the characterization choices of *Les Amours*, as well as the majority of its plotting, which has evolved from this myth. The basic legend is that, in happier times, Elizabeth gave Essex a ring which he could return to her, no matter what, and she would come to his aid. There's even a ring said to be the one of the legend which is in the Chapter House Museum in Westminster Abbey. The rest of the tale is that Essex, while he was imprisoned in the Tower, managed to give the ring to a boy who was to take it to Lady Scrope who could then give it to the Queen. Unfortunately, the boy gives the ring to the Countess of Nottingham by mistake.

This Countess of Nottingham happens to be the wife of Essex's enemy, so she keeps the ring and only confesses what she has done to Elizabeth when the Countess is on her death-bed. The Queen then states, "May God forgive you, Madam, but I never can."[22]

When viewed in light of this story, it's easier to understand why, along with Elizabeth and Essex, the other two main character roles in *Les Amours* are the Countess of Nottingham and her husband, rather than some of Elizabeth's more well-known courtiers who figure largely in other adaptations. The real Earl of Nottingham, Charles Howard, was a cousin to Elizabeth and was formerly the same Lord of Effingham whose admiralship of the English navy contributed to the defeat of the Spanish Armada. He is, of course, not shown in this role in *Les Amours* as it would have significantly complicated the plotting, and Sir Francis Drake and Essex are given the credit for the Armada's defeat, with no mention of Effingham. The historical Countess of Nottingham, Katherine Carey, was also Elizabeth's cousin and one of her close female friends. There is no evidence either that she considered Essex an enemy or that she was ever involved romantically with him. As for the confession and the Queen's subsequent rejoinder, this also is a dramatic plot device which has no basis in fact; Elizabeth did attend the death-bed of her friend, but there were no confessions, and the Queen was devastated by the Countess's death to the point that it is thought by some to be a contributing factor in Elizabeth's own final illness. This myth of the ring was first recounted in *The Devil's Law Case* in 1620, but became an ingrained fixture in the lore surrounding Elizabeth with the publication in 1695 of the fictional *The Secret History of the Most Renowned Queen Elizabeth and the Earl of Essex, by a Person of Quality*.[23]

Since the stage has been set with foreshadowing galore, it's now time to send Essex off to Ireland as Lieutenant-General so that the intrigue which will result in his downfall can begin. The viewer is given a screen shot of the order, signed by Elizabeth, and Essex's public leave taking, after which Elizabeth collapses onto her throne, visibly distraught. Essex may have made his public exit, but he still has a private meeting with the Countess of Nottingham in store. This scene provides some of the most overstated, mime-like acting to be found in *Les Amours,* courtesy of Monsieur Maxudian. Essex pauses in the hallway before the Countess's chamber (which one enters through a conveniently placed curtain). He looks into the chamber, pauses again, dramatically considering, and finally makes up his mind to enter. The Countess within is despondent, and after talking with her, Essex embraces her with what presumably passed for the portrayal of passion in the Edwardian era. Their physical contact is always chaste; there is a full six inches of space between them, and though arms and hands clasp expressively, bodies do not touch. Meanwhile, the Earl of Nottingham has come down the hall and, like Polonius with only slightly more favorable consequences, is listening behind the curtain. He opens the curtain and his reaction is overstated to the point of being unintentionally comedic. There is a reason the phrase "like a silent film villain" instantly conveys the meaning it does — Maxudian hams up his role as his eyebrows crawl up and disappear into his hairline, his eyes pop out, his mouth drops open, and he draws back and grandly throws his arms wide. He actually does a triple-take. The viewer is then shown what has shocked him so — the sight of his wife seated in a chair, while Essex leans over her and ... holds her hand. Though the throwing about of the curtain and Nottingham's spastic movements would have alerted

"A gloriously handsome young man with a magnificent faith." The Earl of Essex (Lou Tellegen) takes his leave of a love-struck Queen Elizabeth (Sarah Bernhardt) in *Les Amours de la Reine Élisabeth*. (Histrionic Film/The Kobal Collection)

the dead to his presence, Essex and the Countess never notice him, and he secrets himself as Essex leaves. Nottingham then comically starts at every kiss Essex blows to the Countess on his way out. Nottingham draws his sword as if to pursue Essex, but then thinks better of it as Francis Bacon wanders in. The title card has told the viewer, "Nottingham swears vengeance on Essex and confides his plans to Lord Bacon, the bitter enemy of Essex." There's much fist pounding and gesticulating as Bacon and Nottingham discuss what has happened and formulate their nefarious plan, then shake on the deal.

Out of the vast panorama of Elizabeth's courtiers, the inclusion of the character of Francis Bacon as the secondary villain, who makes his first appearance in this scene, bears scrutiny. The viewer is told by the title cards that Bacon, who has been converted into a lord (the historical Bacon would not be created a viscount until the reign of James I) is the "bitter enemy" of Essex. In actuality, the relationship between the two men was far more complicated. Francis was the son of Nicolas Bacon, Elizabeth's Lord Keeper of the Seal, but his father's death left him with few financial resources and even less opportunity for preferment. Though he became an MP, his opposition to some of Elizabeth's policies, most notably her taxation program, slowed his political progress. Knowing that he would require a patron if he wished to advance himself, in the early 1590s Bacon attached himself to the court's rising star and became Essex's confidential advisor. Essex worked hard for his friend in this area, providing him with a seat on the Learned Council as well as a property to increase his revenue in lieu of the title and position Essex was unable to secure for him. Bacon would eventually begin to distance himself from Essex as the Earl became more and more volatile. When Essex was arrested for treason (examined in greater detail later in this chapter), Bacon held the unenviable position of being assigned to gather evidence, interview witnesses, and prosecute his former friend and benefactor. Elizabeth, in what has been described as one of her bouts of contrariness, assigned Bacon to represent her in the case against the Earl. Bacon has been vociferously condemned for this "betrayal," but the historical evidence seems to show that it was a duty most unwillingly undertaken, and Bacon even requested that he be allowed to absent himself from the proceedings at times — a request which Elizabeth denied. In this tragic end to the relationship between Bacon and Essex, one can see the motivation for Moreau's characterization of Bacon as a villain. The unwilling prosecutor becomes the "bitter enemy" of the dashing Essex, who in this version is responsible, along with Nottingham, for framing an innocent victim, as well as seeing that he is convicted.

The way in which Nottingham and Bacon bring this about in *Les Amours* is remarkably simple. After Essex has left for Ireland, Nottingham, with help from Bacon, writes an anonymous letter to the Queen accusing Essex of treason. Essex appears to have left and returned in an instant, for the treason of which he is accused by the villains consists of "returning from Ireland after having betrayed the interests of his country." Bacon places this letter on a table where Elizabeth later finds it. She reads it, then tosses it aside with little reaction. Essex's arrival is announced, and he's greeted warmly by Elizabeth; there's much plucking of clothing, hand-holding, and touching. The Queen then leaves the Countess of Nottingham alone with Essex, and the two sit together and embrace. Elizabeth returns to the room just as they kiss and discovers them. The viewer is told by the title card that since the Queen has discovered that Essex is "unfaithful.... She then believes the anonymous letter and orders his arrest."

Events switch into overdrive as Essex is "taken to Westminster to be tried." When the participants file out of the trial, including the headsman with his axe, Elizabeth watches the scene through a window and violently pantomimes distress when it becomes obvious that Essex has been found guilty. Though this is what Elizabeth herself has brought about by ordering his arrest, it seems that she was not seriously intent on his execution, given her reaction and subsequent behavior — a nod to the historical Elizabeth's vacillation. Bernhardt flails her arms, throws her hands over her face, and smacks her forehead with a clenched fist hard enough to give herself a concussion. She promptly sends for the Countess of Nottingham, who appears before her in an aspect of mourning, wearing a black dress and a long, black veil. The Queen is imperious with her, but she sends the Countess to persuade Essex to send back her ring as "a sign of submission." It seems that salvation is in store for Essex, but Bacon has been listening, unobserved by the women, at stage left. He hurries off to warn Nottingham of the Queen's intention to pardon Essex.

Essex makes a good show of stubbornly demonstrating his pride — for a few seconds. He ignores the begging Countess by staring straight ahead, arms crossed over his chest, but then gives her the ring. The Countess hurries off in search of Elizabeth, only to be stopped by her husband, who's waiting for her in the hallway. The Countess staggers in, hand to her heart, noticeably overwrought. The Earl violently throws her to her knees, loosening her hair and veil in the process, and wrests the ring from her. He then hurls it out the window into the Thames. This scene provides some of the most dramatic acting which Mademoiselle Romaine displays in *Les Amours*. She remains on the floor, heaving with sobs, and then faints. Her husband has two pages come in, pick her up, and carry her off like a sack of potatoes.

Meanwhile, Elizabeth has signed Essex's death warrant because she believes him to be too proud to ask for clemency. It's the invidious Bacon who brings her the warrant, which she threatens to tear up, but eventually signs. Essex stoically bears his execution while Nottingham and Bacon look on. Elizabeth then visits the body in its remarkably well-lit crypt. Essex is laid out on a bier, with a line around his neck to indicate that his head is no longer attached, though when Elizabeth, in the throes of her emotion, grasps his head and tugs, it's painfully obvious that it is of a piece with his body. By now, Elizabeth has discovered that her ring is not on Essex's finger, and rather than simply assume he forgot to wear it what with all the dying he had to do that day, she "forces the horrible truth" from the Countess of Nottingham. Elizabeth then, via title card, provides the only dialogue in the film when she proclaims the apocryphal "May God forgive you. I never will!"

The last scene of the film, that portraying Elizabeth's death, takes place in the audience chamber set. The viewer is immediately struck by the incongruous, gigantic pile of pillows placed directly in front of Elizabeth's throne. The Queen enters, helped in by a lady-in-waiting. A sword, which the viewer can assume to have belonged to Essex, is brought to the Queen. Elizabeth is assisted around the mountain of pillows to stand in front of her throne. In a spot of less than subtle symbolism, Elizabeth motions for, and is handed a mirror, setting the precedent for a trope that will appear time and again in almost every film version of Elizabeth's life. Holding it at arm's length, she looks at herself and then throws the mirror away, her vanity unable to cope with the image of the old woman she has become. In the film's most unintentionally humorous moment, Bernhardt throws her arms wide, flaps them around in circles as if about to take flight, and then slaps her hand to her breast. Nottingham enters long enough for the Queen to point accusingly at him, and then she returns her attention to dying. With her arms wide, she falls forward face-first, stiff as a board, belly-flopping onto the enormous mound of pillows. Her courtiers, as one, rush forward and surround her, then all fall to their knees but Nottingham, who solemnly walks to the window and opens it. The final title card reads "Sic transit Gloria mundi" which translates as "Thus passes the glory of the world." This Latin phrase is usually used to imply the impermanence of the things of this world and the futility of clinging to them, but in this case, the word "Gloria," since it is capitalized, could be interpreted as referring to Gloriana herself, and thus is a more personal comment on the passing of the Queen and the world's loss of its "glory," Elizabeth.

As always happens when a literary work is adapted for the screen, what the viewer sees in *Les Amours* and can glean from its pantomimed action is only a small part of the more complicated plotting from the original play. When one is aware of this play's plotting and dialogue, some added understanding for a number of the elements of *Les Amours* can be garnered. The play opens with the same setting, but there is more background information about the invasion and the unreadiness of the English, and Elizabeth's state of mind is made apparent. Elizabeth is in despair, and a "gloriously handsome young man [Essex] with a magnificent faith gives her courage." The play also relates that "this young lover will remain for Elizabeth the embodiment of the glorious day of victory." The dialogue is frequently flowery, with Essex making (rather ironic) statements such as, "How beautiful you are, Madame, in this aureole of glory, and what a misfortune it is not to be able to shed one's blood for you!" Essex's "misfortune" will be short-lived.

The play is especially helpful in providing a deeper look into character relationships. The Lady Howard (Countess of Nottingham) is apparently Essex's cousin and a close confidante of the Queen, to whom Elizabeth has confided that she has doubts as to the constancy of Essex. This makes Lady Howard's betrayal even more unexpected and alarming to Elizabeth. Lady Howard also throws the ring into the Thames herself, though her "devouringly jealous" husband has forced her to do so. The play also hits closer to the historical mark with its more complicated examination of the events leading up to Essex's arrest and execution. In the play, Essex is not merely an innocent victim of malicious court intrigue—he smoothes the path to his downfall by his own actions. According to the play, Essex "feebly" combats the rebels in Ireland before returning home without orders to preposterously propose to Elizabeth that she should establish home rule in Ireland. Elizabeth is understandably surprised, but takes this in stride until she happens upon Essex and Lady Howard. She then becomes furious, summons her court, and accuses Essex of having made an illegal pact with the Irish. No anonymous letter written by his enemies is needed to condemn Essex; he does good work on that score himself. Elizabeth throws her glove in Essex's face, and he draws his sword on her, whereupon he's promptly arrested on the Queen's orders. The rest of the story is similar to *Les Amours*, but the play intimates that Elizabeth has had both Lady Howard and her husband tortured for their part in Essex's execution.[24]

The portrayal of the downfall of the Earl of Essex in the play is much closer to the historical truth than that depicted in the filmed version of *Les Amours*. The historical Earl of Essex, Robert Devereaux, was first the ward of William Cecil, Lord Burghley, and later the stepson of Elizabeth's first and longest-lasting favorite, Robert Dudley, Earl of Leicester. Leicester advanced the boy at court, where he came to Elizabeth's notice when he was about 20 years of age. Essex was popular mostly for his "goodly person" and "innate courtesy," two traits essential in a courtier, and which Tellegen aptly personifies in *Les Amours*. Unfortunately, the real Essex was also reckless, possessing a near-irrepressible ego and volatile temper that he had difficulty controlling. His desire for power and prestige led him to impinge further and further upon Elizabeth's goodwill, which in the beginning seemed almost boundless. His career began promisingly enough, as he acquired domestic power and became a popular hero for his attack on the Spanish port of Cádiz. However, he pitted himself against Robert Cecil, who had replaced his late father Lord Burghley as Elizabeth's most trusted counsel. When the Earl of Tyrone began a rebellion in Ireland that threatened to overthrow English dominion there, the glory-hungry Essex took a calculated risk and volunteered to command the army sent to defeat Tyrone. Essex failed miserably, never truly engaging the Irish, and eventually concluding an unauthorized truce with them before returning home to England without being recalled — two actions which absolutely infuriated Elizabeth. He did not help his case by bursting into her private apartments unannounced, catching the elderly Elizabeth in her chemise. His favor with the Queen all but exhausted, Essex was deprived of his offices. He decided to try one last, desperate gamble. Thinking that he could regain Elizabeth's favor if he removed the enemies he felt were misrepresenting and sabotaging him with the Queen (i.e., Robert Cecil and his faction), Essex and a few of his fellow noblemen, such as the Earl of Southampton, attempted to institute an armed uprising in London to capture the Queen's person and force her to take on new advisers, namely Essex and his coterie. Essex had seriously misjudged the power of his popularity with the people of London, who closed their doors to him. With the city's population refusing to rally to his cause, Essex was quickly captured. His trial, with Francis Bacon as the main prosecutor, was swift and the outcome a foregone conclusion. Essex was condemned and executed on 25 February 1601.[25]

As has been noted, *Les Amours*, like other early melodramas, was a remake of a stage play that had already proved its appeal to audiences.[26] Although these early films share similar primitive filming techniques, *Les Amours*, more than any of the others, is obvious as a stage play that has been filmed. The look of the film and the scene composition will be completely alien to modern cinema viewers. There's no such thing as a close-up in *Les Amours*, and even mid-range shots are seldom in evidence; the majority of the scenes are filmed from a considerable distance with a wide, or cover, shot in order to include all the actors "on stage." The equivalent would be the point of view of a theatergoer seated in the center of the auditorium. It's ironic that Bernhardt felt this film would immortalize her; one could insert a man in a dress in her place and the viewer would not be able to distinguish the difference due to the remoteness of many of the shots. All aesthetic concerns aside, this type of cinematic composition is problematic in two major respects: the revolutionary close-up shot which allows actors to convey so much emotionally cannot be utilized, and likewise the reaction shot, another staple of contemporary filmmaking, which helps to engage the viewer and provide a clearer picture of all emotions conveyed, not just by the principal actor, but by those observing and responding as well.

The subsidiary, background actors in *Les Amours*, as in the theater of the time, are used for set dressing, and they often stand almost motionless, a tableau vivant, while the principal actors deliver their lines and perform prescribed actions. When they do move, it's frequently as one, much like a Greek chorus. Edwardian theater playing, or acting techniques, appear highly stylized, and there is a considerable feeling of staginess conveyed to modern viewers who are more accustomed to naturalistic acting. To a viewer with this perception, Bernhardt's acting style in *Les Amours* will seem blatantly exaggerated. In 1912, Bernhardt's high-style acting would have been familiar, and thus more appealing, to upper-crust viewers who were patrons of the theater. Also, Bernhardt is not the only offender in *Les Amours* — all the actors engage in hand-wringing, amplified arm gestures, overstated facial expressions (when they can be distinguished), and sometimes amusingly overemphasized double- and even triple-takes. To risk understatement, Bernhardt, Tellegen and the other actors of *Les Amours* overplay their parts. It has been noted that this overacting is emphasized "precisely because the camera had not yet learned to help the actors."[27] The cinematic style makes it difficult, if not impossible, for the viewer to supplement all the hand-wringing with facial expressions, and thus the actors appear to portray caricatures of emotions, rather than the emotions themselves. Even in Bernhardt's time, a more naturalistic acting style was coming into vogue, and this can be seen to a certain extent in *Les Amours*. Some of the actors, such as Mademoiselle Romaine (the Countess of Nottingham) have a softer, more subtle style, while others, such as Monsieur Maxudian (the Earl of Nottingham) are clearly at the other end of the spectrum, bordering on Snidely Whiplash-like caricature. Though it was still acceptable in 1912 for an actor's movements and gestures to be more pronounced and demonstrative than in real life, Bernhardt, Mercanton, and the Film d'Art were behind the times. Other filmmakers had quickly realized that actions which might look realistic or only slightly exaggerated on stage could easily border on the ridiculous when viewed on film. Also, the new, solely film-going working-class audiences who were unfamiliar with stage tradition found the high-style inappropriate and incomprehensible. They expected the intense but more naturalistic drama which characterized the playing of actresses such as Eleanora Duse. A French stage actress, Madame Simone, defined the new acting style in an article published in the *New York Dramatic Mirror* in 1912: the new film acting style had no grand entrances, stagey exits, grandly declaimed dialogue (actors still said their lines even though the films were silent), or rooms full of hushed, statuesque observers listening intently to the conversation of two people. Why? Because none of this occurs in real life.[28] Verisimilitude had become paramount.

The critical reception which *Les Amours* received was varied, but in general contemporary critics were kind. In *Moving Picture World*, W. Stephen Bush wrote of the film, "Historical accuracy, swift and clear action, sustained splendor of settings and the supreme art of Sarah Bernhardt combine to make this play stand out as a rare and most creditable achievement.... The whole performance is marked by dignity and an unmistakable care in the preparation of every detail. The most remarkable part of this play is its accuracy in historical detail." Bush goes on to describe certain scenes as a "masterpiece of historical cinematography."[29] Presumably Mr. Bush was not a historian, for *Les Amours*'s lack of the very historical accuracy for which Bush so vociferously praises it is painfully obvious to anyone with any knowledge of the Elizabethan period. However, compared to the other films being produced at the time, the level of detail in the sets and costuming is impressive, despite how they would be disparaged by modern reviewers with higher expectations.

But what of Bernhardt's theatrical portrayal of Elizabeth? A reviewer for *Theatre Magazine* wrote that Bernhardt "proceeded to give one of the finest performances of which this greatest living artist is capable."[30] Bush, the same critic who praised *Les Amours*'s historical accuracy, wrote, "So superb is the art of Sarah Bernhardt that she made her conception, which is that of a passionate woman dominated wholly by her affections, seem not impossible." A passionate woman dominated wholly by her affections is not only "not impossible," it's common enough to be hackneyed. It's also inaccurate to portray Elizabeth in this one-dimensional manner, as she consistently demonstrated her ability to overrule her affections with reason when the situation demanded it. It was not yet the Jazz Age, and the times were not ready to showcase a woman who could be both passionate and logical; logic resided firmly within the male realm. The focus on the passionate woman was also Bernhardt's strong suit and role of choice, as it closely resembled her own personality. Bush goes on to state that Bernhardt "won from her audience such keen sympathy and compassion as the real Elizabeth could never have expected." Though it's impossible to judge audience reaction at a century remove, this statement could quite possibly be true. However, the real Elizabeth wanted neither compassion nor sympathy from her "audience"; she demanded loyalty, love, and obedient respect. Bush also states that there are scenes in the film that are "especially pathetic," one of which is the final scene portraying the death of the Queen. Evidently Bush meant this in its "causing or evoking pity or sympathetic sadness" definition since he paired it with adjectives such as "impressive," but it would perhaps be more accurate to describe the death scene in *Les Amours* using the alternate meaning of pathetic. Other reviewers espoused this view, with one stating, "And by the way, if you run *Queen Elizabeth,* stop with the scene before the last, cutting out that absurd death flop into a pile of cushions placed before the throne for no other reason than to save the Bernhardt bones. It gives a comedy finish that is hurtful."[31] The mountain of pillows may have saved Bernhardt pain, but watching her nosedive into them is certainly painful for the viewer.

The quality of the early silent film acting in *Les Amours* makes it much more difficult to decipher the version of Elizabeth that Bernhardt was attempting to put forth, and no commentary by Bernhardt on the subject has been discovered. Taking the performance as a whole, Bernhardt's Elizabeth comes off almost as happy-go-lucky, with little of the serious or mercurial sides of the temperament often attributed to the historical woman. Though Bernhardt is roughly the right age for the part, in appearance she looks very little like the representations of Elizabeth from her portraiture, and the rather peculiar costuming does not help to further the illusion. As is typical in many film adaptations of Elizabeth's life, the actress playing Elizabeth is strapped into emoting only where her relationships with males are concerned. *Les Amours* follows this pattern to the letter, with the focus being Elizabeth's relationship with her male love interest, the Earl of Essex. All other action, from the attack by the Spanish Armada to the rebellion in Ireland, serves only to advance this romantic plotting. Elizabeth has no real interaction with the female courtiers who surround her; indeed, even the Countess of Nottingham's prominent placement occurs only insofar as she helps to further the romantic plotline by serving as a rival love interest for Essex. Often in film adaptations, much is made of Elizabeth's vanity, and *Les Amours* gives it a flyby in the last scene by having Bernhardt toss away the mirror. Despite the reviewer comments above, Elizabeth does not seem vain or particularly passionate. The physicality of her relationship with Essex is indistinguishable from what it might be with a brother or son, and she certainly displays her passion sparingly. Until tragedies befall her, Bernhardt's Elizabeth is seen enjoying life to the fullest — she celebrates the victory over the Spanish Armada with obvious relish, she sedately delights in the company of Essex, and she enjoys watching Shakespeare's plays and graciously overseeing the entertainments of court life, with her greyhounds at her feet. Even in situations where one might expect to see the famous Tudor temper full-on, it's nowhere in evidence. For instance, when Elizabeth happens upon the anonymous letter accusing her favorite of treason, she shows very little emotion: puzzlement and consternation at most. She does not angrily confront Essex. She is amiable and friendly. The whole event seems to be ignored until she sees him in the arms of the Countess of Nottingham. Even then she calmly orders the distraught Countess out of the room before she confronts Essex. It's only after the Countess has withdrawn that the Tudor fire surfaces, with Elizabeth actually throwing a glove at Essex, who draws his sword against her (a dramatization of an historical event which resulted in Essex's temporary banishment from court). The only other flash of temper Elizabeth exhibits occurs when she confronts the Countess about the disposal of the ring. One might also expect Elizabeth to vent her fury in some way against the Earl of Nottingham and/or Francis Bacon, since these were the prime movers in conspiring to have Essex unjustly executed, with the Earl being as good as guilty of his murder. Nothing of this sort is shown, however, and it can be inferred that, unlike in Moreau's play, Nottingham, at least, has suffered no disfavor, since he is present at court in a prominent role in the last scene when Elizabeth makes her final, uniquely cushioned exit.

Much has been made of Bernhardt's theatrical personality, though many of the more bizarre acts attributed to her are exaggerations or falsehoods which she either intentionally perpetuated or ignored because they suited the image she wanted to convey. In a particularly enlightening essay on Bernhardt's stage techniques, Robert Horville provides perhaps the best description of Bernhardt's appeal: she gave her imagination full rein by "submerging the character to be played in her own personality," and the public was both in awe of and in love with that personality. At the same time, however, critics pointed out that this was also Bernhardt's burden: "The basic fault of Madame Sarah Bernhardt is in never adapting herself to a role but adapting the roles to herself and playing herself all the time. Her interpretation is of value only if there is some point of correspondence between her own experience and that of the character."[32] It's a perennial problem with actresses who play Elizabeth — she seems to attract those with strong, inflexible personalities (see later chapters on Bette Davis and Glenda Jackson), and in this case, it provokes the question of whether there is a point of correspondence between the divine Sarah and Gloriana. On the occasion of her sixty-eighth birthday, the London *Times* ran an article summarizing Bernhardt's career and appeal, and the picture it paints of the actress is useful for comparison with the character of the historical Elizabeth which she portrayed. The piece, written by the *Times*' dramatic critic, begins by describing the "strange charm of her voice, her sinuous grace, her attenuated form, her orchidaceous air" which made Bernhardt the talk of London even when she was only a secondary player in the Comédie Française. The critic continues:

> Her freaks and extravagances and quarrels and advertisements bewildered and fascinated both hemispheres. She became a kind of high-priestess of romance: gratifying in her person, in her *faicts et gestes*, the secret yearning of humdrum work-a-day humanity for the irrational and the fantastic.... She found a dramatist to write plays [']round her own personality, her cooing softness, her nerve-storms, her sudden caprices.[33]

In this picture of Bernhardt, much of the historical Elizabeth and the contemporary perception of Gloriana can be seen. Elizabeth also fascinated by her "freaks and extravagances and quarrels," and as is evidenced by the multitude of books written about her which focus on her romantic relationships, she has become "a kind of high-priestess of romance" while at the same time maintaining her image as an icon of virginity. Elizabeth, too, provides something as far away from "humdrum work-a-day humanity" as it's possible to find, and it's partly in this gratification of a desire for the uncommon, the unattainable, that her ability to fascinate lies. While Bernhardt found dramatists to write plays around her personality, Elizabeth tailored an entire court, government, and country to hers, which could also be described at times as "cooing softness, nerve-storms, [and] sudden caprices." In light of Elizabeth's later years, during which she transformed into Gloriana, the critic's words regarding Bernhardt ring with particular resonance: "At an age when most ... would have faded into a mere reminiscence, she is still a living force. This, after all, is the most wonderful thing about her." In *The Art of the Theatre*, written in the last years of her life, Bernhardt said of the art of acting: "Its ideal is to achieve glory. Its glory is to realize its ideal."[34] Elizabeth might have said the same about her reign as Queen of England.

THE VIRGIN QUEEN (1923)

Though it lacked the signal importance of *Les Amours*, there was another film produced during the silent era that featured Elizabeth as the main character. This film, entitled *The Virgin Queen*, was released in 1923. Though *Les Amours* and *The Virgin Queen* both belong to the era of silent film, much had happened in the interim between the films, most notably the First World War. Throughout the decade of the 1920s, both the British and French film industries attempted unsuccessfully to recover from the war, and they effectively lost their dominance to American films. The British and French films that saw the close of the era were of a markedly different caliber from offerings such as *Les Amours,* while American filmmaking only became more accomplished:

> Technically the late American silent film is often close to perfection. The luminosity of the photography and an imaginative but unshowy use of composition were welded into narrative by editors whose understanding of rhythm and dramatic tension remains extraordinary. Intertitles were reduced to the minimum, and not only had the barnstorming histrionics gone, but players were able to convey with only slight gestures a whole range of emotion — though whether, given the subject matter, the expertise was worthwhile is debatable.[35]

While American films were improving, those produced in Britain were often of poor quality due to the post-war condition of the industry. Whether *The Virgin Queen* conforms to this diagnosis or that of its late-silent era American contemporaries is a matter of conjecture since, unfortunately, the film is no longer extant. Because of this, unless/until some long-buried print of the film is unearthed, one can only make general observations about *The Virgin Queen* based on information pieced together from contemporaneous sources. Complete, detailed information on plotting, characterization, costuming, etc. is not available, and the survival status of the film is classified as unknown.

The Virgin Queen starred Lady Diana Olivia Winifred Maud Manners Duff Cooper (1892–1986) who, as her lengthy name suggests, was a member of the English aristocracy, a daughter of the Duke of Rutland and sometimes styled the Viscountess of Norwich. Often referred to as the "Lady Di" of her era, evoking the glamorous life of the late former Princess of Wales (although Cooper is accounted by all to have been much cleverer), Cooper epitomized the new Jazz Age socialite. Born into the aristocracy of Edwardian England, Cooper was known both for her eccentricity and for her beauty, as well as for her coterie, which contained the exalted and artistic. Cooper was close to members of the British royal family (at one point it was thought that she would marry the Prince of Wales) as well as notable figures of her day, including poet Hilaire Belloc, designer Cecil Beaton, and novelist Evelyn Waugh. Waugh even went so far as to model one of the characters in his novel, *Scoop*, after the unconventional aristocrat.[36] In 1919, Cooper bobbed her hair and thumbed her nose at her parents' wishes by marrying Alfred Duff-Cooper, a man with exalted ancestry, but no money, who was employed as a low-level diplomat after finishing his tour in the army during the First World War. Duff, as he was known, released a highly sanitized autobiography of himself (*Old Men Forget*), but more light on his and Diana's characters and relationship was shed with the publication of his full diaries, which only occurred in 2005. Duff was a war hero who received the Distinguished Service Order, an MP, Secretary of State for War, and eventually First Lord of the Admiralty; unfortunately, his diaries show that he was also a "compulsive philanderer whose persistent infidelities caused his wife ... deep distress."[37] There are multiple references in the earlier diaries to Diana's use of morphine and her abuse of alcohol to combat her unhappiness, although Duff never managed to connect this behavior in his wife with his multitudinous affairs. The Coopers were also, by the standards of their set, extremely poor in these early years due to Duff's dismal Foreign Office clerk salary. Thus, though she was a daughter of the aristocracy, Cooper was often on the lookout for opportunities to make a little hard cash in order to maintain the lifestyle to which she had been accustomed since birth. One such opportunity presented itself in the form of a film director named J. Stuart Blackton.

James Stuart Blackton (1875–1941) was an English native whose family had immigrated to the United States around 1885. Blackton began his working career as an illustrator and reporter for the *New York World*, and it was this employment that, by happenstance, provided him with his true calling. He was sent out to interview and sketch inventor Thomas Edison for the newspaper, his editor throwing in, "And oh yes, by the way, you might just ask him about that newest invention, moving pictures."[38] After purchasing a Projecting Kinetoscope from Edison, Blackton began making his own short films around the turn of the century. These shorts included newsreels, and it is in these newsreels that Blackton experimented with the revolutionary close-up shot, more than ten years before D.W. Griffith would develop and adopt it as a standard for use in films. For this reason, Blackton is considered to be an innovator and pioneer in the field of motion picture cinematography. Also, Blackton co-founded the Vitagraph Company, incorporated in 1900, to produce and distribute his films. In addition to the close-up, Blackton was also involved in the first films to employ single-frame animation (e.g., *The Haunted Hotel* [1906]) and dialogue in subtitles. Credited as being one of the burgeoning industry's foremost directors as well as cameramen, as the Vitagraph Company grew larger, Blackton stepped back and left the direction of some of his films to others while he supervised, effectively creating the position of producer, as it would later come to be called. Blackton was also a trailblazer in that he, along with members from six other companies, helped to organize the Motion Picture Patents Company and, in 1910, he founded *Motion Picture Magazine*, the first magazine ever published for film fans. He was also the first president of the Motion Picture Board of Trade of America.[39]

Despite all this, Blackton was forever overshadowed by other directors, and he eventually decided to leave the rapidly growing film industry in Hollywood for his native England. His greeting there was all he could have hoped for; he told his daughter, "I got a wonderful reception in England. Everything is set for me to make the world's first all-color, feature-length picture."[40] This project, *The Glorious Adventure*, would be bookended by another historical feature-length film, *The Virgin Queen*, and they would both share one star: Lady Diana Cooper.

Cooper was an author as well as a socialite and actress, and her rather verbose chronicle of her exploits (part biography, part travelogue) spans three volumes (*The Rainbow Comes and Goes, Trumpets from the Steep,* and *The Light of Common Day*), but devotes a mere two pages to *The Virgin Queen*. Admitting that Blackton had made her a "handsome offer," Cooper was still very dismissive in her description of him:

> He was said to be the first man to put a story on the screen. Up till then it had been documentary, street scenes, some reels of the Delhi Durbar, and budding slapstick. But Hollywood had risen above Mr. Blackton and he had come to England ("there the men are as mad as he") to try again with my help. He made me a preposterously big offer for two films, to which I, as usual, said "Snap." There was no deflecting him from his plans, which I could see needed adjustments that were never made. But what did it matter? It was exceedingly exciting and amusing and anachronistic and profitable.[41]

In her biography of her father, Blackton's daughter notes that Lady Diana Manners (as she refers to her) had quite a reputation, even on the American side of the pond, "I had read a great deal about ... her recklessness, her flaunting of conventions.... Lady Diana was somebody." Blackton seemed to agree with his daughter's estimation of the socialite's character and public persona, and what's more, he saw in it something that could be transferred to a great film personality as "she has everything ... charm, beauty, grace, intelligence, breeding."[42] Blackton was especially keen to test out his theory that, as a socialite, giving Cooper the starring role in his films would draw the upper crust of British society, the aristocratic movers and shakers, to the theater. He planned to use her already very public persona as a box-office draw. But the real question, as Blackton's daughter asked the director himself, was could Lady Di act?

The first film in which Cooper was to star, *The Glorious Adventure*, was released in 1921. A romance/adventure tale set in Restoration London during the reign of King Charles II, *The Glorious Adventure* had the distinction of being one of the first feature films to appear in color. From the very first days of cinema, experimentation had been done on adding coloration to silent films, but this was accomplished using non-photographic and often painstaking methods applied after the film had been shot. These methods included hand-coloring individual frames or adding monochrome color, achieved by bathing the film in chemical salts, to certain sections of the film in order to reflect the mood (e.g., blue for night scenes).[43] *The Glorious Adventure*, however, was shot in Prizma Color, a new subtractive process, a version of which was still being used as late as the 1950s. Blackton even mined the American film industry to find a color camera specialist, W.T. Crespinal, as well as his cameraman, Nicolas Musurca, and transported them to England to work on *The Glorious Adventure*.[44] Some of Blackton's later projects, including *The Virgin Queen*, would also be partly in color.

Despite the fact that *The Glorious Adventure* was not an unqualified success, Blackton sought to continue the formula with another costume drama as a vehicle for Cooper, albeit this time a slightly more historical one. He enlisted Harry Pirie Gordon, a noted English historian, to come up with an idea for a plot for this film that would revolve around Queen Elizabeth. Blackton's perennially skeptical daughter had this to say about the idea, "I'd read enough about Good Queen Bess to know that Diana, despite her reputation for private devilment, lacked the dramatic fire to give a convincing portrait of the bold, tempestuous, superlatively vital Queen." She felt this disadvantage would only be heightened under her father's direction, since Blackton enjoyed directing women, regardless of the characters they were playing, as breathlessly subservient to the men they loved.[45]

Interestingly enough, the English nobility not only wished to fill the theater seats for a picture about Queen Elizabeth, they wanted to act in it. Blackton's casting department was deluged by offers from members of the English aristocracy (many of whom were, like Cooper herself, less than financially solvent) who wanted to participate in the film by playing members of Elizabeth's court. Though Blackton could not resist casting many of these aristocrats, he was wise enough to give at least some of the major roles to actual actors. Carlyle Blackwell, an American actor, was chosen to play the part of Elizabeth's love interest, the Earl of Leicester, and Norma Whalley was cast as the Countess of Lennox. Blackton found the nepotistic urge to people the cast with his own family irresistible; his 12-year-old stepdaughter was cast as lady-in-waiting Lettice Knollys, who defies Elizabeth's dictates and chooses to wed, leading to "excruciating" love scenes with her romantic interest, played by a much older actor. Blackton also cast his daughter, Marian, in a small role as another lady-in-waiting.

Because of this (though no copies of the film are now extant), Marian Blackton's recollections provide an idea of some of the general plot points and feel of the filming. One scene, featuring yet another of Blackton's children as a the son of the prison warden, has a young Princess Elizabeth, imprisoned in the Tower of London by her sister Mary, using the child to sneak notes to her lover, Robert Dudley, who shares a cell near hers. There were also river scenes that showed the Queen, in her Royal Barge, being rowed up what was supposed to represent the Thames. A coronation scene was shot, featuring Cooper dressed in a gown replicated from the historical Elizabeth's coronation portrait. This historical drama also featured the Duke of Rutland engaging in a sneak attack against the forces of Mary, Queen of Scots. It's interesting to note that while Cooper made sure to mention more than once that the film was anachronistic, Marian Blackton illustrates the attempt at historical accuracy, at least in visuals, that her father applied to the film. The scriptwriter and historian Gordon noted that the horses used had cropped tails, which would have been unknown in the Elizabethan era, so Blackton re-shot the scene after having a wigmaker lengthen the horses' tails since it was too problematic to find 300 more horses on such short notice, and filming was already delayed. Rushes were viewed in the Old Town Hall, and the filming took a little over two months from start to finish.

The Virgin Queen was shot at Beaulieu, which borders on the New Forest. Blackton paid to rent the entire estate, both castle and abbey, from its owner at the time, Lord Montagu. Since the real Elizabeth had vacationed there, Blackton felt it would lend an authentic setting to his story. Also, the abbey, according to the historian Gordon, resembled closely enough the real setting of Elizabeth's coronation to be used for that scene. The Blacktons and some of the members of the cast actually lived on the estate during the filming of *The Virgin Queen*, much to the chagrin of Lord Montagu's staff and some in the nearby town.

Marian Blackton admits to mixed emotions about the film's star, whom her father had to "handle" in a "firmly suave" manner with "admiration of her beauty, envy of her social nonchalance, stern disapproval of her 'reputation,' and a slight, shamed, skulking awe of her noble pedigree. As a titled beauty Diana impressed me. As an actress I considered her definitely a flat tire."[46] Cooper herself describes the irritation occasioned by long waits for the weather to become decent enough to allow for filming, "I learnt patience, which is an all-important virtue if one is immobilized in farthingales and ruffs and collars like tennis racquets. Bewigged and caked in a yellow mask of paint, I would wait." Marian Blackton's descriptions of how pleasant Cooper was to work with and her lack of complaint seem to bear out her patience with her role, a quality which would not always be shared by later actresses who suffered for the art of playing Elizabeth. Despite her aristocratic pedigree, Cooper was not high-handed and readily took direction from Blackton, resulting in an atmosphere among the entire cast and crew that was, for the most part, easy and agreeable. The only tension was occasioned by Cooper's penchant for jet-setting, which resulted in filming delays because she looked too "wilted" after a night of partying to be filmed, regardless of make-up and gauze over the camera lenses.

Though neither of the films was a resounding success, *The Glorious Adventure* fared somewhat better than its successor, *The Virgin Queen*. Blackton's daughter, after noting that the film opened at the Empire Theatre, calls its reception a "mild success" which extended to audiences' responses across Britain and Europe; no American distributors were interested in opening the film in the United States. Some hailed the films as "ambitious costume spectacles with huge sets, crowd scenes, involved plots, and enormous casts supporting the fashionable and celebrated leading players," but at the same time denigrated them as "monumentally slow and dull and the use of color disappointing ... despite society premieres they were not especially successful."[47] Others were even less kind. A collection of essays on undocumented areas of silent film pronounced, "Whatever directorial techniques Blackton had learned in the United States, he seemed to have forgotten once he returned to his native soil, and ... [the film is] more exemplary of British film at its most mediocre rather than American film production at its worst. [*The Virgin Queen*] garnered poor reviews from *Variety*'s London correspondent."[48]

Though *The Glorious Adventure* was picked up by Allied Producers and Distributors and premiered in New York in April 1922, Blackton's promising new beginning in England had ended in, at best, mediocrity; he returned home to the United States and Vitagraph in 1923. The company was sold two years later to Warner Bros., and Blackton bankrupted himself with real estate and other investment speculations before dying in a car accident in 1941.[49]

In her autobiography, Cooper closed the chapter in her life which *The Virgin Queen* occupied with these words: "The second film was less propitious. I was cast for Queen Elizabeth and in spite of a red wig and shaved eyebrows my full young face could not give a suggestion of her fleshless aquilinity.... I had little hope or faith or charity for *The Virgin Queen* with all its grotesque anachronisms, but I delighted in it as an inartistic lark."[50] In this rather apologetic and self-aggrandizing summation, Cooper intimates that her less-than-laudable performance as the Virgin Queen was due to historically inaccurate plotting and her being too attractive for the part, rather than any dearth of acting ability from which she may have suffered. Despite being so dismissive of her stint as an actress, Cooper still felt that cinema was "the most real form of romance modern life expresses," illustrating something Cooper and Queen Elizabeth had in common — they are intensely romantic figures, both for who they were, and for the time periods they represented.

CHAPTER 3

Hollywood's Golden Age:
Bette Davis and
Big-Budget Historicals

The 1920s, when *The Virgin Queen* was produced, though separated by only a single decade from the next iteration of Elizabeth onscreen, may as well have been light-years distant due to the changes that had taken place in the film industry and the world at large. The decade of the 1930s saw the United States hit full-force by the Great Depression, which modified the social and political landscape beyond measure, and this would be followed up by the equally world-altering rise to rearmament and World War II. By the end of the 1920s, two major changes had come about in the Hollywood film industry. The first was that it had evolved into an industry completely dependent on star power. Sarah Bernhardt, always before her time, had been the precursor of the silent era film stars, and since the phenomenal success of Mary Pickford, those who now shared the most power with the studio executives were not the directors, but the actors. This power was always inextricably linked to the actor's popularity, and could therefore be lasting or extremely short-lived. The second factor that forever changed the face of cinema was the advent of motion picture sound. In 1927, *The Jazz Singer* revolutionized filmmaking with its synchronized speech, music, and sound effects, and marked the end of the silent film era.

America may have been crushed under the weight of the Depression, but the film industry was booming. "Audience enthusiasm for the talking picture was such that the Depression, arriving simultaneously, had little effect on cinema takings," wrote David Shipman.[1] It did, however, have an effect on the types of films that were being made. The earlier melodramatic adventure and historical films no longer fit the mindset of a nation under the pall of the first years of socio-economic destruction, and they were replaced with a slew of gangster films and romantic comedies. There was also a focus on the "new woman," an evolution begun by the less morally constricted Jazz Age flappers. In the period between *The Virgin Queen* and the implementation of the Motion Picture Production Code of 1930 (also known as the Hays Code) which truly flowered in the mid–1930s, a large number of films emerged showcasing strong, independent women who were often frank and unrepentant about their forward-thinking sexuality. Their onscreen male counterparts were no longer gentlemen, often exhibiting brutality and callousness, which they frequently exercised without facing the morally edifying, punitive consequences of their actions. The combination of "morally dubious" films with highly publicized scandals surrounding major film stars caused the U.S. government to take note and, rather than wait for the government to censor its films, Hollywood chose to censor itself. By the mid–1930s, the "recommendations" for what was acceptable in films had become much stricter. This quashed many of the staples in characterization and plotting for gangster films and vehicles for uninhibited female protagonists, which paved the way for a return to more "innocent" comedies, dramas, and historicals. The years 1933–34, in particular, saw a resurgence in historical drama, beginning with the tongue-in-cheek, extraordinarily successful *The Private Life of Henry VIII*, and went on to encompass such films as *The Rise of Catherine the Great*, *The Private Life of Don Juan*, and *The Scarlet Pimpernel*. *The Private Life of Henry VIII*, starring Charles Laughton as the redoubtable Tudor monarch, is particularly notable in that its success encouraged its producer, Alexander Korda, to pursue another Tudor-related film, this time starring Henry's fiery daughter. Elizabeth and her father, however, were not the only Tudor-period royals to benefit from this new focus on historicals. While Korda was putting the finishing touches on his version of Elizabeth, her Scottish cousin beat her out of the gate.

MARY OF SCOTLAND (1936)

It may seem strange to include examination of a film whose title would appear to eschew a focus on Elizabeth in favor of her cousin, Mary, Queen of Scots. However, *Mary of Scotland* was seminal in the film "career" of Elizabeth for a number of reasons. It was the first American film to feature a major characterization of Elizabeth. It is also interesting in that it, as would other later film versions of Mary's life, treats Elizabeth's problematic relationship with her royal cousin, thereby illustrating another facet of the Hollywood version of Elizabeth: the great rivalry between the two queens. Did Elizabeth, or did she not, want Mary dead?

Roderick Graham, the producer of the miniseries *Elizabeth R* (examined in Chapter Six) has called Mary's life "far more intriguing" than her English cousin's, and yet in examinations of Mary's life, both literary and film, Elizabeth "keeps running onto the stage when she should be in the wings."[2] Entire books have been written about the relationship between these two women, Mary and Elizabeth, who, according to the historical record, never actually met.[3] Comparison would seem inevitable — they were both queens, less than a decade apart in age, who together ruled two countries that made up a single island. They were also cousins: Margaret Tudor, one of Henry VIII's sisters, was Mary's paternal grandmother. This familial connection created a peculiar sort of dichotomy. It provided a bond which linked the two women together, but at the same time made them rivals — because they shared the same bloodline, they both had claim to the same throne. They also had one more aspect in common: by the time they ascended their respective thrones, they were both orphans.

Mary's father, James V of Scotland, died a mere six days after her birth. Her mother, Marie de Guise, came from the powerful French house of Guise, rulers of the French province of Lorraine. Widowed the first time at the age of 21, Marie de Guise quickly found herself back on the marriage market. James V of Scotland was also recently widowed, and he wished a French wife for himself to further a Franco-Scottish alliance that would provide a counterbalance to the power of his neighbor to the south, Henry VIII. Henry attempted to forestall this by tentatively seeking Marie's hand for himself (he had recently buried wife number three, Jane Seymour), but Marie and her family, given Henry's marital track record, cited fear for Marie's neck and wisely chose the Scottish match. Marie and James produced two sons, but neither boy lived long enough to meet his sister, Mary, who was born in 1542. When James died soon after, Mary succeeded him as his only living heir.

Mary was sent to France to live at the court of her husband-to-be, the Dauphin Francis, heir to the French throne. In Mary's absence, Marie de Guise served as regent, fostering an even closer relationship between Scotland and the French. She moved French courtiers into high-ranking government positions. This, along with the rise of Protestantism in Scotland led by firebrands such as John Knox, ensured that the regency was rife with political and religious unrest. By 1558, the year of Elizabeth's ascension to the English throne, the political instability in Scotland threatened to bloom into open revolt.

When the inevitable insurrection occurred, Elizabeth and the English, not surprisingly, sided with the Scottish Protestants — though Elizabeth had no love for Knox (his *First Blast of the Trumpet against the Monstrous Regiment of Women* had done him no favors with her), she did hold religious sympathy with the Protestants and political animosity for the French. She needed to destroy France's foothold in Scotland, which placed the French almost at her doorstep. The end result was the Treaty of Berwick, English backing for the Scottish Protestants, and the forming of a separate peace with a provisional Scottish government after Marie de Guise's French troops and mercenaries retreated. Matters were simplified when Marie died, probably of dropsy, in 1560.

The year 1558 had been a banner one all around — in addition to Elizabeth's ascension, it was in this year that Mary had married Francis, guaranteeing that, in addition to being Queen of Scotland, one day she would also be the Queen of France. "One day" perhaps came sooner than Mary could have anticipated; Henry II died in 1559, leaving Francis as King and young Mary as Queen of France. It was a time of loss for Mary: shortly after Henry's death she lost her mother, and six months later she also lost her young husband. With nothing left to keep her in France and Scotland in need of a ruler, Mary set sail for a home she barely remembered.

One of the main factors that draws historians, biographers, and filmmakers to the story of Elizabeth and Mary Stuart is its potential for contrast — while even Elizabeth's staunchest critics admit her reign to be a success, even if only in the elementary sense that she managed to retain her throne and keep England's enemies at bay, Mary's reign is considered an unqualified failure. The responsibility for this failure and, by extension, portrayals of Mary herself, varies accordingly. On film, she's most often characterized as a sympathetic, tragic figure: beautiful, young, charming, educated and accomplished, and yet still unable to stay afloat politically due to her propensity for making decisions based on emotion rather than intellect, choosing the heart over the head. Elizabeth is the icy, shrewd Virgin Queen: Mary is passion wedded to naïveté. There's also a tendency to depict Mary as an innocent victim of circumstance — manipulated by both Elizabeth and the cantankerous Scottish nobles surrounding her, a helpless dove in a court full of raptors. The contradictory interpretation is the tireless plotter — a queen more French than Scottish, never satisfied with only a backwater Scottish throne and unrelenting in her attempts to get rid of those in her way, whether it be her spouse or her royal English cousin, even to the point of assassination.

Interpretations are myriad, but the facts of Mary's reign are simple, and it started off promisingly enough. Mary was acknowledged to be uniformly charming, and though Catholic, she did not attempt to widen the religious rift in her kingdom. Like Elizabeth, she had no desire to make windows into men's souls. Though the Scottish nobility was notoriously difficult to deal with, Mary did make a short-lived and ultimately unsuccessful attempt at unity. It was Mary's private life (if there is such a thing in the life of a queen) which would in due course sow the seeds of her destruction.

Mary realized that she needed to produce an heir to continue her line, and unlike her English cousin, she was not averse to marrying in order to further this and other ends, both political and personal. Various suitors for the young, attractive queen had been put forth; Elizabeth even (outrageously and offensively, in Mary's opinion) suggested her Master of the Horse and favorite, Robert Dudley, Earl of Leicester. Mary's suitors equaled potentially dangerous Catholic continental support for Scotland (e.g., Philip II's son, Don Carlos), and Elizabeth had a need to forestall this, if possible. The person Mary eventually chose to wed would end up being even more detrimental to the Scottish Queen's interests than any husband Elizabeth could have selected for her.

Henry Stewart, Lord Darnley, was a great-grandson of Henry VII, giving him a claim to the English throne. He had been sent to France and was educated there before being later recalled; his mother, the powerful Lady Margaret Douglas, Countess of Lennox, had hoped he would succeed Elizabeth. As soon as Mary was freed by Francis's death, the Countess of Lennox began maneuvering to marry her son to Mary, thus cementing both their claims to the English throne. Elizabeth, as can be imagined, was less than pleased with these machinations, which resulted in Darnley and his mother, both English subjects, being briefly imprisoned by Elizabeth in 1561.

Not long afterward, the Countess of Lennox and her son were released, and eventually made their way to Mary's court in Scotland. By early 1565, Mary was already seriously considering a match with Darnley. Sources differ on Elizabeth's reaction to this; she reportedly recalled Darnley and his family to the English court because she condemned the match, though her orders were ignored. Some contend that, in a burst of reverse psychology, Elizabeth pretended to disparage the match so that Mary would feel she had the upper hand and go through with the marriage, which Elizabeth knew would be disadvantageous for Mary. Others argue that Elizabeth truly did object to the match, but was powerless to stop it, while still a third contingent see Elizabeth's council (led by Lord Burghley, who spent his career attempting to destroy the Scottish Queen) as engineering it either in spite of Elizabeth's disapproval or with her secret blessing. Regardless, though the hoped-for heir would be quickly provided, the marriage was to be an unqualified disaster for Mary. It was the beginning of the end for her.

On the surface, Darnley had everything to recommend him. He was a few years younger than Mary and was, by all accounts, tall and handsome. He had been educated in France, which gave him something in common with Mary, who was decidedly French in her upbringing and background. Darnley was also considered to be, at first blush, quite charming. This, coupled with his bloodline, produced a favorable initial verdict. Yet the two were, in temperament, completely unsuited. Both were immature and prideful, and Darnley could be spiteful and vindictive, especially when his desires were not immediately granted. His rowdy coterie of friends posed yet another problem. By most accounts, the main motive behind the match was political; Mary also, however, fell headlong in love with the handsome young man, although this passion was as brief as it was shallow. How he felt about her at the beginning of their relationship is far less certain, but his sentiments would soon become unmistakable.

Mary and Darnley wed in July of 1565, and it did not take long for the romance to sour beyond salvaging. Darnley had firmly believed that he would be immediately given the crown matrimonial—made King of Scotland in his own right, not just the Queen's consort. He also expected to play a major role in the political arena and the governing of the country. This did not prove to be the case, and his reaction to this setback to his ambitions is illustrative of his character in general. Darnley was increasingly contemptuous of his wife while foolishly aggrandizing himself, and they quickly became estranged. Darnley was not helped by the counsel he received from the sycophants with whom he surrounded himself or the Scottish nobles who had their own, rather than his, interests at heart. Matters soon went from bad to worse.

Enter Mary's secretary, an Italian named David Rizzio.[4] Mary and Rizzio were close, and this, coupled with the fact that Rizzio was a foreigner who had a tendency to slight high-ranking nobles in favor of acquiring power for himself, made him extremely unpopular. Unsubstantiated rumors flew that he and Mary were lovers, and the nobles also resented him for reaching beyond his station. Darnley was convinced that Rizzio's behavior towards his wife was personally insulting, and it took little for Darnley to make the leap from there to murder. He entered into a conspiracy with a group of Scottish nobles, and they dashed into Mary's chambers, dragged the terrified Rizzio from her presence, and brutally murdered the Italian secretary. Mary, fearing for her own life, played her husband for a fool—pretending a reconciliation, she flattered and promised until he gave up his fellow conspirators and even helped Mary move to a safer location.

As soon as his assistance was no longer needed, Darnley discovered that his wife's newfound affection for him was as ephemeral as it was insincere. She had already formed a connection with one of her nobles, the Earl of Bothwell who, it was rumored, was heading up a plot to murder Darnley. Finally realizing on what tenuous ground he trod, Darnley decided to flee Scotland. Before he could do so, however, he fell ill, some said as the result of poisoning, or perhaps venereal disease. Mary visited him, and they were supposedly reconciled yet again. This reconciliation was to be even briefer than the previous one. The royal couple traveled to Edinburgh and were installed in a house at Kirk o' Field. Leaving her convalescent husband at home, Mary went out for the evening. And then the house blew up.

From that February night in 1567 to today, historians have debated what level of involvement, if any, Mary had in the murder of her husband. The house at Kirk o' Field was exploded with a hearty dose of gunpowder, but Darnley did not die in the explosion; he was found some distance from the house, strangled, probably after attempting to escape. It's accepted as fact that the murder was carried out by the Earl of Bothwell, who had risen up as a protector of sorts to Mary after her estrangement from her husband, but whose real goal was most probably the throne of Scotland. To compound matters, Mary quickly married Bothwell after he disposed of his present wife (by divorce rather than gunpowder) and carried Mary off to his estate to "ravish" her. The Scottish nobles finally had a common cause under which they could unite: the destruction of Bothwell. Civil war ensued, a war which Bothwell and Mary lost. He escaped, leaving Mary alone and unprotected. Mary was forced to abdicate, and her infant son, James VI, became King of Scotland.

Watching all of this from her seat on the throne of England, Elizabeth must have been astounded, and perhaps bemused as well. Most historians agree that, at least based on what is now historically extant, Elizabeth's policy towards her Scottish cousin was confusing at best, and inexplicable at worst. As one source states, Elizabeth "recognized the threat, but she was emotionally and perhaps politically unwilling to question the authority of another legitimate sovereign."[5] This may be an oversimplification of the situation, for Elizabeth's viewpoint was not the only one that influenced English policy towards Scotland. One possible explanation for the confusion with regard to Elizabeth's policy is that it may represent two separate opinions — what has been called an "ideological rift" between Elizabeth and her chief minister, William Cecil, over how to deal with Scottish affairs. In a memo written by Cecil to Elizabeth on the subject, he chastises her for dealing with Mary as if "she meaneth to reclaim her by gentleness and benefit," a course of action Cecil felt was unwise and dangerous, and one he tried to thwart wherever he could.[6] In addition to her familial ties with Mary, Elizabeth may have also seen in Mary a reflection of her own worst fears — she faced the same type of scheming and court intrigue, and Elizabeth's hold on the English throne was, at times, tenuous. There was also the knowledge that, as part of a royal sisterhood governing by divine right, undermining the rule of one endangered the authority of all. In the same way the French and American revolutions would later feed off the same set of ideals, so could unrest of the type that threatened Mary spread to Elizabeth. In short, Elizabeth did not want her subjects getting ideas from the Scots. For these reasons, Elizabeth's "policy thus vacillated between attacking Mary when she was strong and aiding her when she was weak."[7]

Mary was certainly at her weakest point when she escaped from her confinement in Scotland and fled to England, thinking her royal cousin would aid her and she could recover her throne. Her track record for choosing poorly was officially proven. Elizabeth would ensure that Mary was to spend the rest of her life in England, whether she wished to or not. Though it was in comfortable surroundings, Mary was nevertheless a prisoner, and it did not take long for the Catholic plotting to begin. Mary placed Elizabeth in a most awkward position. Elizabeth saw the danger in restoring her to the Scottish throne or any position of power; Mary had systematically refused to renounce her right to the English throne, and she fully expected to succeed after Elizabeth's death ... natural or otherwise. The English Catholics saw in her an alternative, a Catholic queen to replace the

Protestant currently on their throne. Various conspiracies surfaced; Mary was to be married to the Duke of Norfolk (a divorce from Bothwell had been obtained in 1570), and she was to take the English throne while a Spanish expeditionary force invaded. Mary found, ultimately, that the Duke of Norfolk was not suitable for marrying—as it turned out, he was dead; his machinations had cost him his head, and also resulted in Mary being moved to more secure quarters. Plot after plot surfaced, some in which Mary seemed to be implicated, others where she was simply the unwitting banner under which others pursued their goals. Parliament called for her execution, Elizabeth vacillated. She would take almost 14 years to finally make up her mind about the Scottish Queen.

Elizabeth's spymaster, Sir Francis Walsingham, ultimately provided the nails for Mary's coffin. After uncovering the details of a lamebrained scheme known as the Babington Plot, Walsingham insinuated one of his agents into the conspiracy and managed to entrap Mary and finally obtain irrefutable evidence of her treason against Elizabeth. Mary signed her name to a letter consenting to the assassination of Elizabeth, and in essence, signed her own death warrant. With this evidence in hand, it could no longer be doubted that Mary was guilty of treason, and she was put to trial.

Parliament had long wanted her dead, as had Elizabeth's advisers. It's debatable whether Elizabeth felt more anxiety and conflict over the killing of her cousin or having to face the responsibility for it in the court of European royal opinion, but she finally signed Mary's order of execution. Still Elizabeth delayed, but her council took matters into its own hands by delivering the warrant to Fotheringhay Castle, where Mary was imprisoned. She was beheaded post haste, dramatically wearing a red gown, the color of Catholic martyrs. When the news reached Elizabeth, she pretended fury—she ranted that she had not yet planned to send the warrant, she bore no responsibility for Mary's death. But she must have been, on some level, relieved that the needed action had finally been taken. In this rivalry, there could only be one winner, and it was certainly Elizabeth.

This idea of success as a queen or woman is one that has been widely explored in literature. The concept that the two are mutually exclusive is disproven by many examples, not the least of which is Queen Victoria. Elizabeth and Mary, however, are often used to illustrate opposite sides of this royal issue which is unique to female monarchs. Mary represents success as a woman: she married (not once, but three times) and became a mother. As a queen, however, she was a dismal failure. Elizabeth, on the other hand, remained the eternal virgin, eschewing marriage and motherhood. She failed as a woman, but her rule was a success. All of this presupposes that what women desire more than anything else, and thus the yardstick against which their success is measured, is a husband and children. While in the modern era this traditional view of a woman's chief purpose has evolved almost to the point of irrelevancy, this was certainly not the case in Elizabethan England. For this reason, the adjective "unnatural" was often applied to Elizabeth, whereas Mary represents the "natural" woman. Despite this, taking an empathetic view of Mary Stuart is relatively recent and certainly revisionist—for most of the past 400 years, Mary has been cast as "wanton and cruel"; it was not until the late Victorian era that her reputation underwent rehabilitation. As has been noted, the decision to focus on "such an uneven, questionable female ruler as Mary Stuart indicates a more questioning approach to women's history than the early twentieth-century feminists who tended to focus on Queen Elizabeth as an exemplary, capable woman ruler whose intellect and strength of will equaled any man's."[8]

Due to the opportunity provided for comparison as well as their ties and the role Elizabeth would play in the latter years of Mary's life and in her death, it is unsurprising that Elizabeth figures as a major player in most film adaptations of Mary's life, often almost equaling Mary's screen time. There are two ways to form an accurate perception of an object or an individual — by knowledge of what it *is*, or by employing reverse logic, contrast based on what it is *not*. Many facets of Mary's character are reverses of Elizabeth's, and in the examination of this contrast, Elizabeth is illuminated. In fact, these films are often just as much about Elizabeth as they are about Mary. They display a decided bias, a tendency to "canonize Mary and caricature Elizabeth."[9] Some go beyond caricature and stop at nothing short of Elizabeth's total vilification. Such is certainly the case with *Mary of Scotland*.

Mary of Scotland was based on a play of the same name by Maxwell Anderson which had experienced great success when it opened in theaters in 1933. A screenplay for the film version was adapted by writer Dudley Nichols, who eschewed the poetic blank verse of Anderson's original in favor of more modern dialogue. In most other respects, however, it remains faithful to the play. Katharine Hepburn (1907–2003) was one of the many theatergoers who saw and loved the play, and she was convinced she could successfully play the role of Mary Stuart for the film version. She wanted director George Cukor, but the last film he and Hepburn had made together, *Sylvia Scarlett*, had not been a critical success, and had been damaging to Hepburn's starlet reputation (she played a woman posing as a boy in the film, and her androgyny did not sit well with the moviegoing public). Instead of teaming her with Cukor again, RKO executives decided to put director John Ford (1894–1973) at the helm, and they were thrilled when he agreed.[10]

At the time *Mary of Scotland* was made, Ford was considered by many to be the greatest director since D.W. Griffith. His forte, however, was always the American Western, and *Mary of Scotland* is considered one of his poorer films. He was in the midst of, in its most innocuous rendering, a passionate admiration for the movie's star, Katharine Hepburn, and this comes across in the cinematography of *Mary of Scotland*. It feels like a visual lovesong to Hepburn — there are a plethora of softly focused close-ups of Hepburn's/Mary's face, haloed in light, her eyes shining with unshed tears and her chin trembling, a beautiful and almost saintly figure. Ford may have been expressing his infatuation with the countenance of Katharine Hepburn, but what this translates to onscreen is a devotion to and purifying of the image of the historical woman Hepburn is ostensibly portraying — a canonizing of Mary. Elizabeth, played by Florence Eldridge (1901–1988), certainly receives no such gentle cinematic treatment. The film's bias is readily apparent from the initial scenes of the movie, which feature Elizabeth in council with her advisers.

The opening titles inform the viewer that Mary Stuart and Elizabeth Tudor have appeared in the 16th century "like two fateful stars" to reign over two great nations in the making. The melodramatic star-crossed imagery appears in other film adaptations of Mary's life, and it continues in *Mary of Scotland* when the titles state that the two women are "doomed to a life-and-death struggle for supremacy, a lurid struggle that still shines across the pages of history." Despite this, the viewer is told that after more than three centuries "they sleep side by side, at peace" in their tombs at Westminster Abbey. The set-up has thus been made for a monumental struggle, but one whose end result is peaceful and cathartic.

Double doors are pushed open, and guards zig-zag through them as if choreographed, after which the angle changes to show Elizabeth's court — several dozen gorgeously dressed ladies and gentlemen, murmuring excitedly. They fall to the floor in unison as Elizabeth is announced, and she strides purposefully through the room, ignoring them all, calling loudly for Lords Burghley and Randolph. They follow her into the council chamber, where she plops into her chair and slaps the table, obviously agitated. The entire entrance transmits a sense of urgency, movement, and irritation. The tone has been set for the portrayal of Elizabeth in this film — the two emotions she most often conveys are irritation and displeasure.

Eldridge's Elizabeth certainly looks like the historical woman — more so, perhaps, than many of the other actresses who played the part, the marvels of modern movie make-up notwithstanding. Though she looks little like the historical monarch in other films in which she appears, when gowned and bejeweled, her wig in place, Eldridge's facial structure convinces — it is more handsome than beautiful, and her eyes seem right, as does the way she applies her gaze. Even historical portraits of the Queen vary so much that using them for comparison is difficult, but Eldridge, in costume, bears a remarkable resemblance to the Elizabeth of the "Darnley Portrait," Nicolas Hilliard's "Phoenix Portrait," and the "Sieve Portrait" by Quentin Massys the Younger.

What has so agitated Elizabeth soon becomes apparent. Sir Nicholas Throckmorton explains that Mary Stuart has sailed from France for Scotland. Mary has defied Elizabeth's wishes and, what's more, has refused to recognize Elizabeth as the rightful Queen of England. "What are we to do?" Elizabeth intones. Her advisers have little helpful advice — in a statement that the historical Burghley, given how he viewed Mary Stuart, would have choked on, the film Burghley offers, "She's the true heir of Henry VIII and she must be acknowledged." "Not by me!" Elizabeth barks back. The film Burghley goes on to "state facts": that in the eyes of Europe Elizabeth is a pretender to the throne because the marriage of her father and Anne Boleyn is deemed invalid. Using Burghley for this type of exposition is incongruous; one has a difficult time picturing Elizabeth sitting idly by while he questions her legitimacy and her right to rule by stating facts of which Elizabeth is already well aware. The film version of Elizabeth, however, does just that; she sits silently in her chair, looking pensively angry, her lips pursed, and lets him go on. He then warns that Mary Stuart will use the throne of Scotland as a stepping stone to the throne of England, as if Elizabeth didn't know. Finally, Elizabeth has had enough. In a strident tone, she makes it clear she wants Mary Stuart captured at sea, and the dutiful Lord Randolph hurries from the chamber to find Captains Hawkins and Drake and instruct them to do just that.

The scene switches to the coast of Leith, where Mary's ship glides safely through the mists to land in Scotland. Mary steps regally onshore, immediately kneels and, her eyes moist with tears, prays. She gives thanks for her safe voyage, implying that God has been on her side since Elizabeth's best laid schemes to waylay her have gang aft agley. Unlike

Elizabeth, Mary is humble, and implores her Maker to "counsel my heart, guide my steps in this land of my birth, that I may rule with piety and wisdom." This is no selfish and silly creature. Overcome with earnestness, Mary allows her tears to spill over as the camera zooms in on her perfectly angled, angelic countenance, and the scene fades out.

The contrast between the first glimpses of each queen is indicative of their characterizations—Elizabeth is shown striding about in the artificial setting of her glittering court milieu; the lighting is bright, harsh, and it illuminates every line when she creases her brow or purses her lips in displeasure. Mary, conversely, is outside, at night, a natural setting, and the lighting is subdued, softly focused on her face, which seems to glow. Elizabeth's expression is most often a furrowed brow coupled with the corners of her mouth turned downward; she very seldom smiles, unless it's at something unpleasant, usually the idea of Mary's destruction. Mary, on the other hand, switches between earnest tearfulness and sincere smiles that showcase her perfect white teeth. The clothing of the two women is also a study in contrasts. Elizabeth sports tight puffs and rolls—she literally drips with jewels. The overall impression is of something dazzling, but sharp, hard, inflexible, and unyielding, as well as unpleasant. Even the clacking and jangling of her jewelry is harsh to the ears. Mary's costuming, on the other hand, is less flamboyant and much softer; her traveling gown is made of velvet, adorned only with a reserved patch of gold embroidery down the front of the bodice. She rustles softly when she moves; she does not clack. Mary also wears surprisingly little jewelry. Though this is partially due to setting—riding habits and travel garments must necessarily be less elaborate than court gowns—this is a costuming choice that's made throughout the film. Even when Mary is shown at court, in council, still her costuming is relatively simple and her jewelry understated. Elizabeth is all artificial glitter with only anger and jealousy underneath; Mary is a beautiful woman, touchable, soft, and desirable.

There is also great disparity shown between the Scottish and English courts. Holyrood, to which Mary travels, is a dark, sparsely furnished castle, compared to the bright, grand interior spaces of Elizabeth's palace. Holyrood is a threatening place; this is an environment which is dangerous for the gentle Mary. Elizabeth, by contrast, is completely at home in her glitzy court; the spaces and everything in them are there to suit her fancy. The councilors who populate Elizabeth's court are shown to be deferential males; they may occasionally state their opinions, but are quick enough to hold their peace when Elizabeth flashes with irritation. They are also well-mannered and richly dressed. They sit at Elizabeth's side, holding her fluffy lapdog, a symbol of subservience which appears again and again in Elizabeth films, as well as being an appellation applied directly to the favorites themselves. The first view of the Scottish nobles stands in sharp contrast to this—they wear kilts and rough furs, repeatedly starting up from their seats to argue and gesticulate with one another while their huge hunting dogs bark, so that nothing can be distinguished above the testosterone-fueled din. Where Elizabeth's court is mannered and decorous, the Scottish court is chaotic. One man sits at the table, quietly watching this chaos: the Earl of Moray (Ian Keith).

James Stuart, the Earl of Moray, was Mary's half-brother, the illegitimate son of James V and Margaret Douglas. In the oft-repeated confusion of royal bloodlines, this was the same Margaret Douglas, Countess of Lennox, who would later become Mary's mother-in-law when the Scottish Queen married her legitimate son, Lord Darnley. James Stuart had an even better pedigree than Darnley for claiming the Scottish and English thrones, but the fact that he was born on the wrong side of the blanket eliminated any possibility of capitalizing on it. So Moray chose a different route to power — he stood with the Protestant Scottish nobles against the regency of Marie de Guise. Upon the death of Mary's mother, Moray served as regent, but when Mary returned from France, he initially supported her rule, despite the fact that she was a Roman Catholic. Their falling out came over his support of the rather caustic reformer John Knox and, perhaps even more, his opposition to the marriage of Mary to Darnley. He tried to rouse the citizens of Edinburgh against Mary, and she repaid him by declaring him an outlaw and forcing him to flee across the border. She pardoned him the very next year, and he returned to Scotland. Moray would find himself regent once again when Mary abdicated, and it was his forces that quashed any final chance his sibling had at regaining her throne, turning the tables and forcing Mary to flee across the border. Mary would have the final word, however, for she would survive her half-brother, who was assassinated by one of her supporters in 1570.

While Moray sits watching, but not taking part in the fray in the council chamber, a messenger arrives with the unwelcome news that Mary has landed in Scotland and is on her way. The nobles pretend to have gathered to greet her, and Moray cautions them, "Remember, you lords are the real power of Scotland. You can afford to hold your tongues." Elizabeth is the power at the English court; her nobles dance to her tune. In Scotland, Mary is meant to be merely a figurehead for the powerful nobles who will hold her puppet strings. The only one who does not seem to understand this is Mary herself. Moray goes into the courtyard to greet her, and through their conversation, the viewer learns that, as a child, Mary looked up to and admired Moray. Mary's exuberance is somewhat subdued when she enters the council chamber. None of the lords even acknowledge her until one staunch supporter, Lord Huntly, goes down on one knee. Mary greets them with a speech that is supposed to set her up as someone who has always bowed to the wishes of others for the greater good, "It was not of my own choice that I went away, but it is of my own choice that I've returned. You'll find me young, perhaps, inexperienced, but with the support of all of you and the Earl of Moray at my side, I shall rule fairly and justly." The impression is that, with a little help from her friends, Mary will make one heck of a queen. This demonstrates the naïveté under which Mary labors, and she's soon made more aware of how things stand. The impact of her inexperience and the part it will play in the death of Rizzio is immediately foreshadowed; one of the Scottish lords asks that they be allowed to greet the Queen without the presence of "foreigners," but Mary bids Rizzio remain, even after he, wiser than she, attempts to go. The lords then lay their "differences" before her — namely that she practices the old religion. They encourage her to be more like Elizabeth, who was "born in the old faith, like you, my lady, but she gets off a ship when it sinks." Elizabeth is thus shown to be opportunistic and unprincipled, and Mary is indignant at the comparison. Her religion is "no garment to be put on and off with the weather." They try a different tact, moving on to the subject of her marriage. Mary sarcastically says, "I suppose you've decided on my husband." They certainly have, and inform her that they have chosen Lord Darnley. Mary, still sarcastic, says that she cannot give herself out to be a virgin queen like her cousin Elizabeth, but "suppose I don't choose to marry at all?" This sounds much more like Katharine Hepburn than Mary Stuart. The film version of Mary, however, has "never done anything of my own wish. The ambition of other men carried me to France as a child, the ambition of other men married me to a dying boy who became King of France. I wasn't asked. But I'm through! I'm going to live my own life, do as *I* say! I refuse to marry! I love no one and I shall marry no one! I'm going to begin to be myself, Mary Stuart!" Her passionate and adolescent outburst for independence complete, Mary storms up to her room, followed closely by Rizzio, her black-clad shadow.

Speeches like this delivered with the conviction Hepburn conveys certainly have appeal; however, they ring absolutely false given the facts about the historical Mary, and even as compared with Hepburn's Mary in later scenes from the film. The historical Mary always looked to the "nearest, strongest man" for help, and she certainly never refused to marry.[11] In fact, it was her hopping into the matrimonial state so quickly that got her into trouble — she did not wait for a dispensation from the pope for her marriage to Darnley (necessary because the two were cousins), and her marriage to Bothwell, the alleged murderer of her husband, happened with a rapidity that "unseemly" does not even begin to describe. Many of Mary's nobles were against the Darnley match, and Mary herself, infatuated with the superficially charming young man, chose to go ahead in spite of this. Darnley certainly was not served up on a platter and force-fed to an unwilling Mary by Moray and his contingent.

Mary's comments about her religion are also interesting in what they insinuate by comparison to Elizabeth's. Mary's statements set this as a conflict, not between a Protestant Elizabeth and a Catholic Mary, but rather between a monarch who staunchly adheres to her beliefs versus a hypocritical queen whose religion is a sham — Elizabeth holds no steadfast faith, she follows no conscience, but merely molds herself to whatever seems most advantageous at the moment. The Scots, even the bombastic Knox, are portrayed as Protestants of conviction, but Elizabeth is a Protestant of convenience.

While Moray is downstairs assuring the contentious nobles that he will keep Mary well in hand and protect their interests, peasants begin to file into the courtyard. In one of the most contrived scenes in the film, they burst into a song of devotion to their queen, the "fairest ever seen," complete with solos and harmony more suggestive of the London Philharmonic Choir than a ragtag bunch of Scottish peasants. Mary watches from her window, raptly, eyes yet again shining with tears, and sighs, "Now I'll find a way to win." Before her case of the warm fuzzies turns terminal, the peasant choir is interrupted by a bearded, wild-eyed John Knox. He hushes the crowd and then begins to harangue them, calling Mary the "Jezebel of France" and going on about how her mother, Marie de Guise, burned his mentor, George Wishart, at the stake. In mid-harangue, there's yet another interruption; the Earl of Bothwell arrives and has his men play the bagpipes loudly enough to drown out Knox, who nevertheless continues to rail while Bothwell laughs at him most heartily. Mary comes down to engage Knox, and while one could see Elizabeth reading him the riot act for such a show of defiance and then having him thrown into the Tower, instead Mary gently entreats him to come inside with her where they can speak in private.

Mary was not the first that the historical Knox likened to Jezebel — in his *First Blast of the Trumpet against the Monstrous Regiment of Women*, Knox wrote "most especially against that wicked Jezebel of England," Queen Mary Tudor, for her persecution of English Protestants. The historical Mary Stuart and Knox spoke on more than one occasion, at length, and he never gave way. His pronouncement with regard to the Queen was that she had a "proud mind, a crafty wit, and an indurate heart against God and His truth."[12] Knox was certainly not known for mincing words, and more than one account has Mary in tears because of it. The film version of Mary's encounter with Knox takes place in the hallway at Holyrood, and she begins by appealing to his emotions rather than his intellect. Asking him to look at her, she asks: "Can you believe I'm as wicked as you say?" This statement is absurd on its face; one need not have memorized *The Picture of Dorian Gray* to know that beauty and a pleasant manner can mask a multitude of sins. Mary states that she wants to be loved by her people, that she "needs their support." She reiterates an earlier statement that if she plans to keep to her religion while still allowing the Protestants to practice theirs, cannot Knox show the same toleration? Of course, he cannot. He *will* not. He leaves a depressed Mary alone in the hallway with Bothwell, who has witnessed the exchange.

This need for the "love" of their subjects is a theme that appears often with regard to female monarchs. It is less apparent with their male counterparts who, because of the traditional male hierarchy, demand to be obeyed, their authority inherently respected; they have no need to manipulate others into doing their will by means of a positive emotional response. Ruling queens had no such natural authority, and so they look to love, expressed by them for their people in a maternal context, and given back to them by the people as their devoted children. The imagery is readily apparent in many of Elizabeth's speeches: her people may find better princes, but never one that loves them more. She firmly believed in her divine right to rule, but Elizabeth also understood the political value of popular support. Mary's plea in the film, however, seems more of an emotional necessity than a political one. This woman is emotionally needy — she wants to be loved, by her people, by her nobles, by her suitors, and even by Elizabeth.

After Knox's tongue-lashing, the emotional Mary is, yet again, on the verge of tears when Bothwell engages her, bringing her out of her blue funk. When she accuses him of being a "very outspoken man," he tells her that it's a privilege he's always retained, but he served her mother loyally and pledges the same to Mary. Bothwell then immediately stalks into the council chamber, where the nobles are forming Mary's council without her input. Slamming a shield with his sword as a sort of gong to quiet them and, accompanied by his large dog, Bothwell informs them that he will be taking the position of Lieutenant General, since Mary has appointed him as such, though she never actually mentioned it. At their astonishment, Bothwell launches into a hearty belly-laugh while the scene fades out.

This characterization of Bothwell, portrayed with flair by Frederic March, shows him as a plain-spoken Scotsman, intelligent, forceful, but an amiable and loyal rogue, a man's man deserving of respect. The historical Bothwell was almost certainly less palatable. Though a Protestant himself, he did support Marie de Guise's regency and was a member of Mary's Privy Council. However, as early as 1562 he was accused of plotting to kidnap the Queen, which resulted in his imprisonment. He managed to escape and fled to France in 1564. It was not long before his services were needed again. When the Earl of Moray began his rebellion against the marriage of his half-sister to Darnley, Bothwell was recalled to aid Mary. By the time of David Rizzio's murder, Mary considered Bothwell to be almost indispensable, and they were probably already romantically involved. When Mary's marriage to Darnley became untenable, Bothwell was at her side yet again. He was acquitted of Darnley's murder, but it's generally accepted that the trial was rigged and the outcome a foregone conclusion, much like that of the investigation into the mysterious death of Amy Robsart, the wife of Elizabeth's favorite, Robert Dudley. Bothwell was already married, but when Mary conveniently lost her husband, Bothwell quickly divorced his wife (although he kept her as a mistress) and wed Mary. Protestants and Catholics alike were united by their hatred of Bothwell, and led a successful rebellion that resulted in Mary's abdication, on the condition that Bothwell be allowed to escape. He did, to Denmark, where he would spend his remaining years insane, in solitary confinement, until his death. For her part, Mary had their marriage annulled in 1570.

This honest man's man at Mary's side is contrasted with Elizabeth's favorite, Robert Dudley, Earl of Leicester. He lounges in Elizabeth's apartments, petting her lapdog and cattily discussing the return of Lord Randolph from Scotland. It's obvious he's jealous of Randolph, and Elizabeth delights in torturing him. She fawns all over Randolph until it dawns on her that he has fallen under the Scottish Queen's spell. Randolph makes the mistake of mentioning Mary's beauty and charm, and Elizabeth, her tone playful but dangerous, says, "Is she as pretty as they say?" Randolph sidesteps the issue by allowing Elizabeth to judge for herself— Mary has sent a miniature of herself as a gift for Elizabeth. Her brow furrowed in displeasure, Elizabeth examines herself in the mirror, then looks at the miniature, comparing. "Girl, not a queen," is her contemptuous appraisal. Randolph has other unwelcome news as well, that Mary may wed Darnley. Elizabeth admits him to be a "weakling drunkard" but confesses she will be in "double-jeopardy" if he weds the Scottish Queen. Randolph then goes on to describe Bothwell's contributions, making him out to be a most heroic figure who has restored order and done what no one else could, won the Queen's heart. Randolph stupidly insists that Mary "is a creature of love ... she wins men to her side in gentle ways." The implication is that Elizabeth is anything but gentle, commanding obedience where Mary inspires devotion. This is illustrated through Elizabeth's actions — she is shown grabbing her lapdog by the scruff of its neck and tossing it out of her chair. The laws of physics not being what they are, one could also see her doing the same to her male courtiers. This is a woman who is not kind. Now certain that he's too sympathetic towards Mary's cause, Elizabeth relieves an astonished Randolph of his post, appointing instead Sir Nicholas Throckmorton, a "cold fish" who will be less susceptible to Mary's charms. A satisfied Leicester comforts Elizabeth as she sinks into her chair, head in hand, and sighs, "Am I never to have peace?" Burghley states with finality that Mary must be defeated, and his recommendation is to do it by force, a complete turnaround from his earlier demand that she be acknowledged as heir to the English throne. Elizabeth demurs, "War. Is that all you men know?" Elizabeth shows herself to be a better judge of character and a craftier stateswoman with the plan she lays forth. She says quietly that she knows what it is to be illegitimate, how it "makes ambition burn." She then casually asks after the illegitimate Earl of Moray. Elizabeth knows he hungers for the power he had before Mary's return to Scotland, and she judges, rightly, that he would be willing to solve her problem for her in order to get it back, killing two birds with one stone. She is still watching herself in the mirror, and one half expects her to inquire of it, like the wicked queen in *Snow White*, who is the fairest of them all.

Meanwhile, in Mary's apartments, Rizzio is desperately trying to convince her to wed someone who is *not* Bothwell. He has respect for Bothwell's abilities, but knows how disastrous such a match would be for Mary. Darnley is his choice, but Mary sighs, "Why must I marry at all?" This allows Rizzio to read off a grocery list of possible suitors, listing the advantages of each, while Mary teases him, playfully dismissing each one with defects such as "his ears!" and "he snores!" until Rizzio, frustrated, storms for the door. Mary apologizes, still laughing, but Rizzio is in deadly earnest — only when she is married will she be safe. The fatal flaw in his logic will only come later, but for now, he encourages, "Marry Lord Darnley. There is no one else." Mary, resigned but none too enthusiastic, agrees and starts to send Rizzio for Darnley, but then stops him cold at the sound of the pipes, Bothwell's pipers. He has returned, and her countenance lights up immediately, all thoughts of Darnley forgotten. Her love has come home.

Queen Elizabeth (Florence Eldridge), the calculating spider, waits to trap the saintly Queen of Scots in her web in *Mary of Scotland*. (RKO/The Kobal Collection)

"In some measure," wrote J.M. Tasende, "almost all of the films by [John] Ford have something to do with his personal experiences."[13] Ford was certainly having a "personal experience" with Katharine Hepburn that manifests itself in this film, but the *characters* of the Elizabethan panorama were something else entirely. These beings were "historically distanced" from Ford in such a way that he could not relate to them. "The three centuries that separate him from Elizabeth of England and Mary Stuart is too much time to penetrate the collective or individual psychology of the protagonists."[14] They escaped him. And this is perceptible in *Mary of Scotland*. Other film adaptations manage, while sacrificing, condensing, or rewriting actual events, to present a somewhat convincing *feel* for the historical person experiencing them. *Mary of Scotland* does not.

This is partially due to Ford's direction, but an even greater fault lies with the woman portraying Mary, Queen of Scots — Katharine Hepburn. Hepburn was a member of a prominent New England family (she's often described as "patrician") which embraced the triune values of independence, education, and social responsibility. Hepburn would fulfill the second through her education at Bryn Mawr College, but she would focus most on the first of these, independence. In the early 1930s, after appearing on Broadway, Hepburn was offered a role in the film *A Bill of Divorcement* (1932), and the acclaim she received landed her other film roles. By her third film, she had been awarded her first Academy Award for Best Actress. Hepburn would continue to juggle both stage and film throughout the 1930s.

Due to her upbringing, innate intelligence, and personal temperament, Katharine Hepburn exuded both confidence and competence. She has been described as "a strong-minded independent woman, [who] governed her life and her career to suit herself."[15] In effect, she was the antithesis of Mary, Queen of Scots. Many actresses manage to subvert entire swathes of their personalities in order to believably portray a certain character — to be a proficient actress is to possess the ability to become someone else onscreen. As her four Academy Awards for Best Actress attest, Katharine Hepburn was, by all accounts, exceptional at her chosen craft. However, many of the roles she played most successfully were more in keeping with her personality and worldview. *Mary of Scotland* categorically was not. Hepburn's strength lay in embodying a vigorous female lead, from screwball socialites to daring old maids; portraying a naïve and vulnerable monarch did not play to her strengths. One of Hepburn's critics joked that "if she were cast as Little Red Riding Hood, she'd end up by eating the wolf."[16] Hepburn had little respect, if not outright detestation, for the historical Mary, saying of her, "I thought she was an ass.... I would have rather played Elizabeth, who, after all, was the powerful one."[17] She might have made an exceptional Elizabeth; such is not the case with her portrayal of Mary.

Due to the conflict between Hepburn's personality and that of the historical monarch, her Mary exhibits a strange sort of duality, resulting in a portrayal that is, at best, incongruous. Mary is often on the verge of tears, her chin quivering, uncertain and powerless to resist the forces around her, but Hepburn sometimes looks half disgusted with herself, as if she refuses to believe a woman could be so weak. Despite her acting efforts, Kate shines through the Mary façade, imbuing the Scottish Queen with more strength and intelligence than the historical woman ever actually possessed, and it seems at odds with the decisions the Queen is making. Her affect is inappropriate.

This certainly appears in the film with regard to her marriage to Darnley; this Mary has his number from the very beginning. Unlike other film representations of Mary and the historical record, Hepburn's Mary has no desire for Darnley — how could she for someone so weak and effeminate? It's always Bothwell, her true love, that she wants; she only bows to her greater responsibility, her love for her country, in marrying Darnley. In contemporary parlance, she takes one for the team, and it's quite a sacrifice; there is nothing whatsoever attractive about this film's Darnley. As played by Douglas Walton, he's thin, foppish and simpering, not to mention a gape-mouthed fool. When he enters the audience chamber where Mary's ladies-in-waiting are arranging her canopy of state, he says, "Ah, the four pretty wenches." With a grin, one of them replies, "Five, milord, now that you're here." He takes the comment as a joke rather than what's actually intended, namely contempt. The contrast is all the greater when Bothwell stalks in, accompanied by his huge dog, attired in his kilt. He warms himself in front of the roaring fire, fanning his kilt vigorously enough to make viewers uneasy that they may be about to accidentally find out what's underneath. It's part of his masculine image, and he says to the ladies-in-waiting, "Someday you'll meet a man who won't take no for an answer." He's rewarded with a coy, "And?" and he replies, "And I'll be the godfather." Bothwell's words are teasing, but his tone is serious; it's clear that he sees women as beings to be pursued and conquered, not wooed.

The reason Bothwell and Darnley have been kept waiting is because Mary is in conference with Elizabeth's new cold-fish ambassador, Throckmorton. Mary lays it out on the table for the viewer, "You tell me again and again of Elizabeth's friendship. I, too, give Elizabeth my friendship. We're two rulers in two adjoining countries. We're related by blood ties. There's every reason for friendship based on understanding. But how can there be understanding without frankness?" In this way, yet another unfavorable comparison is made between Mary and Elizabeth. Mary is open, honest, without guile. Her cousin is devious and evasive. It's clear with whom the viewer is meant to sympathize. Throckmorton informs Mary that Elizabeth will recognize her as heir to the throne if only she will marry a man of Elizabeth's choosing. Mary demonstrates her foolish pride and lack of diplomacy when she replies, "My succession was ordained by circumstances out of her control. I don't *need* her acknowledgment." When Throckmorton offers up the Earl of Leicester as Elizabeth's choice of husband for Mary, she explodes, "She's flaunted him before all England! Her favorite! Her leavings! ... and now she wants to cast him off on me? Make me a laughingstock before the world?!" This, at least, rings true — the historical Elizabeth did suggest the Earl of Leicester as a potential husband for Mary, and the offer was met with scorn and derision, as she, no doubt, suspected it would be. The idea was, with Leicester on the throne as King of Scotland, Elizabeth could trust him to act in the interests of England. She may also have seen it as a measure to placate his ambitions for a crown of his own without it having to be hers. As both the gentleman in question and Mary were vehemently opposed to the match, however, the scheme never came to fruition.

During the entirety of Mary's conversation with Elizabeth's ambassador, Rizzio stands behind her in frame, clutching the large cross he wears around his neck. Rizzio, as played by the lanky John Carradine, looks much like a mournful but not unappealing crow. He's dressed from head to toe in black, his long, thin legs like stalks. He's devoted to Mary, whom he calls "Madonna," in keeping with her almost saintly imagery in the film. The only jewelry he wears is a large cross, which he constantly clasps. To the Protestant lords, he personifies the darkness and corruption of the Catholic Church, but the viewer sees him in a much more sympathetic light — his courtly rather than physical love for Mary (the most he ever does is gaze at her and kiss her hand), his concern for her safety and happiness, and his subjugation of his own desires (namely, to return home to Italy) in order to serve her.

As Rizzio looks on, the power behind the throne, Mary concludes her interview with Throckmorton, "My cousin Elizabeth has never taken a single step that wasn't political," she says contemptuously. Mary is, of course, correct. Elizabeth is always considering the political repercussions of her actions. It's why her rule is viable while Mary's flounders. The irony is that Mary is too naïve to see that she should take a page from Elizabeth's playbook — she would be a much more successful ruler if she acted politically rather than emotionally. To act in this way, however, would show her to be like Elizabeth — calculating and unfeminine; as Mary says, it is "not in my nature to play politics," a rather ridiculous statement for a monarch to make. Mary then goes on to say, conversely, that she's about to do just that, marry Darnley for political reasons. The impression she gives is not one of making a dispassionate political decision, but rather acting yet again on her emotions: Elizabeth has angered her, and she will marry Darnley because she knows it's the last thing Elizabeth would have. In short, she will marry him out of spite. Throckmorton begs her not to be so rash, but she dismisses him and sends Rizzio for Darnley. During this entire exchange, Mary haughtily enjoys her moral high ground, and she sits in her chair, sewing, the very picture of feminine domesticity, an attitude which Elizabeth is never shown displaying.

Into this domestic scene strides Bothwell, blustering about how his "girl" won't see him. Mary is indignant, "Your girl?! Is that the way you speak of me outside?" This is about as strong as Mary gets, however; it quickly becomes clear that she's no match for Bothwell. She stands, moving away from him as if retreating before an onslaught, while he bellows, "I'm a soldier, I love ya'!" Mary's voice is barely a whisper as she squeaks, "You take everything by storm." Bothwell asks her if she knows any better way, then grabs her. By this point, she's pinned against the wall, and breathless, she says, "You forget I'm your queen." Bothwell replies that he has never forgotten, but "you're also a woman." Mary "commands" Bothwell to leave her, but her commands carry no weight; her tone is faint as she keeps repeating that she has made up her mind to marry Darnley. The viewer cannot help but agree with Bothwell when he says, scornfully, sadly, "Darnley. Why didnya pick a *man*?" When Mary murmurs about what is best for *her* kingdom, Bothwell, finally disgusted enough to leave, throws back, "Yours for how long?" Bothwell and the viewer already know what Mary cannot seem to grasp — that she is too weak to rule on her own. She requires a man to shore her up, a strong man like Bothwell, and she has made the wrong choice in Darnley.

A devastated Mary is seated in her chair, face in her hand, waiting passively for Darnley. When she tells him she has decided to marry him, he melodramatically intones, "Oh! I love you. I'll keep you! Defend you!" As Bothwell has already pointed out in case the viewer had any uncertainty, Darnley is incapable of doing any of these things. The lighting in this scene is strongly reminiscent of noir — with no readily recognizable outside impetus, it changes from light to almost complete shadow, turning the figures of Mary and Darnley into silhouettes, representative of the darkness that has entered Mary's life with this choice of husband. The only illumination comes in the form of bars of light across the two characters' eyes as Mary kisses Darnley, with distaste, then turns away.

Her fatal decision made, it only remains to be seen exactly how bad things will get with Darnley at the helm. Mary is shown in council, yet again sewing passively, as her councilors stare at her. Finally, Moray volunteers, "It's our rightful duty for us to shape your policies and for you to accept them." Mary has different ideas; one might expect her to retort that it's her job to lay down her policies and the council to follow them since she's queen. Instead, she looks to yet another man, taking the advice of Rizzio. Her tone is needling, baiting, as she refuses to get rid of Rizzio: "I have been a fool. I lost Bothwell, who kept you all in check. I thought I was ruling Scotland, but it was only his strength behind me. But I still have David." The name of her husband as protector and adviser never enters into matters, and the reason quickly becomes apparent. Darnley, obviously drunk, staggers in. Open-mouthed and mooning about, he's totally absurd as he slurs to her, "I'm king now. Even if someone doesn't seem to know it." He goes on about the state of his marriage, accusing his wife of being cold to him while she thinks of someone else, Bothwell. All the while, Mary keeps her eyes, which yet again have filled with tears, on her embroidery. By this point, her modus operandi has been proven: everything is met with passivity. Finally, she picks up her sewing and hurries out, locking Darnley out behind her. The council all put their hands to a bond to murder Rizzio, and convince Darnley to do the same, a conversation which Rizzio overhears.

Later, in Mary's chambers, she sits surrounded by her faithful and loving ladies-in-waiting, while Rizzio strums his lute, gazing into the fire, and sings in a wavering baritone about how he misses his home. Mary finally agrees to let him return there, sighing, "You're my only friend, and they're driving you away." What Mary means is that he is her only male supporter now that Bothwell is gone, for it is always men to whom Mary looks; she has neglected to mention her ladies. Mary is surrounded by four women who love and loyally serve her, but Rizzio is her "only friend." It's interesting to note this dynamic, for Elizabeth is very seldom shown with *any* close female relationships in film adaptations of her life. Though the historical Elizabeth possessed such relationships, it's also seldom covered in the literature, although one recent offering has attempted to bridge that gap.[18] Mary, on the other hand, is often shown surrounded by the "four Marys"—her ladies-in-waiting, Mary Seton, Mary Beaton, Mary Fleming, and Mary Livingstone. The implication is that Elizabeth views all females as rivals for the affections of her male favorites and thus cannot trust or befriend them. Mary has no such insecurities—being a "real woman," beautiful, charming, and desirable, she need have no fear or jealousy, and she inspires love in the females around her as well as the males. While Mary may have these female friends, she views them the same way she views herself, powerless without male support, and so never looks to them for aid.

Into this peaceful scene bursts Darnley, the conspirators hard on his heels. Rizzio, calling for his Madonna, hides behind her skirts. When it becomes obvious she will be unable to protect him, he kisses the hem of her gown and tries to run. Mary can see what's going on in her bedchamber through the doorway, but the conspirators hold her back. In a spate of histrionics that would make Sarah Bernhardt proud, she throws her hand over her face and collapses to the floor. Rizzio, clutching his cross, begs for justice, but the conspirators stab him to death (symbolically, on Mary's bed) and then throw him out the window. Mary immediately turns on an open-mouthed Darnley, finally showing some spirit, spitting, "God forgive you. I shan't, nor forgive myself for marrying you." The conspirators demand Mary sign a full pardon for them all, but she steadfastly refuses until they threaten Bothwell's life, and then her surrender is immediate and unconditional. The conspirators conveniently leave to engage Bothwell. Mary asks Darnley how long he thinks they will tolerate him once she's out of the way, and his about-face is lightning-quick. "You forgive me, Mary? You'll not leave me?" he whines, and Mary swears to him that she'll never leave him. She conveniently ignores his query about forgiveness, but the foolish Darnley does not seem to notice. The guards are easily duped, and the noble Bothwell awaits in the courtyard to spirit them to safety. He and his men engage in a battle with the conspirators while Darnley slinks off into the shadows, demonstrating himself to be a coward as well as a fool.

Without showing how much time has passed, the scene shifts to Elizabeth's court, where she happily dances with Lord Randolph. Throckmorton whispers into her ear and she shrieks, then runs from the room. Her bedchamber is in darkness as she sinks to the floor at the foot of her bed. Her ladies have run after her, but in keeping with the theme of her being isolated from her fellow women, they do nothing but bring candles and watch her; they are also faceless, mere silhouettes shot from behind or the side. Elizabeth, utterly dejected, says to them that while Mary Stuart has a son, "I am only of barren stock," clutching at her stomach. "I've failed. Failed." Elizabeth is a strong, intelligent woman effectively ruling her country, but she considers herself a failure because Mary Stuart has been able to do what she cannot: have a son and heir. It is Elizabeth's one moment of weakness in the film.

Meanwhile back in Scotland, Mary is surrounded by her women and playing with her son, is the very picture of domestic felicity. To show exactly how deep is Mary's need for male protection, as she bounces the baby on her knee, she coos, "He's going to grow up into a great big man and take care of me when I'm an old woman." Even in her baby son, she looks for protection and support. The irony is that, like all the other men to whom Mary has looked, he will ultimately be unable or unwilling to provide it. James VI, raised by the Protestant nobles after his mother's abdication, would never offer her assistance. Bothwell, true to his nature, brings a large sword into this charming domestic scene, giving the baby a Claymore that belonged to Mary's father, stating that little Jamie will need it when he grows up. Darnley enters, drunk, and the baby immediately starts to cry. He peers at the baby as if it were some strange insect, and expresses no desire to hold the child. Instead, Mary quickly sends the baby away as Darnley gives full vent to his paranoia. He fears assassination, stating his intention to leave Scotland. He accuses Mary of never having loved him, and since Mary is so "frank," she does not deny it, but rather tells him that she loves his son, and he should think of the child. This is another manifestation of Mary's naïveté; Darnley has proved himself irrevocably selfish again and again, and he's interested in nothing but his own welfare. Appealing to his nonexistent love for a child he has no desire to even touch is the wrong stratagem. "I'll disown him. I'll deny I'm his father! Try and make him King of Scotland and England then!" he crows, before staggering out of the room, leaving Bothwell and Mary alone together. She confesses that she has kept her word by not leaving him, endured his every insult and humiliation, "I've done everything but love him." Mary passively accepts all the degradations to which her husband subjects her. Trapped in a marriage with a drunken, cruel buffoon, she's deserving of every sympathy. More importantly, however, she is *innocent*.

In keeping with the saintly version of Mary this film puts forth, it would be unfeasible for her to have any hand in the murder of her husband. More than this, it would be impossible for her to condone the murder of her husband by knowingly marrying his murderer. The film neatly sidesteps all such troubles by having Darnley murdered by the conspirators he double-crossed, led by Lord Ruthven. The film version of Darnley dies in bed, mouth agape and head cocked to listen to the sound of the fuse right before the gunpowder explodes the house at Kirk o' Field and blows him to kingdom come. Neither Mary nor Bothwell are aware of, or have anything to do with, the plot to murder Darnley. Instead, using Knox as their instrument, the conspirators convince the Protestant firebrand of Bothwell's guilt and then he conveniently blasts it from his pulpit to rapt audiences just itching to go out and avenge Darnley's death.

Mary is out riding with the loyal Huntly when Bothwell takes them "by force" to his stronghold at Dunbar. It soon becomes apparent that he and Mary have orchestrated this kidnapping ruse. In her passive role yet again, Mary stares into the fire, saying nothing, allowing Bothwell to argue with Huntly. "How do you expect to fool all of Scotland when you cannot pull the wool over my eyes?!" Huntly rails. Bothwell assures him that no blame will attach itself to Mary if he marries her "by force." Huntly, exasperated and saddened, says to Mary, "You're the Queen of Scotland, and you let the woman in you blind your senses." This could very well serve as Mary's epitaph. She has lost her staunchest supporter, she has sealed her fate, but still she remains silent, passively staring into the fire.

Mary and Bothwell later share a tender moment on the turrets of Dunbar Castle, where she murmurs to him that "from the very beginning, I've always belonged to you ... perhaps I didn't really exist until I met you." This is how Mary sees herself, not as an independent woman, but as an extension of the man she loves. To make this Mary less co-dependent and more palatable, however, it's necessary to leapfrog over the historical Mary's three husbands and alleged affair with Rizzio. In the film, it's always stressed that she loved only Bothwell; this is a matter of true love conquering all. For this trope to work, there needs to be no other deep romantic attachment for Mary. Thus her courtly relationship with Rizzio, her complete lack of positive feeling for Darnley, and even so far back as her marriage to Francis, when she reminisces, "I was sixteen. It was just an arrangement ... I was never in love." With it established that Mary is only following her heart, which has always been true to a single love, she and Bothwell marry. Bothwell's putting away of his wife is not addressed; in this film he seems not to have one, and Huntly, silhouetted against the wall, leaves the ceremony and breaks his sword over his knee. Mary has put all her eggs in Bothwell's basket.

Back in England, Elizabeth's mood has improved dramatically. Everything is falling apart for Mary, and Elizabeth is both amused and satisfied by her cousin's stupidity. She laughs, "And I believed I'd failed," and goes back to looking at herself in the mirror again, smiling this time. She knows Mary's downfall is imminent, and she takes great pleasure in it, like the Wicked Queen she's made out to be.

Since the film chooses to show Mary with Bothwell as Moray's troops surround them, a comparison can be made between her attitude towards martial matters and Elizabeth's. As will be seen again and again in later Elizabeth films, screenwriters and directors enjoy portraying the "brave head of the troops" Elizabeth: her speech at Tilbury or equivalents frequently appear on film, often delivered while wearing an armored breastplate. This is part and parcel of Elizabeth's masculine side, a side which is nonexistent in Mary. By contrast, as Mary stands awaiting Moray's terms, Bothwell asks her if she is frightened, and she can barely stutter out, "Yes, t-terribly." She certainly does not inspire confidence, and it's readily apparent that the troops respond to the brave Bothwell, not their queen. Moray agrees to all of Bothwell's terms, specifically that Bothwell will leave if the council swears not to encroach on the Queen's sovereignty. It is Bothwell who attempts to save the Queen's throne for her; she's a completely emotional mess. In tears yet again, she clings to him, crying, "Let me live and die at your side. I love you.... What's my throne? I'd put a torch to it for any one of the days I've had with you. They've been so few ... take me with you!" It is Bothwell who has to shake her off, tell her that she is the Queen of Scotland, that this is her destiny, and then leave her standing numbly in the courtyard as his men march away to the sound of the pipes. Mary is incapable of the strength it would take to face her duty on her own, so Bothwell gives her no choice.

The council, naturally, has no plans to follow through on its promises; the impression is that Bothwell has not been gone five minutes before they inform a tearful Mary that she will be abdicating in favor of her son. She refuses, and playing the ultimate damsel in distress, she says, chin quivering, "Come, lock me up. I'll bide my time to wait for Bothwell." During the reign of her sister, Mary Tudor, Elizabeth spent her own share of time imprisoned, but unlike Mary, she saved herself. Without a male protector (or protector of any sort), she utilized her intellect to combat the intensive questioning to which she was subjected. She never admitted anything, and maintained her innocence in passionate and carefully worded letters to her sister. Elizabeth affected her release by her wits; Mary chooses to wait for outside aid. Though the aid she seeks is Bothwell, surprisingly, the aid she is offered is Elizabeth's. Throckmorton has informed Elizabeth of Mary's abdication, and that she asks for Elizabeth's support. As if she were unaware, Elizabeth's advisers inform her that, if she "favors rebellion in Scotland, you may eventually see it in England." Elizabeth confesses that she hates the very word, so she decides to oppose Moray publicly while offering him private support. At the same time, she sends a ring to Mary, a token of her friendship. While the naïve Mary believes she has been saved at last by the compassion of her sister queen, a self-satisfied Elizabeth is informing her council that "we'll procrastinate. Months, years! There's security in *that*." Though it seems less than credible to picture the historical Elizabeth explaining one of her favorite tactics in such a blatant manner, she often did use delay, procrastination and equivocation to excellent effect, and it rings true in this instance as well.

When Mary arrives in England, she's apprehended by Elizabeth's men. Mary still does not understand her position; it is not until she's left with her "host," Francis Knollys, that she finally realizes the situation she's in. To her question, "Am I a prisoner?" she gets no answer, and she sinks into a chair as all light fades from the room, hope leaving her life. Bothwell has not done much better; it turns out that he, through the machinations of Moray, is imprisoned and insane in Denmark, where he dies. There will be no white knight to save Mary from the duplicitous Elizabeth; she simply does not know it yet.

Though she refuses to recognize its jurisdiction, Mary is tried before an English court for plotting to have Elizabeth assassinated so that she can ascend the English throne. Mary believes that she will finally see Elizabeth at her trial, but even here Elizabeth is present only symbolically — her scepter and crown laid on an empty throne. Still foolishly believing that Bothwell will come to save her, Mary stands defiant before her judges. The entire set-up and framing of the scene serves to further Mary's martyr image. Her judges sit on a bench so high that Mary must constantly turn her face heavenward. The camera often angles from on high, over the judges' shoulders, so they seem to dwarf Mary from their high perch. She is clad entirely in black, with no jewelry except an enormous cross around her neck, and she carries a Bible. She also wears a black veil. The effect of this costuming with the lighting serves to highlight Mary's face as she retorts to the judges' talk of jurisdictional precedents, "Go back to Pontius Pilate, who condemned a sovereign greater than the world has ever known. And remind Elizabeth of what happened to the memory of Pontius Pilate." As if the imagery created by the lighting and cinematography were not enough, the sham trial is compared to that of Jesus Christ, making Mary not just a martyr, but a Christ-like figure. The Babington Plot, which is what has brought Mary to this state, is glossed over. Mary describes Babington as "a true friend who sought only to release me from unjust imprisonment," and it's revealed that Babington, who could "prove me innocent," has already been executed. Mary's eyes are wet, her chin quivers as she tries to turn the tables on Elizabeth; Mary accuses Elizabeth of plotting to take *her* life. Though Mary admits to smuggling out letters, she sidesteps accusations of approving Elizabeth's assassination, telling her judges the accusations are "as true as to say you are honest men." When confronted with the letter in question, Mary calls it a forgery, and asks why they are prolonging this mockery of a court, that Elizabeth only waits to have her executed because she's afraid of Bothwell. The final blow is struck when Mary is finally informed that Bothwell is dead. The change in her demeanor is immediate. Her strength came from the knowledge that Bothwell was alive and coming to save her; she has no strength of her own. Once she learns he is dead, she crumples completely. "Now I see. Now I understand. Condemn me. Kill me. I don't care." She finally sits, and the scene fades out with the only light being that focused on her face as she looks heavenward.

It's difficult to portray a rivalry from afar, with no physical confrontation, and this has always been the case with Elizabeth and Mary. The historical record is clear that the two women never met in person, but this is a historical detail that is almost universally ignored in adaptations of both women's lives. The face-to-face confrontation between the two is something that filmmakers simply cannot resist. As one reviewer put it, "Dramatists writing of this period always contend that the two should have met — since it makes for better dramaturgy."[19]

Filmmakers choose a variety of settings for this fictional meeting, and *Mary of Scotland* has the two meeting in Mary's prison chamber — whether she is at Fotheringhay and Elizabeth has traveled to see her or whether her imprisonment has been moved to the Tower of London is never made apparent. There is also no clue as to the amount of time that has passed. This is true throughout the movie, since none of the characters age. Mary may have been imprisoned a week or decades; it's impossible to tell. She kneels at a prie-dieu, praying, clad in a simple black silk dress. Elizabeth, resplendently attired, enters, and the two slowly approach each other. To symbolize that here are two opposing sides, the scene is framed so that they are separated by a table between them, on which sits a single, smoking candle. Elizabeth tells Mary quietly, "I see now why men love you." Mary replies that "even now, standing where I am, my last night in this world, I wouldn't change places with Elizabeth. I might've known you'd come to gloat like this, stealthily, under cover of night, as you've done everything to destroy me." Mary is playing the wronged victim to the hilt, clutching her huge cross in a gesture very reminiscent of that employed by Rizzio, another unjustly murdered Catholic. She admits nothing; she has done nothing wrong, simply followed her heart. Elizabeth assures Mary that her life has always been a threat because she was born too close to the English throne. Echoing the star-crossed imagery set forth in the film's opening titles, she pronounces with finality, "It was you or I." Mary denies having wished Elizabeth's assassination, but Elizabeth is no fool: "But you would've taken it if it came," she replies. Mary is repulsed, telling Elizabeth, "You're not even a woman." Elizabeth is unperturbed: "I'm a queen. You've been a woman. See where it's brought you." Even at the end, the romanticized figure of Mary clings to her view of love having conquered all. She has done the feminine thing, the right thing — her choices have "brought me happiness you'll never know. I wouldn't give up the memory of one day with Bothwell for a century of your life." The simple fact is, however, that Mary does not know what she's talking about, and Elizabeth shows her as much: "What do you know of my life? ... What do you know of the struggle for power?" Mary was born a queen, but Elizabeth had to struggle against the taint of illegitimacy and many other circumstances working against her. She came up the hard way, but she learned her lessons well: "I learned how a woman may be a queen one day and stand on the scaffold the next. I know what prisons are ... but I fought my way upward, inch by inch, until I wore the crown. I gave my love to no man, but to my kingdom. To England! And you prate to me of love. What do you know of my life?" Though it's obviously not the filmmakers' or the intent of Anderson's original play, in comparison with this, Mary's infatuation for Bothwell looks shabbier by the second. Mary calls Elizabeth a "magnificent failure," but Elizabeth retorts that it is Mary who has failed, "You threw away a kingdom for love." During this exchange, Elizabeth has seated herself, but Mary has not. From her literal and figurative high ground, she looks down self-righteously upon Elizabeth, and it's clear that not a single word has made a dent. Mary counters, "Aye, and I'd do it again a thousand times ... you know my blood will stain you, you'll never wash it off. And the pity of it is, Elizabeth, that you and I might have been friends." Mary demonstrates with this simplistic statement what her failure has been all along — putting the personal over the political. Even as death hovers, she still fails to understand. Elizabeth, in a gesture that seems inconsistent given every other aspect of her characterization in this movie, earnestly entreats Mary to save herself by renouncing her claim to the throne. Elizabeth has Mary where she wants her, but she's willing to show mercy. Mary's pride gets the better of her, and she stupidly baits Elizabeth, even at the end: "You've always loved power. Cherished it fiercely. I've loved as a woman loves, lost as a woman loses, but still I win. I win. My son will rule England. Still, still I win!" Her victory is certainly a pyrrhic one, and Elizabeth has walked out of the room while Mary yells her gloating words after her. Mary's kingdom is lost, her lover is dead, she is utterly alone and about to be decapitated, but there's never a searching self-examination of this situation as a result of her own conduct. She has "loved as a woman loves, lost as a woman loses," so she can go to the block content, her conscience clear, and the responsibility for her death laid firmly at Elizabeth's door.

In the morning, the candle on the table has burned itself out, just as Mary's life is about to be snuffed. She makes her way to the scaffold with quivering chin, but manages enough bravery to continue with her martyr motif, praying while holding her crucifix, "Even as thy arms were spread on the cross, so receive me into the arms of mercy." It's a long ascension to the scaffold, giving plenty of time to focus on Hepburn's luminous face as the wind blows her hair about her. All the others fade into the background as Mary hears the pipes, symbolizing Bothwell, with the implication being that she's happily going to join her love in heaven. She clasps her hands and the camera pans up to the lightning in the clouds as the film ends.

Though Ford's directorial abilities border on legendary, *Mary of Scotland* is far from his most impressive work. As one of Ford's biographers observed, "*Mary of Scotland* feeds into Ford's worst artistic impulses ... sentimentally biased toward the lost cause of the martyred Catholic queen, the film comes alive only when Ford moves his camera in as close as possible to Hepburn's glowing face, allowing her to fill the screen with a tremulous religious fervor that strongly resembles sexual ecstasy."[20] This he does with predictable regularity, to the point where it almost feels as if this is the entirety of Mary's role, and the intercut scenes of Elizabeth and her spitefulness border on refreshing. It's obvious that Ford's objective with this film parallels that of most filmmakers and many biographers when it comes to Mary and Elizabeth's relationship, "Ford preferred to delve within these two women to give their struggle an essentially emotional character within [a] historical conflict."[21] Thus, the overall characterization of Mary in *Mary of Scotland* is that of a beautiful, sympathetic woman who loved not wisely but too well. *Mary of Scotland*'s Elizabeth, by contrast, is devious and disingenuous, a woman who never makes a move without first calculating its outcome. On its face, she is selfishness personified — she pursues only what serves her own best interests, the security of her reign, her own vanity. Mary, though it is unintentional in the characterization, is also selfish in her own way. She marries Bothwell even after being warned it will ruin her; she pursues what she wants, the love of this man, regardless of the consequences to herself personally or to her kingdom. When those consequences overwhelm her, she plays the martyr; she never takes responsibility for the role her own actions have played in her fate. The impact of this is to contrast the passivity of Mary with the action of Elizabeth. Mary sits back and passively allows what happens to her; she is ruled by the men in her life — the Earl of Moray, Rizzio, Bothwell. Elizabeth *acts*. She plans, she calculates, she sets events in motion. The characterization of Elizabeth may be unpalatable, but at least she thinks, she *does*; she does not wait until events overwhelm her and then play the innocent victim. At its simplest, Elizabeth is strong where Mary is weak.

For this reason, several different actresses sought the role of Elizabeth in this film, even though it was a secondary one and might be accounted that of villainess — actresses from Bette Davis to Ginger Rogers expressed interest in playing the role. Florence Eldridge, though possessing nowhere near the star power of these actresses, does not fare the worse for it; she did the best that could be done with the material she was given. It's interesting to note that those critics who had seen the play were much less complimentary towards the portrayals in the film version than those who had not. One stated that those who enjoyed the "dry, sharp Elizabeth" (played by actress Helen Menken in the stage play) should "stay at home and read a good book when the Hollywood version gets around to the neighborhood theater." Otherwise, they could enjoy "an exceedingly pleasant, if slightly maudlin, evening" and at least Eldridge's Elizabeth "pouts rather effectively."[22] Other critics not comparing her portrayal to Menken's reacted more favorably to Eldridge, stating that she was "a splendidly serpentine and crafty Queen Elizabeth"[23] and that she "catches both the dignity and the undercurrent of hypocrisy that are Elizabeth ... [she] is properly spiteful."[24] They were less kind to Hepburn: "We were conscious of definite defects in her characterization. She may be a courageous Mary, perhaps a valiant one, but scarcely a fighter who gives no quarter and asks none."[25] The fact that they expected this type of Mary, a "fighter," shows either how little knowledge viewers had of the historical Mary or how little importance was placed on the expectation that the film Mary would be somewhat like her. It has been noted of Mary that she "always sublimated her own will to that of the men in her life. She looked to men for guidance, protection, and adulation."[26] If that is the historical Mary, Queen of Scots, then this film does manage to convey at least one aspect of the historical woman. In this film, Elizabeth, by contrast, only looks to men for adulation, not protection or guidance, and adulation is demanded, not requested or won. This creates a distinctly dissimilar atmosphere at the respective courts. Whereas the men at Elizabeth's court learn to get what they want through the Queen, Mary's court works on the opposite dynamic — it is the Queen who tries to get what she wants through the males of her court.

Overall this is a highly romanticized, very sentimental version of Mary's life. She's a figure of infinite sympathy — she makes all the wrong choices, but always for the right reason: love. By comparison, Elizabeth is cold and calculating — she is brilliant, but she is unsympathetic. Elizabeth, who is "virginal and Puritan, appears insensible and evil, in complete contrast to the innocent purity that the sensual Mary projects."[27] Hepburn spends much of her time in soft-focus close-up, her eyes filled with tears that threaten to spill over, her chin quivering, the very embodiment of female weakness in need of protection and comfort. Even those who denigrated her portrayal as being "pure Hepburn" still conceded her a "vital, sincere, and impressive performance."[28] Certain aspects of the historical women's characters are illustrated by this film's contrast of the two queens, perhaps more so in Mary's case than Elizabeth's, but taken as a whole, it does not provide anything close to a credible likeness of either.

FIRE OVER ENGLAND (1937)

Hard on the heels of *Mary of Scotland* came the next film to star Elizabeth in a major role, and the feel of both the character and the entire film is completely divergent from Ford's interpretation. By the time production began on *Fire Over England*, its director, Alexander Korda, was influenced by a factor that had emerged in world politics and which would greatly affect the British filmmaking of this period: rearmament. Korda, born

Sandor Laszlo Kellner (1893–1956), was of Hungarian extraction, and though he started out as a journalist, when he saw his first moving picture in 1908, he decided to channel his not-inconsiderable passions into the art of filmmaking. He made his first films in Hungary, and eventually ended up in England, under contract to Paramount British. The British film industry of the time was at one of the low points in its relatively short history and played an obvious second fiddle to the supremacy of Hollywood. In an attempt to combat this, Korda launched his own production company, London Film Productions, which employed such actors as Merle Oberon (whom Korda would later marry) and Roland Young. It was London Film Productions that would see the genesis of Korda's *The Private Life of Henry VIII*, which outstripped all expectations, eventually earning its star, Charles Laughton, an Oscar for his blustering yet affable portrayal of the titular monarch. The film, as would be the case later with *Fire Over England*, is now considered a classic historical drama, but it had a "clear political agenda ... reflecting a distinct line on British foreign policy, and intervening directly in the internal battles raging within the Conservative party in the early 1930s."[29] In fact, a number of articles have been written addressing the film's political slant and value as propaganda. Much is also made of Korda's friendship with Winston Churchill, who wrote the nationalist dialogue for Korda's later film, *That Hamilton Woman*. With *The Private Life*, Korda demonstrated that he had no problem with advancing "The Projection of England," a more innocuous way of describing pro–British propaganda, in his supposedly historical films. Critics noted that "the historical situation the film reflected most obviously was that of 1933, not 1533."[30]

The Private Life of Henry VIII, in addition to bolstering the entire British film industry with the money it brought in, was also the first British film to jump the pond and make a strong showing in the American film market as well. As a contemporary *Newsweek* article put it, "Alexander Korda's memorable study of King Henry VIII put English films on the American map" and paved the way for a film focusing on "the pallid-faced, carrot-haired daughter of that lusty ruler."[31] Due to the phenomenal success of *The Private Life*, Korda was actually hailed as the savior of the British film industry, and he was offered a lucrative contract by United Artists. This contract provided more than mere temporary financial solvency—it allowed Korda access to stars such as Douglas Fairbanks, and he used this to make British films, many of them historical in nature (e.g., *The Rise of Catherine the Great*), which were aimed at the American market. After a series of respectable successes, Korda returned triumphantly to Hollywood to continue to pursue his partnership with United Artists. As he garnered more and more success, Korda became more involved in administration and less with the actual filmmaking process which, it has been suggested, was all to the good: "Korda's work as a director was polished and pictorially beautiful, but lacked vitality, and his real genius was as a producer and impresario."[32]

Though Korda was the generative genius behind *Fire Over England*, it was truly an international effort, co-produced by the German Erich Pommer, directed by American William K. Howard, and co-written by Clemence Dane and the Russian Sergei Nolbandov. The film was based on an historical novel by author A.E.W. Mason (1865–1948). Though Mason wrote in a variety of genres, including detective and adventure fiction, he is perhaps best remembered for his historical fiction, most notably *The Four Feathers*, which has been adapted for the screen multiple times (incidentally, most recently under the auspices of director Shekhar Kapur, who would go on to direct two feature films focusing on Elizabeth). Mason's *Fire Over England* was first published in 1936, and is a combination romance/adventure story. Mason's version centers around a young student who has developed a deep loathing for Spain due to his father's death there, and he becomes instrumental in helping England defeat the Spanish Armada. The film adaptation of Mason's novel, though sharing the same basic plotline, has little else in common, stylistically or in characterization, with the book. As one critic noted, "The epic sweep of ... swashbucklers and adventure yarns filmed by Korda in the late 1930s created a new 'image' for Mason which the books themselves are hardpressed to live up to."[33] Mason's novels tend to be, by modern standards, affected and overly formal; there's much repetition and a focus on period detail so meticulously strict that it often detracts from the enjoyment of the plotting. Korda's version of the story eliminates all of the stiff composition for which Mason's works are sometimes denigrated, and replaces it with a simplistic, purely romantic, swashbuckling storyline, which nevertheless fails to belie its less-than-subtle propagandist themes.

Korda had his film crew, now he needed actors. For the role of the main protagonist, Michael Ingolby,[34] Korda selected one of his contract players, a young British actor by the name of Laurence Olivier (1907–1989). Olivier was already familiar with some of those working on the project, such as Erich Pommer, whom he'd met in 1930. Olivier was fresh off of two films to which he himself stated he had "contributed nothing remarkable," *The Conquest of the Air* and *Moscow Nights*, and he looked forward to working with Korda on this new historical drama. Olivier's excitement over the project was based on what he knew of Mason's original novel, and when Korda and Pommer had the story essentially rewritten by Clemence Dane, Olivier felt that it "could not even be called a version of the Mason book" and "neither added a point nor made a mark."[35] In his autobiography, *Confessions of an Actor*, Olivier makes it quite clear exactly how important he felt the film was by the amount of coverage he gives it — two paragraphs. He mentions it mostly as a segue to the introduction of one of the film's players who would have much more than just a professional impact on his life: Vivien Leigh.

Vivien Leigh (1913–1967) was one of many as-yet unknown actresses under contract with Korda, and as she hadn't worked in almost a year so feared her contract might not be renewed, she was thrilled to be cast as Cynthia, lady-in-waiting to the Queen and one of Michael Ingolby's love interests. Though the part was far from Oscar-worthy material, the general consensus is that the young actress made the most she could of it: "While she did not consider the decorative part of the Queen's lady-in-waiting any great achievement, she was pleased to find that she had not been entirely lost in the general colour and spectacle. She had been able to instil Cynthia with a sense of humour, and had not left her just a prettily-dressed cardboard heroine."[36]

Cynthia (as portrayed by Leigh) is certainly no cardboard cutout, but she does come across as very young, unseasoned, and (a fault shared by even the great Olivier in this film) overly exuberant. Her curtseys have her flopping to the floor and popping back up again as if she were on springs, and she spends a significant portion of her onscreen time rushing breathlessly about, skirts flying, on errands for the Queen.

The filming of *Fire Over England* took more than three months, and during that time, Leigh and Olivier, by necessity as the two romantic leads, had to spend a good deal of time with each other. They soon developed what one biographer called an "indefinable sympathy for which there was only one interpretation."[37] Though both were married at the time, they began an affair which went on for two years before they both confessed to their respective spouses. It would be an even longer period before both could obtain divorces and be married to each other. For this reason, biographers are keen to note that "their love scenes in the film bear eloquent witness to what was going on offscreen."[38] They also note the fact that Olivier was keen to do all his own stunts in the film to impress Leigh. In one particular scene (shot, as was most of the film, at Denham Studios), Olivier had to jump overboard into a net from the deck of a galleon which had been set aflame. During one take, when the water hoses failed to put out the flames, he came very close to serious injury.

While Olivier and Leigh provide passable performances, the acting style employed by both, but especially by Olivier, has not translated well by modern standards. Even at the time, the young Olivier's flair for melodrama was as yet untempered by experience, and he admitted, "Korda provided me with a very good costume part in *Fire Over England* with Vivien (and Flora Robson as Queen Elizabeth), but I emoted too much, and in the American version they had to cut one of my scenes because the New York preview audience got the giggles."[39] His performance occasionally comes off as overblown to the point of being ridiculous. The exuberance of his and Leigh's acting in the film is shown to even greater disadvantage when compared to the quiet competence evinced by the woman chosen to play Queen Elizabeth.

For the role of the Queen, Korda needed an actress with both the gravitas to inspire as well as the flexibility to make the fabled monarch seem human. At the beginning of her career, it seemed almost a miracle that Flora Robson (1902–1984) had ever become an actress to begin with, much less one of the caliber which Korda sought for his film. Though at a young age Robson was enthralled by stories of the theater and famous stage actors, she had none of the assets needed to get one's foot in the theater door. Eric Johns, author of *Dames of the Theatre*, had this to say about her: "Of all the actress–Dames, Flora Robson must have gone through the toughest struggle to get a start in the theatre … she had no theatre connections … furthermore, she had no money, no looks, and no idea about dress. She never understood how to make the best of herself."[40] In this way, she may seem as dissimilar from the historical Elizabeth as it is possible to be. Despite all these strikes against her, however, Robson did manage to make her way in the world of the stage. She began with bit parts, including her first speaking part, a one-line stint as the ghost of Queen Margaret in *Will Shakespeare*, a play written by one of the authors of *Fire Over England*'s screenplay, Clemence Dane. Though there were setbacks, slowly but surely, and despite her "arrestingly plain face," Robson's career in the theater progressed until, in the early 1930s, she joined the company of the Old Vic as a leading lady. Though she had seen success in roles as Lady MacBeth and Gwendolyn Fairfax, Robson still found herself barely able to make ends meet. Enter Korda, who recognized Robson's value as a character actress and offered her a four-year contract generous enough to make her financial troubles a non-issue. As Janet Dunbar observed in her biography of Robson, "Soft-spoken, kind, and one of the most likeable men in the film world, Korda had a way of making a generous offer sound as if its acceptance conferred a favour on him."[41] Robson made a start with the role of the Russian Elizabeth in Korda's 1934 historical, *Catherine the Great*, and when he began considering actresses for the role of the Tudor Elizabeth in his new film, he felt Robson was a natural choice. When he offered her the role, the script had not yet even been written, so Robson, with Korda's permission, took on other plays while waiting to begin the filming of *Fire Over England*. One of these would prove of great use to Robson in crafting the character of the Tudor Queen. Serious about all the parts she chose to take on, Robson had immersed herself in learning all she could about Elizabeth's life. Absorbed in this study, she was particularly interested when she was offered the titular role in a play by Wilfred Grantham called *Mary Tudor*, about Elizabeth's older half-sister. As have various other actresses, authors, playwrights, and historians, Robson found the contrast between the two queens to be fascinating. Grantham chose to portray Queen Mary sympathetically rather than as a religious fanatic, with Elizabeth as a clever but scheming rival. Though the critical reception of the play was lukewarm at best, Robson herself was well-received in this role, and the play ran until the death of King George, which devastated the theater industry and resulted in the closing of the play. Like many of the stage and screen adaptations of her sister's life, the concentration in *Mary Tudor* was on the personal more than the political, and it focused on Mary's unfulfilled longings for both love and a child. Robson identified with the unhappy queen, and drew on her own desire for the son she did not have to add depth and emotion to her portrayal. Critics praised Robson's interpretation of the role: "The play is well worth the attention of those interested in Tudor times; for those who are not, there is the presence of Flora Robson, in some lovely Tudor dresses, to offer as fine a piece of acting as she has ever given us. There are no high points in her part; it is a sustained journey on the lower slopes of dramatic emotion, but it is sure footed travel."[42] Though the play's performance at the box-office of the Playhouse was less than stellar, Robson had garnered significant praise for the role and, perhaps more importantly, gathered valuable insight into the character of Elizabeth by looking at her from another perspective — that of her sister. After four long years of waiting, it was finally time to begin filming *Fire Over England*, so Robson applied herself to what was to be, for her, a difficult filming.

Though she was not unfamiliar with costume dramas (e.g., her role in *Catherine the Great*), Robson, as had others before her and as would others that came after her, found all the accoutrement that came with playing Queen Elizabeth to be tremendously difficult and uncomfortable. Her filming days were long, usually lasting at least 12 hours. Robson would arrive in the make-up chair early in the morning to have her trademark Elizabethan make-up, along with a false nose, applied. Robson looked little like portraits of the iconic queen, and so an American expert was shipped over to craft the complex make-up Robson would wear. In order to accomplish this, he used as a template a mask of Elizabeth, from the famous effigy in Westminster Abbey. The major offenders were Robson's eyebrows, since the Tudor Queen had none, and her nose. The film's director was willing to overlook the issue of the nose, but Robson wanted to look as authentic as possible. Accordingly, Robson's eyebrows were shaved off, and an elaborate contraption of putty, cotton lint, and latex was fashioned into an Elizabethan "nose" and glued onto her face, a process which took three hours every day.

In addition to the discomfort occasioned by her make-up, like Lady Diana Cooper before her, Robson also had to deal with the misery of her costumes. Just as the real Elizabeth had been, Robson was actually tied or sewn into her gowns, so was forced to wear them until the close of filming each day. Boned, stiffened, wired, and sewn in as she was, Robson had to spend any "resting" moments sitting awkwardly on a backless stool since her enormous skirts made chairs impossible. The gowns were extremely heavy (one weighed over 100 pounds), as were the jewel-encrusted wigs and headdresses. Trussed up in this way, Robson spent the majority of the shoot in pain that could not be ignored.[43] Both cast and crew noted that it adversely affected her demeanor in a way she could not hide, and though she remained professional, she was sometimes irritated and brusque.

In addition to the bother of the costumes and make-up (she felt her false nose looked ridiculous in profile, which is very often how she ended up after scenes were blocked), Robson had originally believed her part would be much larger than it turned out to be — that Elizabeth would be the centerpiece of the film, the way Laughton's Henry VIII had been in Korda's previous film. She was disappointed to learn that this was not the case, especially given how much preparation she had lavished on her part. But perhaps even more than this, Robson also took issue with the way she was being directed to play her role. She believed that, given all the research she had done and her success with other Tudor period roles, she was perhaps more qualified than *Fire Over England*'s director, W.K. Howard, to make decisions about how the monarch should be portrayed. She felt she was regarded only as a "puppet" to be positioned, and that her skills at her craft were viewed as completely coincidental. All this changed on a single day of filming. The scene was one in which Queen Elizabeth dresses down the Spanish ambassador, and it was to be shot in the audience chamber set, requiring the use of hundreds of expensive extras. Robson and Henry Oscar, the actor portraying the ambassador, were loathe to flub their lines in front of such a large audience, so they rehearsed tirelessly together when they were not needed for filming. The result was a perfect delivery on the very first rehearsal with all the players, and it earned Howard's respect; from that point on, he chose to let Robson basically direct herself. Thanks to the actress's professionalism, Howard got a scene with which he was more than satisfied by mid-day on the second day of filming when it had been scheduled to take at least a week. This saved the production an enormous amount of money (though the extras were less than pleased at losing a week's work) and cemented Howard's respect for Robson's abilities.

Howard's backing would prove extremely important to Robson's interpretation of the part, because she even went so far as to rewrite her dialogue. As time neared to film a scene which often appears in motion pictures about Elizabeth — her famous rallying speech to the troops massed at Tilbury — Robson became more and more uneasy about the dialogue. For the screenplay, Elizabeth's historic, dynamic speech had been condensed by Clemence Dane down to four short lines. Robson went to the source; she started by speaking with Dane about including more of the original speech, but Dane had been advised to keep dialogue to a minimum by the film's producer, Erich Pommer. Not to be deterred, Robson then consulted Charles Laughton, who had played Henry VIII, for his opinion. He suggested she learn the entire Tilbury speech, request that Howard film it, and then show it to Pommer. The day arrived for the filming of the scene, and it was much less than ideal. Due to the unseasonable heat, Robson's fake nose was in danger of melting right off her face, and her armored breastplate, uncomfortable in the best of circumstances, was almost unbearable, making it very difficult to move. The horse Robson had ridden in previous scenes and which had been slated to be her mount for this scene came up lame and so was replaced with a much more skittish creature. Despite all this, Robson waited until she was astride and ready to film before she broached the subject of the dialogue change to Howard. Robson declaimed the full speech for Pommer, and he agreed that Howard should shoot the scene with Robson's version of the dialogue. This included more iconic and stirring turns of phrase, with Elizabeth vowing "to lay down for my God and my kingdom and for my people, my honor and my blood, even in the dust. Not Spain nor any prince of Europe shall dare to invade the borders of my realm.... We shall soon have a famous victory!"

This new, rousing version of the scene proved so appealing when the rushes were viewed that Pommer and Howard decided another display of pomp and circumstance with Elizabeth as centerpiece should be added into the screenplay. Originally, Robson's part ended with the scene at Tilbury, but Dane crafted a new scene set at St. Paul's Cathedral. Here, Queen Elizabeth appears at the center of a grand display of pageantry, giving a rousing prayer of thanks for the English victory over the Spanish. She kneels, with the throng following suit, and prays, "We thine humble and unworthy servants, do give most hearty thanks," ending the film with bells pealing and music swelling to the final fade-out and the beginning of the credits.[44]

In *Fire Over England*'s attempt to further a pro–British agenda in the most simplistic manner possible, Elizabeth herself is sometimes lost. One Robson biographer observed that W.K. Howard "seemed interested only in making the film comprehensible to farmers in the Middle West of America who had never heard of Elizabeth, rather than to anyone who might expect an intelligent character study."[45] Rather than an in-depth examination of the historical woman, the "real" Elizabeth is often crammed into a simplified mold so that a particular audience demographic — the average 1930s moviegoer — can understand and relate to her. However, "A primary function of the narrative art is to produce empathy in those who may otherwise lack the ability to understand what it is another person feels or thinks,"[46] and in this, Robson went beyond Howard's simplifications to create an Elizabeth with more depth. The preparation Robson took to make herself ready for the part — reading all she could find not just about Elizabeth, but also about her sister, Mary, and other contemporaries — gave her the historical knowledge she needed to craft a believable version of the Virgin Queen. The question remains, in the canon of film Elizabeths, how does Robson's interpretation fit?

In his seminal essay "A Queen for All Seasons," Thomas Betteridge viewed Robson's portrayal as powerful, but at the same time, constrained because this power "is represented as being deployed through traditionally feminine traits. She persuades, cajoles and seduces her subjects into doing her bidding."[47] *Fire Over England*'s portrayal of Elizabeth comes, as does the formation of opinion on almost any person, from two separate sources: scenes of Elizabeth herself, and scenes where Elizabeth is not present but is being discussed by others. As is often the case, there is some disparity between the two pictures that emerge. At the beginning of the film, young lady-in-waiting Cynthia is shown rushing about the palace in a desperate search for a single pearl, lost from the back of the Queen's dress. The audience is told, in Cynthia's dialogue to Burghley, that the Queen is keeping the Spanish ambassador waiting because she wants to wear "the French dress." Leicester states that the queen has 3,000 dresses, but Cynthia assures him she will have none of it, and she will definitely know the pearl is missing because she has eyes in the back of her head. From this one smattering of dialogue, the picture meant to be conveyed is of a woman exacting, demanding, vain, and extravagant. However, in the first scene in which the Queen actually appears (in which Robson so impressed Howard by her flawless execution of her lines), she holds her own with the Spanish ambassador, showing her imperiousness, but also intelligence, subtlety and diplomacy.

The film returns to the popular theme of vanity and adds a dash of aging when Elizabeth is being undressed in her rooms. Her wig and make-up gone, she looks in the mirror and asks the beautiful young Cynthia, "Do you like what you see in the glass?" This and statements like it are often made by screen Elizabeths, and Elizabeth sends Cynthia off for the Earl of Leicester. He has grown old with the Queen and thus not only understands her feelings but commiserates on the subject of lost youth. Elizabeth says, "This mirror is old and blemished ... no, the Queen's face is blemished, not the mirror. Well, fetch me my disguises." Robson, never considered a beauty herself, manages to convey with these scenes a wistfulness that makes the Queen seem more sympathetic than vain. Her treatment of this aspect of Elizabeth's personality is certainly more palatable than similar scenes with other actresses who would come after her, such as Bette Davis.

Robson also crafts a queen whose condescension (she looks down her nose at Leicester and states imperiously, "I am England!") is tempered by personal compassion. Though instances are scattered throughout the film (such as Elizabeth spoon-feeding a sick Burghley, something the historical Elizabeth is said to have done), there are two separate scenes that particularly highlight this aspect of Robson's portrayal. The first is an assassination attempt as the Queen returns through the throng to the palace. A crazed old woman leaps out at her, and is wrestled to the ground by Ingolby. The woman, a devotee of the executed Mary, Queen of Scots, accuses Elizabeth of her murder. This scene kills two birds with one stone, as it tangentially touches on the execution of Mary Stuart (allowing Elizabeth to express regret at not having "saved" her cousin) while also allowing Elizabeth to show her compassion as she gives the failed assassin safe conduct out of the country to her friends in France. The second scene involves Cynthia's distress at the Queen's having sent Ingolby off on his dangerous errand to discover those plotting against England. Though in other scenes Elizabeth has been angry and envious of Cynthia's relationship, when Cynthia says she's off to find a quiet corner in which to cry, Elizabeth tells her, kindly, to "cry here" and holds her.

Overall, Robson's portrayal of the Queen, while showing the contradictory nature of the woman, is much less mercurial and fiery than other, later portrayals. Robson's queen can be passionate, but she's more often tempered by caution and logic. The *New York Times*, in its review of the movie, declared that Robson had taken a "middle course between caricature and glorification" and went on to praise the Elizabeth she had crafted as "torn between her dignity as a queen, her frailty as a woman; tender yet ruthless, ambitious yet weary, vain yet honest." The performance was described as "sincere and eloquent

... one of the best of this year." This review of Robson's performance is telling in that it highlights something Robson herself must have realized in all her research into Elizabeth — the dualities of the queen's character. It's perhaps less than accurate to say the historical woman was torn between her "dignity" and "frailty"; Elizabeth seemed to use the contemporary stereotype of women's "frailty" more to manipulate the males who held power in her world, rather than because she truly believed herself to be a "weak and feeble" woman. As historian David Starkey observes, "Elizabeth uses everything ... everything is used to manipulate."[48] However, the other adjectives applied to Robson's portrayal could very well stand up to scrutiny about the historical Elizabeth.

In the area of historicity, like most films, *Fire Over England* is a unique study both for the Tudor period it was attempting to portray, and the era which it actually reflected — rearmament leading up to World War II. As has been mentioned, filmmakers have a

"Do you like what you see in the glass?" Beautiful, young lady-in-waiting Cynthia (Vivien Leigh) looks on as Queen Elizabeth (Flora Robson) is reflected in that ubiquitous symbol of vanity, advancing age, and mortality: her mirror in *Fire Over England*. (United Artists/The Kobal Collection)

penchant for molding the events of the Tudor period to promote an agenda and make them relevant to a contemporary audience, and nothing had greater immediacy in the 1930s than the rise of Hitler's Germany. According to British newspapermen, Adolf Hitler not only saw *Fire Over England*, but enjoyed it so much that he watched it over and over again.[49] This is particularly ironic given the fact that the film is now put forth as a prime example of British nationalist propaganda at its finest. Later, when England was at war with Germany, parts of the film (e.g., Elizabeth's Tilbury speech) were even used in documentaries chronicling the British fighting spirit.[50] The film's nationalist slant is made all the more interesting given its multinational crew and production team, some of whom, such as Pommer, were German.

The historical parallels portrayed in *Fire Over England* between the villain, Philip II and his Spain, and Hitler and his Germany, are quite unmistakable. Author Gore Vidal, in his work *Screening History,* devotes an entire essay to the film, which he opens with these words, "Movies changed our world forever. Henceforth, history would be screened ... the world's view of the world can be whatever a producer chooses to make it."[51] The makers of *Fire Over England* definitely had views they wished, they *needed,* others to share.

At this point in the progression towards World War II, there was much debate in the United States as to whether or not to take part in what was considered a foreign war. Obviously, Great Britain was doing everything in its power to influence the United States towards the status of active ally, including what Vidal terms a "propaganda barrage" that permeated U.S. culture through the medium of British films, of which *Fire Over England* is a prime example. These "gallant little England" pictures served the purpose of glorifying English culture, showing a plucky can-do attitude when it came to war, while at the same time presenting England as somewhat of a damsel in distress — one who could be rescued by the courage and valor of a champion such as the United States. Like other Elizabeth films that would follow (e.g., *The Sea Hawk*), *Fire Over England* equates a tyrannical Philip II with Hitler; to rousing but slightly ominous music, the title cards at the beginning of the film spell everything out for the viewer, as does much of the dialogue. Phillip rules by "force and fear" and the only challenge to his tyranny is provided by the "free men" of a "little island, England." Lord Burghley even uses a globe while pontificating to Leicester just "how small we are, how wretched, how defenseless" and then details Spain's assets of money and power and its insidious trend towards territorial expansion, the sixteenth-century Spanish version of *Lebensraum.*

Danger also lurks below the surface of the court itself. England is rife with those serving Spanish interests, and in keeping with the theme of court intrigue, plotters are introduced immediately in the person of Hilary Vane (a young unbilled James Mason). Vane has been carrying secret correspondence to and from the Spanish court regarding a plot to murder the Queen. While these machinations go on, Elizabeth, in her first appearance in the film, argues with the Spanish ambassador over the work of El Draco, Sir Francis Drake, who has been looting and burning Spanish ships. Her diplomacy walks a fine line between concession and defiance — while disavowing Drake and assuring the Spanish they can punish him if they can catch him, she nevertheless refuses to close English ports to him and accuses Spain of flinging "my honest merchants to the Inquisition to be burned alive," a statement that is graphically illustrated by the fate of Ingolby's father. Alone in her chambers with Leicester, the Queen admits she's afraid of invasion, that she has been "too bold." Leicester assures her that boldness is exactly what's needed. This echoes the concerns and fears of British conservatives in the wake of rearmament, as well as that of isolationist America. Though, if some commentators are to be believed, the entirety of the movie's agenda was lost on U.S. audiences, as one reviewer noted, "American press coverage of the film, even articles focused on it as an example of Hollywood's interest in British history and culture, did not connect the film to the political affairs of modern Europe."[52]

The storyline switches from Elizabeth to Ingolby who, along with his father, has been captured after a battle with a Spanish ship. Ingolby escapes by swimming to shore and being taken in by an old Spanish friend of his father's, whose beautiful daughter, Elena (Tamara Desni), helps care for him. While Ingolby is wasting time singing love songs and roasting potatoes with Elena, he notices smoke on the horizon. Though his Spanish love assures him "it's only smoke," the viewer knows differently — it is his own father being burned alive. Ingolby's father has sent a message for his son that sounds as if it could have been drafted by Churchill himself: "It isn't our quarrel. It isn't the Queen's quarrel. It's a war of ideas ... you can't burn ideas." This concept of a "war of ideas" is interesting in that terminology such as this was meant to, and did, inspire 1930s audiences to nationalist fervor. By contrast, in a 2009 compilation of comments to President Barack Obama made by citizens through a government website, despite the wide range of topics from health care to technology upon which comments were solicited, the one concept the majority of citizens wished to convey to their newly elected president was "no more wars fought over ideas."[53] The concept of fighting for an ideal is something which, apparently, no longer holds the sway it did a half century ago, and viewing *Fire Over England* highlights this change in perception.

When Ingolby learns of his father's death, he stops his dallying and escapes back to England, bringing news of the events in Spain, stating, "In Spain they herd souls as we herd cattle.... Spain is the prison of all freedom, Spain is horror!" The scenes, weirdly prescient, bring to mind Jews being herded into cattle cars to feed the furnaces of Auschwitz, with the smoke and the ash of human bodies falling like snow. Elizabeth, however, meets his passion with clear-headed planning, discussing troop numbers and other logistics — the practical side that accompanies the fervor of warfare. The rhetoric is never completely laid aside, however, as an emotional Ingolby insists to Elizabeth, and by extension the England she represents, "You are the world's hope!" Ingolby's passion is necessary, but he must "be prepared to bring his extreme political beliefs under control so that they can be of use to the commonwealth. It is the example of Elizabeth and the sacrifices her queenship demands of her as a woman that teach Michael to control his feelings."[54]

In another scene with Lord Burghley on the eve of her departure for Tilbury, Elizabeth echoes what many must have felt on the eve of World War II: "I have seen blacker fears turn to hope. Hope on til there is none." Also as evidenced by current events (e.g., the 2008 U.S. presidential campaign) the idea of hope in an uncertain world is a very appealing one, especially as part of a political agenda. *Fire Over England* certainly emphasizes this point. However, unlike some modern political rhetoric, the film makes clear that this hope cannot come without sacrifice and action from average citizens. In a "for mom and apple pie" moment, Ingolby and Cynthia confront the need for him to do his duty rather than stay and marry her. The Queen walks in on them and asks for Ingolby's service and obedience. He readily agrees, and is sent off to the Spanish court, posing as the plotter Hilary Vane, to uncover the conspirators. With his duty done and death, once again, narrowly averted, he returns just in time for Tilbury and to command these same plotters, pardoned by a magnanimous Elizabeth, who allows them a choice: "How will you die — in sunlight or in darkness? For a free world or a world where your thoughts are rationed like prison bread?" The sorely repentant conspirators, under Ingolby's command, destroy the Spanish Armada with a handful of small fireships, and the day is won.

Since English films of the period immediately preceding the production of *Fire Over England* had been so resoundingly disappointing, critics were generally positive in their response to the film as a whole. The film is an historical spectacle, with striking sets and costumes and an impressive amount of action. While praising it for this, at the same time, there was a tendency to be dismissive about the film or sprinkle the praise with qualifiers: "The film is exciting and colorful on the lines of Henry VIII when content to remain a piece of derring-do. At other times it appears too self-conscious a piece of special pleading in a significant period of contemporary dismay. Laurence Olivier is magnificently acrobatic. He is not called on to be much more."[55] A contemporary *New York Times* review stated that "Erich Pommer's rich production has all the solid virtues of the better British pictures. It is dignified, sound, carefully filmed, extremely well played, and reasonably faithful to the events it sought to reenact. It has, too, a curious lack of vitality for all its wealth of vibrant material.... Mr. Olivier is properly impetuous, and Vivien Leigh and Tamara Desni are lovely as the fortunate chap's two leading ladies. The materials, in brief, were there; only the vital spark to fuse them into a stirring historical drama was missing."[56] Others described the acting as "far better than we are accustomed to in English films. Mr. Laurence Olivier can do the hysterical type of young romantic hero with ease, Mr. Leslie Banks is a Leicester who might have been on the board of governors of any school, and Mr. Raymond Massey presents a fine and plausible portrait of King Philip. Mr. Massey is the only memorable thing about the film."[57] These contemporary appraisals represent an unfortunate snubbing of Flora Robson's characterization as Elizabeth, since it was this role that made her reputation as an international star. It was noted by a few of the more perceptive critics — perhaps one even made all the discomfort of Robson's false nose worth the trouble with his pronouncement: "Historic detail is handled with reverence and awe. Elizabeth's nose, carried defiantly by that excellent actress Flora Robson, is precise in size and proportion to the last millimeter."[58] Another contemporary article posited that Alexander Korda had "put English films on the American" map with his "memorable study" of King Henry VIII in 1933, and went on to say that *Fire Over England* was "chiefly notable for Flora Robson's portrayal of Queen Elizabeth."[59] As will be examined in the last chapter of this book, with the benefit of hindsight, later commentaries, as well as the average modern viewer, would prove to be far more enthusiastic in their estimation of Robson's performance in this film and her later reprisal of the role in *The Sea Hawk*. The more versions of Elizabeth that have appeared, the more favorably Robson's has been viewed. Comparison has bred greater admiration, and of the many actresses who have portrayed Elizabeth, Robson's version now appears as one of the best to be found in the canon.

THE PRIVATE LIVES OF ELIZABETH AND ESSEX (1939)

The year *The Private Lives of Elizabeth and Essex* was produced, 1939, has been called the *annus mirabilis* of Hollywood films. In addition to the phenomenally successful *Gone With the Wind*, the year also saw the release of the critically acclaimed *Stagecoach*, *Mr. Smith Goes to Washington*, *Dark Victory*, *Of Mice and Men*, *Ninotchka*, *The Women*, *Wuthering Heights*, and *The Wizard of Oz*.[60] *The Private Lives of Elizabeth and Essex* fits in with none of these films, and does not fare particularly well by comparison. In films of its own genre, it's a far cry from the dewey-eyed romanticism of *Mary of Scotland* or the themes and nationalist propaganda of *Fire Over England*. In fact, it has been called a "direct response" to that film, radically apolitical, that "the world of politics [was] consistently upstaged by the queen's private relationship with Essex."[61] Whereas the two romantic leads in *Fire Over England* developed an offscreen romance to parallel their onscreen wooing, *Elizabeth and Essex* would see the flowering of a relationship that was exactly the reverse — what came to be called a "Battle Royale" between its two stars.

At the height of his popularity, Errol Flynn (1909–1959) was one of the biggest box-office draws in the United States, and when *Elizabeth and Essex* went into production, that popularity was at high tide, with no ebb in sight. Flynn was known, however, for his swashbuckling, not drama or intricate portrayal of historical character. He was also known for his charming, fun-loving, but impulsive character, which he coupled with a lackadaisical attitude towards his roles — he did little or no research and often did not bother to learn his lines. At the other end of the spectrum was Bette Davis.

By 1939, Bette Davis (1908–1989) was already the acknowledged queen of the Warner Bros. studio. Like such viragos as Joan Crawford, her temperament was legendary — she was known to be a demanding perfectionist, by turns snidely condescending and explosively angry towards those she felt did not meet her expectations. She was thrilled about playing the role of Elizabeth, one she felt was worthy of her grand talents. Unlike in *Fire Over England*, Elizabeth was to be one of the two main protagonists of this onscreen iteration. Who was more important, Elizabeth or Essex, Davis or Flynn, became the first bone of contention between the two.

The Private Lives of Elizabeth and Essex was based on another Maxwell Anderson play, originally titled *Elizabeth the Queen*, which was written alternately in prose and blank verse. In addition to *Mary of Scotland* and *Elizabeth the Queen*, Anderson would author other plays with Tudor/Elizabethan-era settings, providing plenty of fodder for later films; he also authored *Anne of the Thousand Days*, which was adapted for the screen in 1969.

Elizabeth the Queen had been a hit on Broadway in 1930. Since then, Metro-Goldwyn-Mayer had had box-office success with films based on the lives of female monarchs, such as *Queen Christina* (1933) starring Greta Garbo, *Marie Antoinette* (1938) with Norma Shearer as the French queen, as well as Hepburn's *Mary of Scotland*. Paramount had also embraced this trend with Marlene Dietrich as Catherine the Great, *The Scarlet Empress*, in 1934. These films inspired not only the executives at Warner Bros., but also its stars. Davis had expressed an interest in playing a screen queen as far back as the casting for *Mary of Scotland*; she interviewed with the film's director at her request, but Ford abruptly cut the interview short by telling her she talked too much.[62]

Warner Bros., however, had Davis in mind from the very start for the role of Elizabeth; the studio purchased the rights to Anderson's play in 1938 specifically to showcase Davis in her first Technicolor film. In her time, Davis was unique as a star actress for several reasons, not the least of which was the fact that she did not shy away from roles that portrayed her in a less than flattering light. While this may seem unremarkable in modern-day Hollywood where actors relish challenging or unsympathetic roles, in Hollywood's golden era, there was great danger of an actor being identified personally with a role, of "the public, ever prone to confuse the star with the on-screen character," which could damage one's box-office appeal.[63] This was especially true of actresses. Yet Davis did not let this frighten her away from difficult roles. She much preferred them to the stock romantic heroines that pervaded Hollywood films of the time period. As one commentary puts it, "She built her reputation on roles that nobody else wanted and turned them into *tour de force* performances."[64] Though it would be inaccurate to say that no one else wanted the role of Elizabeth, it's a certainty that no one else wanted to portray Elizabeth in the *manner* Bette Davis played the role.

Elizabeth and Essex was not the first film on which Davis and Flynn had both worked—just the year before *Elizabeth and Essex* began filming, they had acted together in *The Sisters*. It's unsurprising that Warner Bros. sought this pairing; Davis and Flynn were their two largest box-office draws, and having them together in one film seemed a formula for certain success. In *The Sisters*, described as a "standard women's film,"[65] Flynn played Davis's love interest. He had demanded and been granted top billing, a fact that did not sit well with Davis or her ego. The same problem was encountered with *Elizabeth and Essex*; Flynn felt the original title, focusing as it did solely on the Queen, needed to be modified to reflect the importance of Essex's (i.e., Flynn's) role. In a way, he was to get top billing again when Warner Bros. decided to call the film *The Knight and the Lady*. This satisfied almost no one but Flynn; it was argued that it was ridiculous to refer to Elizabeth simply as "the lady" (Davis called it "horrific," stating that a more undignified title could not be found), and Essex was an earl, not a knight. Davis demanded top billing, but did not wish to go against the title order lest her fans think she was vain. She told Warner executives, "You force me to refuse the picture unless the billing is mine."[66] *Elizabeth and Essex* seemed preferable, but as Lytton Strachey had published a book with that exact title, and with the success of *The Private Life of Henry VIII* still in mind, the film was finally dubbed *The Private Lives of Elizabeth and Essex*.

The squabbling over title and top billing was not the only issue (Davis was eventually given billing over Flynn); there was also the problem of Davis's "nerves." In a parallel to the historical Elizabeth, who could either pretend or actually make herself violently ill when it suited her, Davis could use her physical wellbeing as a manipulative tool. The associate producer on *Elizabeth and Essex*, Robert Lord, was so concerned about the state of Davis's nerves that he proposed taking out health insurance on her. In a memo to Jack Warner, he wrote, "How about health insurance on Davis? Once she starts shooting we have no work without her. If she folds up, we stop shooting. I have been studying the lady and in my opinion she is in a rather serious condition of nerves. At most she is frail and she is going into a very tough picture when she is a long way from her best."[67] Though Warner refused to get insurance on Davis since he suspected she was only pretending sickness, he did go so far as to test Geraldine Fitzgerald for the role of Elizabeth. No one but Bette would do, however.

There was also contention over who was to play Essex. Davis wanted and requested that Laurence Olivier be given the role. In addition to her personal dislike of Flynn, she felt he was too shallow to play the part, and she had been impressed (though one wonders exactly why) with Olivier's work in *Fire Over England*. Instead Flynn was cast, and to say that neither Flynn nor Davis looked forward to the experience of working with each other again would be an enormous understatement. Davis stated that, in all her scenes with

Flynn, "I used to dream that Laurence Olivier was Essex."[68] In his autobiography, *My Wicked, Wicked Ways*, Flynn described the situation from his point of view: "Now Bette was a dynamic creature, the great big star of the lot, but not physically my type; dominating everybody around, and especially me, or trying to."[69] In addition to the title shenanigans, Flynn states that Davis was also upset over the question of salary — though she had, by that point, two Academy Awards under her belt, Flynn was making almost $1,000 a week more than she. Warner Bros. executives tried to placate her with a resplendent dressing room, far superior to Flynn's (who said he didn't care if he was given a park bench), but this did little to alleviate the situation.

At the heart of the matter, much like the portrayals of Elizabeth and Essex in the film, was the fact that these were two individuals with widely disparate working philosophies and personalities. Flynn states several times in his autobiography, self-deprecatingly, that he does not consider himself to be an "actor," and he readily admits Davis's superiority in this arena. His working philosophy was of the "live and let live" variety, whereas Davis saw nothing wrong with contemptuously pointing out the flaws of any and all she thought were beneath her, and she placed the majority of the planet's population in this category. One reviewer summed up the plot of *Elizabeth and Essex* as "the public quarrels of two prides,"[70] and this could just as well have been applied to the two actors playing the parts. As another critic put it, "The mix of Davis and Flynn ... does *not* work. Davis was driven and über-professional. Flynn was larky and full of fun."[71] Their animosity established, Flynn took every opportunity to playfully irritate Davis; he yawned off camera when she played her scenes, smacked her on the rear end (one instance of which made its way into the film), and made silly gestures at her. For her part, she reacted with "paroxysms of fury" to his shenanigans.[72] This resulted in a working relationship that was strained at best, and at times, almost unbearable. As soon as a scene finished shooting, Flynn and Davis would walk in opposite directions away from each other.

Flynn and Davis weren't the only ones unhappy on the set of *Elizabeth and Essex*. Olivia de Havilland was, by this point, typecast as Flynn's love interest, having already served this role in several other films. She had had some difficulty finagling her career-defining role as Melanie in *Gone With the Wind* due to her contract with Warner Bros. — *Gone With the Wind* was a David O. Selznick/MGM picture and Warners had to agree to loan her out. Not willing to suffer an actress who did not acknowledge her place, Warners executives attempted to reinforce to whom de Havilland belonged. She would eventually go on to sue over the issue of contracting, and win a court case that freed actors from some of the previously standard, more oppressive elements of studio contracts — in essence, giving actors more control over their own careers. This is a battle the great Bette Davis herself had fought, but not managed to win. Though de Havilland made the best of it, she was miserable with the very small role she was given for *Elizabeth and Essex*. The director, Michael Curtiz, was also not a friend of Davis, though in this case, with her ire focused on Flynn, he was a lesser target.

The film, much like *Les Amours de la Reine Élisabeth*, opens jubilantly: the year is 1596, and the Earl of Essex is returning home in triumph. He and his retinue march through the adoring throngs on the streets, pennants waving, to Whitehall, where he's certain he will receive a warm welcome from his monarch. Olivia de Havilland, in her role as Lady Penelope Gray, leans out a window to admire the handsome young Essex, stating, "It must be wonderful to be a man, and a hero." All is not what it seems, however. Elizabeth's counselors, led by Robert Cecil (Henry Daniell), watch from another terrace and express their contempt for Essex, while at the same time conveniently providing the needed exposition and backstory: "Our queen can be difficult, even on the best of days ... something's got to be done to tarnish him, or we'll have him sharing England's throne with her, and then where shall we be?" With the exception of Lady Gray and Francis Bacon (Donald Crisp), Essex's self-aggrandizing and somewhat petulant demeanor has not won him many adherents — almost the entirety of the court is scheming to bring him down.

Thus established that Essex has few friends and more powerful enemies at court and is suspected of having his eye on the throne, it only remains to see how he and the Queen get on. The air of expectancy is heightened when the audience is allowed to hear Elizabeth, but not see her — the first scene with her is staged in her private apartments, where she's being dressed. As Francis Bacon desperately attempts to convince her not to "put down" Essex in public, Elizabeth appears only in silhouette, although a readily recognizable one, a shadow against the wall, cast from behind her dressing screen. To Bacon's plea, she replies, "The necessities of a queen must transcend those of a woman.... My personal feelings must not enter into this."

Thus, Elizabeth is allowed to speak before the audience is allowed to see her, and the first glimpse of her is iconic — as she sits on her throne, the camera starts with one bejeweled shoe, pans up past silken skirts, jewels, and ruff, until finally and majestically fixing on her face. Bette Davis was in her early thirties when she first played an Elizabeth who was, in 1596, over 60 years old. In order to bridge the gap, Davis took an active role in directing Warners' make-up chief, Perc Westmore, on exactly how her make-up should look, based on a series of royal portraits she had examined.[73] Davis insisted not only that her eyebrows be shaved, but also that her hairline be shaved back a few inches, so that she would appear to be bald underneath her Elizabethan wigs. Hal Wallis and other studio executives were appalled (at the time, no other Hollywood actress had appeared bald in a film), but under a barrage of temper from Davis, they finally agreed.[74] Though Davis had shaved her eyebrows and hairline and donned the white mask, the representation is still far less than convincing. That some film critics disagreed, however, is perhaps not surprising, given statements such as, "Deviations from history ... do not matter, for Michael Curtiz has directed an interesting, intelligent picture." One reviewer felt that "Bette Davis's vain, cruel Elizabeth, made up like an ugly embryo, is the real thing."[75] Her portrayal is also, from a dramatic standpoint, one of the most idiosyncratic — she's constantly opening and closing her palms and fingers, fidgeting and twitching, jerking her arms, and walking about briskly only to stop abruptly at no particular destination. One commentary notes that Davis's Elizabeth "storms and strikes, fidgets and fingers.... Davis's mannered performance distracts, and we see only glimpses of the brilliant, charismatic stateswoman and intuitive, wise ruler."[77]

Davis was helped by the gorgeous costumes created for the film by designer Orry-Kelly. Before beginning work on the gowns, he did extensive research into the Elizabethan period and Elizabeth's wardrobe. Davis, as she had with Westmore, also took an active role as oversight committee on her costuming by "comparing them stitch by stitch, paste jewel by paste jewel, with the various royal portraits."[78] Orry-Kelly's work appears to marvelous effect onscreen and in Technicolor; he enlisted every seamstress the studio had available to work on a variety of gowns — a green brocade riding habit, quilted white satin embroidered with pearls, bronze taffeta with a large, delicate ruff. This attention to detail would provide Davis with her share of the discomfort that comes with Elizabeth's accoutrements. Filming in the summer heat without air conditioning, encased in several layers of stiff material and heavy jewelry, was an extremely unpleasant day's work. Rather than being pleased with Orry-Kelly's amazing costuming, when he saw the screen tests, Curtiz expressed the feeling that the gowns were *too* historically accurate — to be precise, too big, in the skirts and in the ruffs. To get around this, Orry-Kelly had two sets of costumes made: his historically accurate creations for use in the actual filming, as well as scaled-down versions of the gowns for the screen tests. Like Flora Robson before her, Davis found it impossible to sit in a regular chair with the huge skirts, but a simple, uncomfortable stool would not do for Warner's queen. Accordingly, the studio's carpentry department built a long wooden bench that was designed specifically for Davis and could handle the large circumference of her beautiful costumes.[79]

The costumes went a long way towards transforming Bette Davis into Elizabeth Tudor. Even Flynn admitted that when "Bette assumed her place on the throne, dressed as Elizabeth, with big square jewels on her hands, and on her wrists big heavy bracelets, she was living the part. She *was* Elizabeth."[80] Elizabeth, thus attired and regally seated on her throne, reprimands the surprised Essex when he strides through her courtiers to meet her. Others are praised; Essex is reproved. Though he has defeated the Spanish, he has failed to capture the Cádiz treasure fleet, which the Spanish sunk themselves rather than have it fall into the hands of the English. They had time to do this because Essex and his machismo were busy storming the town. Though he protests that he acted "for the glory of England," Elizabeth insists, "Essex first, and England second!" He, furious, turns his back on her, and she slaps him for this offense. He fumes, "I would not have taken that from the king your father, much less will I accept it from a king in petticoats!"

This particular scene shows some of the personal animosity between the film's two stars. In his autobiography, Flynn vividly depicts how, on the first rehearsal of the scene, Davis actually hauled off and slapped him with her heavily be-ringed hand — so hard that it left him seeing stars and caused ringing in his ears. Knowing he would be forced to do the scene several times and fearing irreparable damage to his ears if not his already alcohol-soaked brain, Flynn decided to speak to Davis about it. She was unsympathetic, ridiculing him for not being able to "take a little slap," which resulted in a yelling match between the two. Flynn stormed out of her dressing room, telling himself, "If she hit me, and I knew she was going to, I would have to whack her and drop her — and I believed that if I did, after what I had just been through, I might break her jaw." Luckily for Davis's jaw, Flynn's yelling had the desired effect; she pulled her punches in subsequent takes.[81]

With Essex publicly reprimanded, Elizabeth goes even further by promoting Sir Walter Raleigh, who is no friend to Essex, and relieving Essex of his post. Essex, in a fit of pique, retires to his country estate at Wanstead, planning to stay there until the Queen regrets her treatment of him and apologizes. This is unwise, for while he's away from court, his detractors, led by Raleigh and Cecil, may scheme, sabotage him with the Queen, and plot his downfall with impunity. Bacon travels to Wanstead to warn Essex, attempting to convince him to return to court before his enemies are successful in having him removed not only from the Queen's council, but also from her good graces, permanently. Essex will have none of it — he has a grand opinion of himself and his heritage. He's also quite the chauvinist; it's clear that he considers himself to be superior to Elizabeth simply because he's a man, and he denigrates the way she has deployed her forces in Ireland, calling it a "silly, frightened, womanish" war that she's been waging. The film often portrays this contrast between Essex's male viewpoint and that of Elizabeth; the way in which Essex builds himself up by decrying Elizabeth's feminine weaknesses may have been more impressive to 1930s audiences than it is today. Still, it rings true from a historical viewpoint, and it fits with Flynn's personality, since he has been described as "a magnificent specimen of the rampant male."[82] The glory Essex wishes for himself is never implied; rather, the film constantly states it outright. Essex certainly lacks the subtlety and cunning imperative in a successful courtier. When Bacon says, "You are not forthright with yourself ... you wish to climb to the pinnacle of fame," Essex unwisely borders on treason as he brings up the Queen's illegitimacy, stating, "I come of better blood than Elizabeth." They discuss the fact that Elizabeth loves Essex, but she also fears him (he is a man "not easily governed") and the popularity he has inspired.

Though Essex so far has displayed precious little loyalty to his supposed beloved, he attempts to quantify his feelings for her, and things seem even stranger. He says he loves her, and would "even if she were my mother's kitchen hag, toothless and wooden-legged ... she's a witch, she's got a witch's brain" and she makes all other women look "pale and colorless." In typical melodramatic fashion, he then declares, "I love her, I hate her, I adore her." One commentator quantified Essex's feelings as a response to sheer force of personality: "So vivid is her personality, that though she bears no beauty, true glamour envelops her, and Essex's love at once becomes understandable."[83] Level-headed Bacon has more sense, however, and his response to Essex's outburst is, "Don't count too much on the love of queens."

The insight this provides into Essex's relationship with Elizabeth is not particularly enlightening given the fact that it's quintessentially dysfunctional. Perhaps the best that could be said is that Essex is awed by what Elizabeth represents — all the glamour and glory of royalty, rather than her own physical appearance or personality, and he's also overpowered by her intellect, while at the same time denigrating it because she's merely a woman. In short, Essex is completely out of his depth, but feels that he's in control of the situation because he's absolutely confident of Elizabeth's affection for him. Due to Elizabeth's womanish weakness, Essex feels certain she will put her love for him before anything else, and through this love, he can control her. Elizabeth has already stated that such is not the case, and even had she not, it soon becomes obvious that Essex's confidence is one that, as the much put-upon Bacon tries to warn him, is terribly misplaced. Bacon returns to court, torn between loyalty to his friend and benefactor and the danger by association to which Essex's hotheadedness and lack of wisdom could expose him.

Back at court, in Elizabeth's chambers, she and her women are doing what they often do in Elizabeth films — sitting around, idly killing time while waiting to be informed that something has happened. Lady Gray and Elizabeth are engaged in a game of chess, and Elizabeth displays her jealousy by stating, with added meaning, "So you would take the Queen's knight?" Elizabeth ends up losing the game and shows her bad-temper by sweeping the pieces violently to the floor. Lady Gray, in a cruel and dangerous show of passive-aggressivism, sings a song about how "love cannot endure without its youth," mocking the aging Queen to her face. Elizabeth, her vanity and insecurity fully revealed, takes out her fury on that omnipresent symbol of advancing age, the looking glass, and breaks all the mirrors in her apartments.

As already evidenced by *Les Amours de la Reine Élisabeth*, *Mary of Scotland* and now *Elizabeth and Essex*, mirrors and scenes where they are either destroyed or ordered removed is a motif that is repeated in almost every film featuring Elizabeth. It's a dramatic device that simply and effectively conveys the female monarch's anguish and anger at the process of her own aging. The historical Elizabeth is believed to have, in a fit of self-pity, commanded all looking glasses be removed from her apartments. As evidenced by today's booming cosmetic industry, beauty is not timeless, but the desire for it certainly is. Almost anything the Queen desires is hers for the asking, but no one can turn the clock back and make her as attractive as her young ladies-in-waiting. Elizabeth dons her make-up, wigs, and elaborate court costumes as her armor, her disguise, but no one is fooled. As Davis's Elizabeth describes herself, she is "a glittering husk."

Though female characters in Elizabeth films almost universally appear as rivals for the affections of the males whom Elizabeth loves or dominates, the historical Elizabeth was not so bereft of loyal female companionship. Not all of Elizabeth's ladies-in-waiting in *Elizabeth and Essex* are so contentious either. Young Mistress Margaret Radcliff (Nanette Fabray) gives Elizabeth a chance to show her softer side. After tearfully confessing her love for one of Elizabeth's courtiers who serves in her forces in Ireland, Elizabeth comforts her, assuring her that she will recall him to England so they can be together. She says, "When he takes you in his arms again, thank heaven you're not a queen. To be a queen is to be less than human, to put pride before desire, to search men's hearts for tenderness, and find only ambition ... she must give up all that a woman holds most dear." With this and other such speeches, Elizabeth continually reinforces the notion of a woman alone and apart, surrounded by men who manipulate her feelings only to further their own ambition and jealous women who undermine her relationships with those same men. This theme of jealousy manifests itself not just in the females who serve Elizabeth. The animosity here is personal — it revolves around feeling, sentiment, and emotion towards the male courtiers whom these women love. But there is also great professional jealousy to be found in Elizabeth films, and this is reserved almost unanimously for the men. While the women play for love, the men play for power. Essex is jealous of Raleigh's promotion, Cecil is jealous of Essex's favor with the Queen. It's this explosion of jealousy that feeds the court intrigue which advances the plotting in the majority of Elizabeth films.

Her waiting at an end, a courier finally arrives to inform Elizabeth and Bacon that something has happened — Sir William Bagenal, commander of Elizabeth's forces in Ireland, has just been defeated and killed, his forces completely annihilated by the Earl of Tyrone, who leads his Irish soldiers in rebellion against England. Elizabeth's first impulse is to retreat, completely pull her forces out of Ireland. Bacon counsels otherwise, lest Philip of Spain use it as a base from which to attack England. Elizabeth despairs, "I'm only a woman; must I carry the weight and agony of the world alone?"

Dialogue such as this paired with Davis's acting choices provide one of the neediest onscreen versions of Elizabeth to be found in any film. It's especially apparent in the closing scene of the film, and it strains credibility; a historical Elizabeth of this caliber would never have been able to survive. It does, however, serve to further a construct that's familiar in literature and film. It could be argued, with the rise in popular culture of the idea of the "cougar," that an older woman romantically involved with a younger man is becoming less pejoratively viewed than in the past. Hundreds of years of ingrained sentiment are not easily dispelled, however, and it certainly still possessed overwhelmingly negative connotations in 1939. Elizabeth's clingy dependence on a much younger and less intelligent Essex reinforces the idea that "an older woman who loves a younger man is always pathetic and ridiculous."[84] Elizabeth is made to seem diminished by her love for these young court favorites; it is evidence of her self-delusion and weakens her position. She may be the most powerful woman in the world, but her love for a man less than half her age is still pitiful. What's strange about the concept in this film is that Elizabeth and her supposedly much younger love, Essex, are in actuality the same age — Davis and Flynn were both in their early thirties when *Elizabeth and Essex* was made. Despite the make-up, it's obvious that Davis is no 60-year-old woman pursuing a man young enough to be her grandchild.

Essex, showing how manly and independent he is by comparison, is blithely out hawking when the news of England's defeat reaches him. He's adamant about teaching the Irish a thing or two, but Bacon, suspecting that Essex's thirst for glory in Ireland could be used to devastating effect against him at home, cautions, "If you lose your head now, you'll lose it in earnest later." Again, Essex imprudently ignores Bacon's sage advice. Upon his return to court, he tirelessly mocks Sir Walter Raleigh over a suit of silver armor in which he struts about, a gift to Raleigh from Elizabeth as a token of her esteem. The characterization of Sir Walter Raleigh (Vincent Price) in this film is an interesting contrast with that to be found in later onscreen versions, such as Richard Todd's portrayal in *The Virgin Queen* or Clive Owen's in *Elizabeth: The Golden Age*. In his essay, Thomas Betteridge divides the spaces to be found in Elizabeth films by gender: the court is overwhelmingly feminine, and everything outside it is masculine. The court is enclosed, constrictive, formal, but battles in Ireland, the high seas, these are places where "masculinity holds uncontested sway." Betteridge notes that those characters who are content to exist at court are less than completely masculine. He specifically notes the character of Sir Walter Raleigh in *Elizabeth and Essex* who "although invariably viewed in history as a decidedly masculine figure, is portrayed, rather uneasily by Vincent Price, as an effeminate dandy."[85] Flynn and his Essex, by contrast, represent unbridled masculinity, so it's inevitable that his feelings for Raleigh manifest themselves in contempt and anger. These "hopelessly feminized"[86] men are not Essex's equal, but neither can he survive in their world of deceit and flattery, since his straightforward masculinity precludes him from possessing the necessary dissemblance to effectively combat them. With his foolish quarreling, Essex makes an implacable enemy of Raleigh. Bacon, at his wits' end, admonishes him, "When will you realize how vital it is not to make enemies at court?" Essex laughs off his advice for a final, fatal time, "I'll make friends and choose enemies to please myself."

Knowing his hot temper and impetuous nature, Elizabeth appoints Essex to the post of Master of the Ordnance for the Irish campaign; in this way, she plans to keep him safely in England and out of the fray in Ireland. Essex's enemies on the council, however, see their golden opportunity — using Essex's ego against him, they formulate a plan to manipulate him into doing exactly what Elizabeth has tried to prevent: convince him to lead an expedition to Ireland to engage the Earl of Tyrone. His chances of success, they know, will be abysmal, and meanwhile they can discredit him with the Queen in his absence.

The scene in the Queen's private chambers where Essex and Elizabeth finally reconcile is an odd mixture of forced laughter, tenderness, anger, and playfulness. As one critic put it, "Bess and Robert love and spit at each other in classical language.... Elizabeth resents the empty husk of solitary queenhood, [parrying] with ambitious Essex who refuses to stand *behind* her throne."[87] While Davis hurls her lines in a compelling manner, critics noted the lack of vitality in Flynn's delivery (although the general consensus is that he still looks good doing it), no doubt a reflection of his apathetic feelings towards the film. The ire between Davis and Flynn is more than evident in the portrayals, and it creates an altogether antagonistic atmosphere. While this might, at first blush, seem antithetical to what should be portrayed between the two lovers, it's not as out of place as it at first seems. For those with strong, disparate (or conversely, too similar) personalities, love often expresses itself in volatility. This is a pair that's tragically mismatched, which is understandable given the differences in their ages, temperaments, and motivations. This quintessentially unhealthy relationship consists of the two of them constantly baiting each other, with the Queen obviously the intellectually superior of the two. Essex alternates between being condescendingly playful (he smacks the Queen of England on her royal rump) and constantly provoked to anger by her. For her part, Elizabeth will not leave well enough alone, until finally even she tires of the antagonism, and says, "Robert, let us be kind for a moment ... you're young and strangely sweet, and my heart cries out to you. And there's something in me that draws you, too. The same lovely, dreadful thing that draws us together." This paints the two as the stock ill-fated lovers familiar to any student of Elizabethan tragedy. It is not, however, fate that keeps them apart, that dooms them, but rather Essex's ambition and pride. Elizabeth voices her fears: "I fear you because you're flattered by the praise of fools, til you think you'd make a better king than I a queen. You think you'd rule England better because you're a man." Essex, with the fatal honesty that seems to be his one redeeming character trait, replies, "I do indeed. And that's exactly where you'll fail, because you can't think and act like a man." If thinking and acting as Essex does is considered manly, then it's definitely a good thing Elizabeth is a woman. While she admits that one of the things she loves most in Essex is his honesty and reckless pride, in classical tragic fashion, these are the two aspects of his character that will ultimately destroy him.

Scenes such as the above feature lengthy dialogue and little or no action. As a matter of fact, *Elizabeth and Essex* diverges from *Fire Over England* and its successor, *The Sea Hawk*, in this area — this is much more a drama than an action film. Which would be all to the good, were it not for the fact that Errol Flynn is an action hero. He is, therefore, unquestionably out of his element in *Elizabeth and Essex*, which is made evident by his

The queen of Warner Brothers enthroned in Technicolor: Elizabeth (Bette Davis) and the Earl of Essex (Errol Flynn) enjoy a romantic fireside blaze and an interminable conversation about pride, ambition, and the throne of England in *The Private Lives of Elizabeth and Essex*. (© Turner Entertainment Company)

lackluster performance. This is also a very wordy film, a state of affairs which even "action" scenes of the campaign in Ireland can do nothing to alleviate.

The scene which takes place in the council chamber showcases Essex's foolhardiness; his enemies on the council easily play upon his biggest weakness, manipulating him into thinking that it would be an insult to his pride not to take over as Lord Protector in Ireland. Elizabeth, much wiser, attempts to warn him as to their motives, but Essex has his mind made up. Exasperated, Elizabeth shouts, "Go to Ireland, and go to the devil, too!" As has been established as typical in their hot and cold relationship, she quickly relents and they embrace. Physical contact between Elizabeth and Essex is awkward; it's clearly difficult for the two actors to engage with each other. Certain aspects of the costuming, specifically Elizabeth's huge ruffs and skirts and the jewels on her bodice and hands, make it problematic for Essex to get close to her in a manner that seems anything but clumsy. Finally resigned to the idea of Essex's departure and aware of what will probably happen, Elizabeth gives Essex one of her rings. As in *Les Amours de la Reine Élisabeth*, this is a "pardon" ring — an Elizabethan version of the "get out of jail free" card. Elizabeth informs Essex that, no matter what he has done, if he wishes to be forgiven, all he needs do is send the ring to his queen and she will pardon him.

Resplendent in his new piece of jewelry, off Essex goes to Ireland and to the devil. The Queen, though she fears he's doomed to failure, ultimately does not stop him from going. With Essex hopelessly mired in Ireland chasing the elusive Tyrone, who's always two steps ahead of him, Essex's enemies in England are free to strike. Even those whom Essex counted among his friends are made to further the ends of the plotters — Francis Bacon finally bows to the futility and danger of attempting to help the self-sabotaging Essex, and Lady Penelope Gray, due to her jealousy of his relationship with the Queen, also aids in the plot. She intercepts and withholds letters between Essex and the Queen, ensuring that they become estranged through miscommunication.

The scenes set in Ireland, though meant to relieve some of the film's long spates of dialogue, are not particularly action-packed. They mostly consist of the English troops marching slowly through bogs, with a few being felled by arrows from unseen Irish enemies. Elizabeth, convinced that Essex is ignoring her letters, orders his return to England. Bacon, knowing he can no longer protect Essex and that promoting Essex's interests will result in his own downfall, hides his knowledge of the conspiracy and the withheld letters from Elizabeth. In her agony of indecision, Elizabeth turns to Bacon, as Essex's "friend." He admits that Essex is "a dangerous man to befriend," and Elizabeth confesses that she feels trapped and strangling in a jungle of lies and deceit. She bemoans the plight and fear of every queen regnant when she declares, "He never wanted me. He wanted my kingdom."

Essex, meanwhile, is mired in Ireland, unsuccessful in isolating the Earl of Tyrone and angered because he believes Elizabeth has abandoned him, ignoring his requests for aid. Yet still he plays the tragic hero — a man betrayed by circumstance rather than the victim of his own incompetence. After a brief battle, Tyrone lures the trusting Essex into a truce, then burns his camp. Tyrone is portrayed as a good-natured rogue by Alan Hale, Sr., a rare role for this actor who usually served as a loyal sidekick in Flynn vehicles. Having tricked Essex, he then offers him his "pride against the life of every last man in your command," and though Essex's first impulse is to fight a battle he knows he cannot win, for once, he chooses what's best for others over his own pride. After his humiliating surrender, he returns home to England. Believing himself betrayed by Elizabeth, he and his men march on the palace. As Elizabeth's frightened courtiers gather in her audience chamber, she enters, to a regal theme, a woman alone but showing no outward signs of fear. When her fluttering courtiers inform her that Essex is on his way and she must allow them to protect her, adopt defensive measures, she replies contemptuously, "This court wriggles like a mess of eels." It's one of the few instances in the film where Davis conveys anything like the historical queen's strength of character.

By the time Essex arrives, still Elizabeth has done nothing to defend herself. She allows him into the audience chamber, and carefully lulls him into a sense of total security. Rather than rail at him, she tells him, "I have a great fondness for rebels, being frequently one myself." She tells Essex that he's the only honest man around her. The irony of this statement is that, because of its truth, Essex will pay the ultimate price. His faults are many, but dishonesty is not one of them. They spend an extended time alone together — she on the throne, him kneeling at her feet, clasping her. There's a great deal of talk about love and trust, and Elizabeth offers Essex as much as she is willing to give: "Take me, my life, my present, my future" but only on the condition that he stand *behind* the throne so that they can build England up together. Essex refuses to be satisfied with this enormous concession, and ever honest, admits as much. What Elizabeth offers is not enough for him; he must be the ruler, not the ruled. He even admits that his ambition is stronger than his love for his queen. One of the most interesting and anachronistic (as well as contradictory) statements he makes is that he knows "if this were a freer time, where people could elect" their own governance, they would choose him. In essence, the film presents a sixteenth-century English nobleman propounding the prevailing mid–twentieth-century American worldview of democracy as the ideal for governance, with Essex in the role as elected president. When Elizabeth asks him what his plans are, he states that he has none. Unlike Elizabeth, he's incapable of foreseeing outcomes, of planning towards achievable goals. He knows what he wants, but once he has it, he knows not what to do with it. He has taken hold of the Queen's person, the throne of England is within his grasp, yet he cannot think what to do next.

Elizabeth, realizing that their differences are irreconcilable and that she must save herself, promises to share her throne with Essex. He takes her at her word, and Elizabeth convinces the naïve Essex to dismiss his soldiers. She then immediately has him sent to the Tower. For all his faults, it is Elizabeth who's the deceiver, the liar — Essex is ever honest. This side of Elizabeth, the prevaricator, is not an attractive one, but it's the reason why she will survive and Essex will not. It's the same dynamic illustrated by Florence Eldridge's Elizabeth in *Mary of Scotland*. "A ruler must be without friendship, without mercy, and without love," Elizabeth intones, as the camera pans past her to her silhouette, and outside the palace walls it begins to storm.

Elizabeth waits in a throne room of the Tower, and in an attempt to save Essex, Lady Gray tearfully confesses about the intercepted letters and begs for his life. At first, Elizabeth refuses to send for him, but finally relents. She sends Lady Gray away, thinking that her youthful beauty will provide too much of a contrast with the Queen's aging face. Essex arrives, ascending through a trap door in the floor. In a scene remarkably similar to that right before Essex is arrested, he and the Queen rehash the same subjects — she offers to pardon him, he will not accept it unless the offer also includes her throne. His ambition knows no bounds, even at the cost of his life. For her part, Elizabeth shows herself to be desperate to save him. She literally begs him to accept her pardon, and whines, "I'm old. With you I could've been young again." Essex as much as admits that death is the best thing for him, since he will never give up his ambitions. He turns his back on her and descends into the dungeon as she wails, "Take my throne, take England, it is yours!" Essex is allowed a heroically brave death on the scaffold, kissing the pardon ring Elizabeth has given him before he readies himself for the executioner's blow. But it is Elizabeth the camera focuses on, in her darkened throne room, as the abrupt end of the drum roll signals her lover's death. She sits numbly, a tear rolling down her face as the movie ends. It's a final portrait that is oft repeated in several Elizabeth films — the Queen on her throne, unhappy and very alone.

To risk stating the obvious, the emphasis of *Elizabeth and Essex* is not historicity. Even as the film's trailers try to convince viewers that what they will see is history, at the same time, they make statements which illustrate that any historical fact which happens to appear is merely background, set dressing. Prominence is given to the love story: England is a "restless kingdom ruled by a lonely woman" who is "jealous of the heritage of the lowliest woman in her realm: the right to love. Freely. Completely." This is the story of "a love affair that changed the course of history." Essex is "one of the most adventurous warriors ever to lead an army to victory" and serves as the "dashing knight of Elizabeth's roundtable." Evoking the brave knights of the roundtable is particularly incongruous, as it implies a brotherhood of brave men, selflessly fighting together for a common goal under the auspices of a single, male monarch. The men of Elizabeth's court cannot be further from this ideal, especially as depicted by the portrayal of characters such as Raleigh, Bacon, and Cecil. They neither work together nor, ultimately, for the Queen — they all pursue their own ends. Against this backdrop, Essex does stand out because of his masculinity, though the nobility with which Flynn imbues him is tempered by his insatiable ambition.

That the historical Elizabeth and Essex engaged in a physical romantic relationship cannot be stated with any certainty. The historical Essex was much more the courtier than Flynn's impersonation — though he certainly had his enemies, Robert Cecil chief among them, he was suave rather than intentionally antagonistic, and utilized the patronage system to his advantage. His stepfather, Robert Dudley, Earl of Leicester, first introduced him at court in 1584, and by 1587, when he was 20 years old, it was evident that he was a favorite of the Queen. What this relationship actually entailed, however, is unclear. While Victorians and Edwardians such as Lytton Strachey preferred a romantic interpretation (as they did with regard to just about anything), modern historians often lean towards a less salacious construal. Historians such as Alison Weir suggest that the 60-something Elizabeth viewed Essex as more of a son than a lover. It's not impossible that Essex played both roles for the aging queen, but given that he was the stepson of Robert Dudley, the closest thing the childless Elizabeth ever had to a lover, the role of son would be a natural one for him to fill. He married, and his career did not suffer for it. Perhaps at this remove, all that can be stated with conviction is that Essex and the Queen spent a great deal of time in each other's company, and she was very fond of him, to her political detriment.

One historical aspect Flynn's portrayal does get right is Essex's desire for military glory. Robert Cecil and his faction on the council advocated domestic concerns over fighting foreign wars, making Cecil and Essex diametrically opposed. Essex became the figurehead for the war party, and his position with Cecil became untenable. When his attempts at reconciliation failed, he mounted an armed uprising against the Queen's advisers, not the Queen herself — his stated goal was to force her to take on a new council, presumably led by himself. The distinction is important, because whereas the film Essex will go to the block rather than stand behind Elizabeth's throne, it seems that this is exactly the position the historical Essex had in mind.

In their examination of *Elizabeth and Essex*, Ford and Mitchell take a stand not shared by other reviewers of the film: that Flynn surpasses Davis: "Flynn's Essex trumps Davis's Elizabeth, despite the character's intelligence and strength, with a charm and nobility the real Essex never possessed" and Flynn "steals the film."[88] While Flynn does bring his innate charm to the role of Essex, their argument that Flynn's heroic demeanor and exploits (e.g., the opening in Cádiz) "assures Flynn's importance over [Elizabeth]" is contrary to almost all other critical interpretations of the film, and certainly falls flat given Flynn's undistinguished performance. He is, admittedly, a more likable characterization than Davis's Elizabeth, but his charm cannot overcome the sheer force of Davis's portrayal, nor does Flynn even attempt it. As one critic put it, "Flynn isn't diminished by his pairing with Davis—he's too good-looking and easy in his role—but he doesn't shine either. Davis wants a co-star who's less a star than she is—a Glenn Ford, a Paul Henreid, a George Brent. She wants and needs the movie to be hers. Bette Davis was never once part of a power duo of dynamic star casting. She couldn't accept an equal."[89] In this, she and Queen Elizabeth were ideological soulmates. Another reviewer summed it up thusly: "Errol Flynn is prettier than Cinemactress Bette Davis, but not such a good actor.... Davis dominates the picture as single-handedly as Elizabeth dominated England."[90]

Flynn makes no attempt at historical veracity for his version of Essex; as one commentator noted, "He is always transparently Errol Flynn—all masculine bravado and dynamism, ruined by his unwillingness to bend to the old, feminine world of the queen and her court."[91] Davis, on the other hand, took her roles seriously, and she did her homework for this one. In addition to studying various portraits of Elizabeth, she also supposedly read several books on the Queen. Which books these were is uncertain, but the determination of Elizabeth's character Davis gleaned from them was that she was "flinty, overbearing, and harsh."[92] These adjectives could just as well be applied to Davis herself, and as with Hepburn's portrayal of Mary Stuart, it is often Davis that shines through the façade of Elizabeth. The result is interesting—Davis and Elizabeth did share strong personalities with some similar elements, so her Elizabeth is less unconvincing than she is incomplete. The elements she shares with Davis were nowhere near the entirety of Elizabeth's temperament; Davis only manages to illuminate a small part of the historical woman, and that most idiosyncratically. Davis fails most dramatically to capture Elizabeth's femininity, innate intelligence and charisma. Davis and Flynn's personal distaste for each other negatively affected what Davis was able to accomplish in portraying Elizabeth's emotions with regard to her favorite: "She seems as if she doesn't really approve of him even in the scenes in which she's supposed to be blindly loving him."[93] Davis had proved in earlier films (e.g., *Jezebel*, *Dark Victory*) that she enjoyed playing women who were "as masculine as they were feminine," but the only feminine aspects she chooses to highlight in this film are "heightened emotion and vulnerability,"[94] leaving the picture of Elizabeth unfinished. Instead, Davis "acts nothing so well as a neurotic tantrum," and thus "scratches, claws, snarls and romps"[95] her way through the film and her characterization of Elizabeth. This film is not kind to Elizabeth, and the general consensus is that Davis's version has "too strident and coarse an edge, and because of Flynn's indifference, which made his Essex weak, soft, and self-indulgent, *The Private Lives of Elizabeth and Essex* emerged as a stiff and awkward pageant, dead under its lavish trappings."[96]

THE SEA HAWK (1940)

Given the positive reaction to her portrayal of Elizabeth in *Fire Over England*, it's unsurprising that Flora Robson was asked to reprise this role. What is surprising, perhaps, is the rapidity with which that reprise occurred. Less than five years after the release of *Fire Over England* and only a year after *The Private Lives of Elizabeth and Essex*, yet another picture with Elizabeth as a main character (although, again as with *Fire Over England*, the role was secondary to that of two fictional lovers) would be produced: *The Sea Hawk*.

As had been the case with *Fire Over England*, Robson's theater work would be in conflict with a proffered film role. She had just been asked to appear in the play *Ladies in Retirement*, and Robson always preferred theater work to that of film. When Hollywood came calling to offer her a role in *The Sea Hawk*, she was obliged to turn it down because of the play. She had no idea how badly she was wanted for the role, however; company executives came immediately to see her, assuring her that they would arrange the shooting to fit her schedule. They were willing to fit her scenes into a short time span to get things done as quickly as possible, and there would also be new costumes for the part. Doubtless the fact that she would not have to endure the painfully heavy gowns and stiff ruffs again helped sway her; the new costumes were designed with zippers as well as softer materials so that they would be easier to get into and out of, and more comfortable to wear. Though these were resoundingly positive aspects to the role, Robson still feared she would find "this Elizabeth far less inspiring to act than the other; the script was not so well written as Clemence Dane's."[97]

Scripting aside, *The Sea Hawk* had other features to recommend it. For one, it was helmed by none other than *Casablanca* director Michael Curtiz, himself no stranger to directing Elizabeth pictures since he was fresh off the set of *The Private Lives of Elizabeth and Essex*. *The Sea Hawk* was based on a novel of the same name by author Rafael Sabatini (1875–1950) who, in the early 1920s, had come into his own in America. Before this, since the turn of the century, he had been writing historical adventure romances that were garnering popularity in England, but he had difficulty finding an American publisher for his work. In 1921 he published *Scaramouche*, which cemented his commercial success, and finally the American publishers came calling. Sabatini found them eager to reprint his earlier works, among them a novel he had published in 1915, a swashbuckling adventure romance called *The Sea-Hawk*.

Sabatini was influenced by both Alexandre Dumas and historical romance writer Mary Johnston, and his research into the period he was attempting to portray was careful and thorough. After this research, his "inventive and convoluted incidents were bathed in rich prose, which was carefully structured to complement his themes of injustice, revenge, and reconciliation."[98] Thanks to the popularity of adventure novels and Sabatini's particular brand of escapist melodrama, as well as actors such as Douglas Fairbanks who could bring it to life on the silver screen, the cinematic swashbuckler flourished in the silent era. Due to its focus on action, swashbucklers also fit well in a medium where spoken dialogue was nonexistent. Though this particular genre fell out of favor for a few years after the advent of motion picture sound, it soon found its way back with the arrival of a new swashbuckling star.

While *Fire Over England* may have had pretensions to being a swashbuckler, Laurence Olivier could never compete in this arena with swashbuckling personified — Errol Flynn. Flynn had made a name for himself with adventure tales such as *Captain Blood* (1935) and *The Adventures of Robin Hood* (1938), and the motion picture version of *The Sea Hawk* was an attempt to exploit his trenchant popularity in this genre. *Captain Blood*, another adaptation of a Sabatini novel, had been especially lucrative, raking in huge profits for Warner Bros., and *The Sea Hawk* was company filmmaking at the height of the phenomenon. Though this would render *The Sea Hawk* not much more than a formulaic Flynn vehicle, it was a formula that had already proven to be enormously successful with audiences. Moviegoers on the brink of war welcomed the simplistic, escapist themes these adventures provided, with their black/white villains and heroes and pat, happy endings. It would also be a much more appropriate role for Flynn than that he was forced to endure in *Elizabeth and Essex; The Sea Hawk* played to his strengths.

Like Robson's role, *The Sea Hawk* itself was a reprise of sorts — the First National Company had originally acquired the rights to Sabatini's novel, and in 1924, had produced a silent-film version that was relatively faithful to the book and was well received. It made nearly two million dollars, which was a substantial sum for a film to gross at the time. Warner Bros. bought the rights and acquired First National in 1929–1930, and set writer Robert Neville (and later others) to work on a treatment for a remake of the film.

The original book revolves around the story of an Englishman from the Cornish coast named Sir Oliver Tressilian, whose half-brother falsely accuses him of murder. This same half-brother has him kidnapped and sent to sea; his luck goes from bad to worse when his ship is attacked by the Spanish and then the Moors, and he ends up as a galley slave. The Moorish captain soon promotes him, allowing him feats of derring-do that gain him the appellation "Hawk of the Sea." Tressilian learns that his beloved fiancée is about to wed the same half-brother who betrayed him, so he sails to England and abducts them. Bloody sea battles abound, and the half-brother finally admits his crimes, which allows Tressilian to return to England and live happily ever after with his love.

The evolution of Sabatini's novel into what would become the film version of *The Sea Hawk* is itself quite a journey. Film history courses sometimes use it to illustrate the complicated process a book can go through before becoming the finished script for a film. The first writer to be assigned the project, Robert Neville, added many elements completely absent from the novel, most notably creating Queen Elizabeth and the Earl of Essex as major figures in the story, as well as introducing Sir Francis Drake and the Spanish Armada. Though, in Sabatini's original, the main character converts to Islam and becomes "The Scourge of Christendom," Neville completely removed this element from his version.

So Robert Neville is to thank for the introduction of Queen Elizabeth as an integral character in *The Sea Hawk*, and later treatments may have kept her due to the influence of the "biography" of Elizabeth written by Lytton Strachey[99] which proved to be a bestseller, as well as to add the element of pageantry which viewers had enjoyed in *The Private Lives of Elizabeth and Essex*. When Neville presented his finished treatment to Hal Wallis, Warner Bros.' executive producer, staff writer Delmer Daves was immediately assigned the script and told to start from scratch.

Daves scrapped Essex, and though he allowed Elizabeth to remain, he greatly reduced her role in the film. Daves was not particularly impressed with Sabatini or the outcry over altering a beloved novel for a film adaptation. As a matter of fact, he even wrote an article for the trade press detailing original dialogue from the book and contrasting it with the more streamlined, realistic film version, highlighting how "extravagant and flowery scenes from the book ... would have turned the so-called drama into a farce."[100]

Escapist adventure fare was at the height of its popularity, but rather than move forward with *The Sea Hawk*, Warner Bros. executives chose instead another Flynn vehicle, *The Adventures of Robin Hood*. This would still affect *The Sea Hawk*, for one of the writers of *Hood*, Seton I. Miller, was asked to look at *The Sea Hawk* and give an approach for the material. Miller's draft diverged even more widely from Sabatini's original than the previous two, focusing on Queen Elizabeth and the Spanish Armada—his version has Philip II playing the peace card, pressuring Elizabeth to reign in her privateers and not build a navy, all the while planning to destroy England with his Armada. Enter Captain Geoffrey Thorpe, who attempts to convince the Queen of Philip's evil plans. With the Queen's blessing, Thorpe plans a raid on a Spanish treasure shipment in Panama, the proceeds from which Elizabeth can then use to build England's navy.

All does not go according to plan, however. Due to court intrigue, Thorpe's plans become known to the Spanish, who capture him and his men, sentencing them to be galley slaves, one of the few nods to Sabatini's original story. While the script went through yet another iteration with writer Howard Koch (who worked with Orson Welles on the iconic 1938 *War of the Worlds* radio broadcast, and with Julius and Philip Epstein on *Casablanca*), Flynn was cast in *Elizabeth and Essex*. Finally, with Miller and Koch sending contentious memos back and forth about writing credits, the script reached its final draft. This last version of the story bears little resemblance to Sabatini's novel, but studio executives retained the right to use the title, and they wanted Sabatini's name to use in conjunction with the film, feeling that it would help draw viewers. After reading the script, Sabatini refused, feeling that it diverged too widely from what he had written to even be recognizable as his work. During a reissue of the film in 1947, however, the studio's publicity department mistakenly added Sabatini's name to the advertising, and the studio later worked out a deal with Sabatini to use it for this distribution of the film.

Captain Thorpe is certainly no re-named Oliver Tressilian; he's easily recognizable as a romanticized version of Sir Francis Drake. As a matter of fact, in the script, he's actually referred to as both Francis and Geoffrey Thorpe, with Geoffrey settled on right before filming. Miller even wrote an introduction to the film that declared "the story of this picture finds its origin in the exploits of Sir Francis Drake, under whose leadership Elizabethan England challenged the supremacy of the great empire of Spain." Due to this connection, studio executives worried somewhat over two British films that had recently been released, *Drake of England* (1935; released in the United States as *Drake the Pirate*) and *Fire Over England*. It was felt that there might be too much overlap between the films, from a legal standpoint. After having Warners' lawyers examine all the films, however, it was decided that no legal entanglements were likely to ensue, and work could proceed on *The Sea Hawk*.

Though others were briefly tested for the role, Captain Thorpe was always meant to be played by Errol Flynn. This was more problematic than it at first might seem, for though Flynn was Warners' biggest box-office draw at the time, he felt he was underappreciated by Jack Warner, a fact which he resented. Also, though all involved knew he was perfect for the role of Thorpe and he eventually signed on, Flynn himself was not particularly keen on a role in another costume drama so soon after the arduous filming of *Elizabeth and Essex*. Olivia de Havilland, his romantic interest in that film, *Captain Blood*, *Hood*, and other successful vehicles, might have been thought to be the obvious choice for his costar in *The Sea Hawk*, but neither she, nor Flynn, nor the studio executives wished her to be cast in the role. Instead, it went to a new contract player the studio was promoting, Brenda Marshall (1915–1992). She had appeared in only one other film.

As has been mentioned, based on her portrayal in *Fire Over England*, the studio wanted Flora Robson for the role of Elizabeth. Though she was strongly preferred, Robson was not the only actress under consideration for the role; Warners also looked at Judith Anderson, Gale Sondergaard, and Geraldine Fitzgerald who, oddly, was also under consideration for the love interest, which was eventually offered to Marshall. *The Sea Hawk* was not the only picture in Robson's deal; Warner Bros. also contracted her for another film, *We Are Not Alone*.

Robson's contract also stipulated that, if production on *The Sea Hawk* were canceled, she would be offered another role in lieu. Due to the volatile situation in Europe, Robson was extremely anxious to get her contract fulfilled so that she could return home to England as soon as possible. The Second World War intervened, however, so Robson made the best of a bad situation by seeking a career in America for the time being. Luckily, Warner Bros. did choose to go ahead with *The Sea Hawk*, so she did her screen test for the part of Elizabeth. For the test, she wore the costumes that had been made for Bette Davis in *Elizabeth and Essex*. Since Warners had been so easily persuaded on the matter of the scheduling for shooting her scenes, Robson knew how greatly desired she was for the part, and took the opportunity to ask that they make all new costumes for her role as Elizabeth. Warners gladly conceded this point as well, and everything was set for Robson's performance.[101]

The Sea Hawk was on a 48-day shooting schedule, and due to her theater commitments, Robson's scenes were to be shot first. From early on in the pre-production process, Warners' executives looked to cut corners where they could due to the production budget of *The Sea Hawk*, which was more than substantial by the standards of the time ($1.7 million).[102] One way to do this was to reuse as much as they could from other films. Most notably, they planned to use many of the sea battle scenes Curtiz had shot for *Captain Blood*. In addition to this, there were also the sets and costumes from *Elizabeth and Essex*, some of which could be reused or retooled for the new film. Most of Robson's scenes would be shot in sets representing palace interiors, and these were cleverly modified and redressed from the palace sets of *Elizabeth and Essex* by art director Anton Grot, who had also worked on that film.

These sets did not even attempt historical accuracy: "Queen Elizabeth's palace interiors as rendered are not to be taken as realistic, detailed reproductions of any of the royal palaces of her time."[103] This is a perennial preference — the majority of film versions featuring Elizabeth choose to stylize palace interiors for dramatic effect, rather than attempting to use extant Tudor architecture or recreate Tudor-period buildings from historical information. Grot was quoted as saying he didn't particularly care for "extremely realistic" sets. This is certainly reflected in the court scenes from both *Elizabeth and Essex* and *The Sea Hawk*, where pristine flooring is polished to a high gloss and rooms are enormous, with ceilings that seem to stretch to infinity.

The sea battles, sets and their dressings weren't the only things to be recycled for *The Sea Hawk*. Though Robson had negotiated for all new costumes for herself (and some of the other major characters also got new wardrobe as well), Orry-Kelly was able to rework many of the other costumes he had designed for *Elizabeth and Essex* for use in *The Sea Hawk*.

As has been mentioned, the costuming Robson endured for *Fire Over England* was extremely uncomfortable. This was due, in large part, to the British mindset behind the costuming — it was made in a much more historically authentic manner than might be expected. Robson had to be cut out of the costumes because the lacing was too elaborate to get her out any other way. The lace ruffs had been made using original Elizabethan patterns and manufacture, ensuring that they quickly wilted under the heat of the studio lights and were unpleasant to wear. Hollywood, however, would have no qualms about sacrificing historical authenticity in favor of functionality. Robson's new costumes were adapted to meet the rigors of Hollywood filming — the ruffs were made from shapes padded with horsehair that were finished in lace to give the appearance of an Elizabethan ruff, and zippers were added to get Robson easily in and out of her gowns. In addition, the application of Robson's make-up for this film was much less complicated and took far less time.[104]

Not surprising for a film directed by Michael Curtiz with Sol Polito directing the photography, *The Sea Hawk* was also notable for its cinematography. Though one might have expected another Technicolor pageant along the lines of *Elizabeth and Essex*, especially given that some of the same sets and costumes were used, this is not the case; the film was shot in black and white. One major reason for this was most probably the studio's desire to intercut new naval battles scenes with those from the earlier films such as *Captain Blood*, which was filmed in black and white.

The Sea Hawk, although widely divergent from the "gallant little" *Fire Over England*, does share some of its anti–German themes and often lapses into allegory. This is most candidly illustrated with the film's opening scene: the setting is King Philip's palace, and the viewer first sees a map of the known world (circa 1585), where countries under Spain's possession are denoted by dark gray, and the rest of the world by white. Philip informs the audience that Spain's "arms are sweeping over Africa, the Near East, and the Far West ... invincible everywhere but on our own doorstep," England. The reason for this metaphorical chink in Spanish armor is a "puny, rockbound island, as barren and treacherous as her queen," and Philip rages that he will never keep northern Europe "in submission" until he has a "reckoning with England ... with England conquered, nothing can stand in our way." The scene closes with the darkness of Philip's shadow eclipsing the map, slowly overshadowing the entire world, while he croons that one day soon "it will have ceased to be a map of the world. It will be Spain." The implication is obvious: Philip is a proto–Hitler, with the Spanish forces his own version of the Nazi armies marching across Europe in an attempt to hold the entire world in their thrall. As it was in *Fire Over England*, also recognizable is the feared and hated Gestapo, symbolized in both films by the Spanish Inquisition.

This is contrasted in the next scene, where Doña Maria Alvarez (Brenda Marshall), a beautiful, carefree young Spanish noblewoman, niece of the Spanish ambassador, plays shuttlecock on the deck of a Spanish galleass while her uncle and the captain discuss her fate. She is to be a lady-in-waiting to Elizabeth, and the viewer learns tangentially that the Queen "surrounds herself with beauty in the hope that it may be contagious." Even this sunnier view of Spanish life is overshadowed, however, when the camera pans down to the ship's hold to show that it's powered by galley slaves, captured English sailors sentenced by the Inquisition, who pull at their oars while being cruelly whipped by their Spanish captors.

Enter Captain Geoffrey Thorpe, who sails in on the "breath of Satan," swooping down to capture the Spanish ship. This is a nod to Sir Francis Drake, known as El Draco ("the dragon" in Spanish, much more impressive than the English meaning of his last name — a male duck), who was said by Spanish sailors to possess the very powers of the Devil himself. Though *Fire Over England* had its share of shipboard melee, *The Sea Hawk* demonstrates its higher production values in this area especially — these and other later naval scenes are cited by critics as some of the most impressive work of this kind ever to be put to film. Warners even built an entire maritime sound stage that could be flooded with 12 feet of water and filled with ships built to scale. Two such ships were constructed for the naval battles portrayed in *The Sea Hawk*. In addition to this, Flynn makes a far superior action hero than his predecessor in *Fire Over England*, Laurence Olivier.

After the derring-do of taking the Spanish galleass, Thorpe is magnanimous with his Spanish prisoners; though he plunders the ship, including Doña Maria's jewels, he saves all aboard the sinking vessel by taking them onboard his ship, and he frees the galley slaves. This time onboard Thorpe's ship, *The Albatross*, gives room for character development — Thorpe and Maria engage in verbal sparring and get to know each other. Maria is righteously indignant but amused by Thorpe in spite of herself; Thorpe, a man among men, behaves like an unsure teenager in Maria's presence. Through their banter, his men let the audience know that the only woman he's comfortable talking to is the Queen, and the masculine facet of Elizabeth's character is illustrated when one sailor jokes, "Man to man, I calls it!" Meanwhile, Thorpe does with a gesture what he can't seem to manage with words — he plays the gentleman by returning Maria's jewels to her from the Spanish treasure he's plundered. Like *Fire Over England*, by this point it's clear that the film will serve as a romantic vehicle for two imaginary protagonists, with the other primary theme being the thwarting of a sinister country intent on invading England and conquering the known world.

It's interesting to note that, in another similarity with *Fire Over England*, the love/hate relationship between England and Spain is paralleled in the romantic relationships of the protagonists. In *Fire Over England*, Ingolby is attracted to the Spanish Elena, but as soon as the veil is torn from his eyes about the true nature of Spain (i.e., when his father is burned by the Inquisition), no matter how kind she has been to him personally, he immediately rejects her outright, his hatred of all things Spanish at a fever pitch. He runs home to the arms of his English-through-and-through love, Cynthia. Perhaps indicative of the more level-headed, subtle propaganda to be found in *The Sea Hawk*, Thorpe is already aware of Spanish cruelty and cunning, yet still he treats the Spanish in his care with courtesy and is tolerant of Maria's Spanish heritage — she's far more vocally critical than *Fire Over England*'s Elena, but he loves her regardless. Unlike Elena, however, Maria has English ties: an English nurse, and though she considers herself Spanish, her mother was English. She must decide which side she is on, and ultimately she chooses the right one — Thorpe and England.

By this point in the film, before she ever appears onscreen, the audience has learned that Elizabeth is barren and (if Philip's estimation is to be believed) treacherous, and that she's vain, wishing for herself a beauty that she does not possess. Based on the sailors' comments, she is perhaps even a bit mannish. In the first scene in which Elizabeth appears, this less than favorable secondhand impression is not much improved — she is displaying, as the screenplay intimates, another "of her temperamental tirades." The subject of this particular outburst is building a naval fleet, something her advisers press her to do, but for which she cannot see her way to find the funding. She may complain about lack of funds, but both she and her court are costumed resplendently. When the Spanish ambassador arrives along with his niece, whom he presents to the Queen, she intones wistfully, "You are very beautiful," then immediately launches in to a brusque interrogation regarding King Philip's grievances. When the ambassador speaks of "justifying this [Thorpe's] murderous assault" on his ship, Elizabeth cuts him off imperiously with, "The Queen needs justify nothing!"

Thorpe is summoned, and in his explanation to the Queen of his capture of the Spanish ship, he makes another German allusion very easily translated to 1940s audiences. When Elizabeth asks him if he imagines that England is at war with Spain, he replies, "Your Grace, Spain is at war with the world." The Queen disavows his actions but later, in her private chambers, the public persona is set aside and she shows her softer side. Her displeasure has been a front, and she seems downright avaricious when Thorpe gives her a large tear-drop shaped pearl, flattering her. Koch's screenplay calls her reaction "sheer, feminine delight" since, naturally, all females are delighted by jewelry. A note of whimsy is added when she also shows herself to be greatly amused by Thorpe's pet monkey, which she appropriates for herself. Thorpe, the Queen's feigned displeasure avoided, suggests a daring plan — he will attack the Spanish treasure caravan in Panama, and she can use the plunder to build England's much-needed naval fleet. Elizabeth counsels him that "our safety lies in diplomacy, not force," but Thorpe knows that diplomacy with the treacherous Spain is an exercise in futility. As in *Elizabeth and Essex*, Flynn's character represents the masculine need for action (read war), while Elizabeth's femininity prefers negotiation. Robson's Elizabeth is much more feminine than Davis's, making the contrast appear to better advantage. All the while he's detailing his plan, Elizabeth primps in front of her mirror, powdering her face. The Queen tells him that, if caught, she must completely disavow him, leaving him to his fate. Thorpe goes on his way, leaving the Queen to stand and look after him, holding her pearl necklace, as the screenplay pronounces, "Both her feminine vanity and her queenly pride have been gracefully complimented."

Based on the dialogue and snippets like the above from the written script, this version of Elizabeth would seem to be nothing more than a disingenuous, prideful, and vain ruler, one easily distracted from her purpose by any trinket that appeals to her feminine nature — in short, a woman shallow and unlikable. It's a testament to Robson's acting ability that, despite this intent for the characterization by the screenwriters, she manages to imbue the Queen with a sense of humor, to present her as clever and effectual, a woman of level-headed conviction who exercises her "tirades" more for rhetorical effect than from any true sense of anger. She also portrays Elizabeth as one whose desire for personal beauty conveys more wistfulness than vanity. Robson communicates the Queen's nervous need for action by a few well-placed fidgety movements, but avoids the unintentionally comedic spasms with which Bette Davis characterized her version of the monarch.

Thorpe and his men are off to Panama, but all is not well. What goes on at court illustrates another facet that often appears in Tudor period films — the "inaction" of the court contrasted with the derring-do of those outside it. This seeming inaction is simply a veneer — intrigue churns beneath the surface. The treacherous Lord Wolfingham and his cronies, in the pay of the Spanish, have discovered Thorpe's purpose, and he and his men are walking into a trap. While Thorpe and his crew are making their disastrous raid on Panama, the Queen and her ladies are sitting about in her apartments, waiting for something to happen and idly listening to Maria sing. The topic, not surprisingly, is love, allowing Elizabeth to pronounce, "Each of us must choose between loving a man or ruling him. I prefer to rule." Again, while the dialogue might seem to present a domineering virago, Robson delivers it with a melancholy wistfulness that manages to convey just the opposite, that she has chosen this path by necessity rather than due to personal preference.

The Spanish ambassador enters and informs Elizabeth of Thorpe's capture, implying that his raid was conducted with her blessing. He expects to catch the Queen unawares so that she might give herself away due to her emotions, but it's Maria who faints; Elizabeth maintains her composure. In yet another scene created to showcase Elizabeth's supposedly mercurial temper, the Queen's response begins with nonchalance, quickly progresses to irritation, and ends with the imperious, "Has Philip gone mad? Does he imagine he can dictate to the Queen of England?!"

Meanwhile, unbeknownst to all, Thorpe has miraculously escaped and is making his way back to England, with papers proving the existence and purpose of the Spanish Armada. Once he arrives in England, with the help of Doña Maria, Thorpe manages to reach the Queen with his evidence, after neatly disposing of Lord Wolfingham in an exceptional sword fighting scene. The dramatic lighting of this scene, during which much of the action is conveyed through the actors' shadows, is striking but also necessary, as are sweeping wide-angle shots — Henry Daniell, the actor playing Wolfingham, was helpless with a foil. His close-ups had to be shot from the elbows up, and the rest of the duel was shot using extras. The traitor thus dispatched and Elizabeth warned, there's nothing left but to neatly tie up the ending with a patriotic plug.

Robson's Elizabeth displays none of the historical monarch's much-touted indecisiveness — once she has concrete evidence of the Spanish plan and Philip's duplicity, she's all business. The last scene takes place onboard *The Albatross*, where Elizabeth bestows the knighthood on Thorpe. The Queen, after knighting Thorpe, with the other Sea Hawks ranged about, makes her most patriotic speech yet. This particular piece of dialogue was not included in the American release; it was directed solely at the British moviegoing public: "And now, loyal subjects, we must prepare for a war that none of us wants, least of all your queen. We have tried by all means within our power to avert this conflict.... But when the ambition of one man threatens to engulf the earth, it becomes the duty of

"For England and the Queen!" Flora Robson reprises her role as an Elizabeth who offers hope to an England preparing for war. Surrounded by her court and the privateering Sea Hawks, she knights the heroic Captain Thorpe (Errol Flynn) on board the representation of England's rise to naval supremacy — his ship *The Albatross* in *The Sea Hawk*. (Warner Bros./The Kobal Collection)

all free men, wherever they may be, to affirm that the earth belongs not to any one man, but to all men, and that freedom is the deed and title to the soil on which we exist." She goes on to pledge to build a navy that will be "foremost in the world — not only in our time, but in generations to come." To Erich Wolfgang Korngold's swelling score, the film then ends with the crowd crying, "For England and the Queen!" When shown during its theater release, the film was then followed by a newsreel with coverage of the Battle of Britain. Like *Fire Over England* before it, *The Sea Hawk* appeals to the patriotic impulse and offers courage and hope to a country facing war.

Biographer Janet Dunbar notes in her work on Flora Robson, "Flora has seldom looked happier than she does in *The Sea Hawk*. She is relaxed and confident and consequently gives what may be her finest performance as a screen actress."[105] Dunbar gives several reasons for this, including Robson's relief at the more comfortable costumes, stating that she knew she looked superb in the part, and didn't have to suffer for it. Another major reason was that the part was one Robson already knew; having previously portrayed Elizabeth lent her additional confidence, and she already had the research she had done for the earlier part at her disposal to inform her characterization. And lastly, there was Robson's relationship with Errol Flynn.

Dunbar states that many of Flynn's biographers are surprised by Robson's memories of the man. Though it's a far cry from how biographers choose to portray him and from how Flynn chose to portray himself, Robson remembers him with fondness, as "charming and gentlemanly." He treated her with respect and consideration. Though Flynn was notorious for not bothering to learn his lines, when Robson mentioned her concern that this might delay the film and make her miss her theater work, Flynn astonished everyone by taking the time to perfect his dialogue so that filming would finish on schedule. The offscreen rapport Robson and Flynn shared translates to their onscreen performances, making "one of the delights of the film ... the warm and flirtatious relationship" between Thorpe and the Queen.[106] Flynn, with his famously mischievous nature, even convinced Robson to help him execute a few pranks on the film's director (one of which, a humorous change of dialogue, caused Curtiz to leave the set in tears). This is certainly quite a divergence from Flynn's relationship with his former queen, Bette Davis, which also imbued both of their performances, but in a resoundingly negative way. As one critic noted, whereas Robson "conveys level-headedness with flashes of temper," Davis "projects distinctly neurotic and indecisive aspects of the character."[107]

The film was well-received for what it was, a "blood-and-thunder adventure film" that excels by staying within this prescribed medium.[108] Some disliked the court aspect of the film for focusing too much on dialogue and not enough on action. Flynn and the film's dramatic action scenes, especially the sea battles, however, more than satisfied most viewers' desire for swashbuckling.

Robson's two turns as Queen Elizabeth, though not as familiar to modern audiences as those by actresses such as Davis or, more recently, Cate Blanchett, nevertheless have garnered her long-lasting acclaim by film historians, as well as some of her more perceptive contemporaries. It has been said, "Miss Robson proved long ago that no one else should ever be allowed to play Elizabeth on the screen." Others were just as fulsome in their praise, stating that Robson "handles the Queen entirely from the scholarly standpoint rather than from the bumptious one and endows her with the mentality of a stateswoman rather than making sport of her shortcomings as is usually the case when this unique monarch is depicted dramatically."[109] Unlike Sarah Bernhardt or Bette Davis, Flora Robson was neither a great star nor a diva. When one watches her portrayal of Elizabeth, it is *Elizabeth* one sees; Robson never peeks out through the historical façade. This is due primarily to Robson's skill as an actress, but another factor may be the lack of a focus on Elizabeth's romantic relationships in the roles as written. Both films, *Fire Over England* and *The Sea Hawk*, feature romantic plotlines, and there is a degree of attachment especially between Elizabeth and the character of Thorpe, but the love story does not truly include Elizabeth. It is left to her young courtiers, and unlike some other Elizabeth films, she evinces little to no jealousy; there is no triangle. Because of this, Robson's portrayal focuses on Elizabeth's regality and political acumen, on Elizabeth as stateswoman. As has been argued conversely for other portrayals that focus on Elizabeth almost entirely as frustrated lover, a concentration entirely on the political is just as incomplete — it is less than the whole woman. This side as Robson portrays it, however, appears very seldom in these films, and while she excels at it, she also couples it with glimpses of the personal. For this reason, what she brings to the canon of film Elizabeths is both unique and notable.

YOUNG BESS (1953)

Young Bess is a distinctive Elizabeth film due to the fact that it focuses entirely upon Elizabeth's life *before* she came to the throne. Other adaptations show snippets of Elizabeth's life as a princess, but only as brief precursor to her time as queen. The fact of the matter is, however, that Elizabeth lived 25 years before she came to the throne, a substantial portion of her life, and one that has ample potential for dramatization. The plot arc of *Young Bess*, unlike other adaptations, focuses on Elizabeth as princess, and revolves around one man whose tenure in Elizabeth's life was brief, though his impact would be substantial — Thomas Seymour.

Thomas Seymour was born and raised in Wiltshire, the son of a knight, Sir John Seymour. The Seymour family had remained on the fringes of the court of Henry VIII until Anne Boleyn's star began to rise. Thomas's younger sister, Jane, had served Henry's first wife, Catherine of Aragon, and later Queen Anne as lady-in-waiting. During this time both Thomas and his older brother, Edward, began to learn the ins and outs of Henry VIII's court. By 1535, it was apparent to this team of powerful brothers that Anne Boleyn's star had fallen, past any hope of redemption. Knowing that Henry's roving eye never stayed idle for long, they began to push forward their younger sister, and Henry predictably took the bait.

Accounted by most to be sweet-tempered if not overly intelligent, Jane Seymour was ill-equipped to effectively manipulate Henry. Fortunately she had no need to, for her father and brothers were more than capable of doing it for her. Having learned their lesson from Henry's countless discarded mistresses and taking a page from Anne Boleyn's playbook, Jane was counseled to encourage the king, but never accept the position of mistress — hold out for marriage and the crown. This she did ably, and though it would doubtless have come about without Jane, this helped speed Anne Boleyn and her little neck to their appointment with the executioner's sword. A mere eleven days later, Henry and Jane wed in a private ceremony.

Jane's actions speak to her amiable disposition; she did her best to reconcile Henry to his estranged daughter, Mary, and heal the rifts in his family. She was also able to give Henry what no one else had: a son and heir. Her duty thus discharged, Jane might possibly have been the one success story in Henry's book of wives, keeping her husband as well as her head. History will never know, however, for she died twelve days later of puerperal fever. A little over a year was too soon for even Henry to have a chance of tiring of his new spouse, and he was genuinely distraught at her death.

Jane's ascendancy had made her brothers' rise to power possible, and it might be expected that they too would fall with her death. This was not the case, however, for Jane had left behind her a great deal of royal goodwill for a job well done as wife, as well as a surrogate to ensure the Seymours' continued relevance at court — the heir to the throne, little Edward. His uncles continued to enjoy Henry's favor until the very end of his reign, through three more wives. The last of these wives, Catherine Parr, would have a particular influence on the course of Thomas's life.

Thomas Seymour had received appointments at court, including being sent on diplomatic missions abroad, as early as 1536. He was eventually appointed the commander of the fleet stationed in the English Channel to combat the French. He became a suitor to the recently widowed Lady Latimer, Catherine Parr. Most accounts agree that Catherine was more than amenable to Seymour's attentions, and looked with favor upon his marriage suit. Forces beyond both their controls, however, would compel them to abandon their marriage plans. King Henry VIII had decided that he liked the cut of Catherine's jib, and he did not take disappointment well.

Abandoning his pursuit so that his monarch could have the prize, Thomas left Catherine free to marry the king, which she did, perhaps reluctantly, on 12 July 1543. By this time, Henry was ailing from a wound that would not heal, an ulcerous sore on his leg, and was not in the best of temper, even for a man who was known for his dangerous bad humors. Catherine was calm and intelligent, and dealt with Henry as best she could. Her influence was a beneficial one on all members of Henry's family. An avowed humanist, she encouraged the educations of Elizabeth and Edward, and did what she could to bring peaceful reconciliation to all three of Henry's children. She did her best to be a good wife to a difficult husband and a surrogate mother to his much tossed-about children.

Despite this, there were those in Henry's court who plotted Catherine's downfall, and Henry himself was a ticking time bomb when it came to wives. It took all of Catherine's tact and intelligence to diffuse several tense situations with Henry, and it seemed that she might also end up on the scaffold. Luckily for her, her royal husband was not long for this world, and he died on 29 January 1547, before he could add a third name to the list of wives slaughtered.

When Catherine Parr, most likely with a prodigious sigh of relief, relinquished her duties as queen, she moved from the royal residence and invited young Elizabeth to live with her. Though she had buried multiple husbands, Catherine was still only 35 years old, and her ardor for Thomas Seymour remained undiminished. How Seymour, who has been described as combining "the audacity of a successful ladies' man with the insouciance of a reckless youth"[110] felt about Parr is a matter of speculation — at the very least, his priorities were more political than romantic. This is illustrated by the fact that he had considered both Mary Tudor and Elizabeth as possible brides, but in the face of what seemed insurmountable opposition, he chose to secretly marry Catherine a mere five months after Henry VIII's death. If a princess was not to be had, a queen dowager would have to suffice.

This marriage placed him in Parr's household and in contact with the barely teenaged Elizabeth. The result would be extremely dangerous for Elizabeth and fatal for the dashing Seymour. Under his wife's nose, and occasionally even with what seemed her complicity, he courted the young princess. Several incidents would later be revealed by Elizabeth's servants under intensive questioning: Seymour came into Elizabeth's rooms early, in only his nightshirt, before the princess was dressed, and tried to tickle her in her bed; he slapped her on the rear end; Catherine held Elizabeth while Seymour playfully cut her gown to ribbons. Many different explanations have been offered for why the kind and devout

Catherine chose to participate in some of these activities rather than discouraging her husband, though at this remove, all explanations are mere speculation. It is possible that she saw them as harmless frivolity until something made her change her mind. Regardless, at some point, the situation became untenable—Catherine was pregnant, and Elizabeth removed to a different residence. Catherine did not long survive the birth of her child, leaving Seymour free to pursue the young princess in earnest. His machinations would result in his execution, and for Elizabeth "this was the first episode in which she was genuinely in political and personal danger."[111]

Due to the opportunity it provides for character development, other offerings choose to treat this situation (e.g., *Elizabeth R*) and its political fallout for Elizabeth. *Young Bess*, by contrast, turns the entire incident into a clichéd, tragic love story. The film adaptation is based upon a novel of the same name by Margaret Irwin (1889–1969), published in the 1940s, the first in a trilogy about Elizabeth's life. Irwin was not the first to treat the Seymour situation; it had proved to be a popular topic in Elizabethan fiction as far back as the 1850s.[112] Irwin's novel, however, had an advantage the others did not: timing. On 2 June 1953, a second Queen Elizabeth was crowned in England, and America, as well as much of the rest of the world, came down with a near terminal case of Anglophilia. According to its trailers, *Young Bess* was six years in the making, but its release was a matter of careful precision—it was timed to coincide with and capitalize on the wave of royal mania sweeping the world in conjunction with the ascension of Elizabeth II. This is readily apparent when one looks at contemporary reviews of the film; the issue of *Newsweek* in which *Young Bess* was reviewed has as its cover illustration a gorgeous photograph of Elizabeth II looking off into a distance filled with promise. Young, attractive, dignified—she serves as an appealing symbol for an appealing monarchy.

Metro-Goldwyn-Mayer had, for some time, made a point of contracting British stars "to make the kind of movie that British stars, in their eyes, were more suited to than many of their own domestic stars: historical dramas, period costumers, movies with a European background."[113] *Young Bess* fits this mold, so MGM's choice to cast British actor Stewart Granger (1913–1993) as the dashing Lord High Admiral Thomas Seymour is unsurprising; he was under contract for just such roles. Granger has been called the last of the swashbucklers, and Elizabethan films often feature this as an element (e.g., *Fire Over England*, *The Sea Hawk*), so Granger would seem a natural choice. In addition to playing action roles of this kind in other historical films, his offscreen persona was also that of impetuous action hero—he made a point of being photographed hunting big game and was known for his "extravagant ways and risky business ventures."[114] He cherished a penchant for being portrayed as an alpha male of the first order. *Young Bess*, however, is a historical drama; there is no action whatsoever, and Granger's swashbuckling talents are completely wasted. He's not called on to be much more than dashing and handsome, but that he manages well, conforming to what Hollywood's idea of an English actor should be: "well-spoken, with matinee idol looks, a certain gravitas and a gentlemanly air."[115]

Granger also had one more asset—his wife. At the time *Young Bess* was made, Granger was married to British actress Jean Simmons (1929–2010). Though various actresses from Elizabeth Taylor to Deborah Kerr were considered for the film's title role,[116] it went to Simmons, an actress whose career MGM was attempting to promote. The film is primarily a vehicle for Simmons, and it has been argued that Granger's taking the role of Seymour was as much an attempt to control his wife's burgeoning career as to help boost it.[117] Though Deborah Kerr lost out on the role of Elizabeth, she still features in one of the other main roles of the film, that of Elizabeth's stepmother, Catherine Parr. Charles Laughton, who made his mark in *The Private Lives of Henry VIII*, reprises his role in *Young Bess*.

That *Young Bess* will wallow in a morass of cliché is apparent from its opening credits, which claim that "her father, Henry VIII, called her Young Bess. Her mother, Ann Boleyn, ended on the block." Elizabeth has been "born at a time when heads were falling around her like cabbage-stalks" and "to grow up at all was an achievement: to grow up to greatness was a miracle." The film opens on the day before Mary Tudor's death; Elizabeth's governess Kat Ashley runs up the stairs to inform the keeper of the household accounts, Thomas Parry, that he need no longer worry with the unpaid bills, for "Queen Mary is very ill," and "Young Bess will be queen before the dawn breaks." They have a drink together over the prospect, which Ashley modestly attributes all to herself: "When she sits on the throne, I can safely say I did it." In rather silly fashion, she and Parry dance and sing a children's song about going up and down, then Ashley begins to reminisce about the ups and downs that have brought Elizabeth to this point — the entire story is a book-ended flashback.

According to Ashley, "To start with, we were our father's darling," and Laughton's boisterous Henry VIII is shown holding the baby Elizabeth up and laughing, "Your future Queen Elizabeth!" to the cooing ladies of the court. He also makes the comment, "No mistaking her fatherhood!" Though various statements against Anne Boleyn are made in the film, it's never implied that Elizabeth is illegitimate — quite the opposite, in fact. Great pains are made to compare her with both her mother and father. Even when it's stated explicitly that she has been declared illegitimate, it is made clear that it's simply a matter of barring Elizabeth from the throne, not that her parentage was actually being questioned. This is emblematic of what has been described as the film's "inbuilt reverence for the British monarchy."[118] Certain lines are never crossed. Even Anne Boleyn, who finds herself so often maligned in film adaptations of Elizabeth's life as "the great whore," is carefully euphemized in this film. She "laughed once too often, and with the wrong people," thus was sent to the block; her inability to quickly give Henry a male heir is never mentioned or implied, and Anne took three lovers with her to the scaffold because "old Harry did things in a big way." He is shown caressing the laughing Anne's neck, and then the scene immediately cuts to that same neck being lowered onto the block for execution, with its owner no longer laughing. The scenario is repeated exactly for Catherine Howard — a cut from Henry caressing her neck as she laughs to her neck on the block. Anne of Cleves is not shown at all, merely a German voice to which Elizabeth, now a young child, listens, as Ashley evinces an unquestionably post–World War II anti–German sentiment when she warns her, "Now remember, this one is German. But it's not her fault." These brief scenes of stepmothers coming and going and Elizabeth's concurrent comings and goings (after each stepmother is dispatched, she's summarily sent packing to Hatfield and recalled when a new stepmother arrives) are a flyby attempt to show the instability of Elizabeth's childhood and its affect on Elizabeth's psyche and her resulting attitudes. When told that she has been recalled to court yet again, the surly little Elizabeth spits in contempt.

The years pass, and Elizabeth is recalled for a final time to meet her latest stepmother, Catherine Parr. She refuses to go, so Thomas Seymour is sent by the king to bring her to court. By this point, the little girl has grown into a supposedly teenaged Elizabeth, but there is no attempt made at authenticity — the 20-something Simmons is obviously not 13. She has shown herself to be strong-willed even as a child, and now her petulance continues; she has locked her door, and Seymour has to charm and cajole his way inside. He does this by using her feelings for her mother to manipulate her and by appealing to her adolescent insecurities — though Simmons is attractive, *Young Bess* makes various statements meant to show that Elizabeth is not considered a beauty. Simmons's hair has been dyed auburn in a nod to the historical Elizabeth, but she still sports dark brown eyebrows and distinctly 1950s make-up. Her costuming, as is that of all the women in this film, is a rather hasty interpretation of Tudor period with modern elements — dresses are all one-piece and strangely color-blocked, and a pillbox hat actually makes an appearance. The overall effect is less than convincing. Seymour declares, "I want to see the shape of your face, the color of your eyes," and Elizabeth lets him in when he admits that his reason is "because of a woman I once knew and liked and laughed with. I know the king has banned you from the court because you are too much like her." Throughout this first exchange, Elizabeth makes comments that are contradictory to her demeanor — she doesn't need Seymour's "friendship" or "pity" because she can take care of herself. Yet despite her prickly statements, Simmons comes across as more needy than independent. Much is made of her "loneliness" by Seymour, and she ends up literally running after him so she can go to court with him. Seymour notes that she's "exactly like the king," sharing his stubbornness and suspicion. Simmons does manage to look wary, but also vulnerable, and as he holds her chin to look at her, Seymour pronounces that Anne Boleyn "turned men's heads with that smile of hers. Someday you're going to be as beautiful as she was and everyone will fall in love with you. And that, Your Highness, will save you from ever being lonely, as you are now." Despite the silly sentimentality of his words, Seymour is an intensely romantic figure — the age difference is less pronounced than the historical three decades, and he is both handsome and engaging. The formula is thus complete: a young, vulnerable and lonely girl and a dashing older man who affectionately (if carelessly) flatters her. The outcome is never left in doubt.

If there is one thing that this film does manage to accomplish, it's to give a feel for the security that Catherine Parr most probably represented for the historical Elizabeth — the first in her young life. When Elizabeth arrives at court, Seymour shows her into a lovely room, complete with new gowns and hoods all laid out on the bed for her, gifts from the Queen. To make sure the point is not missed, Elizabeth says, "There was another Catherine, and I'd no sooner grown to love her than my father sent her to the scaffold and me back to Hatfield." The fear and suspicion bred in the historical Elizabeth by all this instability is echoed by this film; she's afraid of attachments, for it has been her experience that they are quickly and violently severed. Queen Catherine, as played by Deborah Kerr, is dignified and kind, gentle with the suspicious young princess, who instantly warms to her. She goes so far as to comment that Elizabeth can be her sister or daughter, for she knows that Elizabeth will make a "charming companion." Kerr and Simmons got along famously; Kerr remarked that Simmons was "the one pleasant thing" about *Young Bess* and that she found her "enchanting,"[119] and in their scenes together in this film, of which this is a good example, there are glimmers of the affinity the two women felt for each other.

One of the more painful elements of this film, along with certain bits of dialogue which leave the viewer accidentally snorting frosty beverages through the nose, is the portrayal of Elizabeth's little brother, Edward. Rex Thompson is a less than convincing child actor, and his version of Edward is at once terribly acted, querulous and spoiled. It also stretches credulity that he knows more about the goings on of the court than does his older and more intelligent sister. After the ubiquitous mirror-gazing scene (this time to check her nose, since Seymour has commented on it), Elizabeth moons about how happy she is and that she and the Queen will "be great friends," and it is little Edward who shatters her illusion by pronouncing, "She won't last." As she seems to do throughout this film, Elizabeth pulls out her stock reaction, which is disbelief. The lines, "I don't believe you!" and "You lie!" often erupt from Simmons's mouth. Edward is shaping up to be a tyrannical little carbon copy of his father; Parr's fault is that "she contradicts the king, and no one's supposed to do that. When I'm king, if anyone contradicts me, I'll have them executed, too." To illustrate his point, he takes Elizabeth down a secret passage to listen at a door, while on the other side Henry berates a silent Catherine for her support of Anne Askew.

It seems that Catherine may indeed be about to follow her predecessors to the block. In an extremely unlikely scenario (even Henry asks "Is this a war or a picnic?"), Archbishop Cranmer, Elizabeth, Catherine, Henry, and Edward Seymour, the Duke of Somerset, take the air onboard Thomas Seymour's flagship as he scouts for the French, who have been threatening England's coast. This gathering of all the major players allows for a quick run-down of the two Seymour brothers' relationship — Somerset calls his brother a vainglorious fool and in return Somerset is a "spoilsport." Henry anachronistically states that the two fight like "Kilkenny cats" and everyone knows what happened to them (i.e., they killed each other). The question of religion and Catherine's marital issues are elucidated in one fell swoop when Henry confronts a seasick Archbishop Cranmer, whom he accuses of having had the Bible translated into English without the king's knowledge or approval. The Queen speaks up, gently (and unwisely) reminding her husband that it is she who held the power of regent while he was away. Elizabeth looks more and more concerned as Henry makes statements about Catherine instructing rather than being instructed and how there are heresy laws which may apply to her. When he reaches out to caress Catherine's neck in a duplication of earlier scenes with Anne Boleyn and Catherine Howard, the terrified Elizabeth lets loose with a bloodcurdling scream. Henry threatens to send her back to Hatfield, and she flatly refuses to go, facing him down. Both mirror each other with their stances — hands on hips, legs spread wide. Throughout the film, Henry and Elizabeth's distinctive (and affected) posturing is impossible to miss and is meant to associate them with each other — to convey that here is an apple that has not fallen far from the great tree. Henry angrily blusters that Elizabeth would "shape the world as it suits" her, to which she replies, "Why not? Didn't you?" His anger turns to uproarious laughter before he suddenly collapses. He shows approval of Elizabeth's spirit; her defiance amuses him, because he sees in it a reflection of himself. Other portrayals of Elizabeth show her as, at best, in awe of her father, if not terrified by him, but Simmons's

Elizabeth is continually pitting herself against him. As he lies dying, he calls his other two children sheep—Mary is a "crazy" sheep and Edward a "frightened" sheep, but he has no words for Elizabeth, who assures him she's the black sheep. At that, he crows, "I wish you were a boy," and admonishes Seymour to watch her grow up and keep an eye on her, for she will make them all jump. "I wish I were there to see the fun," are his final words on the subject before he succumbs.

This means yet another move for Elizabeth, and her first panicked utterance is, "I'll never see him again!" She rushes through darkened corridors in her nightgown to Seymour's room. In a complete divergence from the historical Seymour, it is he who advises Elizabeth of the impropriety and danger of her actions, of them being together in a bedchamber while in their nightclothes. Her girlish impetuousness has endangered them both. "Use your head and allow me to keep mine on my shoulders," he tells her with a smile. This is just one of several instances in the film where, as one commentary noted, "Seymour is presented as the man who must look after and protect the young, imprudent princess."[120] Elizabeth tells him, "I'd rather die than be lonely all my life," and Seymour, oblivious to the cause of her passionate outbursts, assures her, "You'll not be lonely, Bess. And remember, no fear any longer." After promising to find a place for her to stay where he will visit her, he condescendingly chucks her chin and bids her to "run along now." Though she is clearly not a child, Seymour treats her as one even while paradoxically acknowledging that she is not—if it were not perceived as a potentially sexual situation, there would be no danger involved in her being in his room.

To illustrate this, Elizabeth's visit has not gone unobserved. If Catherine Parr is the good stepmother, the Duke of Somerset's wife plays the part of the wicked one. She questions Elizabeth about her visit to Seymour, and the end result is yet another attack on Anne Boleyn, which Elizabeth meets by throwing an inkwell at the Duchess before leaving in a huff. While the historical Elizabeth was tellingly silent on the subject of her mother, choosing always to identify herself (at least in public pronouncements) with her father, Simmons's Elizabeth is fiercely sensitive and protective where Anne Boleyn is concerned. Her reaction to attacks on her mother is always defensive anger. The entire incident is later used to bait Seymour, who lightly says that if he wanted a love affair, he wouldn't search for it in the nursery. Somerset warns that this path is dangerous, to which the cavalier Seymour replies, "I love danger" and laughs the whole thing off as his private business. The problem is, when it comes to the marriage of the heir to the throne, private feelings are always trumped by politics. The portrayal of Seymour in this film lends him nothing of the historical man's grasping foolishness—Granger's Seymour recognizes the danger, but seeks to gratify personal desires rather than political ones. His main fault seems to be willful ignorance of the fact that the council will not see things the same way, and a desire to infuriate his brother even at great cost to himself. He stokes the sibling rivalry; where it would be wise to placate his brother, instead he baits him.

Elizabeth has been happily living with Catherine, spending her days dreaming about Seymour's arrival and torturing her tutor. The historical Elizabeth was acknowledged as a brilliant scholar even by her detractors, but Simmons's Elizabeth is only interested in love. When her tutor attempts a lesson on Caesar's campaigns, Elizabeth demands to hear the "important part"—his love affair with Cleopatra. "I've often wondered what was the fascination she held for a man so much older than her ... how was she able to hold a man like that?" Elizabeth answers her own question, "She had brains enough to show him she shared his interests." In this case, since he's Lord High Admiral, those interests tend toward the maritime, so before one can say avast, Elizabeth has familiarized herself with everything there is to know about ships and the English fleet. As Ashley says, "You work 24 hours a day to fit yourself for an admiral's wife." The somewhat ludicrous implication throughout this film is that the rise of England as a maritime power under Elizabeth, and indeed, even the defeat of the Spanish Armada, can all be traced back to Elizabeth's all-consuming love for Thomas Seymour. In true romance-novel fashion, she passionately declares, "I love him. I love him dearly. I shall love him til I die ... because we match." Gone is the grasping admiral old enough to be the father of the teenaged girl he pursues for political gain. On offer instead is a true-love match between two equal souls, even if one does not yet know it. Elizabeth "gets" Seymour in a way he does not yet understand himself, but things are complicated by the fact that there's someone who has a prior claim on him. Thus, the triangle is complete: the dashing older man, the wife who may love him but does not understand him, and the girl who not only loves him, but shares his passions and is his equal.

"I'd rather die than be lonely all my life!" Princess Elizabeth (Jean Simmons), as damsel in distress, displays all the accoutrements of the clichéd romantic heroine in *Young Bess*. (MGM/The Kobal Collection)

Elizabeth receives the news of the "other woman" with typical passionate disbelief, mirroring her father's gestures yet again as she angrily emphasizes her words by pointing with her thumb. When she sees the evidence for herself (observing from her window Catherine and Seymour running to embrace each other) she remains stoic, and it's Elizabeth who brings about their marriage by manipulating her brother into commanding that the two marry, since she cannot bear their clandestine meetings.

The plotting is furthered through entries in King Edward's diary; Seymour secretly gives him pocket money, and Edward chronicles the situation, scribbling such enlightening political statements as "More power to Uncle Tom" in his journal. Besides the little puppet king, there are also the people to consider — mirroring the tone between Elizabeth and Essex in other film adaptations, Seymour is becoming too popular with the people for the de facto ruler of the realm, his brother the Lord Protector, to countenance. Seymour returns home from his sea voyages in triumph, and encouraged by the cheers of the crowd, Seymour declares to his brother and sour sister-in-law, "We're on the eve of great things," to which she replies that these great things may "sweep you right to the steps of the throne." Rather than attempt to deny this or be discreet, instead Seymour merely raises his eyebrows and admits it to be "a fascinating idea."

Things on the home front are also progressing. The Duchess of Somerset has already snidely stated that Seymour has "two wives at home," and the dynamic has changed — Elizabeth is no longer a child. Though he acknowledges that during his absence, Elizabeth has grown up, Seymour still treats her with the unrestrained affection he would show a child, playfully throwing his arms around her and kissing her on the lips. Catherine stays passively at home while the two of them ride out together and spend time sailing on his flagship, where Elizabeth greatly impresses him with her technical knowledge of maritime minutia. For no apparent reason, since the king appears the picture of health, Seymour pronounces that Edward "won't make old bones" and Mary is "a fool," so Elizabeth's ascension is a sure thing. A sexual component to their relationship has begun to develop, even if Seymour still remains too willfully blind to acknowledge it. There is much talk of "excitement" which is directly linked to Elizabeth's power. Elizabeth says that "it excites me to think what we could do — you and me and England," and Seymour is "excited to hear you talk like that" when Elizabeth speaks of her plans to send him sailing to the New World, as "her admiral," when she becomes queen. Throughout their conversation, this idea of possessiveness is put forth by Elizabeth: that Seymour belongs to her, and because she couches it in terms of queen and subject rather than lady and lover, it's never gainsaid by Seymour. Seymour funnels the excitement and exuberance Elizabeth provokes in him into the only acceptable outlet — his wife. After their lovely day, he cheerfully embraces Elizabeth and holds her just a bit too long before running up the stairs to Catherine, whom he has called "beautiful, absolutely beautiful." The camera focuses on Elizabeth's stoic gaze as he and Catherine are heard canoodling and exchanging sweet nothings. In typical high-school fashion, Elizabeth decides to apply a little jealousy of her own to bring Seymour around.

She writes to the Lord Protector encouraging his Danish marriage plans for her, and at a banquet with the Danish ambassador her conspicuous flirtation achieves its desired effect. Seymour, stuck on the other side of the table, cannot take his eyes off her. He confides to the little tyrant Edward, "Your Majesty's sister is very beautiful tonight. And very foolish." Elizabeth ups the ante by dancing with others in front of him while enticing him with her gaze, and she plays her final card by kissing a page at a location where she knows Seymour will walk in on them. It is not Seymour who happens upon them, however, but the Danish envoy, which kills two birds with one stone — the Danish marriage suit is off, and Seymour is still made aware of the kiss. On the boat ride home, he's angrily silent, and Elizabeth is prodigiously pleased with herself, laughing hysterically as she crows, "Tom Seymour, the great Lord Admiral, is jealous!" This is the final straw, and Seymour slaps her, which pleases her more than anything. His abject apologies turn into a passionate kiss, and she confesses her love for him.

This arc for Elizabeth and Seymour's relationship is in keeping with this film's reverence for the monarchy. Unfavorable circumstances are mitigated, and the entire affair is rendered in the most innocuous of terms. Elizabeth loved Seymour before his marriage to Catherine and with no knowledge of a prior attachment; she did not willfully pursue a married man. Neither did Seymour intentionally court her; his affection for the child grew into love for the woman as Elizabeth aged. Seymour is not an unfaithful scoundrel — he appears to love both his wife and Elizabeth, and though, as Catherine says, Elizabeth's "name was never mentioned," when Catherine realizes the situation, he neither lies to her nor attempts to manipulate her. Catherine is not hurt, she does not rage; as she has been in everything, she is gentle, kind, and even understanding. Seymour makes himself scarce while she and Elizabeth have a little talk, woman to woman. Catherine "needs" Seymour: "I can't afford to lose him. I'm not like you, strong and independent." Elizabeth shows her strength and independence by choosing the noble route — to go. Seymour dutifully stays with his wife, caring for her when she becomes ill. There's no pregnancy or child, for that would only complicate the romantic storyline, and in her fever, Catherine asks the question that will set the audience's mind at ease, "You don't want me to die because you want to marry Elizabeth, do you?" Seymour's earnestness in denial leads her to confess madness for even asking, and she gently comforts him with, "You're not the first man to be in love with two women at the same time" before conveniently dying with the beneficence of a saint. The situation has not been ideal, but all involved have acted with sincerity, civility and honor — a blameless affair of noble hearts. It's a far cry from the historical Seymour sordidly pursuing an adolescent girl under his pregnant wife's nose.

To show how properly Elizabeth and Seymour conduct themselves, Seymour spends an entire year at sea after his wife's death before he comes back to see Elizabeth, who has waited for him, growing pale with her lovesickness. He has sent her a letter, intercepted by the Lord Protector, but Elizabeth is informed of its contents by her brother, who pronounces that it's a nice letter, and "Uncle Tom likes you very much, I think, and that's why Uncle Ned wants to kill him." Seymour sneaks into Elizabeth's rooms at Hatfield by night, and they stay together until dawn. There's much soft-focus camera work as they kiss and embrace, with Elizabeth (for all her much-touted strength and independence) sobbing statements such as, "When shall I see you again? Oh Tom, I love you and I'm frightened!" For his part, Seymour holds her while nobly looking off into the distance, spouting idealistic phrases about popular support for their cause in his beautiful baritone voice. Off he must go to rouse the people, and he's soon captured.

Elizabeth is immediately questioned by the Lord Protector and his ilk. She gives as good as she gets, stating, "The people will set him free," and warning the Lord Protector that he'll answer for his deeds with his head. She also admits her feelings for Seymour. One commentary noted that this is "in stark contrast to the historical record, since we know that during questioning, Elizabeth repeatedly denied any interest in Seymour."[121] Handled in better fashion in other offerings (e.g., *Elizabeth R*), the goal of questioning Elizabeth was not to entrap Seymour as *Young Bess* portrays — his guilt was not in question — but to determine Elizabeth's own involvement in an effort to implicate her and bring her down with him. Elizabeth met the situation with cunning and a resolve to save her own skin, not a young woman's emotional desire to defend her "lover." Simmons's

Elizabeth is only momentarily cowed by mention of her "shameless" love affair before passionately accusing the Lord Protector of attempting to murder his brother because of his "ignoble envy"—the quintessential Cain and Abel story. She ends her diatribe by smacking the Lord Protector with a riding crop (that just happens to be lying on the table) and solemnly walking out of the room, only to faint dead away in archetypical romantic fashion as she ascends the steps to her room.

Elizabeth is delayed by illness and the Lord Protector, and by the time she sets her brother to writing an order for Seymour's release, it's too late. In the Tower, Seymour recalls Henry's words about Elizabeth and the "fun" there will be in England. Unfortunately, he won't be around to see it, to which news his reaction is, "It's hard to believe this could be the end." His last words for Elizabeth are equally brilliant: "Tell her from me. Tell her ... well, never mind. I think she knows." He goes to the block, and as a numb Elizabeth leaves the palace, her silhouette looms large over the Lord Protector's cowering wife, denoting the power and influence she will soon exert. The flashback over, the camera cuts back to Ashley as she voices a statement (according to one commentator) "whose absurdity is in keeping with the atmosphere of the rest of the film."[122] Ashley says sadly that "she never mentions his name. That's how I know that, in her heart, he's still alive." Ashley ties up any loose ends for the viewer by mentioning Edward's death and the Lord Protector's execution, and she and Parry have a dance before falling to their knees as, to a regal theme, Elizabeth enters. Upright, clad in black, her gaze remains expressionless as she walks out onto the balcony to the cheering of the crowds. The wind begins to blow, whipping her hood around her, as the camera pulls in on her sad face—another picture of Elizabeth as a woman in mourning for a love sacrificed so she can be wedded to the realm. To make sure the point is not missed, the film then fades to a close-up of the British crown before ending.

The trailers for *Young Bess* reached shameless heights of hyperbole ("a galaxy of pictorial brilliance"), although hailing it as being of "epic size and high emotion" does bear some resemblance to the actual film. With the exclusion of the costuming, there are glimpses of epic-size production values—palace interiors and shots of Seymour's tall ships are impressive. High emotion hits closer to the mark; Jean Simmons's Elizabeth is nothing if not a creature of extremes. She seems to exhibit three moods: passion, passionate anger, and passionate disbelief. To this trinity she occasionally adds an outburst of fear. For his part, Granger "had little to do as Seymour other than look suitably handsome and be his usual slightly arrogant self,"[123] and this he manages with aplomb. What he cannot seem to accomplish is a portrayal of charm plus ambition. The historical Seymour was a manipulator and schemer of the first order—and his scheming was always in service of self, never others. Granger's Seymour is more palatable, but he's also less than convincing. The viewer is led to believe he's ambitious by the statements he makes to his brother, but he displays little action to match his words, making his portrayal, at best, incongruous.

Since Granger and Simmons were man and wife at the time the film was made, the chemistry between them is apparent, despite the trite stylings of the film's love scenes. Simmons has stated that she felt more "self-conscious"[124] playing love scenes with Granger after they were married than she did before, but it seems to have had no negative effect on their rapport in *Young Bess*. This is not the only area where film borrowed from reality, however. One biographer of Granger noted that *Young Bess* "does reflect in an odd way some of the issues between Granger and Simmons in real life."[125] Granger was older than Simmons, by some 16 years, and he did display some of the condescension towards her that comes across in the film with Elizabeth and Seymour's relationship. Unlike in the film, however, it was more Granger's alpha male personality rather than the age difference that seemed to drive his treatment of his wife. When he wooed her (while he, like the historical Seymour, was married to someone else), he used his charm and flirtation to manipulate the feelings of a girl who was, at the time, not out of her teens. By the time *Young Bess* was made, however, Simmons had matured and was coming into her own with regard to her film career, resulting in "definite issues about possessiveness and power within their marriage" which the atmosphere of *Young Bess* sometimes reflects as Elizabeth grows from impressionable young girl into a woman who can talk of what she will command of Seymour when she becomes queen.

If there is one actor in this film that does deserve praise, it's Deborah Kerr, for her portrayal of Catherine Parr. One wonders, despite its sentimental and silly dialogue, what Kerr would have been able to do with the part of Elizabeth, a puzzle Kerr herself must have pondered, since that was the part she originally sought. Kerr hated being pigeon-holed into the dignified, genteel roles which Hollywood kept offering her, roles of which her turn as Catherine Parr is a prime example. "Now I was down to playing a minor part in the film *Young Bess* ... another long-suffering woman. I had done so many of them, the thought of them made me ill."[126] Kerr wanted sexier, stronger roles, and she may have been able to successfully meld the passion called for by the part with more of the historical Elizabeth's deliberation and intelligence. As Catherine, she exhibits the perfect mix of dignity and kindness, and if there's any defect in characterization, it's that she's *too* mild and detached — no doubt a choice made for contrast with the supposedly temperamental Elizabeth, but one that belies the passion that led the historical queen dowager to quickly and secretly wed a man of whom she knew the council would not approve.

Contemporary reviews of the film were, on the whole, favorable. *Newsweek*, while admitting it to be "an exceedingly free improvisation on Elizabethan themes" still pronounced that it was a "handsome Technicolor show window for the smoldering grace of Jean Simmons" and that she was "beautifully expert" in her seething.[126] *Variety* called it "remarkably engrossing," since "romance phases are rich in emotion; court intrigue conjures suspense, and there is a suggestion of action throughout."[127] Clearly, the film decided not to act on the suggestion, for *Young Bess* features no action scenes whatsoever.

The yardstick used to measure the film, however, was as a romantic drama by the standards popular during the 1950s — in short, clichéd and sentimental. In hindsight, it has not fared as well. A biographer of Stewart Granger remarked that "the treatment is nothing if not hackneyed and there are no surprises in this pageant, only tired predictability.... There is no real pain or deep emotion in the movie — all is surface and outward show — so that there is a deadness to the whole proceedings that the actors cannot break through."[128] Add to this some truly embarrassing bits of dialogue, and the overall impression is that this is a film that may succeed as a shallow romance, but fails miserably as an historical drama.

In an examination of the canon, *Young Bess* has been called one of the "weakest" films made about Elizabeth's life.[129] The film utilizes historical characters, but condenses everything down to three simplistic themes: love first and foremost, but also a Cain and Abel sibling rivalry and the elevation of the tradition of the British monarchy. In Irwin's original novel, published during World War II, "The person of the future queen was far less important ... than was the theme of redemptive sacrifice."[130] This is a theme echoed in other Elizabethan film offerings influenced by the Second World War, most notably *Fire Over England*, but it's not as apparent in the film adaptation of Irwin's novel. With the war over by the time the film was made, a more romantic theme could become the focus, and the result is a stock romantic storyline with stock romantic characters which bear little resemblance to their historical counterparts or to earlier, more patriotic versions of Elizabeth's, such as Flora Robson's.

The film's ending (which has Thomas Parry grandly stating, "It's a new day") is obviously meant to parallel Elizabeth's ascension to the throne with that of the second Elizabeth 400 years later—a new day for England, one that opens with promise and will result in glory, a second Golden Age of Elizabeth. However, as one commentator noted, using this particular incident in Elizabeth's life to highlight the coronation of Elizabeth II is a bit of a backhanded compliment, for "it was not a pretty story and it wound up with Seymour's execution for treason ... whatever statesmanlike qualities the sixteenth-century Elizabeth possessed ... she also displayed a public and private immorality which hardly bear honorable comparison with the exemplary conduct and high moral purpose of the present queen."[131] Another contemporary examination of the film is particularly interesting in hindsight. Noting the final scene in *Young Bess,* which leaves Elizabeth "alone and lonely" in her "destiny of greatness," and drawing the comparison between the two Elizabeths, the reviewer remarked, "Perhaps, many years from now, we shall have another romantic movie about a great Queen Elizabeth, and I hope it's a happier film."[132] One wonders what the reviewer would have thought of Helen Mirren in *The Queen*. The second Elizabeth is far from "alone and lonely" given her husband, children, and grandchildren; but the public scrutiny, often with disastrously unfavorable results, which more than one member of her family has brought upon the institution of the monarchy begs the question of whether the first Elizabeth didn't have it easier being "alone."

THE VIRGIN QUEEN (1955)

Like Flora Robson before her, Bette Davis chose to give an encore performance as Elizabeth; however, unlike Robson, significant time had elapsed (16 years) between Davis's first and second turns in the role. This provides an interesting perspective in that the historical time frame of the second film is set earlier than *Elizabeth and Essex—The Virgin Queen* predates it by more than a decade, but the woman playing Elizabeth was 16 years older. As this put her closer to the right age of the historical Elizabeth, one might expect a corresponding increase in the authenticity of her portrayal. One's expectations would be disappointed.

The Virgin Queen was based on a short story entitled "Sir Walter Raleigh," and from the beginning, the focus was to be on Raleigh, not the Queen. Raleigh had appeared onscreen in other Elizabeth films, such as Vincent Price's milquetoast portrayal in *Elizabeth and Essex*, but with this film, 20th Century–Fox's intentions were for the spotlight to be directed on the male lead, for Raleigh to be the focal point of the film. Perhaps the executives at Fox were unfamiliar with the aphorism about the road to hell and paving materials.

The first hurdle came with the film's name — studio executives were worried that its pronunciation would provide some difficulties. Speakers of American English and British English tend to pronounce "Raleigh" differently, and as *The Virgin Queen* would have a cast made up of both British and American actors, some sort of uniformity had to be enforced. Ultimately, the studio chose the British pronunciation, but they still wished to avoid having Raleigh's name in the title of the film.

As had been the case with *Elizabeth and Essex*, the deciding factor in the titling of the film came from the force of nature playing Elizabeth: Bette Davis. A script for a film tentatively titled *Sir Walter Raleigh* was sent to Davis in the summer of 1954, and negotiations were concluded in the fall. Once she became attached to the film, the name was quickly changed to *The Virgin Queen*, and Raleigh threatened to follow the path of Flynn's Essex, disappearing beneath the very long shadow cast by Bette Davis.

Luckily for Raleigh, the Bette Davis of 1955, while not a different creature in essentials from the woman who had first played the Tudor Queen, was at a decidedly different point in her career and her personal life. Davis had adopted a child, Margot, who turned her life upside down (the child was mentally ill and violent) to the point where she had to give her up by sending her off to a special school. This devastation came hard on the heels of Davis's physical difficulties: an infection in one of her teeth abscessed, causing her almost unbearable pain and making it difficult for her to work. She finally had to have a major operation to remove it and address the underlying cause, osteomyelitis, a bone disease. Hollywood tabloids erroneously reported that she had cancer, an assertion which greatly disturbed Davis and caused her much time and effort to refute. She had also gained weight. Add to this the fact that the reviews she had received for her last work, a Broadway musical, were mostly negative, and Davis was at a physical and psychological low point, a far cry from the undisputed queen of Warner Bros. and the industry that she had been in 1939.

Due to these factors and a need to convalesce, Davis did not take on any new motion picture work for an extended period of time. When she decided to begin working again after an almost two-year hiatus, she enlisted the help of studio executive Darryl F. Zanuck to find a vehicle worthy of her return to the screen. It was Zanuck who introduced Davis to the script for *The Virgin Queen*, and she responded favorably. This script was created under the auspices of a writer named Charles Brackett, whose critically acclaimed work was diverse enough to include atmospheric film noir such as *Niagara* (1953) and the extraordinary pathos to be found in *Sunset Boulevard* (1950). Brackett was known for his storytelling ability, and has been described as a man quite content to "twist the history of England to tell a good story."[133] After signing on to do *The Virgin Queen*, Brackett found that he was too busy to write the script himself, so he hired screenwriter Mindret Lord[134] to write while Brackett would produce. The language Lord employed for the dialogue in the script is exceptional; he retains the beauty and cadence of sixteenth-century

English, while unobtrusively modernizing it enough to make it palatable to 1950s audiences. Lord was assisted in crafting the dialogue by writer Harry Brown, who was "pleased that Brackett had let him 'mess around' with the Elizabethan idiom."[135]

The dialogue was not the only unusual aspect of this film. It also benefited from a relatively new process of cinematography called CinemaScope. In the 1920s, a French physicist named Henri Chrètien invented a technique that utilized a special camera lens to allow a wide picture to fit on standard 35-millimeter film. A special projection lens was then utilized for screening the film; this lens allowed the film to be expanded to widescreen without any loss of clarity or ratio distortion. Twentieth Century–Fox bought the rights to CinemaScope and used it to adapt an older, anamorphic process. The studio then patented the process and first used it for the American screen with the successful biblical film, *The Robe,* in 1953.[136]

The studio wanted the pageantry and grandeur of *The Virgin Queen* to be filmed in CinemaScope, but many directors lacked the expertise needed to successfully frame for the new widescreen process. The director of *The Robe,* Henry Koster, had shown great creativity and success with the new process and produced a stunning result. As is often the case when one excels at something, one finds oneself deluged with requests for repeat performances. Koster became 20th Century–Fox's first choice to direct expensive or important pictures using the CinemaScope process, and his skills were solicited for the production of *The Virgin Queen.*

Directors were not the only ones who found working in CinemaScope to be a challenge — actors also experienced difficulty with the constraints it engendered. Filming in CinemaScope could be almost identical to stage work with regard to blocking; actors often had to learn full scenes, including exits and entrances, without the safety net of cutting. Since Bette Davis's last stint had been on Broadway, she did not find this to be particularly difficult, but other actors took some time to adjust to it. Not surprisingly given her personality, Davis did have other objections — she resented the bluish tinting produced by the use of DeLuxe Color and also the lighting. Claiming that her eyes were very light sensitive, she objected to working in the sun (and several scenes in *The Virgin Queen* are shot outdoors) and to the use of other powerful lights, both indoor and out. Charles G. Clarke, the cameraman for *The Virgin Queen,* explained, "The stronger the sun, the deeper the shadows, and the great problem with lighting exteriors is filling the shadows. Bette didn't like the bright lights too much. She kept saying to me they were too intense for her. And she thought she knew something about cinematography and lighting. A few times she'd try and tell me my job, but I don't put up with that kind of business."[137]

Davis clashed with Clarke as well as other members of the production team, making the working environment almost as difficult as it had been on the set of *The Private Lives of Elizabeth and Essex.* The difference was that, as has been mentioned, Bette's position had changed since 1939. As one Davis biographer noted, "The brutal fact was that she no longer occupied the supreme position in Hollywood that would justify behavior acceptable at Warners in her heyday."[138] Koster tried to diffuse the tension as best he could and get on with the film. Koster, who had made a name for himself in the American film industry with the Deanna Durbin musical pictures, was known to be a workmanlike director, with an ability to take on and complete large-scale technical projects while still bringing a human face to them.[139] This he attempted to do with *The Virgin Queen* while placating Davis and juggling the animosity she often provoked in the cast and crew.

With the role of Gloriana filled, it was now important to find the right Walter Raleigh. In the early stages of the project, Richard Burton was under consideration for the role, but it would ultimately go to Richard Todd (1919–2009). Todd was a native of Ireland and the son of an army officer; his formative years were spent in Ireland, England, and India. Like Raleigh, he had seen his share of combat and was a war hero himself, having parachuted onto the beaches of Normandy during the D-Day invasion. The film and stage roles at which he excelled were those of military or otherwise heroic men, and he was nominated for a Best Actor Academy Award for his turn in *The Hasty Heart* (1949). After the war, he landed the title role in *A Man Called Peter* (1955), and it was this performance that seemed to mark him out for bigger things. He was then cast as the lead in *The Virgin Queen*. Like others before him, he would find that regardless of his performance, playing opposite Bette Davis was not a formula for greatness in a male lead. His career would never regain the impetus for stardom it had possessed immediately following *A Man Called Peter*.

Todd was being groomed by 20th Century–Fox to be a major star, but Davis allegedly "didn't think much of Richard Todd as Essex [sic] and said, 'Compared to Errol he's a milquetoast. Elizabeth would have dumped him in five minutes flat.'"[140] This was according to Davis's daughter, however, who exhibits a tendency to get her facts incorrect, not the least of which was what role Todd played in the film. It also seems ludicrous to call Raleigh's performance that of a milquetoast, even when compared with Errol Flynn — what little swashbuckling Todd is allowed to do in the film is impressive, and his character is as strong-willed as Flynn's Essex, just as assured, and certainly cleverer.

Though dramatized and romanticized, the court milieu that *The Virgin Queen* depicts is indicative of what the historical Elizabeth must have endured. One commentary on the film, while providing a laundry list of Elizabeth's male courtiers from Edward de Vere, the Earl of Oxford to Robert Cecil, notes, "By the time she met the virile Devonshire rogue Walter Raleigh in 1581, Elizabeth was a seasoned politician, maintaining the delicate balance of her court and courtiers like a vaudeville plate spinner."[141] Given the plethora of ambitious men all surrounding one throne, struggles for power were inevitable, though after many years in Elizabeth's service, most of her senior advisers had managed to find common ground, and a balance was more or less preserved. When a newcomer was thrown into the mix, however, especially one of Raleigh's character, "The snarling and posturing began anew." Illustrating this concept with the "latest cock of the walk," and its effect on Elizabeth's court is, according to Ford and Mitchell, the film's "one strength." This view is unfair to *The Virgin Queen*— it does have other strengths — but it's an overarching theme which the film aptly demonstrates.

Indeed, to pigeonhole Raleigh as but the latest in a long string of Elizabeth's male admirers would be a disservice. As one biographer stated, "In many ways, Sir Walter Raleigh symbolizes the energy, indeed even the hubris, of the Elizabethans. He was by turns poet, historian, philosopher, scientist, soldier, sailor, courtier, legislator, explorer, entrepreneur, and colonial administrator."[142] Another called him "the ideal Renaissance version of the valiant English knight."[143] A true Renaissance man, it is not difficult to see how Elizabeth would be drawn to such a character. Though Raleigh was accounted by most to be darkly handsome and his penchant for derring-do was already well established by the time he and Elizabeth met, more than anything else, it seems theirs was a meeting of the minds. This particular aspect of their relationship does not appear to best effect in *The Virgin Queen*. Raleigh is no fool, but it's clear that Elizabeth is always the intellectual superior, and she often leaves him confused. More than that, they do not seem to connect on an intellectual level or enjoy each other's company, a dynamic that is more aptly portrayed in other Elizabeth offerings (e.g., *Elizabeth I: The Virgin Queen* or even *Elizabeth: The Golden Age*).

Walter Raleigh (also spelled Ralegh) was born in Devonshire, probably in 1554, the youngest son of a not so well-to-do country squire. He did have some valuable maritime connections, however—he was related to Sir Francis Drake, and Sir Humphrey Gilbert, the renowned navigator, was his half-brother. Raleigh attended Oriel College but never received a degree, instead running off to join the foreign wars for religion; he fought with the Huguenots in France. When he returned to England, he attended the Inns of Court, though it's doubtful that he ever had serious designs on a career in the law. It's more probable that he considered knowledge of the law as an asset he would need to get on at the court of Elizabeth. He remained on the fringes of the court for a few years before joining an expedition, led by Sir Humphrey Gilbert, to the New World. The expedition experienced one setback after another, until finally Raleigh and the few other surviving members of the expedition dragged themselves back to England in disgrace. Raleigh's luck seemed at an all-time low, and he dealt with his disappointment and frustration like a sensible young man—he ended up imprisoned more than once for fighting and disturbing the peace.

His luck changed when he was fortunate enough, under the auspices of the Earl of Leicester, to be sent to Ireland to help suppress a rebellion. In a side of Raleigh's character seldom examined in film treatments, he exhibited absolute ruthlessness in crushing the Catholics, even to the point of massacring over 600 people, women and children among them, at a garrison at Smerwick. When he returned from Ireland in 1581, he was something of a heroic figure, and attracted the Queen's notice. There was an age difference of over 20 years between Raleigh and the Queen, but their rapport was immediate and they quickly became quite intimate. Royal favor had its rewards, and Raleigh was appointed captain of Elizabeth's guard, knighted, given a magnificent house in London, and lucrative licenses and monopolies. His appointment as Captain of the Guard was especially notable, as it was one of the most important positions at court, giving him unimpeded access to the Queen. It also made him the object of incandescent hatred for many of Elizabeth's jealous male courtiers.

Raleigh had his finger in several New World pies, and though Elizabeth provided some funding and ships, she would not allow him to sail himself, preferring to keep him near her. Raleigh is often cited as bringing both tobacco and potatoes to England, but in fact, he was simply the promoter—the plants themselves were the result of one of the colonization expeditions to Virginia with which Raleigh was associated; the colonists brought them back to England after being rescued by Sir Francis Drake in 1586. All the settlers who stayed behind, as well as 100 more left at Roanoke from a later expedition, disappeared without a trace, and the expeditions cost Raleigh a fortune. He went on to experiment with the planting of tobacco and potatoes and did his best to popularize them.

By the year of the Spanish Armada, 1588, a new cock of the walk had appeared to challenge Raleigh's position as queen's favorite — Robert Devereaux, Earl of Essex. It was not a male rival, however, that came between Raleigh and the Queen, but a female one. The Queen learned that Raleigh had secretly married Elizabeth Throckmorton, one of Elizabeth's maids of honor and daughter of the ambassador to France, Nicholas Throckmorton. Elizabeth was irate and had them both incarcerated. She eventually allowed Raleigh his freedom to lead a new expedition to Venezuela, and he, along with the Earls of Essex, Nottingham, and Suffolk, also participated in a raid on the Spanish port of Cádiz, the homecoming from which is so vibrantly portrayed at the beginning of *The Private Lives of Elizabeth and Essex* and features in later miniseries. The English won a major victory, but failed to plunder any Spanish treasure. The capture of the Spanish treasure fleet was the impetus behind the attack, and the primary motive driving a cash-strapped Elizabeth. She was irate when her captains returned home without the least bit of swag to match their swagger. Raleigh managed to weather the storm and retain enough of Elizabeth's favor to last him throughout her reign, but he would not fare so well when her successor, James I, came to the throne.

Due to the machinations of Robert Cecil, son of Lord Burghley, upon James's succession, Raleigh was almost immediately imprisoned for treason, accused of plotting to put James's cousin, Arabella Stuart, on the throne in his stead. Despite an impressive defense of himself, Raleigh was playing to a tough crowd — he was judged by his enemies, Cecil amongst them, and found guilty. Rather than being immediately executed, Raleigh spent 13 more years in the Tower. He did not languish away; waited on by multiple servants and visited daily by his wife and family, Raleigh's was more of a house arrest. In 1616, he was released and immediately went venturing again, despite his 62 years. This would be his last voyage. Raleigh, too ill to continue himself, placed the expedition under the command of a subordinate, who promptly engaged in a skirmish with a Spanish fort which, as well as being against King James's express orders, resulted in the death of Raleigh's eldest son. The search for gold being fruitless, Raleigh returned home to England to face the music one last time. He was arrested and, in an attempt to avoid war with the Spanish, James had him executed. Over the years, the historical perception of Raleigh has experienced various revisions, but he always emerges as a romantic and intensely masculine figure.

Compared with this historical version of Raleigh, Vincent Price's uninspiring characterization in *Elizabeth and Essex* is even more inexplicable. Richard Todd's rendering hits closer to the mark, though it's still but a two-dimensional reflection of a vibrantly three-dimensional man. It is also, as are most film representations of historical persons, intentionally manipulated to make only certain hand-picked character traits the focal point — in this case, Raleigh's masculinity and insatiable desire for adventure.

The Virgin Queen opens much less triumphantly than *Elizabeth and Essex*; titles set the historical context when they tell the viewer that "in 1581, all the roads of England led to London — for better or worse." It's pouring down rain, and a speeding carriage barrels into frame and quickly becomes stuck in the mud. The carriage's occupant is an aging

Robert Dudley, Earl of Leicester (played with quiet gravitas by Herbert Marshall), and he is on the Queen's business. He seeks help at the local tavern to free the carriage, where Walter Raleigh and his Irish friend, Lord Derry, each with a wench on his lap, are among the carousers. Raleigh immediately recognizes Leicester and knows his position at court. Others are not so savvy — the first tavern patron of whom Leicester requests help, a grizzled man with a patch over one eye, replies cantankerously, "Last time I went out on the Queen's business, was to the Irish wars I went, and here's all I got for that," indicating his lost eye. In this one exchange, and the fact that no one contradicts him, it is conveyed that there's ill-feeling about the Irish wars which extends to Elizabeth herself. Invocation of her name does not command instant obedience. In fact, the only one willing to help is Raleigh, and it soon becomes apparent that he has ulterior motives.

The film manages to work in a rather irrelevant action scene between the Eye Patch and Raleigh to showcase Todd's heroic combat ability; he must defeat the Eye Patch in a brawling swordfight before the other tavern patrons will help free the carriage. This action sequence is remarkably well choreographed and realistically acted, and Richard Todd proves to be a much more convincing action hero than predecessors such as Olivier; Todd is arguably on par with Errol Flynn when it comes to action heroism. This scene is admirable for the way its sparse dialogue sets up the current state of affairs for Raleigh. When the Eye Patch has surrendered at sword point, Raleigh says to him, "I, too, am late come from the Irish wars and as poor as you." On common ground and laughing, they go out to free Leicester's carriage, the viewer now aware that Raleigh is a poor soldier, but clever and brave.

Leicester offers Raleigh a bag of gold for his help, but he refuses, stating grandly, "To serve my queen is reward enough." Leicester asks him, "Do you not recognize me?" Raleigh coolly lies, and feigns surprise when Leicester introduces himself as the Lord Chancellor of England "amongst many other things." He offers to do Raleigh a service if he will wait on him at Whitehall Palace. This is what Raleigh has been attempting to finagle all along, and he quickly agrees. When an incredulous Derry tries to get him to take the bag of gold, he shoves him into the mud, saying, "My hopes soar higher than that."

The characterization of Raleigh that has so far emerged in the film is completely disparate from the historical individual. The screen Raleigh is back from the Irish wars, a brave soldier, but virtually penniless, rough, with no sense of style and only the threadbare clothes on his back, an ensemble not fit to appear in at court. By contrast, the historical Raleigh had, by 1581, become known because "he outdistanced every fashion. His jewelled shoes were said to be worth more than 6,600 gold pieces, his hatband of pearls, his earrings, the silks and damasks he wore and the ornaments with which he bedecked himself were worth a king's ransom. And he had the pride of the peacock he appeared."[144] Perhaps Hollywood thought audiences incapable of relating to so complex a character — a man's man who, simultaneously, possessed a fashion sense impeccable enough to provoke the envy of metrosexuals everywhere. Regardless, Todd's Raleigh is simplified to represent the masculine, which allows, later in the film, for greater contrast with Elizabeth's other male courtiers.

When this neatly masculine Raleigh waits on Leicester at Whitehall, the Lord Chancellor offers him promotion first in the army and then as a civil servant. Raleigh wants neither — instead he asks to be introduced to the Queen. Like others before him, he knows the way to his ambition lies in currying favor with the monarch. And what is this ambition he cherishes so? "I've long had a dream — to sail to the new world in ships of my own design. I feel the Queen would share that dream." Raleigh is not quite the starry-eyed adventurer, but he also does not realize the enormity of that which he pursues; Leicester is not so naïve. Though he admits Raleigh may find favor with the Queen, he warns, "She is a woman of both whims and wisdom. But the whims are of the moment. The wisdom will endure when you and I are dead.... God help your pride, if you should find favor with the Queen."

Raleigh may have been clever enough to play Leicester, but within seconds of appearing at court, he makes powerful enemies. When one courtier comments on his cloak, Raleigh lies that he took it off a man he stabbed: "The fellow was bloodless, like yourself." In scenes such as this, Raleigh shows his machismo among Elizabeth's effeminate male courtiers, but he also demonstrates that, like Flynn's Essex, he lacks the advantage of their innate subtlety. Watching this encounter is the young and beautiful Beth Throgmorton (Joan Collins). She boldly approaches Raleigh, who obviously likes what he sees. She begins playfully instructing him in the rules of court etiquette: "1. Keep a blank face like those about you. 2. Be careful to whom you speak and where — the very walls are listening. 3. Do not be seen talking to such as I in the Queen's presence. She will take it amiss." Like most of the other Elizabeth films, *The Virgin Queen* does not see fit to let Elizabeth and her actions speak for herself; before the audience has ever glimpsed her, others have laid out Elizabeth's character for the viewer. In this case, so far she is known to be capricious, and with Throgmorton's warning, jealous of the pretty young women in her entourage. As Throgmorton is speaking, she counts off on her string of pearls like a rosary, and it breaks, spilling pearls all over the floor. As Raleigh is bent over gathering them up, Elizabeth finally arrives. Like the first view of the Queen in *Elizabeth and Essex*, the camera pans from the bottom up — from Raleigh at her feet to her skirts and then her face. Her first words are acerbic: "Mistress Throgmorton, is this your swine?" When Raleigh is introduced to the Queen, it's apparent that he stands out. Elizabeth says, "I am surrounded by dancers. It will do me good to talk with a blunt man of war."

A blunt man of war and quick to anger Raleigh certainly is, but he can also be cleverly gallant. In a scene borrowed from the mythology surrounding the historical Raleigh, he throws his cloak (in this imagining a very expensive one he only has on loan) over a mudhole for the Queen to walk across. She seems amused by this, and tells Raleigh, "I'm not sure whether you please me or not. However, you have qualities which the court sadly lacks." This and statements like it show Elizabeth's attitude towards the male sycophants who surround her (personified by the devious Sir Christopher Hatton) to be one of affectionate condescension, occasionally minus the affection. She has cultivated their behavior by her expectations of unwavering and instant devotion, which comes with ample reward for them, yet she is simultaneously irritated by their fawning and shows her contempt by public denigration. Raleigh seems a breath of fresh air, and the Queen invites him to sup with her in private. The conversation they have there is a study in cross-purposes. Raleigh tells the Queen, "My next campaign is you," and she replies, "It takes strategy to reach me." In a spate of metaphor, the two banter back and forth about "citadels" being breached and the Queen "captured." While this may be the screenwriters' attempt to bring to the screen the intellectual affinity which the two historical persons were said to possess for one another, it falls somewhat flat — this Raleigh is no match for Elizabeth's understanding, and where there is no equality of intellect, there is no respect. Elizabeth is obviously referring to romantic love, to the capture of her heart. Raleigh, on the other hand, is thinking only of capturing the Queen's support for his request of three ships to sail to the New World. Raleigh is truly exuberant, becoming increasingly passionate the more he talks of the voyage. Elizabeth becomes more and more irritated with his oblivious refusal to indulge in the pretense of wooing her. When he finishes triumphantly, "Give me these ships, ma'am, and a year in the New World, and before heaven, you'll be glad you met with me this day!" Elizabeth suddenly dashes her goblet of wine in his face. Raleigh, instantly angry and astounded at an adverse reaction the viewer has seen coming from a mile away, starts to storm out of the room. Elizabeth stops him by saying acidly that he'll regret having met with her this day if he leaves without her permission. "I regret it already!" he rails. "I'd thought you'd listen to an honest man." Elizabeth, still harsh, mumbles, "Too few of 'em. I'm out of practice. The court is no place to talk truth." After ordering Raleigh around to perform menial tasks such as filling her wine goblet, the Queen finally gives him permission to leave. He walks through a throng of tittering courtiers, Sir Christopher Hatton among them, who remarks that the Queen only toys with Raleigh. Beth Throgmorton stops to ask Raleigh if he got his ships, and when he expresses astonishment that she could know about them, she replies, "There are no secrets at court." She goes on to ask him if he sat on the green-striped cushion at the Queen's feet. Offended, Raleigh bellows, "I'm not a lapdog!"

This statement sums up one of the major themes in *The Virgin Queen*, one that stands out amongst other Elizabeth offerings — for once, the plight of the male courtier is seriously considered. Typically the focus is on Elizabeth, what she faces at the hands of her grasping male courtiers, how the rivalries and jealousies that swirl at court affect *her*, her desire to be loved for herself rather than her position, the relationships with her male courtiers from her perspective, how all this informs her characterization. *The Virgin Queen* examines the other side of the coin: what these powerful, ambitious men must have felt at being forced to humble themselves to an aging queen who treated them like pets. Raleigh is a most unwilling courtier. As his conversation with the Queen illustrates, what he wants are his ships, not to cajole an old woman, and he naïvely thinks he can simply ask the Queen for what he wants and she will grant it because she has the wisdom to see that it's in England's best interests. He fails to consider Elizabeth's ego and her emotional need for others' subservience; being forced to debase himself before her astounds and angers him. In other onscreen renderings of Elizabeth's court, male courtiers fall all over themselves to win the Queen's favor; they are portrayed as perfectly content to tell her whatever she wants to hear and do whatever is necessary to advance their ambitions. They are very willing participants in the charade of courtly love. In *The Virgin Queen*, this is evidenced in the characterization of Sir Christopher Hatton (Robert Douglas), Elizabeth's reigning favorite before Raleigh arrives on scene. He lolls about in Elizabeth's apartments, reading poetry to her, complimenting her vanity, offering his cloak, and subjugating any anger he feels at her dismissive treatment by channeling it into court intrigues whose only aim is to ensure he keeps the humiliating position he already occupies. Elizabeth is never allowed a glance at his true feelings, whereas Raleigh exhibits the anger and frustration he feels at being subject to the whims of the Queen, a woman. As one historian noted, Elizabethan culture "gave men a patriarchal advantage in the world, but Elizabeth turned this on its head."[145] Todd's portrayal of Raleigh embodies the dissatisfaction that men at Elizabeth's court could feel when forced to accept the commands of a woman, something that turned their worldview upside down. In this way, Raleigh and Hatton provide contrast by representing two different ends of the spectrum. To be found in the middle is the Earl of Leicester, older and wiser than the young Raleigh and Hatton. Leicester appears to possess a genuine desire to serve the Queen; he has had his share of power given at her hands, for which he is grateful. But he also recognizes and readily admits the sacrifice that this has entailed, how much his devoted service to her has cost him. He counsels Raleigh that court is the place for ambitious men, and the way to realize one's ambition is to hold the Queen's favor. But in a world-weary tone that intimates he is speaking from personal experience, he also warns, "In return for her favor, the Virgin Queen demands a devotion that is single-hearted, unwavering, long-suffering." Leicester is all these things; Raleigh is not.

When describing the events with the Queen to his friend Derry, Raleigh says that "there was talk, like a game of chess with no conclusion," but in truth, it was concluded in a way Raleigh does not yet realize. Even though she knows it is an "honor" he does not want, Elizabeth appoints Raleigh to be captain of her palace guard, ensuring that he will be at court and near at hand. Mistress Throgmorton playfully offers him her pity: "You have no ships, and the Queen has a new lapdog." The danger of becoming just like all the other effeminate, submissive males surrounding Elizabeth is a fact of which Raleigh is aware, and one he fears and loathes. His banter with Mistress Throgmorton allows the viewer to know his true thoughts: he hates toadying to Elizabeth, his "heart and soul festers," yet he is helpless to stop it unless he's willing to give up his dreams of the New World. Soon Elizabeth has this brave soldier, this man of action, directing where to put the pasties for the picnic and sitting on the green-striped cushion at her feet like the lapdog he has sworn not to be. Elizabeth may find Raleigh to be a breath of fresh air, yet she still tries to force him into the same degrading attitude of obeisance displayed by her other courtiers. Todd manages to register Raleigh's dissatisfaction with every look and gesture, but he has not yet been pushed far enough to rebel.

Elizabeth is a very harsh taskmaster — it's not enough that Raleigh love her; she also forbids him to have anything to do with any of the court ladies. Seeing how surly all this makes Raleigh, Elizabeth first berates him, but then sighs, "As you love me, speak only gentle words, and I will do the same." Raleigh has, as yet, confessed no love for the Queen, and it's strongly reminiscent of Davis's queen in *Elizabeth and Essex* sweet-talking to Flynn, "Let us be kind to one another." Luckily for Elizabeth, unlike Flynn's Essex whose ambition focused itself on England's throne, Raleigh's aspirations are for adventure, an adventure that will bring glory to England as well as himself, and raise Elizabeth up, rather than wrest her power from her.

Raleigh must have no other love interests, but Elizabeth is supposedly in the marriage market. In the obligatory council chamber scene, the French ambassador arrives to propose, yet again, that Elizabeth marry the Duke of Alençon. This scene is based on the historical marriage suit of the Duc d'Alençon (from 1576 onward, styled the Duc d'Anjou), the fourth and youngest son of Catherine de Medici and King Henri II of France. Born in 1554, Anjou was over 20 years Elizabeth's junior, yet still came closer than perhaps any other suitor to breaching Elizabeth's marital defenses. Though Catholic, he was known to be a moderate and the marriage suit provided the valuable benefit of mitigating the traditional enmity between the English and their neighbors across the channel. In 1579, Anjou managed to succeed in negotiating a marriage contract with Elizabeth, and he visited her in both 1579 and in 1581 (the year *The Virgin Queen* is ostensibly set). Despite the best efforts of the French and some of Elizabeth's advisers as well, the marriage negotiations were never concluded. *The Virgin Queen* has Elizabeth describing Alençon as "a sweet boy, but *only* a boy" before she bellows the French ambassador out of the chamber. Elizabeth then goes on to explain her foreign policy in simplistic detail: for five years she has been writing Alençon "gentle and long" letters to keep France on tenterhooks and prevent it from turning to Spain. "That is policy. *My* policy," she says, with satisfaction.

As illustrated in *Elizabeth and Essex*, the council chamber is the location jealous courtiers often choose to spring the traps they have laid for one another. Hatton takes this opportunity to mention that Elizabeth has an Irishman serving in her own palace guard, and who knows but that this Irishman has designs to murder her? The Irishman to whom he's referring is, of course, Raleigh's friend Derry, whom Raleigh has appointed as his second-in-command in the palace guard. Elizabeth commands Raleigh to arrest Derry, but this is one command Raleigh refuses to obey. He makes the near-fatal mistake of putting loyalty to his friend over allegiance to the Queen. It becomes instantly apparent how Elizabeth reacts when her wishes are not given precedence, and exactly how she views her relationship with Raleigh. With yet more canine imagery, she rages that she will strip him of "every bone I've thrown you," and Raleigh replies angrily that "it's no honor for a man to humble himself. This I've done, time out of mind! I return such honors gladly!" Elizabeth screams, "I took pity on you and *allowed* you to serve me!" Raleigh then makes it perfectly clear what he's after: "I wish to serve England, not you!" Elizabeth may consider her interests and England's to be one and the same, but due to the capricious and selfish nature she has exhibited, it's finally apparent to Raleigh that they are not. Strong-willed men such as Raleigh can not only distinguish between the two, but also choose which they will serve. The idea of the soul-devouring service she requires of her courtiers being a privilege rather than engendering any reciprocal obligation on her part is yet another facet of Elizabeth's selfishness. It's a situation a man of Raleigh's pride finds untenable.

Elizabeth orders Raleigh out of her sight and out of her house, and he storms off, leaving Hatton with a grin that would put the Cheshire cat to shame. Realizing what her own inflexibility and her courtiers' petty jealousies have cost her, Elizabeth seethes, "Little men, little men, you know what you were before I made you what you are. Do not gape so, or by the rood, I'll turn you all out of doors!" She may be violently angry with Raleigh, but even she knows that he's a "real" man amongst all these "little" men, a will to rival her own. The wind suddenly gone from her sails at what she has lost, she collapses into Hatton's waiting arms, a weak and pitiful old woman. With the exception of the film's final scene, this is one of the few instances where Elizabeth's sadness and loneliness are perceptible, where she can be viewed as an object of pity rather than antipathy. Bette Davis's portrayal frequently borders on the repellent, and while her Elizabeth provokes a variety of emotions, sympathy is not often one of them.

Commentators on *The Virgin Queen* have noted that it's an "odd choice" to use Sir Christopher Hatton as the villain of this piece, since the historical Hatton was known for his kindness and was certainly one of Elizabeth's less contentious and grasping courtiers.[146] It would seem a much more logical choice to insert the Earl of Essex in this role — he and Raleigh *were* rivals (a rivalry more closely examined in other offerings, most notably *Elizabeth R* and *Elizabeth I: The Virgin Queen*), and the fact that he does not appear at all in the film certainly seems suspect; the time period when the film is set would have seen his enmity with Raleigh at its height. His personality was such that the historical Essex could be characterized to fit the adversarial mold much more easily than does Hatton. One plausible explanation why this was not done could be the filmmakers' desire to avoid overlap or duplication with the plotting of the earlier film, *Elizabeth and Essex*. This may be the same reason that the raid on Cádiz and its aftermath, integral to the historical Raleigh's life, is missing from *The Virgin Queen*. Regardless, Essex and others, such as Lord Burghley, are conspicuous by their absence in this film.

Raleigh plans to travel with Derry to Ireland, but while he's packing, Mistress Throgmorton arrives to declare her love — Raleigh's public face-off with Elizabeth has impressed her and, his masculinity thus asserted, he's once again a man she can respect and love. Their relationship manifests itself in this way throughout the film, and Raleigh's masculinity meter can be measured by how hot or cold Throgmorton's feelings for him are running. They decide to wed secretly, and it's implied that the marriage is immediately consummated. Before Raleigh can escape to Ireland, Elizabeth sends her soldiers to bring him back to the palace. Mistress Throgmorton fears the worst, saying that the Queen's anger "is like some beast. She lets it feed all day then sets it free to spring. She'll have his head." Throgmorton has put herself forth as someone adept in the ways of the court and its mistress, but with this statement, she shows how shallow her expertise truly is — she's no better at understanding and predicting the Queen's behavior than Raleigh.

Meanwhile, Elizabeth has taken to her bed, pretending to be quite ill. She does look horrific, with stark-white make-up unrelieved by any rouge and a most unflattering pointed nightcap which makes her seem as if she's topped by a dunce's cone. Thus attired, she receives the French ambassador, sending him back to France with news of her ill health as yet another exercise in delay of her marriage to Alençon. The ambassador believes her ruse and after his departure, Elizabeth laughs uproariously at her success in fooling him. It's then on to deal with Raleigh. Rather than "have his head," it seems Elizabeth has decided to forgive him, though Raleigh is self-aware enough to admit and warn her that it will only happen again. In keeping with the ever-present motif of Elizabeth's hollow vanity, she asks Raleigh, "Do you like me as you see me?" Raleigh admits that he admires the woman but "not the wrappings." Though one might expect this forthright answer to annoy Elizabeth, instead she seems satisfied by his honesty, and bids Raleigh kiss her. At first, Raleigh looks dismayed, but then bends to kiss her on the mouth; she stops him by holding out her hand for him instead. Of Sir Christopher Hatton and, by extension, the

The queen (Bette Davis) bestows a title as "empty as air" upon the latest cock of the walk, reluctant courtier Walter Raleigh (Richard Todd) in *The Virgin Queen*. (© 20th Century–Fox Home Entertainment)

class of courtier he represents, Raleigh says, "He acted not in your best interests but his own. Ambition opened his mouth, and jealousy spoke his words for him." Elizabeth is already aware of this, but says with resignation, "But you are *all* jealous, *all* ambitious." She admits that if she gave these grasping men around her all they wanted, she would have to give away half the world, which is not hers to give. Instead, she offers them titles which are as "empty as air," to placate them. Becoming melancholy, she returns yet again to the trope of her aging appearance, saying, "Am I old? Do I look old?" Raleigh tries to put her off by asking if the sun looks old, or the moon, but she will have none of his evasion. Raleigh replies that if she were not Queen of England and he were forming a new company, "I'd have you wielding a broadsword," a young man's weapon. Raleigh couches their relationship, as he did earlier with the talk of citadels, in martial rather than romantic terms, a masculine response to a feminine question. Since Davis's Elizabeth is decidedly mannish, this imagery seems to please her, and she takes a sword the French ambassador has given her as a gift and, from her bed, knights Raleigh with it. He protests — he does not want titles "empty as air," he wants his ships. Finally, she agrees to give him one.

His new title announced to the court, Raleigh meets secretly with Mistress Throgmorton. Rather than be happy at her new husband's success, she's running cold again, jealous of his relationship with the Queen, and she plays the shrew, causing him to leave her in a huff.

Raleigh takes his leave of Elizabeth, with the entire court assembled, and Leicester tells Elizabeth, approvingly, that he has "the highest hopes of this adventure." Elizabeth, however, is about to demonstrate her fickleness yet again. In her apartments, with Hatton reading poetry (somehow unbeknownst to him, written by Raleigh himself for the Queen), Elizabeth's women, including Mistress Throgmorton, scurry about undressing her. Elizabeth lolls, splayed in most unladylike fashion on a couch (incidentally, a garishly recognizable prop that also appeared in *Young Bess*), and unexpectedly says, "Sir Walter will not sail. He'll return here to be with me." She admits she toyed with the idea of letting him go, but she misses him because "he tests me mettle." This is not the only bomb

Elizabeth is to drop; she tells her ladies they have won an all-expense-paid trip to serve at the French court for at least two years. At this, Mistress Throgmorton drops the jewelry she's holding and almost faints, a condition coming on more and more of late and a blatant clue to let the viewer know she's pregnant.

Scenes such as this are illustrative of some of the more unpleasant aspects of Elizabeth's character; she shows herself to be despicable in the way she viciously toys with the lives of others for no purpose more important than her own amusement and emotional comfort. Unlike Raleigh, her word is no bond; she cannot be trusted. She expects unqualified devotion from her subjects, but she shows none in return. *Noblesse oblige* is not her strong suit.

Meanwhile, Mistress Throgmorton's statement about the preclusion of secrets at court proves prophetic — Raleigh learns of his wife's pregnancy through court gossip and rides to her country home to see her. He plans to take her on his voyage to the new world, gambling that Elizabeth's anger will be mitigated by the treasure with which he will return, and all will be forgiven. It's already too late, for Hatton has uncovered all, and he has made the Queen aware of Throgmorton's condition and who's responsible for it. For a queen of Elizabeth's temperament, it's a quick jump from this knowledge to warrants of arrest. In the scene where Elizabeth is informed of Raleigh's "treachery," she shows surprisingly little emotion vocally; she does not yell or rage about, as might be expected. Her posture, on the other hand, is indicative of the change in her feelings. At the beginning of her conversation with Hatton, she's sprawled in a chair, leg up on the table, in a most masculine fashion, displaying her ease and authority. As her former favorite relays his information and understanding dawns, she assumes a much more submissive, feminine posture — she stands, her back against a tapestry-covered wall, for once, her fidgeting practically stilled, a small woman dwarfed by the enormity of her position.

Raleigh is duly apprehended, but with a rousing hand-to-hand shipboard fight scene (since he has promised Elizabeth not to "cross swords" with Hatton), he buys enough time for Lord Derry to escape, charging him with getting Throgmorton safely to Ireland. Derry is killed in the attempt, and Throgmorton is brought back to the palace under guard. In a totally implausible manner, she manages to sneak in to see Elizabeth who is, yet again, in her enormous bed. As if it were a horrific revelation, Elizabeth shows Throgmorton what her bed curtains and nightcap conceal — that she's bald. Even as she begs for her husband's life, Mistress Throgmorton unwisely baits the Queen, endeavoring to stake her territory with regard to Raleigh, and in the attempt demonstrating that her pride, a hollow triumph over an old woman, is worth more to her than her husband's life. Elizabeth remains calm, and it is Mistress Throgmorton who suffers by comparison when she asks her, "Do you think I've put myself in the lists against pretty faces and empty heads? I am Elizabeth Tudor. Men have loved me ... because I struck sparks from their minds, matched spirit with spirit." All Throgmorton has to offer in return is a superior, "But it is I who carry his child." Elizabeth is unfazed, telling her that at age 18 she was informed she could never have children, but she was glad: "England was child enough for me." In her cruelest moment yet, she orders Throgmorton to be taken away, to be executed as soon as her pregnancy has come to term.

Raleigh has been imprisoned and, in a scene which was blasted by historians who noted that an English monarch would never lower herself in such a way, Elizabeth goes to the Tower to visit Raleigh in his cell. It's clear that, whatever his other transgressions, it's his love for Beth Throgmorton that feeds the Queen's anger and is the true bone of contention. When she confronts Raleigh, he says, "Always I was blinded with the fascination of the Queen's Majesty." This may well be true; the glory of Elizabeth's trappings are impressive enough to be fascinating, but it is to a pretty face that Raleigh has given his heart. He tells Elizabeth, "I loved you as a man loves a great queen." This is not enough. Elizabeth replies, returning to her familiar lament, "But I'm also a woman. A woman not too young." Even in the dire predicament in which he finds himself, still Raleigh indulges his obsession with voyaging to the New World. He pleads for the voyage to go on, even if the ships must be sailed by others. Elizabeth does not forgive Raleigh, but she still plans to let him make the voyage, telling him she wants the world he promised her. One might expect Raleigh to be most concerned with the life of his wife and unborn child, but it's almost as an afterthought that he asks after Throgmorton. His tangential references to his wife are also most dismissive; he assures Elizabeth that she will be quick to forget "a dead man whose eye wandered," as if Throgmorton were a passing fancy, already half forgotten. Though this could be interpreted as skilful manipulation of the Queen's character faults — building Elizabeth up by belittling Throgmorton — this is not the way it plays onscreen. Elizabeth does grant a pardon of Throgmorton's execution, at the same time referencing how the death of her mother, Anne Boleyn, affected her: "I was once a brat crying because of the headsman's axe."

The last scene of the film has Throgmorton and Raleigh happily embracing onboard his ship as it prepares to sail down the Thames to the sea. Elizabeth watches them through a spyglass brought to her by the faithful Leicester, and he directs her to look higher — Raleigh is flying a scarf the Queen gave him as a pennant from the topmast of his ship, her consolation prize. Elizabeth sighs to Leicester, "A puking wench, and some waves. I must go on with the business of state." Leicester leaves her writing at her desk, and she puts on a brave front until he's out of the chamber. She then rests her head in her hands, bereft and alone, as the camera pans out for the film's end.

It's interesting that Leicester appears with Elizabeth in this final scene, for it is the only time they are shown alone together, and their interactions should be illustrative of a close relationship. Despite the importance of the historical Leicester and Elizabeth's relationship, however, there is almost no evidence of it in this film. To Raleigh, Leicester may talk of his devotion, of the difficulties of serving his queen, but his demeanor is almost dissociative; for all the emotive value it expresses, he might as well be speaking of someone else. For her part, Elizabeth never treats Leicester like a lover, even a former one, nor a friend. It's almost as if he fills the role traditionally assigned to Burghley, since Burghley does not appear in this film. Elizabeth and Leicester's relationship is completely lacking in the intimacy and familiarity that would be expected, especially on her side, and it is never more evident than in the film's final scene. Leicester is calmly sympathetic, but completely detached, and Elizabeth does not seek comfort from him nor show him her weakness.

Commentators on this film have noted that the focus on Raleigh as a subject rather than a courtier such as Leicester is one that counterpoints "marriage and imperialism," a theme adopted to capitalize, as was *Young Bess*, on the "New Elizabethanism" born of the coronation of Elizabeth II in 1953.[147] The renewed interest in Elizabeth did not necessarily equal audience enthusiasm for *The Virgin Queen*, however. Despite an Academy Award nod for Best Costume Design, one Davis biographer opined that "the picture lacked the physical splendor of *Elizabeth and Essex*. It was a somewhat dowdy production, drab and pedestrian, and the public notably failed to respond at the previews. The result was that the studio virtually threw the picture away, and it lost money, a sure sign that Bette's star was rapidly fading."[148] Despite this, many contemporary reviews were, on the whole, positive. In hindsight, however, "*The Virgin Queen* scans like a bad stage play with its painted backdrops and overblown acting."[149]

Richard Todd does make his mark as a relatively convincing Raleigh who is hard pressed to match Elizabeth's swagger, and whose masculinity manifests itself in combativeness. With men, he engages in physical combat. Due to the strictures imposed by the code of chivalry, this option is not available to him where members of the opposite sex are concerned, so he employs verbal sparring as an alternative. This is evidenced by his bellicose conversations with the Queen and his quick, confrontational exchanges with Beth Throgmorton (of which he often appears to be on the losing end). Joan Collins, as a Hollywood newcomer, does good work with the role she was given in this film, especially when one considers how intimidating and difficult it could be to work with Davis. According to Collins, Davis had a habit of lambasting the young actresses, all in their late teens or early twenties, who played her ladies-in-waiting, yelling at them for infractions as minor as chewing gum when they were not filming. In one dressing scene where Collins was required to lace Davis's shoe, Davis even went so far as to kick her. Despite all this, Collins had great respect for Davis as an actress, calling her "an enigmatic, fascinating, fabulous, and exasperating movie star."[150]

Her young costars were not the only ones dazzled by Davis. The reviewer for the *Los Angeles Examiner* cooed, "Like a magnificent war horse, breathing fire and brimstone, Miss Davis injects life and action into the tale, seeming to inspire everyone and everything about her. What a queen! What an actress!"[151] Since Bette Davis was playing the same character, comparisons between *The Virgin Queen* and *The Private Lives of Elizabeth and Essex* are inevitable. Davis does seem a more self-assured queen in this iteration, but as with her earlier turn as Elizabeth in *Elizabeth and Essex*, the portrayal is again extremely fidgety and idiosyncratic. Regardless of the other acting choices in the film, it was Bette Davis's walk that seemed to draw the most attention. Critics waxed poetic and practically choked themselves on simile to liken it to "an overfed duck walking across a frozen pond; like Groucho Marx; a hopalong walk rather like that of a saddle-sore jockey." One compared her to "an overhearty lacrosse captain in a red wig" and a personal favorite, as though she were "walking not on one artificial leg, but on three."[152]

Davis's distinctive walk is but one of many manifestations of Elizabeth's mannishness in this film. As one historian noted, the historical Elizabeth "blended masculine and feminine power very skillfully.... The only way Davis can portray the power of Elizabeth is to capitalize on her masculine side."[153] Her walk is the most prominent feature of this portrayal, and to it, Davis adds very masculine mannerisms — Elizabeth downs cups of wine at a gulp, throws her feet up on the furniture, bellows loudly, and in general lumbers around like the proverbial bull in a china shop. The contrast created when Elizabeth makes statements about her femininity is almost gruesome by comparison. Whereas the historical Elizabeth used whichever tool was more effective — feminine wiles or masculine posturing, Davis's version seems capable only of the latter. She's distinctly more mannish in this turn than she was in *Elizabeth and Essex.* Davis's Elizabeth frequently mentions that she is a woman, which seems almost necessary given how difficult it is to make such a determination based simply on her physical appearance. The closest Davis's Elizabeth comes to feminine manipulation are the scenes in which she pretends illness, a tool that the historical Elizabeth often employed with great success.

Whereas Davis's portrayal of Elizabeth in *Elizabeth and Essex* could pass as merely idiosyncratic, its evolution in *The Virgin Queen* ripens into full-blown caricature. One review of the film summed it up by stating that Davis "should never have repeated her performance as Elizabeth ... this is a clear case of poor fit between actress and character."[154] Davis stated that she and Elizabeth were "very alike" in many ways and that she felt a "great propinquity" to her character. But even Davis admitted to a certain lack of subtlety in her portrayals of the Tudor monarch: "Both times I played her, I had a whale of a time. Elizabeth I *was* a ham. The script of *The Virgin Queen,* I felt, contained a better character study of her than did *The Private Lives of Elizabeth and Essex.*"[155] It could be argued that Davis's interpretation in *The Virgin Queen* may be a *stronger* character study, but it's certainly not a "better" one. It's also inaccurate to equate it more with the historical Elizabeth. Davis's Elizabeth suffered the same fate as Sarah Bernhardt's — in both *Elizabeth and Essex* and *The Virgin Queen,* Davis's portrayal is an Elizabeth poured into a character mold fitting Davis's dimensions, not the other way around.

CHAPTER 4

Hollywood, A.D.: Elizabethan Career Woman to Pop Culture

The Virgin Queen would prove to be the last of the big-budget Hollywood historicals starring Elizabeth for almost 20 years. Box-office receipts remained relatively unchanged while production costs continued to rise, and the world of film also had to learn to peacefully co-exist with television; the result was that the pageantry of the costume drama all but disappeared in the 1960s, which "deemphasized spectacle and bigness."[1] By the time Elizabeth found her way back onto the big screen in the early 1970s, production values had changed, giving these new historical films a decidedly less "spectacular" feel than their predecessors from Hollywood's golden age. Also, the confusion and uncertainty of the 1960s and 1970s affected the perceptions and, consequently, the tastes of the average moviegoer. Filmmakers' desire to connect with this audience, which differed from their more morally certain golden age predecessors, produced a different type of historical drama. As one commentary noted, "Beginning in the turbulent 1970s, the royal characters who caught Oscar's eye tend to be flawed creatures, humanized superiors, people of privilege whose lives are in turmoil — just like ours."[2] This fostered a tendency to distill from the regal something more personal and approachable. In addition, changing perceptions of the female role which came with the Women's Liberation movement would greatly affect characterizations of Elizabeth in particular — she evolved from a female frustrated in love into a symbol of feminist independence. This change in perception is never more evident than in Glenda Jackson's portrayal of the Virgin Queen in two separate realms, the mini-series (*Elizabeth R*, covered in Chapter Six) and yet another film about the life of her most contentious cousin, Mary, Queen of Scots.

MARY, QUEEN OF SCOTS (1971)

Mary, Queen of Scots was based on a best-selling biography of the titular monarch written by popular historian Antonia Frasier. Like its predecessor from the 1930s, *Mary,*

Queen of Scots, while ostensibly a biopic about Mary Stuart, is in actuality the story of Elizabeth and Mary's rivalry. Given the importance placed on the relationship between these two women, it would seem more logical to title these films to reflect Elizabeth's role. The use of only Mary's name in the title, however, clearly shows where the viewer's sympathies should lie. This is apparent from the opening titles of the film, which is set in 1558. After explaining how England and Scotland are torn apart by "family and religious wars," the titles go on to say that Mary becomes involved in a fight for power with Elizabeth and that this "is the story of the fierce struggle between the rival queens." Though other offerings choose to gloss over Mary's tenure in France, focusing solely on her life after her arrival in Scotland, *Mary, Queen of Scots* chooses a different approach, opening in France, where Mary is still living happily with her young husband. This allows for contrast of her existence in France, presented as almost idyllic, with the harshness of her life in Scotland and later England. France represents light and freedom, two concepts that will disappear entirely from Mary's life once she returns to Scotland.

There is great disparity between the characterization and the first glimpses of Mary in *Mary of Scotland*, and her first appearance onscreen in *Mary, Queen of Scots*. Katharine Hepburn bore little resemblance to the historical monarch, but at least her coloration was roughly accurate — the historical Mary had auburn hair. Vanessa Redgrave portrays the Scottish monarch in this representation, and her blond hair and blue eyes ensure the likeness is nonexistent. Whereas Hepburn's Mary, with her perfectly angled face and sculpted expressions, was directed and shot to best showcase a poised and, at times, saintly demeanor, the one trait that comes across in Redgrave's Mary is a sort of flushed childishness, apparent from the film's opening scene. While the credits are still rolling, Mary, her hair loose and clad only in her flowing white chemise, frolics with her young husband, François, in an ideal natural setting. They hold hands and run through the gardens of a French chateau, row together in a boat, young, untroubled, and conspicuously in love. This carefree existence is almost at an end; François immediately grabs his head and keels over. Mary soon finds herself in conference with her Guise uncles while François lies on his sickbed. Her uncles are planning for the future, drilling into their naïve young niece that she is the Queen of Scotland, France, and England — especially England. It's too little, too late, however; why they have waited this long to indoctrinate her seems inexplicable, and it's certainly too late to provide her with the educational and ideological tools she will need to effectively govern a country (or three). Besides, she will have none of it; like the love-struck teenager she supposedly is (though Redgrave, in her thirties, cannot quite convince the viewer of this) she weeps that she "will not think of life" without François. It is a statement she will make, in slightly altered form, about several men during the course of this film. Repetition, it turns out, does not make it any more true.

Mary and her uncles do not have much to say of a pleasant nature with regard to the Queen of England; she is "a bastard" who "consorts with her horsemaster" and has no right to the throne. As if to prove the accusation of said consorting, Elizabeth (Glenda Jackson) is then immediately introduced. Rowing peacefully in her state barge, the curtains drawn to provide a sense of privacy around her and said horsemaster, Elizabeth listens to Dudley (Daniel Massey) sing a love song written by her father for his mistress Anne Boleyn, while she gazes raptly into Dudley's face. Her Robin tells her that, when Henry

VIII asked Anne how she liked it, she asked him in return how his *wife* liked it. The two enjoy a hearty laugh over this, a sort of inside joke to viewers who already know that Dudley, with a wife at home, is in a similar situation with his royal mistress. It shows Elizabeth to be, at best, unprincipled. Her characterization will not soften with better acquaintance. Their passionate kiss is interrupted when a message arrives from William Cecil to inform the Queen that Dudley's wife has died.

Elizabeth's reaction is not quite dispassionate — she smashes a lute — but ultimately she subjugates her emotions to political expediency. Cecil has warned her that the French ambassador is already making veiled hints about murder, and despite her belief in Dudley's innocence, she sends him away, for "now will the great scandal begin." Regardless of her personal feelings, Elizabeth offers up Dudley for impartial investigation, refusing to see him unless and until he's been cleared of any accusations with regard to his wife's suspicious death. She does this because she realizes the delicacy of her position, that she cannot afford to be perceived as putting her favorite above the law, or worse, having been a party to murder. Political spin is in order. She goes on to show herself to be contemptuous of the threat to her rule personified by Mary Stuart and her ilk, whose mother "tyrannizes Scotland with a French army. She forces the Catholic faith down Scottish throats. Half her nobles are Protestant and in open rebellion ... she barely survives." This exposition neatly sums up the situation in Scotland under the regency, what Mary will encounter if she returns home, as well as informing the viewer of exactly why Mary on the throne of Scotland represents such a danger to Elizabeth.

Elizabeth is portrayed by British actress Glenda Jackson, who, though an established theater actress in Britain, first came to fame in the United States by playing the same role in the BBC miniseries *Elizabeth R*; this miniseries is accounted by some to be the comprehensive modern portrayal of the Tudor monarch, though such commentaries were written before Helen Mirren's performance in *Elizabeth I*. Critics have described Jackson's acting style as strictly mannered; she "is noted for her full and expressive voice, her theatrical diction, and performances based less on naturalistic precepts than a declamatory theatrical tradition."[3] While this acting style has been disparaged for some of her roles, for the portrayal of Elizabeth it is appropriate. It gives Jackson's version a formality and regality which do not seem out of place for the depiction of the monarch. She couples with this formality the display of flashes of temper — and they are truly flashes, for they burn with violent intensity and just as quickly extinguish themselves — that treat the changeability often described in the historical Elizabeth's demeanor. Physically, Jackson is also convincing; while not beautiful by any means, she can exhibit a certain appeal — the expression of her dark eyes along with her mannerisms and obvious intelligence fit well with the type of attraction the historical Elizabeth might have displayed. However else it may be described, Jackson's rendering of Elizabeth is nothing if not believable.

By contrast, Vanessa Redgrave's portrayal of Mary is anything but mannered. This Mary is a woman who seems to be formed entirely of rushing, raging emotion. There is no subtlety, no duality, no depth. Everything is surface. She is, by turns, ecstatically happy, in the depths of despair, violently angry, and always madly, madly in love. There's no in-between, no shading; she often comes across as hysterical. The overall impression she gives is that of a spoiled child, and she reacts and makes decisions as one would expect of such a child: not wisely, nor well.

Redgrave continues the theme of having Mary look to the men around her for assistance and protection, but she ramps it up to fever pitch. Unlike Hepburn's Mary, who had a modicum of poise and resolve, Redgrave's Mary has no idea what to do with herself. When François dies, she is guided first by her Guise uncles, who bestow upon her David Riccio (Ian Holm) and the Jesuit priest Father Ballard (Tom Fleming), and then by her brother, the Earl of Moray (Patrick McGoohan). With her mother and husband dead, Scotland in need of a ruler and nothing left to keep her in France, the course of action is obvious. Yet still she begs Moray, "Help me. Tell me what to do." Moray looks almost as if he cannot believe his ears, but informs her she should return to Scotland. Of

Elizabeth (Glenda Jackson) at her favorite pastime — plotting the downfall of her unwitting Scottish cousin in *Mary, Queen of Scots.* (Universal/The Kobal Collection)

the million expected responses Mary could have to this, what she produces is, "But will I be happy? Will the people of Scotland love me?" Despite his duplicity, one cannot help but praise the Earl of Moray's self-control in not rolling his eyes and smacking his forehead in exasperation. At this point in the historical Mary's life, she was still a teenager, and perhaps Redgrave's characterization is meant to show the uncertainty of an adolescent faced with an adult role for which she has had no preparation. Given Redgrave's age, however, it's less than compelling for her to play the uncertain teenager.

Mary vows to win Elizabeth's friendship, but the English Queen is implacable; she plans to stop Mary's return to Scotland by force if necessary. It's Moray who counsels Elizabeth otherwise. In a scene which lays out that Moray has more common cause with Elizabeth than with his own half-sister, he warns Elizabeth that to use force against Mary would be unwise and, at any rate, there's no need. "Mary will rule in name. I will rule in fact," he tells Elizabeth, and it's difficult to gainsay him since, based on her behavior so far, unprepared to rule does not even begin to describe Mary. When Mary receives the news that Elizabeth has refused her safe conduct through England, she sticks out her bottom lip and says petulantly, "She hates me." Elizabeth's refusal to be her best friend is but one of Mary's worries; the Earl of Bothwell (Nigel Davenport), who has been sent to France to bring Mary back to Scotland, tries to prepare her for what she will encounter there, the contentiousness of the Scottish nobility. "Will you rule the Scottish lords, or will they rule you?" he asks. Her naïve reply is that she shall rule the lords, but it's obvious that she hasn't a chance. Despite being ill-equipped to rule, Mary is still a danger to Moray and the Scottish lords. As Moray tells Burghley, "With Bothwell to help her, Mary might find a way to finish me and rule alone." Of course, she will not be ruling alone; she is incapable of it. Moray or Bothwell — there must always be some power behind Mary's throne, for she has none of her own.

Mary's arrival in Scotland is staged much differently from that in *Mary of Scotland*. It is not a mist-shrouded night dripping with meaning, but rather broad daylight, and Mary and her retinue mill about uncertainly on the beach. There is no one to greet them, and as if to underline her general cluelessness, Mary asks, "Where are we, in the name of God?" When Moray and the Lords of the Congregation arrive to welcome Mary, she bubbles, "Oh, I understand! Soon there will be gun salutes, the royal carpet!" The enormous burden of ruling a country torn in two has been placed upon her shoulders, but Mary, like a little girl playing dress-up, cannot see past the excitement of queenly ceremony. Even in this she is to be disappointed, and gets her first glimpse of Scottish pragmatism when she's informed that, in Scotland "we can waste no money on idle show." Moray also tells her that the other ship carrying her horses and Bothwell has been captured by the English. In a surprising show of insight, Mary asks him how he can have received this news so quickly, intimating that she suspects he's working with the English.

Back in England, Elizabeth is taking great pleasure in Mary's fine horses, captured from the second ship, along with Bothwell, who languishes in chains in the Tower. Things are going very well for Elizabeth; Dudley is back, having been completely cleared of any implication in his wife's death. Wasting no time whatsoever, Dudley asks Elizabeth to marry him. In an approximation of a statement made by the historical Elizabeth, she replies, "In this land there will be but one mistress, and no master." This statement, which appears in other film adaptations, is often delivered with vehemence and anger. Jackson chooses to dispense it teasingly, laughing. Underneath this light exterior, however, lurks her red-headed temper — when Dudley, frustrated, is unwise enough to defy her, she's instantly furious. From Sweet Robin he's reduced to a "commoner whose head itches for a crown," and he is imperiously ordered back to his "common business," taking care of the Scottish Queen's stolen horses. One half expects Elizabeth to command him to muck out the stables. Unlike some other adaptations, Elizabeth is not dependent; Dudley may be her "eyes," and she loves him in her way, but she's all too willing to humble him, even sacrifice him if need be. Like Eldridge's Elizabeth before her, this Elizabeth is mercenary and cunning. In a sort of theatrical aside out of Dudley's earshot, Jackson muses, "The Scottish Queen ... there's a pretty widow for an ambitious lord." The germ of an idea has taken root: Elizabeth will offer up Dudley as a husband for the Scottish Queen and accomplish multiple goals at once; a foreign marriage prevented, England's interests protected, and a crown to satisfy Dudley without Elizabeth having to give up any of her own power. To Dudley, her anger subsided with her satisfaction at her plan, she says, "You will dine with me, and we shall keep each other loving company 'til morning light." Though the film is ambiguous about a sexual consummation of Elizabeth and Dudley's relationship, lines such as these, along with scenes that show them engaging each other physically, do seem in favor of an intimate physical relationship between the two. Exactly how far the "consorting" goes, however, is left to the viewer's imagination. It works as a counterpoint to the portrayal of Mary's intimate physical relationships.

Like *Mary of Scotland*, *Mary, Queen of Scots* chooses to treat Mary's face-to-face confrontation with the firebrand John Knox (Robert James). Rather than stage the scene inside as a private and more intimate conversation with Bothwell as observer, *Mary, Queen of Scots* has Knox appear unexpectedly on top of a hill, like one of Monty Python's hermits, to rail down at the startled queen, who's passing by with her retinue on the way to Holyrood. His language is also stronger than that of the earlier film. He has "prayed that this queen would die before she set foot in this land." Rather than attempt to engage him, Mary spends most of her time gaping open-mouthed and then crossing herself. Moray keeps urging her to ride on, but Mary has decided to be magnanimous, "I will hear your ugly words, John Knox, for you, like all my subjects, shall have the free use of your conscience. And I of mine!" At this, Moray has had enough, and he grabs her horse's halter to lead her away to Holyrood.

When they arrive, there are no quarreling Scottish lords. In fact, these Lords of the Congregation present much more of a united front (and therefore more of a danger) than their 1930s film counterparts. Though there are leaders who stand out — Ruthven, Huntly — they act almost as a single entity under the guidance of Moray, whom they appear to respect. This Huntly, also, is no friend to Mary; he's one of the more violent of the group, even attempting to kill her as part of the Riccio murder conspiracy.

Moray gives Mary the tour of her new home, and it stands in sharp contrast to the beautiful spaces shown in France. France is a place of sunshine and happiness; Scotland is confinement and gloom. The rooms are small, the furnishings are not rich, the stone walls look cold and bare and their texture rough, like everything in this land. Moray has attempted some comfort for his queen; he has had many of her larger possessions and furniture brought over from France and set up for her, as one would placate a child with toys in the uneasiness of a new environment. This is exactly how Moray treats Mary, as a none-too-bright child. This does not seem an inappropriate approach; given her infantile behavior so far, Mary has shown herself to be nothing more. He tells her, "You shall be happy and have dancing and good eating ... leave the troubles of state to me. We have made a good beginning. Remember, be discrete, and consult me in all things." In Moray's mind, trifling entertainments are all a woman needs in order to be happy, even if that woman is a queen. Mary is insincerely gracious until Moray exits, at which point she explodes to her confidants Riccio and Father Ballard, "Run away and play, he tells me, as if I were a child!" What Mary fails to realize is that she could do worse than to heed Moray's advice, at least until she gained more support in her own right. It would be wise for her to subjugate her emotions and be discrete. Moray obviously has his finger on the pulse of the country as well as a useful intellect; she could learn from his counsel. All this aside, given the fact that it was Mary herself whose only voiced concern was whether or not she would be happy and loved in Scotland, it makes her anger at Moray's concentration on these things seem all the more childish. She has done nothing to earn respect and has shown no authority, something the practical Scottish lords value, yet still she insists they respect her and obey her demands. Mary is every inch the petulant child who wants her way, even if she does not yet know what that way is.

Father Ballard and Mary's little Italian secretary are there to show her, however. The Jesuit tells her that her Guise uncles will solve her problems by finding a husband for her. Unlike Hepburn's Mary, this Scottish Queen is ecstatic at the prospect of a new husband: "I will marry quickly," she says brightly, to which Riccio adds sagely, "Marriage, then, shall be our policy." This policy is the reverse of Elizabeth's. The English Queen knows that security lies in *not* marrying, in keeping her options open; she also is most vociferous in her views about whom Mary should and should not consider as marriage material. As one commentary put it, "Although she did apparently remain a virgin all her life, Elizabeth was fond of meddling in the sexual lives of others."[4] From her throne, Elizabeth pronounces to the gathered ambassadors that the marriage of Mary Stuart to any Catholic prince will be treated as an act of war against England, "We realize our sweet young cousin has been deluded by dangerous and self-seeking men." With this barely veiled insult, Elizabeth shows herself to be at once condescending and threatening towards the "deluded" Mary, but she does offer a compromise of sorts: Dudley. She announces that he will be immediately created the Earl of Leicester in order to make him more worthy of Mary, and should she accept him, her succession to the throne of England will be assured.

Elizabeth sends Leicester to Mary's court: "Go, and go quickly before my heart wins over my head." These words are said with conviction, but when she's alone with Burghley, Elizabeth reveals the extent of her scheming. Burghley, whose self-described duty is to "foresee the result of English policy and convince the Queen," guarantees Elizabeth that Mary will disparage the match. Elizabeth is none too surprised: "Good! For I do not intend for her to have him." Though she will if necessity dictates, Elizabeth would prefer not to sacrifice her favorite pawn; her plan is even more Machiavellian. She sends Bothwell as messenger to offer up Leicester and the succession, but with him she also sends Stewart, Lord Henry Darnley, a man she describes as "the finest flower of our nobility — gentle, brave, and chivalrous" to Bothwell, but to Burghley, she describes him more truthfully as "a weak, degenerate fool."

Elizabeth has never met Mary, but she has no need to — she possesses the ability to accurately read people. So sure is she in her estimation of Mary's character that she wagers 50 gold crowns to Burghley that Mary will choose Darnley over Leicester. "You may be an expert in matters of state," she tells him, "but you know very little of women. Mary is a young widow. Her blood is hot." Burghley is doubtful, with the choice of Leicester comes the crown of England, free and clear. It's the quintessential no-brainer. "No monarch would turn her back on that," he says with authority. But Elizabeth knows that Mary will make the emotional decision rather than the rational, political one: "That 'monarch' is first a woman." Burghley remains adamant: "*You* would never fall for such a pretty fellow." That, certainly, is the very point — as Elizabeth replies to Burghley, she is a monarch first, a woman second, and "win or lose the wager, I cannot lose the game." As is echoed by Hepburn's Mary shouting, "I win! Still, still I win!" to Elizabeth's retreating back in *Mary of Scotland*, the two women's relationship is again couched in terms of a contest, a game with exceptionally high stakes. Elizabeth cannot lose this game because she has stacked the deck. Unlike Mary, who misjudges Elizabeth's motivations and actions time and again, Elizabeth pronounces, "We have never met, and I *know* her."

As played by a young, blond Timothy Dalton, Darnley is certainly attractive, although, to put it kindly, less than completely masculine, and appearing even more so next to the roughly handsome, hairy Bothwell. Elizabeth is immediately awarded the match point when the very next scene cuts to Darnley and Mary frolicking, riding their horses along the beach, obviously attracted to each other and having a grand time. Mary is shown in men's clothing, creating an understated androgyny to match Darnley's effeminate manner. Though the two appear to be alone, Riccio watches with displeasure from the parapets of the castle, as does an incensed Leicester. Darnley takes a tumble from his horse and is knocked unconscious; he's unharmed but plays up his injury while Mary stumbles to the sea to wet a handkerchief and mop his brow, sobbing that she loves him.

An angry Leicester returns home to Elizabeth, barging into her apartments, where she lies in bed in her nightgown, writing on a lapdesk. They seem comfortable with this level of familiarity; apparently Elizabeth is used to Leicester coming and going as he pleases in this manner. She pretends surprise at his rejection as he rails, "She must be demented. Before my eyes she tore up the document of succession and she consorts with that mincing boy. And, by all the saints, madam, she is a woman that needs a *man*." This leads to an examination of Mary's character; Elizabeth wants Leicester's opinion of what kind of woman Mary is. He muses that she's "formed like a goddess," but concedes absently that she has none of Elizabeth's accomplishments; she cannot play well or speak multiple languages. For all this, however, the impression Leicester manages to convey is that one would still choose Mary over Elizabeth due to her good looks and charm. Leicester has been too lost in thought to realize where his musings are taking him; Elizabeth has been coyly smiling. As if instantly comprehending the precariousness of his situation, he quickly retreats: "I found her tiresome." It's too late—Elizabeth hurls herself at him, flailing, punching, while he retreats. She pretends to have forgiven him, he lets down his guard, and she punches him in the stomach, hard, then the face, and throws him out of the room. Her fit of temper spent as quickly as it came on, she says pensively to herself, "May it please Almighty God she hates me as I hate her." This is not just a political struggle; Elizabeth hates Mary on a personal level—she's jealous of her beauty and the response it seems to provoke in men. Not all the men in Mary's life are so impressed by her charms, however.

The viewer already knows, through Elizabeth's revelation of Darnley's true character, that he's weak and degenerate. Exactly how degenerate is illustrated when he's shown in bed with Riccio, using Riccio to further his cause with Mary. The two actors who play Riccio in *Mary of Scotland* and *Mary, Queen of Scots* could not be more physically dissimilar. John Carradine's long, lanky, black-clad Riccio has been replaced by the diminutive Ian Holm who, no matter how serious his expression, cannot escape evoking Bilbo Baggins. The two Riccios are also somewhat divergent in characterization; Carradine's Riccio, with his huge cross and accented English, seemed to personify foreign threat, but even more the Catholic Church. Holm's Riccio certainly does not evoke religiosity, perhaps because *Mary, Queen of Scots* also includes the characterization of Father Ballard to fill this function. Holm's Riccio wears no symbolic jewelry or clothing, and his behavior is categorically unreligious.

The two characterizations of Riccio are disparate, but they also share some similarities — Holm's Riccio may be sleeping with Darnley, but he truly cares for Mary and has her best interests at heart. As he is more than aware of Darnley's shortcomings, he remains reluctant to promote him to Mary as a suitor, not out of jealousy, but out of concern for his queen. Darnley casts Riccio as his only friend, stating, "We are both outcasts in this court." Mary unexpectedly knocks at the door, and Darnley, grabbing his clothes, hides in another room to eavesdrop. She waltzes in, love-struck and giddy, demanding of Riccio, "You must advise me ... what if I married Darnley? I believe it is God's will. Both policy and my deepest longings are fulfilled in him ... it is the fate of queens to choose where other women are chosen. I choose him." The entire time she's delivering this speech, Mary caresses the drapes voluptuously, runs her fingers over the furniture: she is a woman in constant, passionate motion. Elizabeth has been right about her blood being hot. Mary has made one of the most insightful statements she manages in the entire film: that queens can choose where other women are chosen. This is only partially true, for a queen's choice is limited by a variety of political factors; it is not as if she were free to marry whomever she would, to follow her heart. However, she need not wait to be asked, and she had no doubt that, once her choice was made, the man in question would acquiesce. Riccio ultimately decides not to oppose the Darnley match, and a gloriously happy, madly-in-love Mary announces her decision. Moray is less sanguine, and he makes it clear that marrying Darnley is not to be considered. This is in keeping with the historical facts, unlike in *Mary of Scotland*, which has Moray and the Lords of the Congregation choosing Darnley and forcing him upon Mary. However much one is meant to identify with Mary over Elizabeth in this film, the fact remains that this version of Mary makes her own mistakes; she is not a woman forced into a marriage she does not want. She pursues it against advice to the contrary, and is all emotion and no logic when she faces down Moray's opposition. As he does throughout the film, Moray maintains his cool exterior, telling Mary as he would an overwrought child, "I'll speak to you again when you have more control of yourself." Mary, drunk on love and the power she mistakenly assumes the marriage will bring her, crows, "From this day I alone rule in Scotland! Now who is caged, brother?!" Her taunts seem more appropriate to a playground than a queen's audience chamber, and Moray bears them with icy silence. Bothwell has observed the exchange and advises Mary to kill Moray, but she unwisely allows him to live, sending him into exile in England.

Mary's triumph is amazingly short-lived; Darnley does not even allow the marriage feast to conclude before he shows his true colors, forcing the Lords of the Congregation to serve him, caressing Riccio in public and then seating the secretary at the royal table so that the lords, forced to serve someone of such a low station, will be sure to hate him. Mary is soon despondent, and things go from bad to worse when even the loyal Bothwell decides to take his leave. Mary admits that she needs his help to "keep order in this country." Bothwell still supports Mary, but he has grown poor in her service and must marry for money, vowing to return after he has done so. Mary is instantly incensed, yelling that she forbids him to marry without her permission. Her jealousy is apparent, as is the fact that she is already seeking elsewhere than her husband for male solace. She offers Bothwell money, but he prefers to come by it his own way.

The characterization of Bothwell in *Mary, Queen of Scots* is similar to that in *Mary of Scotland*. Bothwell is a plain-spoken, honest man, a virile and intelligent specimen. He is also unfailingly loyal to Mary. Unlike the earlier Bothwell, however, he's not exactly a man of principle — he has no scruples about making love to another man's wife or carrying out the murder of Darnley. His ambition is also more marked. This Bothwell may very well care about Mary, but his ultimate goal is to rule Scotland at her side, as king.

With Bothwell out of the way, a conspiracy immediately unfolds to put Darnley on the throne in his own right. The Lords of the Congregation track Darnley down in a hallway at Holyrood, and he immediately turns from a swaggering bully into a cowering bag of mush, whimpering, "Please don't kill me!" They have no intention of killing him; they need him as a puppet king. Ruthven parrots the contemporary view of Elizabeth as well as Mary when he informs him that "it is an unnatural thing for a woman to rule," and Darnley heartily agrees, putting his signature to a bond to remove Mary as ruler. His only demand is that Riccio be murdered, and that the deed be done in Mary's presence. Even the rough Scottish nobles look askance at such cruel depravity — Mary is several months pregnant — but ultimately agree.

Elizabeth is aware of the plot; indeed, she even has a copy of the bond, and Burghley informs her that everyone at the Scottish court knows of it save Riccio and Mary herself. Elizabeth's view of marriage as policy is illustrated by her cynical reply: "And her loving husband has put his seal to it. So much for marriage." Elizabeth is, oddly, angry as well. In the scheming of Moray and the Lords of the Congregation, she sees reflected the worst case scenario of her own courtiers' ambitions; Elizabeth is also an "unnatural thing," a woman ruling in her own right, and in a burst of angry solidarity, states that she has half a mind to warn Mary herself. She refuses to support a murder bond. Even after Burghley drops the bomb that Mary is pregnant, still Elizabeth refuses, sighing, "How long must I live under the shadow of this other queen? I desire her to be without power but not dead." As has been the case before, it is her sweet Robin who helps make the decision for her by angering her into action. He presses her yet again to marry him and have an heir herself. She puts him in his place by immediately informing Burghley to give Moray the money he needs to carry out his plan.

The characterization of Leicester in *Mary, Queen of Scots* shows him to be more naked in his ambitions, less diplomatic and charismatic than either the historical man or some other film characterizations (e.g., Jeremy Irons's portrayal in *Elizabeth I*). Elizabeth has his number; she knows what he wants — marriage so that he can share the throne of England with her. The more he asks for it, the more she pursues a course of action which is diametrically opposed. Burghley even says a prayer of thanks after one of their exchanges, since Leicester's ambition, and Elizabeth's emotional desire to thwart it, has time and again set her on the proper course when all of Burghley's logic could not accomplish it.

The murder of Riccio is staged in graphic manner, and it feels one of the truest scenes in this film. There's no romanticized death scene on Mary's bed, with her frilly sheets pulled up to hide his innocent face, as there was in *Mary of Scotland*. Riccio, at dinner with Mary, realizes what's to occur and clutches at her skirts, yelling for her to save him. Mary is in immediate hysterics, and in the melee that ensues, it's the cruelly vindictive Darnley who pries the terrified Riccio's fingers from the cloth of Mary's gown and brutally holds her face to make her watch as he's dragged away and butchered. There's a moment of silence as Riccio looks down at the knife that has been thrust into his chest, then he begins screaming like an animal, frantically clawing at the floor and trying to crawl away as he's stabbed again and again by the conspirators. The mood is chaotic, and it is strikingly real in its staging. With Riccio dead, Mary is informed of what her fate will be: she will bear the heir to the throne then be locked away for the rest of her life. Threatened with imprisonment, Mary gives her greatest performance, pretending to go into labor and then throwing herself on Darnley's mercy, convincing him to betray his bond and escape with her. For his part, Darnley sits, morosely holding Riccio's lute and whispering, "Davy, Davy." Dalton manages to convey regret, showing that there might possibly be something besides selfish cruelty in there somewhere. At times, Dalton's Darnley is more pathetic than ridiculous or evil. Though he is, for the most part, loathsome, there is also something of the frightened little boy in this portrayal that gives it a depth lacking in other versions of Mary's drunken husband.

The heroic Bothwell is there to save the day, sitting Mary up in front of him on his horse while he rides her to safety at his stronghold of Dunbar. Mary has just been through a horrible ordeal, her trusted friend and adviser carved up before her eyes, almost murdered herself, and now a harrowing escape on horseback. None of this has brought on labor, but the sight of Bothwell's attractive young wife manages it the second Mary claps eyes on her.

Elizabeth is enjoying herself at court, talking and laughing, when she receives news of James VI's birth. In similar vein to *Mary of Scotland*, she takes a line from the historical Elizabeth when she collapses to the floor and moans, "The Queen of Scots is lighter of a fair son, and I am but barren stock." As in *Mary of Scotland*, Elizabeth's distress is played out on the public stage; in this version, she is not even allowed the solace of her apartments — all her courtiers are in attendance to see the display of defeat, and they watch in silence before finally helping her to her feet.

Elizabeth might not have been quite so distraught if she had any idea of the events unfolding in Scotland. Despite their pretended reconciliation, Mary and Darnley are incapable of tolerating each other. Darnley even goes so far as to attempt to rape Mary in Bothwell's presence. In a surprising show, rather than looking to Bothwell to save her, Mary sends him away and plays her husband yet again — she drugs his wine and leaves him drooling on the floor. This gives the burly Bothwell ample time to make love to an initially half-reluctant but ultimately very willing Mary while Darnley lies insensible in the next room. He also informs her that Darnley has been "vagabonding at night" and is poxed. "He will rot with it," Bothwell pronounces matter-of-factly. This allows Mary to assuage her conscience; she has already decided to murder Darnley, but now she can tell herself it's a matter of mercy, for he will die regardless, and "an honorable end is better than this." Apparently in Scotland, an "honorable end" can be obtained with the judicious application of gunpowder.

Since the house at Kirk o' Field is described as the place where Darnley takes his "whores and young men" and he has already been described as poxed, the entire event of his murder is couched in terms of a combination cleansing and mercy killing. Fire is a purifying agent, so the degenerate and diseased Darnley will be cleansed by fire. The Lords of the Congregation want Darnley dead, and Moray is the mastermind of the method, though they allow Bothwell to help them carry it out. Despite all this, it is Mary herself who authorizes Darnley's murder — she pardons the conspirators who murdered Riccio, including Moray, specifically so they can return to Scotland and kill her husband. Mary's thoughts on the matter are revealed through her love letters to Bothwell, which she writes while Darnley lies sleeping in bed, his face covered to hide what venereal disease has done to it. "I have obeyed you because I believe he is condemned to death by the pox, which is the wrath of God upon his vile nature. So what is planned is no sin ... and you shall be no puppet king but the master. For the first time I am loved and fulfilled. I have turned my back on God for you." Mary seems unconcerned by the contradiction of committing "no sin" while at the same time acknowledging that what she does is so grievous it will separate her from God. Such depth of self-awareness is not in her nature. She has already been shown to be an adulteress, and with these few voiced-over lines, she shows herself to also be complicit in her husband's death.

The characterization of Mary here is antithetical to that in *Mary of Scotland*. Far from being an innocent unfairly accused in the court of public opinion, this Mary is unequivocally guilty. Not only is she guilty, but she refuses to take responsibility for her actions, rationalizing them as "no sin" to murder someone with such a "vile nature." The role Bothwell is expected to play after Darnley's murder is also apparent — he will be king, and not just in name; he will *rule*. Especially telling for a woman who, in other film representations and later in this same film, will cast herself as a Catholic martyr, Mary admits to having turned her back on God for the love of Bothwell.

The depth of Mary's treachery is shown on Darnley's final night, when she sits on his bed as he rests, calmly strumming Riccio's lute and singing to him in French. She assures the frightened, sick, and pathetic Darnley that she will be back soon, bids him a fond farewell, and rides off to a wedding feast as the conspirators busy themselves at their work. When the explosion occurs and everyone rushes to see, she does not even bother to look out the window; she merely exchanges glances with Bothwell.

After the deed is done, she shows no regret, only whiny irritation at Bothwell when she finds out the manner of it: "He was to have an honorable death, be challenged to a duel — you told me so!" The impression is that Bothwell was to be her champion in a matter of chivalric honor; she saw him defeating her sick husband in hand-to-hand combat, then helping himself to the spoils, namely her person and the crown. Bothwell was to fight for her. The fact that Darnley was blown up and strangled in his nightgown does not fit with her romantic sensibilities. The practical Bothwell cuts her off with, "Death is death, however it comes. We must look to our futures."

Elizabeth theatrically makes the most of the situation — for the benefit of the European ambassadors, she and her entire court dress in black to mourn the late King of Scotland "because the Scottish court does not.... We are shocked at his abominable murder. We are astounded at what followed." Naturally, this is all for show and though she may be somewhat surprised — after all, who could have predicted Mary would blow up her husband? — she is more pleased, and also amused. The Queen seems to take particular relish in the fact that Mary has made every misstep, while Elizabeth deftly diverted a similar situation: "It was once said in the Catholic courts that Elizabeth would marry her horsemaster, who had murdered his wife. Then her people would turn her out in favor of Mary. I have not married. Leicester is innocent. My people did not rebel and Mary

Stuart does *not* rule here.... Let the Scottish Queen settle her own affairs as I once settled mine." Elizabeth compares herself directly to Mary and takes great pride in her superior intellectual as well as political abilities; the results are starting to speak for themselves. Elizabeth knows that Mary is incapable of putting her own house in order, and it gives her satisfaction to watch Mary's life implode.

Elizabeth's court may be dressed in black, but glitter still abounds, and her palace is a fashionable place — elegantly attired courtiers, warm wood panels, and polished floors. This is order and efficiency, an effective political machine. In this, it mirrors the disparity to be found between Elizabeth and Mary's respective courts in the earlier film, *Mary of Scotland*. The contrast with Mary's state of affairs in this version, however, is even greater — she's shown in bed with Bothwell in a stone turret, covered with ratty furs, her messy hair in a ponytail and wearing a rough woolen dress. She starts up at the howling wind, crying about how frightened she is. Mary is in need of constant comfort, and Bothwell is there to give it to her, telling her not to be afraid, just as one would hush a child who had had a nightmare. There is no efficient court machine to surround them and through which they can run the country; Mary has no savvy advisers. Riccio was assuredly less than savvy, as evidenced by the fact that he cannot provide counsel from the grave. Father Ballard is no longer in evidence, perhaps fled lest he suffer the same fate as Riccio. Mary is incapable of political planning and Bothwell is not much better, preferring direct confrontation to intrigue and subtlety. They are both out of their depth, as is about to become painfully apparent.

Mary's nightmares come true when Moray turns on them and calls Bothwell out for a duel. Mary locks Bothwell in his room, denying him even the "honorable death" she wished for Darnley, because she's too scared to face the prospect of life alone. Bothwell rages that he "will not be dishonored," but Mary assures him that no one remembers the honor of the dead, an ironic comment from the soon-to-be martyr, and tells Bothwell, "You are no match for the treachery of these times." Mary decides to face the conspirators to buy time while Bothwell escapes, but she lacks the courage. With no male around, she looks for it in a very unlikely place — a woman. She asks the loyal Mary Seton to come with her and "give me courage." Captured by Moray and the nobles, who threaten to publish her letters to Bothwell unless she abdicates, she remains adamant until, just as in *Mary of Scotland*, they threaten her love. Moray assures her that Bothwell will not be coming to her aid, for he has been captured. Mary begins screaming and attacks Moray with a knife. The lords subdue her none too gently with a blow to the back of the head, showing the brutality inherent at the Scottish court, just as did the earlier scene portraying the murder of Riccio.

Mary has been guilty of her own fair share of treachery, but with her childlike mindset, it is always others who are culpable. The ultimate betrayal for her comes when even Bothwell asks her to abdicate, not for his own safety but for hers. Bothwell describes himself as an "ambitious man, hungry for life," but he fears for Mary. In her typically melodramatic fashion, she wails that she cannot exist without him, that she prays for death. As in the courtyard scene in *Mary of Scotland*, it's left up to a man, the pragmatic Bothwell, to lay out Mary's duty for her, since she's incapable of seeing to it herself: "You are Mary Stuart, the Queen! While you live, there is hope. Cling to that ... one day I shall return for you with an army." Thus fortified, Mary agrees to abdicate, and by the time she reaches the English border, is wildly happy, yelling about how free she is, how she will "overcome all and be reunited with my Bothwell. I am but five and twenty years of age; I have my whole life before me! I am free!" It's more evidence of Mary's naïveté. She is far from free; she's simply being moved to a different prison, but is too silly to realize it.

With Mary in England, all that remains is the obligatory secret meeting with her cousin Elizabeth. Accompanied only by the trusty Robin, Elizabeth awaits Mary in a wooded glen. While they are waiting, the conversation between Elizabeth and her horsemaster sets up how Mary has busied herself since last the viewer saw her — her actions have been, as always, unwise. She encourages English Catholics to flock to her and has even gone so far as to hold court at Carlisle. Even Elizabeth, who has so far accurately predicted Mary's every move, is astounded: "Is she mad to behave so blatantly? I fear I may have misjudged her all these years." Leicester makes the understatement of the century when he replies, "She has never learned discretion."

When Mary arrives, the contrast between the two queens is marked. Elizabeth is clad all in green, verdant, like her surroundings, flourishing. Mary is dressed in black, a foreshadowing of the fact that she is already dead, her actions having sealed her fate. The two rivals have nothing but insincere smiles for each other at the start, though Elizabeth makes clear through her veiled comments that she is none too pleased at her sweet cousin's "ungentle demand" that they meet. If Mary were more astute, she would know to be on her guard. Things being as they are, however, Mary is positively exuberant as she explains that the crimes of the Scottish lords are so great that "it buries all past differences between us. I am confident of your help; I ask it as a right." Mary continues to display a dangerous sense of entitlement; from her vulnerable position, she ought to supplicate, but instead she demands. Elizabeth responds wryly, "I see you have courage." It is, of course, not courage Mary displays, but oblivious foolishness. She demands an army, supplies, and money. Elizabeth entreats her to be totally open "for be assured there is no waking hour of the day when you are far from my thoughts. Your fate is linked with mine. We are princes both. We are joined by blood." Mary says she has nothing else she wishes to ask, but what Elizabeth has solicited is an explanation of the circumstances surrounding the murder of Darnley. Mary lies through her teeth as she tells Elizabeth to rest assured that she's innocent in the matter, as if her declaration were all that was needed to put an end to the discussion. She's totally taken aback when Elizabeth guarantees her that she shall have her army and money after she has been "honorably acquitted." As is often the case when habitual liars are caught, Mary becomes instantly indignant, stating that if her word is not good enough, she will go to France. With Elizabeth's stern, "You shall *not*," the atmosphere instantly changes, all pretense of friendship gone. Mary reacts to authority as a spoiled child would, and she rants that she will answer no accusations; she believes herself to be above them. "Who is my equal? Will you do it in public, before the eyes of the world? You lack the courage!" she rages contemptuously. Mary is the one who lacks courage, buoyed only by her misplaced sense of self-importance. Elizabeth finally gives vent to her true thoughts: "It is not enough to speak one's mind in season and out as you have done. It is not the conduct of a queen. It is the conduct of a pampered woman demanding that all indulge her. It does not surprise me that you are here, helpless, and that your brother rules. You are not fit for the high office to which you were born!"

Though spoken out of anger and jealousy, not a single word of what Elizabeth has said is untrue, and she has provided a likeness of Mary more exact than holding up a mirror. Rather than see herself for what she is or even pretend humility in an attempt to manipulate Elizabeth into providing the support she must have, Mary is all impulsive anger. Elizabeth is "the bastard, the heretic, the usurper cursed by God!" Mary leaves no arrow in the quiver, loosing insults about Elizabeth's childlessness from her superior perch as mother of a male heir. Elizabeth will "die a solitary old woman ... and whatever my fate, my son will rule here in time!" Elizabeth bears this without anger, showing little emotion. But she has yet to play her final card. She informs Mary that it was she who intentionally sent Darnley to the Scottish court: "Any queen who could be gulled by such a pretty, wicked fellow and take him to her bed and put a crown upon his head ... inspires pity. You have my pity, madam ... knowing you to be without wisdom, discretion, or any of the attributes of a queen. I see you have learned nothing." And here is another of Mary's chief failings; she is always emotion before reason, but she also does not learn from her mistakes. To learn from a mistake, one must first admit a mistake has been made, and this is something of which Mary is incapable. She's adept at playing the victim, not taking responsibility. As her final blow, Elizabeth declares that Mary is spoken of in all the courts of Europe as "an infamous royal whore." Elizabeth finds this last insult particularly satisfying, for it harkens back to the beginning of the film when Mary and her Guise uncles repeated the current gossip that Elizabeth was a harlot. The tables have finally, completely turned.

Lacking any logical course of action, Mary responds emotionally and with physical violence — she attempts to strike Elizabeth with her riding crop. Leicester stops her, and all that's left is for Mary to threaten Elizabeth's life. Elizabeth is resigned, not angry, as she states, "Now I have no choice. I must keep her prisoner until the day of her death."

Throughout the exchange between the rival queens, one fact becomes unmistakable: Elizabeth's superiority of intellect. She has already proved herself an astute politician as well as skilful in the art of manipulating others (which, some might argue, are one and the same). Her exchange with Mary highlights the fact that, though Mary considers herself to have the moral high ground (her misplaced pride would allow for no less), she is still no match for Elizabeth intellectually, and ultimately she is defeated. This is, perhaps, not entirely Mary's fault. To be fair to her, the impression given through this film is that she had absolutely no training for the role she was to play as queen — she was allowed to play like a carefree child up until the moment she left for Scotland. Even with proper guidance, however, Redgrave's breathlessly passionate Mary seems as if she would be hard-pressed to overcome her emotional unsuitability for the role.

The film fast-forwards a number of unspecified years; unlike in *Mary of Scotland*, the characters in *Mary, Queen of Scots* do age, showing the passage of time. She is older than Mary, but time appears to have been disproportionately unkind to Elizabeth — she's wrinkled and her make-up is garish. By contrast, Mary as heroine simply looks a bit pale and wan. Mary has been imprisoned an untold number of years, and she is about to make her final, fatal mistake. Father Ballard arrives, in disguise, with news of the Babington

Conspiracy, and Mary's countenance instantly lights up. It is Father Ballard who informs her of Bothwell's death, and at this news, she finally displays a sliver of repentance for some of her actions—though only the ones that "brought him to such an end."

Elizabeth, meanwhile, is the picture of unhealthy old age—she's in her nightgown, soaking her feet while attendants bring her tinctures and medicines and Burghley cajoles her to be "sensible" and order Mary's execution. He reminds her of the pope's order, that it is no longer a sin to assassinate Elizabeth: "Destroy Mary, and all problems wither away." Elizabeth steadfastly refuses, "I fear her execution. It threatens me. She is an anointed queen as I am." Burghley promises to provide Elizabeth with proof positive, and finally she relents, "It has always been, from the beginning, her death or mine."

The evidence of Mary's complicity in the Babington Plot is duly discovered, and while they ransack her rooms and discover damning letter after damning letter, Mary does nothing but sit and stare, wide-eyed. Mary may have been able to charm others, but Burghley is immune; he points out that she casts an evil spell on all she meets, save him: "It has taken me years to trap you, madam. Now you will come to justice." He has spent his entire career plotting Mary's downfall, and he now finally has what he needs to fully accomplish it. This particular exchange rings with a certain historical veracity. It has been suggested that Mary Stuart and the threat she represented was the predominant catalyst propelling Elizabethan politics. Certainly, William Cecil spent an inordinate deal of time attempting to address the question of the Scottish Queen, the "S.Q." as he called her. One archivist noted that, based on Cecil's correspondence and memos, "She wasn't just a 'threat' recurring every three or four years ... she was his obsession. Every morning for thirty years, Cecil got out of bed, worrying that S.Q. ... was still alive."[5] With this in mind, his exasperation in the film is all the more pointed when Elizabeth still vacillates, fearing "a terrible retribution" if she signs Mary's death warrant. Even at this late date, Elizabeth is willing to forgive her, so yet another secret meeting is staged, again with Leicester as the only witness.

As at their first meeting, Elizabeth is again in green, but no longer vibrant; now it seems the green of mold and decay rather than verdant growth. Mary is again dressed in drab, a combination of grays and browns. Neither of these are forceful or passionate colors, and they reflect the mood. Enthusiastic hatred has atrophied with the years; all that is left is for Elizabeth to make a last-ditch attempt to save a woman who will make not the smallest effort to save herself. Mary starts off in whiny tone about how she must sit, for the cold and damp of English walls has entered her bones. Elizabeth, while making up a fire for her, is forthright; she wishes to spare Mary, but Mary must beg her forgiveness, in writing. This Mary is, again, no innocent. She readily admits she knew of the plans to assassinate Elizabeth and that she was glad of them. Though seeing Elizabeth in the flesh, she confesses to be oddly happy that they were not successful. In a silly bit of rhetorical meandering, Mary states she will ask forgiveness in person, but refuses to do it in writing, since "it would damn me in the eyes of posterity." Instead, she wants her trial, so she can "die a martyr to the Catholic faith." Elizabeth is unsurprised, and smiles sarcastically as she says, "How little you have changed. How wildly you rush to your destruction." Mary *still* has not learned. Elizabeth plays the last card she has to manipulate Mary, the so-called Casket Letters—Mary's letters to Bothwell that prove her an adulterous murderess, a far cry from the sainthood she aspires to after death. "Your absurd love letters will be read out for the people to gloat upon," Elizabeth warns her. "Will all this treachery and lust rise like a hymn to God, or will it cast you down forever?" Again Elizabeth holds up a rhetorical mirror for Mary to see herself: "For the first time in your life, put aside your personal desires and behave like a queen." Mary is as she ever was, however, and she refuses: "Now I must die. It is my destiny. And it is your destiny, Elizabeth, to kill me. Nothing you can say or do will avoid my martyrdom." Mary tells Leicester, "I will pray for your mistress Elizabeth at the moment of my death." It is evidence of Mary's ingrained self-delusion for her to see herself as a saint worthy to pray for the damned Elizabeth's soul; Mary has done nothing to redeem herself. Her years of imprisonment have fostered no self-awareness, no repentance, no growth. She is, as she always has been, a selfish child. Yet Elizabeth pays her the compliment of saying as she leaves, "Madam, if your head had matched your heart, I would be the one awaiting death."

Though some commentators have praised this line as "resounding with truth,"[6] this statement on Elizabeth's part is a trope by screenwriters to give a sort of wistful "what if" closure to her dealings with Mary, and it rings false. The historical Mary certainly chose emotion over intellect; this fact is undisputed. But when one considers that the film Mary's "heart" has shown itself to be nothing but impetuous and needy, her possession of a mind to match, reckless and selfish, could not have helped her cause, and certainly would not have allowed her to triumph over Elizabeth. Based on Redgrave's portrayal, casting Mary as a great lover is also unconvincing — her love is not of the worthy, selfless kind, quite the opposite, in fact. Her "love" manifests itself as a deep-seated emotional need, a bottomless pit into which her lovers must pour strength and solace and comfort without ever receiving any in return. It is not admirable, and it does not inspire the sympathy with which the filmmakers obviously intended their version of Mary to be viewed.

That Mary is to be seen as a flawed yet sympathetic figure is reinforced by the film's last scene. Mary has gone to her execution, a romanticized affair which conveniently glosses over the horror that attended the historical event. She has worn her martyr's red, commended her soul to God, and gone to meet her Maker. The axe comes down, and the scene switches to a close-up of Elizabeth's tearful eyes, which stare straight ahead. It's strongly reminiscent of the last scene of *The Private Lives of Elizabeth and Essex* — Elizabeth has been forced to condone an undesired execution, and she, as survivor, is bereft. Elizabeth slowly looks down to her hands, in which she holds Mary's Bible and rosary, the symbols of her Catholic martyrdom. Elizabeth sits alone on her throne, just as Mary warned her she would, and the camera pans out slowly to show her in all her dismal loneliness. With the closing titles, the film gives Mary the triumph and last word: Elizabeth "died as she had lived, unmarried and childless. The Thrones of England and Scotland passed to the only possibly claimant, a man, King James I — only son of Mary Stuart ... Queen of Scots."

Roger Ebert summed up the film's ending by saying it was "as it must be, suitably solemn and dignified. It is always that way with historical movies. After two hours of galloping sex and court intrigue, the heroine makes her peace with God, thanks her faithful lady-in-waiting, and goes off to the guillotine."[7] Faithful ladies-in-waiting and guillotines optional, he is essentially correct; historical dramas, especially those with female protagonists, almost invariably tend to end on a solemn note. The *New York Times* review agreed on the solemnity, but chose to explicate less favorably: "It's just solemn, well-groomed and dumb."[8] Closing solemnity aside, reviewers of *Mary, Queen of Scots* almost universally agree that this film is a "blatantly 'Hollywood' conception of Mary, Queen of Scots"[9] and little more than an historical soap opera, one that hits the historical high points, but overall, lacks fire. The screenplay "veered from the banal to the ludicrous; and the direction, by Charles Jarrott, was too lumbering to capture anything of value from the distinguished cast."[10] Despite the less than impressive framework in which they appeared, Jackson and Redgrave's performances, from an acting standpoint, were just as universally praised as the film was dismissed. Redgrave's portrayal of Mary, Queen of Scots was chosen as a Royal Command Performance and also garnered her an Oscar nomination. Ebert called it "finely spirited," and another reviewer praised her face-to-face encounters with Elizabeth, saying they were "electric," while at the same time admitting that the cast could barely overcome "an episodic, rambling story."[11] Redgrave also fared well when compared to her screen predecessor in the role, Katharine Hepburn. Neither *Mary of Scotland* nor *Mary, Queen of Scots* "gives us a truthful account of [Mary]," but, "Redgrave's interpretation comes closer to the mark than Hepburn's ... Redgrave's Mary seems more emotionally fragile than Hepburn's in many respects. She exhibits less control, swinging to extremes from courage to collapse, which is probably the more accurate portrayal."[12] And as one overly fulsome commentator put it, "At least she was tall enough."[13]

Jackson's portrayal of Elizabeth was just as well received, if not more so — she "makes a perfectly shrewish, wise Elizabeth"[14] and presented a "far more well-defined character"[15] than Redgrave's Mary. Jackson herself regretted taking on the role, on a number of levels. She had just wrapped up her portrayal as Elizabeth in the miniseries *Elizabeth R* six weeks before, and she was hesitant about playing the same character again so quickly; she feared mind-numbing boredom. The filmmakers, notably Wallis and Jarrott, made the allowance of shooting her scenes in only three weeks, at great inconvenience to both themselves and the other actors, in order to accommodate her and prevent this. And yet, "The film itself, despite all the concessions made to her, soon died on the actress. She looked back on the project with horror and referred to it as the first film of which she was ashamed to be a part."[16] Jackson disagreed with some of the artistic choices made (most notably the face-to-face meetings between the two queens, though she later defended them in interviews) and felt it was nothing more than a rehash of her previous work, which did not reflect well upon her and might damage her career. Another film Elizabeth, Bette Davis, disagreed: "Glenda Jackson is going to have an incredible career. She makes me think of myself. She hasn't got the motion picture beautiful face, and neither have I. But she cares and is dedicated. That counts."[17] General audiences and reviewers appeared to agree with Davis's estimation. What no contemporary reviewers seemed to note is that this film is a sort of royal sister act — the two characterizations play off each other by contrast, strengthening the overall impression of each. It was left to later commentators and a biographer of Jackson to state that "the two women gave extraordinary and completely different kinds of performances — a contrast that perfectly expressed the differences between the characters."[18]

Mary's flaws in this film are meant to humanize her; by the 1970s, audiences no longer needed a morally perfect heroine — in fact, it was feared they could no longer relate to one. What was needed what not a saint like Hepburn's Mary, but a flawed individual like Redgrave's. If "it is precisely this dichotomy between Elizabeth the successful ruler but flawed woman and Mary the hopeless ruler but real woman worthy of male protection that *Mary, Queen of Scots* depicts,"[19] then Mary is to be viewed as the victim. The problem with this particular characterization is that it's difficult to see her as anything more than the victim of her own obtuse choices. *Mary, Queen of Scots* is presented by those who made it, as are most biopics of this nature, as factual. The promotional trailers trumpeted, "Fiction at the peak of its excitement pales before the facts of her tempestuous reign," though, naturally, the filmmakers chose to fictionalize a great deal of the historical material anyway. The brief blurbs which accompanied the promotional materials for the film were sure to appeal to the 1970s feminist viewpoint by stating that this was the story of "two of history's most powerful women ... Mary Stuart, who was first a woman" and Elizabeth Tudor, who was "first a monarch." This is, at best, a two-dimensional rendering of both women, though it seems closer to the mark for the historical Mary, who exhibited less depth than the historical Elizabeth.

If neither the Hepburn nor Redgrave portrayals suit, viewers may soon have another chance to see Mary Stuart take to the screen. Announced at the 2007 Cannes Film Festival, another iteration of Mary, Queen of Scots is in the works. Scarlett Johansson has been attached to this film version of Mary's story since 2008, although the film has yet to go into production. According to its description, it will be yet another "chronicle of the life and reign of Mary I of Scotland, with a concentration on her strained personal and political relationship with her cousin, Queen Elizabeth I of England."[20] Given the sultry sensuality Johansson cannot help but exhibit onscreen, the characterization of this new Mary may be closer to femme fatale than helpless victim. It also provokes curiosity as to who will be chosen as the latest actress to portray Elizabeth on film. Regardless, given the time elapsed, it will be interesting to see if this postmodern version of Elizabeth and Mary's relationship differs from its predecessors, and how the portrayals of both are shaped by current events and worldview.

ELIZABETH (1998)

Whether due to the changing attitudes inherent in the 20-odd years since Elizabeth had last appeared in a major film role or director Shekhar Kapur's specific vision, *Elizabeth* has generated a significant amount of attention, both positive and negative, in film and historical studies. Much has been made of the film's revisionist, post-colonial view of the Virgin Queen, with some critics even going so far as to call it "something of a post-colonial revenge on Britain's most hallowed myth."[21] Others have credited Kapur (with a little help from screenwriter Michael Hirst) as "vitally reviving" the dying genre of historical drama, using "liberal dramatic license"[22] as his crash cart. This film certainly has a different feel from any other that had come before it, though exactly what that feel is, critics have been hard pressed to agree upon — *Elizabeth* has been called everything from a serious drama to a historical thriller to a bodice-ripper. This is seen as a deliberate strategy by the filmmakers to make *Elizabeth* all things to all potential viewers — to give it appeal for the widest possible audience. Regardless of how it's pigeonholed, *Elizabeth* represents "a new stage in the development of quality 'British' costume drama," and, along with *Shakespeare in Love* (examined in Chapter Five) it became a "cultural presence for a short period."[23] Even calling *Elizabeth* "British" is deceptive, given its Indian director and multinational cast. Due to its tendency to devolve into lush but shallow pageantry, costume drama, British or otherwise, is often denigrated. But it has been noted that "costumes can be used to reveal a subject as well as overdress one. And the Elizabethan era ... would be the richest source for this kind of myth."[24] In his study on the English costume drama, Andrew Higson notes that *Elizabeth* would not have been possible without the success of not only English costume dramas/heritage films of the 1980s and 1990s, but also related films such as *Braveheart* (1995) and *La Reine Margot* (1994). The reception of films such as these paved the way for *Elizabeth* to be made.

One thing is certain — everything is sexier, everything is darker, everything is more sinister than the Elizabethan offerings that preceded this film. Kapur's Virgin Queen is not only decidedly less than virginal, but as one commentator wryly put it, she's "Michael Corleone in Tudor drag."[25] This dark ambiance is apparent from the opening credits of the film — in combinations of red and black, shadowed crosses and superimposed portraits of the historical players float across the screen, titles fade in and out, all while ominous choral music resonates. It is 1554, and as the titles elucidate with frequent full-stops, Henry VIII is dead. The country is divided. Catholic against Protestant. Henry's eldest daughter, Mary, a fervent Catholic, is Queen. She is childless. The Catholics' greatest fear is the succession of Mary's Protestant half-sister. Elizabeth.

As if to show that this is a film that will have its share of blood, it opens with the emphatic pressing of Mary's huge royal seal into a pool of congealing, blood-red wax — an execution warrant. A woman, clad in only a dirty white shift, is having her head brutally shaved, almost scalped, by a soldier using a knife. She and the two men who are to accompany her to the pyre pray ceaselessly. As are a great many of the scenes in this film, the camera angle is high and relatively tight, from above, a God's-eye view, as the soon-to-be martyred Protestants are tied to the stake. One of the martyrs is given a name when a man in the crowd cries, "God bless you, Master Ridley!" This would make him Nicolas Ridley, the Bishop of London. One of the most learned men and finest minds of the Reformation, the historical Ridley had flourished under Edward's Protestant policies. Upon Edward's death, he had supported the ill-fated attempt of Lady Jane Grey to claim the English throne, and was duly arrested. He refused to recant, and with Hugh Latimer, former Bishop of Worcester (whom one can assume to be the other male martyr), he was burned alive for treason and heresy in 1555. Both Ridley and Latimer died a brave death, with Latimer telling Ridley from the pyre that "we shall this day light such a candle by God's grace in England as I trust shall never be put out."[26] The woman upon whom so much in this scene focuses is completely fictitious, added for dramatic effect. A ruler who would burn a woman alive is obviously a monster. Like much in this film, fiction blends with fact, overwhelms it, dates expand and contract, bits and pieces of history are stripped, reconstituted, applied to other contexts. Even the musical score runs the gamut from Tudor-period pieces to Mozart. In short, this film is a mishmash of the first order, and to try to untangle all the factual historical threads from their morass of invention would be counterproductive — historical veracity is not the point. Kapur is attempting to create an emotional portrait, and that he does well; two minutes into the film, England is visualized as a place where answering someone's cry for help means adding fuel to the fire to shorten the torture of his death. Mary is a cruel tyrant; her reign is blood and fire.

That Mary (Kathy Burke) is darkness is illustrated by the spaces she inhabits — she and those around her all wear black, the interiors of her palace are dim and murky, and despite the fact that these are huge spaces, the scenes in which she appears are shot to convey a sense of claustrophobia. The architecture itself represents a literal step back to the Dark Ages; Kapur chooses to use the Gothic arched stone interiors of medieval cathedrals and castles rather than more accurate Tudor reconstructions. Utilizing his God's-eye view, extremely high-angled shots looking down through these immense architectural structures, was a conscious attempt, as Kapur explains it, to "introduce the idea that their [sic] is greater Power operating beyond the human conflict going on in the plot. I called it Destiny but it could go by many other names. All the antagonists and the protagonists were ultimately equal in Death and subject to their Destiny."[27]

Mary's destiny seems assured — she has just announced that she is pregnant. Unfortunately, she's the only one who believes in her pregnancy since the king has not shared her bed in many months. The viewer learns this through hushed conversations in darkened corridors; these occur throughout the film, reinforcing the sensation that everything is observed, spies lurk everywhere, intrigue is unceasing. The Duke of Norfolk, played with an appealing mix of brute force and sensuality by Christopher Eccleston, informs the Queen and King Philip (who is obviously bored and repulsed by her) that he has suppressed the Wyatt rebellion, and Elizabeth should be dealt with. When the Earl of Arundel tentatively offers that there's no proof Elizabeth was involved, Mary, clutching the hand of her dwarf rather than the one her husband has pulled away, explodes "My sister was born of that whore Anne Boleyn. She was born a bastard; she will never rule England!" There's awkward silence as the men in the room coolly study her after this near hysterical outburst; their detached observation provides even greater contrast to her emotional instability. Finally she bids them find proof of Elizabeth's "treachery."

When Elizabeth's world is shown, the contrast with Mary's is absolute — from oppressive, darkened interior spaces the viewer is introduced to an open, sunny field where Elizabeth (Cate Blanchett) and her ladies are dancing and giggling. The effect, which Kapur uses later in the film for more than one transition, is akin to walking out of a darkened house into the whiteout of blinding summer sunlight — the eyes take a moment to adjust, and when they do, a completely different vista lies before them. Robert Dudley (Joseph Fiennes) gallops up on horseback with a breathless young lady, sliding her expertly to the ground as she gasps, "It was so fast!" All the other women run to greet him with the exception of Elizabeth; she waits, alone but still dancing, for him to come to her.

Elizabeth has been shown from afar, but in the first real look the viewer gets of her, she seems to radiate youth and health and light, a total contrast with the bloated, ill Mary. Blanchett has been called "so right" for this role "physically, intellectually, spiritually ... she seems to be channeling Elizabeth."[28] This is certainly debatable; intellectually and spiritually, Blanchett's portrayal is hard fought to live up to historical accounts of the woman, and physically she seems too ethereally beautiful for the part. It might be more accurate to say that Blanchett is "so right" for a romanticized, Hollywoodized version of Elizabeth. Her long, strawberry-blond hair hangs loose to her waist, and she wears a green dress with a bright red sash, growth combined with passion. The costuming of this film is indicative of its divergent feel from previous Elizabeth offerings. Costume designer Alexandra Byrne did have budget restrictions within which she was forced to work (the film's production budget was modest by Hollywood standards — $25 million), but the production values of this film are high, and it was more an aesthetic rather than practical choice that dictated the costuming. *Elizabeth* makes little attempt at historical verisimilitude, and its costumes are no exception. The silhouettes are understated and barely Elizabethan; only at two points in the film is the costuming meant to represent that of the historical Elizabeth, and these are the "portrait" shots, intentional nods to historical portraiture meant to denote Elizabeth's rise to power and lend the film the gravity of historicity. The rest of the costumes, while visually appealing and convincing enough not to jar the viewer out of the period, are what Byrne calls "theatrical" in their look and feel — their stated purpose is not to distract from the plotting of the film, thus avoiding the "frock flick" epithet.[29]

Elizabeth wears no make-up, indicating her lack of artifice, and her skin is luminescent in the dazzling sunshine. The looks she and Dudley exchange seem in danger of starting a conflagration. Dudley is intended to be a figure of romance novel proportions; attired as he is he looks as if he's just stepped off the cover of a bodice-ripper. He wears no doublet, his shirt open to show his chest, as he asks Elizabeth, "May I join you, my lady?" This film often exudes a lush sensuality, and it is nowhere as apparent as in the scene where the two dance with each other for the first time. There are close-ups of hands and bodies brushing, slow turns, lowered eyes and locked gazes, all lit by filtered sunlight. Kapur has a penchant for intercutting disparate scenes, so while Dudley and Elizabeth dance in what almost appears to be slow motion, Kat Ashley (Emily Mortimer) is running at full-tilt towards Hatfield. She must warn her mistress of Mary's soldiers, who are hard upon her heels. When they arrive, they immediately arrest Elizabeth for treason, at which point Blanchett manages to convey barely suppressed terror. She has difficulty looking Dudley in the face as he reminds her, "Remember who you are. Do not be afraid of them." This is yet another male emphasizing to an irresolute woman the duty of her royal position.

Elizabeth is taken by boat to the Tower's Water Gate, and her world literally grows darker as she enters Mary's. She wears a white, shift-like dress, denoting her innocence, as she passes slowly by severed heads on pikes, showing what awaits her if she falters. The scene is again shot from above and harkens back to the martyrs at the beginning of the film as Elizabeth, in her white dress, is circled by three black-clad interrogators. Despite their coercive attempts to elicit a confession, Elizabeth maintains she is "a true and faithful subject" and asks "why must we tear ourselves apart for this small question of religion?" The sinister Bishop Gardiner (Terence Rigby) fixing her with the one eye not obscured by cataracts, spits, "You think it small, though it killed your mother?" It seems a strange statement to make, attributing Anne Boleyn's death to the question of religion. In this film, however, the religious struggle is all, though it's couched less in terms of the individual conscience than a representation of the ultimate struggle for power. Many did not take this viewpoint; *Elizabeth* and its sequel, *The Golden Age*, have been condemned as vehemently anti–Catholic. While Catholics are obviously the villains of the piece, it's less a reflection on Kapur's view of Roman Catholicism than it is a necessary polarization — Elizabeth is the victim/heroine and she was a Protestant. In order for the viewer to see her as a character worthy of compassion, she must have adversaries, and as she was Protestant, they must necessarily be Catholic. It's only logical, but it does have unavoidable corollaries: "In representing the burning of martyrs as unpopular and Mary's court as foreign, it is giving cinematic expression to a Protestant view of the past."[30] Everything is made to fit this religious iconography, including, eventually, Elizabeth herself. Even the windows (holes in the thick medieval stone that seem more like widened arrow slits) are shaped like crosses, and Elizabeth is framed squarely through one as she's shown to her cell, Bible in hand and cross around her neck. She completes the martyr image by stating, "Tonight I think I die."

Elizabeth has been sent for, and her journey seems to be one through hell itself. Safe inside a rushing carriage speeding her God knows where, Elizabeth is driven through tableaux strongly reminiscent of a Hieronymus Bosch painting — a man is hung upside down as his throat is cut, a woman clutches the carriage door and begs to be saved as she's dragged away by a soldier, another is stabbed in the stomach. The city is in chaos, and as if to show the cause, the scene immediately cuts to a tapestried wall in Mary's apartments which depicts the Virgin, breast exposed to suckle an almost grotesque Christchild — the unappealing fruit of Mary's fanatical religion. Elizabeth enters directly through this tapestry, stepping through the barrier created by her sister's Catholicism, and Mary watches her, completely in shadow. Mary is cruel: "When I look at you I see nothing of the King. Only that whore, your mother. My father never did anything so well as to cut off her head." Elizabeth maintains her innocence, and Mary tells her contemptuously, "You speak with such sincerity. I see you are still a consummate actress." Mary is at her wits' end and, despite her demeanor, is a pitifully deluded figure — her husband has gone and "they" have "poisoned" her child, which is in fact a fatal tumor. She points out Elizabeth's death warrant, unsigned on the table. One can see Elizabeth madly thinking as she eyes the warrant — her next words could save or damn her. What she chooses is the same tact Mary Stuart would later employ with the historical Elizabeth: responsibility for the death of God's anointed and one's own kin. "Mary," she says carefully, "if you sign that paper, you will be murdering your own sister." Mary changes approaches, asking Elizabeth to promise her that she will uphold the Catholic faith after Mary's death. "Do not take away from the people the consolation of the Blessed Virgin, their Holy Mother," she begs. One might expect Elizabeth to agree to anything, say anything to save herself. Being an innocent, Blanchett's Elizabeth is not so dishonest. She agrees to "act as my conscience dictates." Mary sends her out, back to her home at Hatfield, but not the way she came in — through the court milieu. "Feed her to the wolves," she says. "Let her see what they are like." The crowd quiets itself and parts for Elizabeth, but all eyes are upon her, and the atmosphere is unquestionably menacing. After she has left the room, though she is still within earshot, they begin to murmur, and the Duke of Norfolk says with contempt, "She is just a child, yet still you piss yourselves." Elizabeth, listening, laughs as she makes her escape, realizing they are almost as afraid of what she represents as she is afraid of them.

This metaphor of the court as a den of wolves is an apt one; nowhere is there safety, and when the courtiers watch Mary, they are literally waiting for her to die so they can metaphorically strip her of her skin, the trappings of power and royalty. Elizabeth fares better, but it's because she, as yet, presents no real threat. As an unknown entity, the court is cautious, circling her. As soon as she ascends the throne and they take her measure, things will change; they will execute their attack upon her. The one thing that has been established is that all eyes are now on Elizabeth.

It becomes clear that Mary is dying, and plans are set in motion. Elizabeth meets in secret with Sir William Cecil (Richard Attenborough), who informs her that her friends are returning from exile and counsels her "these are most uncertain times.... Say nothing and meet no one whose visit may compromise you. Not even Lord Robert." Elizabeth seems very naïve and young when she replies with dismay, "But he is a trusted friend!" Throughout the exchange, Cecil refers to her as "child," and with Attenborough's grandfatherly appearance, the kindly parental dynamic is reinforced, even though the historical Cecil was much closer to Elizabeth's age. He cautions her, "You are most innocent in the ways of this world and we must do all we may to guarantee the security of your throne." Despite Cecil's warnings, the next scene has Elizabeth playing checkers with Dudley, heads together and talking intimately in hushed tones while watched over by one of the Queen's guards. Dudley may be the love of her life, but his counsel is unwise: "Do not listen to any of them. None of them are of consequence when you are queen." They confess undying devotion to each other, eyes wet with unshed tears, as Elizabeth says, "Robert, you know you're everything to me." He replies, "All that I am, it is you." All sentimentality aside, he's more prescient than he realizes, for the time is fast approaching when, without Elizabeth's favor, he will be worse than nothing.

As soon as Mary Tudor releases her last breath, Norfolk pries the ring of state off her pudgy finger and orders, albeit unwillingly, that it be taken to Elizabeth. She's at Hatfield, inside reading, and she walks outside to another one of Kapur's blinding transitions, taking the ring and quoting the historical Elizabeth, "This is the Lord's doing, and it is marvelous in our eyes." Kapur cuts to the coronation, where everywhere there is the combination of bright light and the color red, passion and power. Elizabeth stands out, in her gold coronation dress, her reddish-gold hair loose down her back, as she processes down the red carpet and seats herself on the throne. She is crowned, handed the scepter and then the orb. The scene, shot full on from the front, forms an almost exact replica of the historical Elizabeth's coronation portrait, and the camera lingers to make sure this impression is received and reinforced. It's one of two iconic images Kapur chooses to emphasize in this film; he employs the same technique in the last scene of the film, framing Elizabeth to look exactly like later portraits of the iconic Virgin Queen. Both are representative of her power. In this framing, however, the Duke of Norfolk and the Earl of Sussex stand behind Elizabeth, representing the power behind the throne and dangerously overshadowing the beginning of her glorious reign.

Cecil wastes no time in getting the administrative ball rolling; while Elizabeth removes her heavy crown and coronation trappings, he informs her that she has inherited "a most parlous and degenerate state." There is no money, no army. As Elizabeth watches herself in the mirror, he assures her, "Until you marry and produce an heir, you will find no security." Unlike almost every other representation of Elizabeth on film, Blanchett's Elizabeth has no problem with what she sees in the mirror. She is young and attractive; as yet, the mirror is still kind in what it reflects to her. It will take another film almost a decade later for the mirror to become her enemy. She seems almost not to hear Cecil's advice about marrying as she's already focused on the revelry that will attend her coronation. It's a time of jubilation — despite Cecil's warnings, for the first time, she feels safe and happy. She will soon be shown how illusory this impression is.

The mood borders on euphoria as Elizabeth moves through the crowd at her coronation celebration, glad-handing and greeting. She notices a gentleman who seems to disturb her, moving along the perimeter of the festivities: Sir Francis Walsingham. Cecil informs her that he has "appointed him to have a care for Your Majesty's person." Walsingham observes her calmly, through sheer red curtains that seem to taint his entire field of vision with a red haze evocative of blood. The characterization of Walsingham in this film, consummately portrayed by Geoffrey Rush, is one of its strong points. He has been described as a "superspy, hit man, and guardian angel"[31] all rolled into one. Rush has stated that he loves the Tudor period because of its "wonderful atmosphere of political skullduggery," and his characterization certainly emphasizes this.[32] Walsingham is introduced while still an exile in France, and the first glimpse of him is from behind, his hands folded behind his head, as a boy holds a knife to his throat — Norfolk has paid to have him assassinated before he can return to England. He manages to calmly talk the boy, who may or may not be Walsingham's lover, out of his purpose. Leading him to the window to look out over the city, he opines, "So little beauty in this world, and so much suffering. Do you suppose that is what God had in mind? That is to say, if there is a God." This

"This is the Lord's doing, and it is marvelous in our eyes." An uncertain Elizabeth (Cate Blanchett) takes the throne while the powerful Duke of Norfolk (Christopher Eccleston) overshadows her reign in *Elizabeth*. (Polygram/The Kobal Collection)

characterization of Walsingham as, at best, an agnostic, is one that is reinforced throughout the film by both his dialogue and his actions. It's an interesting choice given the fact that the historical Walsingham was extremely devout, literally puritanical. An avowed family man, his intense adherence to the tenets of Protestantism was his defining trait — it was the impetus behind his tireless pursuit to uncover Catholic conspiracies and those who fomented them. A Walsingham with this kind of religious conviction and familial baggage, however, would never fit with the Machiavellian nature chosen for Elizabeth's spymaster in this film and the tone he brings to the entire production, especially his effect on the characterization of Elizabeth. Of all the men who surround her in this film, including Dudley, it is Walsingham who provides the defining force behind Elizabeth's transition from untried girl to successful monarch. He is ruthless, as is illustrated when he tells his young would-be assassin, "Innocence is the most precious thing you possess. Lose that, and you lose your soul." The boy looks surprised, and when the camera pans down, it becomes clear why — Walsingham has slit his throat. If Walsingham ever possessed innocence, it's long gone, and his soul with it. He is a dangerous and merciless man; one is extremely grateful he's on Elizabeth's side, for he makes a formidable enemy.

As Walsingham and the whole court watch, Elizabeth calls Dudley out to dance with her, and the dance she chooses is the Volta. This is a nod to historicity — Elizabeth was known to have performed this Italian dance with Dudley, but it's also an adept way to indicate the public perception of their relationship. The dance steps are comprised of a series of turns and jumps, and unlike most Tudor-period dances, it requires an embrace, with the man grasping the woman at the waist, underneath the busk of her dress, to lift her for the high jumps. For this reason, it was originally considered quite scandalous. Elizabeth and Dudley romp together in front of her entire court, performing a dance whose social unacceptability mirrors that of their relationship. Dudley takes it a step further when he asks not if, but when he may see her in private. She teases him with, "Have you forgot, my lord, I am queen now." As the dance ends, he kisses her cheek, setting the court to murmuring. It is, apparently, Elizabeth who has forgotten that she is queen, as her behavior soon illustrates.

Elizabeth goes where no other film adaptation has gone before when it decides to show the physical consummation of Elizabeth's romantic relationship with Dudley. As almost every appraisal of this film has noted, it is strongly imbued with a sense of voyeurism — the high-angle shots as well as scenes framed through windows and sheer draperies give the viewer the impression of watching, secretly, something meant to be private. The ultimate expression of this comes when Dudley visits Elizabeth's bedchamber. He must pass by her ladies-in-waiting, all lined up and giggling, and these same ladies watch through ornate portals in the stone wall as Elizabeth and Dudley make love. Even the sheer hangings of Elizabeth's bed provide no privacy and are themselves imprinted with a pattern of eyes and ears, reminiscent of dresses Elizabeth has been shown wearing in portraiture. While the original dresses represented Elizabeth as able to see and hear everything and thus protect her people, in this case, they represent Elizabeth as the object of scrutiny, being watched, listened to. This idea of a total lack of privacy is underlined when Cecil asks to be shown Elizabeth's sheets every morning for "I must know all her proper functions." As Cecil states, "Her Majesty's body and person are no longer her own property. They belong to the state." This is a simplification of the idea, first introduced during the Renaissance, of a ruler's two bodies — the "body natural" (a ruler's physical form) and the "body politic," an invisible body representing the power of the ruler and that ruler's responsibility to his realm. Elizabeth has yet to realize that there is more to her than just her body natural — her physical relationship with Dudley jeopardizes her personal security and that of her realm, a fact of which she is either oblivious or indifferent.

Despite *Elizabeth*'s vagaries with regard to timeline, events, and characterization, this one scene perhaps provoked more comment than any other, for it single-handedly demolishes Elizabeth's virginity as fact and grounds it strongly in the realm of myth. This decision was not without its consequences, as screenwriter Michael Hirst noted, "For putting Elizabeth into bed with Dudley, I have already been branded a heretic." Hirst was unconcerned by the censure, and his deprecating attitude toward historical evidence is apparent in his reaction: "Now neither you nor I, nor any of the rent-a-quote historians know with any certainty whether they were actually lovers."[33] All questions of historical veracity aside, this artistic choice is used within the plotting to further the idea of Elizabeth's transformation from "real" woman into the myth, a progression which is only fully realized at the end of the film.

The obligatory council chamber scene quickly makes clear the dynamics at play within the new government. In her actions as observed thus far, Elizabeth has not proved herself to be ineffectual so much as uncertain. She has managed to defend herself against her sister Mary's interrogators as well as the accusations of Mary herself. In both of these situations, however, she was on the defensive — she had only to *react*. As quickly becomes apparent in her interactions with her advisers, being proactive is not her strong suit; she has difficulty choosing a course of action. The council chamber, like all the other royal settings portrayed thus far in the film, is a large, echoing stone space with tall ceilings, and it is meant to dwarf Elizabeth. The proportions of these spaces "create an atmosphere of ceremonial architecture imposing its will on the queen," and also seem jarringly irrational; the majority of the interior spaces seen in *Elizabeth* "make little sense as dwelling spaces,"[34] despite the fact that the viewer is implicitly expected to accept them as such. This was a conscious choice by production designer John Myrhe at Kapur's insistence in order to give the film a certain tone. Kapur noted, "The architectural design of the film ... by constantly showing Elizabeth as a tiny individual in relationship to the immense stone architecture, it contradicted her rise to Power, often through the very high angle shots of the stone arches in the places that I shot in."[35] The architecture is not the only element which dominates Elizabeth — she sits in her chair at the end of a plank table with simple wooden benches upon which her councilors are ranged, with the exception of the Duke of Norfolk. He stands at the other end, towering over the other councilors, the proceedings, and Elizabeth. He informs them that Mary of Guise is massing French troops, and he demands Elizabeth allow him to raise an army to combat them. He is dismissive and abrupt; when she tentatively offers, "Can we not send emissaries..." he cuts her off, insisting on immediate action. The impression conveyed is that Elizabeth is being forced into a snap decision for which she is completely unprepared; she needs time to think, which Norfolk does not wish to give her. She polls the table to buy time, and all around it, even Dudley after Norfolk's bullying, agree. She then looks to Walsingham. He sits apart from the table, several feet away, to represent his status as outsider — as Cecil points out, he is not a member of the council (though the historical Walsingham was, as well as Secretary of State). Walsingham is the only man strong enough to disagree with Norfolk: "I say a prince should rather be slow to take action and watch that he does not come to be afraid of his own shadow." Ideologically, Elizabeth and Walsingham seem to be in agreement. She says softly, "I do not like wars. They have uncertain outcomes." Despite this, she bows under the weight of Norfolk's imperious demands, and authorizes the forces.

It is readily apparent to the viewer that things will not go well for the English in Scotland — as Elizabeth is slowly undressed by her ladies, she stands, her gaze distant and her face intermittently lit by flashes of lightning in her darkened apartments. It has begun to storm. When the storm blows over, the battlefield in Scotland is littered with English dead. Into this scene rides Mary of Guise (Fanny Ardant); she is an attractive, sensual woman, but she's also a political creature. She spares one of the English soldiers, a child, and sends him back to Elizabeth: "Tell that bastard queen not to send children to fight Mary of Guise," she says contemptuously in French. When Elizabeth receives the news, she storms through the palace, again shot from above, her steps ringing on the stone flags and her ladies trailing behind her like ducklings in a row. She screams for them to leave her as thunder rings out and she finally finds herself alone, in what appears to be an unused portion of the palace. The furniture is covered in dusty cloth, giving the room an eerie, Gothic ambiance. Elizabeth sinks to her knees, crying, and when she looks up, like the ghost of Hamlet's father, she discovers her own father towering over her — she has collapsed at the foot of Holbein's painting of Henry VIII, draped with moth-eaten fabric reminiscent of a shroud. Henry VIII is dead, but he can still cast his shadow over his daughter from the grave — and judge her failures. Elizabeth may think she is alone, but as always, she is being watched. Walsingham stands at the door, and Elizabeth voices her agony and anger: "They should never have been sent to Scotland. My father would not have made such a mistake." Her father is the yardstick by which she measures her successes and failures, and she understands that she has been outmaneuvered — set up to fail. Rather than wallow in self-pity, Elizabeth channels her anger into a flurry of action. She rides out to find Dudley and her councilors, who have been out blithely hunting while she suffers. She immediately agrees to invite the Duke of Anjou and entertain his marriage suit — an attempt to achieve by diplomacy what she was incapable of accomplishing by force.

Things are not going well for Elizabeth — her forces have been defeated in Scotland, the cracks are beginning to show in her relationship with Dudley, and now she must face an icy Parliament and ask them to pass the Act of Uniformity. In the film, it seems to be a combination of this Act with the tenets of the Act of Supremacy, which revived Henry VIII's declaration of the monarch as the supreme governor of the church in England. The Act of Uniformity established the official order of worship (as based on the *Book of Common Prayer*), and it also provided an infrastructure for enforcing doctrinal and liturgical conformity. While the film shows the Catholics firmly against the Act and the Protestants unanimously in favor of it, in actuality many of the more radical Protestants felt it was far too moderate and that more drastic measures were needed. Elizabeth, fresh out of bed and looking disheveled and young, practices different deliveries of the lines she plans to speak before Parliament. In her white chemise, like a lamb to the slaughter, she makes a sharp contrast with the intercut scenes of the foreboding, black-clad bishops who await her in the Parliament chamber. By the time she arrives in the chamber, she's dressed in vibrant scarlet — the Elizabethan equivalent of a power tie for an important board meeting. Thus attired and seated on her throne, Elizabeth listens to the din before finally trying to yell above it. Realizing this will get her nowhere, she resorts to her feminine wiles. When a bishop cries, "You force us to relinquish allegiance to the Holy Father," Elizabeth smiles and replies, "How can I *force* you, Your Grace? I am a *woman*." It soon seems that the tide is turning; with her flirtatious manner, Elizabeth first entices the entirely male crowd to laughter and finally to listen to her, as Walsingham looks on approvingly and Norfolk glares as if he cannot believe his eyes. She whips out her line about windows and men's souls, to which one of the bishops replies that this is heresy. Elizabeth counters with, "It is common sense, which is a most English virtue." She eventually moves on to the question of her marriage, deftly avoiding any kind of assurances. She finishes strong, giving them a sense of empowerment and at the same time laying responsibility at their door by saying, "In your hands, upon this moment, lies the future happiness of my people and the peace of this realm."

This scene represents a turning point in the characterization of Elizabeth in this film. Up until this point, she has been an uncertain young girl; she makes her first tentative steps as monarch when she faces down a contentious Parliament, seemingly alone. It also shows the tools this burgeoning queen will use to rule — her flirtatious wit, self-deprecation about her sex, coupled with an earnestness and the repetition that all she does, she does for the good of her people. The Act passes by a narrow margin, but Elizabeth has only *seemed* alone in her struggle. Walsingham has locked Bishop Gardiner, along with the other most vocal dissenters, in the basement until the vote has passed.

The Duke of Anjou (Vincent Cassel) duly arrives to pay court to Elizabeth, and from his first moments onscreen, it's obvious that he and Elizabeth will not connect — though not unattractive, he's a buffoon, and a crass one. Arriving disguised as a musician, he reveals himself, giggling like a girl, and commences to grab the Queen and kiss her. She gives him an unenthusiastic slap, making him giggle all the more, and he whispers into her ear in French about the things he plans to do to her when he gets her alone, while the exasperated French ambassador rolls his eyes. Elizabeth is partly astonished and even more amused; she cannot take this man seriously and neither can the audience — Anjou is played almost entirely for comic effect. He also serves to underscore how unappealing Elizabeth's "acceptable" suitors could be, thus providing a justification for solace sought in the arms of men such as Dudley. Elizabeth flaunts Dudley before the Duke, lying with him in her boat during a nighttime masque on the river, while Anjou shares another boat with the ambassador and watches from afar. Despite his silliness, Anjou does manage to illustrate the danger of Elizabeth's current course of action when he says, "Her life depends on the feelings of *my* heart, no?"

Dudley has been asking Elizabeth to marry him, unwisely teasing about it to the Spanish ambassador, when an assassination attempt is made on Elizabeth's life. Arrows shoot through the darkness, killing one of her guards and pinning her to the pillows by embedding themselves in the gauze that has surrounded her and Dudley (yet another curtain through which the voyeur watches her private world. Elizabeth's illusion of privacy and safety is as ephemeral as these gauzy curtains). In the chaos that follows, Cecil orders that no one be allowed access to the Queen, including Dudley, which angers him enough to hear out the Spanish ambassador (a slick and menacing James Frain) when he assures Dudley that, if he were to convert, he would find many new and powerful friends to help him "keep" his queen. For the moment Dudley is not willing to listen, but the impression is that if he is pushed much further, things may change.

Even as Elizabeth's ladies try to calm her and remove her blood-stained clothing, Cecil speaks to her of marriage, since it has just been illustrated how pressing the point is. Elizabeth, angry, says imperiously, "Do not presume to know the secrets of my heart." It's Cecil's turn to be angry as he replies, "Secrets, madam? You have no secrets! The world knows that Lord Robert visits your chambers at night and that you ... *fornicate* with him. It's even said that you already carry his child!" Elizabeth seems stunned by this, but it's a wonder how she could be — it's impossible for her to be unaware that she is constantly and closely observed. Neither she nor Dudley have seemed to care. She then makes a strangely contradictory statement, "I live my life in the open! I am surrounded by people! I do not understand how so bad a judgment has been formed of me." This illustrates the theme, glimpsed earlier in the Dudley/Elizabeth consummation scene, that often appears in film adaptations of the lives of royalty — the total lack of privacy that accompanies their position. How Elizabeth can claim not to understand why people have judged her when she knows that her every action has been laid out upon the public stage for just that purpose is illogical, and it is one of the dangers of explicitly showing a physical consummation of Elizabeth's relationship with one of her favorites, as this film does. Cecil has one more devastating blow to deliver: "You *cannot* marry Lord Robert," he says, oddly with tears in his eyes, "He is already married." At this Elizabeth is silent, sinking into her chair, shocked, as her ladies also exchange astonished looks. This and subsequent scenes make a point of presenting Elizabeth and the entire court as unaware that Dudley was married. This is a divergence from the historical record — Elizabeth knew of Dudley's first marriage, to Amy Robsart, as did everyone else. The historical Elizabeth *was* unaware of his second marriage to Lettice Knollys, at least initially. This film chooses to present Elizabeth as an innocent, so making her ignorant of Dudley's marriage furthers the plot by providing justification for her anger at his betrayal. Making the wife Robsart rather than Knollys is yet another instance of Kapur's telescoping of events.

The Duke of Anjou, it seems, may be back in the running, but when Elizabeth unexpectedly visits him in his apartments, he shows himself to be even more unsuitable than one could have imagined. Elizabeth steps gingerly through a scene that warrants the term bacchanalia — the wine flows freely, half-dressed men and women are everywhere, leading up to a dais where high-pitched laughter can be heard from a woman's silhouette behind the (yet again) transparent curtain. When Elizabeth is recognized, the music stops, and the "woman" turns around, revealing "herself" to be Anjou, who has been frolicking in bed with two young boys. The two similarly attired royals face each other, a woman and a caricature of a woman. Fanning himself, he asks imperiously, "What? What? Do you see something ... strange?" Elizabeth replies, deadpan, "You are wearing a dress, Your Grace."

Anjou is unconcerned, "Yes, yes, I am wearing a dress, like this, like my mother ... and you. But I only wear a dress like this when I'm alone. In private, with my friends." Of course, there is no privacy, and the overall effect is comic, a parody of what goes on behind Elizabeth's similarly transparently curtained bed. She tries to hide her smile while speaking about the agony of having to make the decision to "sacrifice my own happiness for that of my people" and refuse his suit. Back in her throne room, she laughs almost hysterically before calling out Lord Robert to dance the Volta with her. Unlike the first scene with this dance, this time around the feel is completely different — combative. When Dudley makes the mistake of cajoling, "You are still my Elizabeth," she shoves him away, awkwardly and abruptly ending the dance, and says loudly enough for the entire court to hear, "I am *not* your Elizabeth. I am no man's Elizabeth. If you think to rule here, you are mistaken. I will have one mistress here, and no master!" She leaves Dudley with tears in his eyes, and it comes as no surprise when he accepts the Spanish ambassador's Faustian bargain.

Unlike other portrayals of Dudley, Fiennes's version is more the smoldering romantic than the grasping politician. Despite what has been said of him by others in the film, he seems to have no ambitions for himself or for power; his main motivating factor in everything is his feeling for Elizabeth. His feelings are the weakness through which he is manipulated, not his ambition. With tears in his eyes, he tells the Spanish ambassador, "I have no need for her love. Have I not suffered enough already for loving her and showing it? Such love is hateful, tears the soul apart." The Spanish ambassador warns Dudley that Elizabeth will soon be dead if Dudley does not unite with Spanish interests to protect her, and it is Dudley's desire to save his love that ironically leads him to betray her.

Yet another attempt is made on Elizabeth's life, this time through the gift of a poisoned dress. This will not stand, something must be done, so to Scotland Walsingham goes to "reason" with Mary of Guise. Mary and Walsingham are of a kind — as she says to him over a candlelight dinner, "I hear you are ... a creature of the world. Like me," while playing suggestively with her knife. These are two feral, sensual creatures, and watching them interact fascinates while at the same time provokes a need to shower; though Mary seems the lesser of the two, both she and Walsingham are polluted souls. Walsingham pretends disloyalty to lower Mary's guard, but one of the statements he makes of his queen is telling because it contains the germ of truth: "Her Majesty rules with the heart, not the head." Mary seems almost sympathetic as she states, "I understand. It is hard for a woman to forget her heart." The statement that Elizabeth rules with her heart is interesting because it is an appraisal most often applied instead to her rival and Mary of Guise's daughter, Mary, Queen of Scots. This film version of Elizabeth has much in common with the Scottish Queen — at times her characterization feels more like Mary Stuart than it does Elizabeth Tudor. She is passionate and reckless, naïve and uncertain of herself, set about and manipulated by the powerful male forces at her court, personified by the Duke of Norfolk. As noted earlier, it is up to Dudley to remind her of who she is, a parallel task often assigned to the Earl of Bothwell for Mary Stuart in film adaptations of that queen's life. Also like Mary Stuart, at least in the beginning, Elizabeth is portrayed as an innocent. That this characterization is not rendered problematic is due to a single factor — Mary Stuart does not appear in this adaptation of Elizabeth's life, so there is no danger of comparison. Mary is only mentioned in passing; it is said the Duke of Norfolk means to marry her and secure the throne for himself through her — but she is not portrayed as the ever-present threat which she appears in other films. As has been seen when Elizabeth addresses Parliament, she is evolving, and her characterization moves away from that traditionally associated with Mary Stuart as she does so. Even in this film's divergent interpretation of her, Elizabeth retains one of her defining traits: she learns from the situations that occur in her life, and she adapts herself accordingly. She does not continue to make the same mistakes, as does her unfortunate Scottish cousin.

The lesson she learns in this case, and under Walsingham's tutelage, is prevarication and ruthlessness. Rather than allow her a natural death of dropsy, this film has Mary of Guise seduced and murdered by the cold-blooded Walsingham. It's unclear whether he has done this on his own initiative or at Elizabeth's behest — regardless, publicly she disassociates herself from this "bloody act." It is certain, however, that the path she has chosen is not one of conciliation. Cecil represents this policy: safety through marriage, security through appeasement. As Elizabeth says to him, "Your policies would make England nothing but either part of France or Spain." To show that the training wheels have come off, Elizabeth forces Cecil into retirement, with the bestowal of the title of Baron Burghley as his gold watch. "From this moment," she states, "I am going to follow my own opinion." He takes his dismissal graciously, though he does point out that Elizabeth is "only a woman." Since Tilbury does not appear in this film, this opportunity is chosen for Elizabeth to snap, "I may be a woman, but if I choose I have the heart of a man. I am my father's daughter. I am not afraid of anything."

The downplaying of Elizabeth's relationship with Cecil in this film is one of its wider divergences from historical fact, and something is lost in translation. Elizabeth never forced Cecil into retirement; he quite literally dropped in the traces. They had a close and enduring relationship, and though they disagreed on certain points and he could find her vacillations apoplectically infuriating, they had an extremely successful working partnership. What is more, Elizabeth *liked* Cecil, which was not a sentiment she expressed towards Walsingham. Walsingham and Cecil also had a productive working partnership — they were certainly successful in aiding each other to bring about the downfall of the Queen of Scots. These two men worked together toward common goals. However, this film is all about dichotomy, so Hirst and Kapur need a Cecil that can be contrasted with the Walsingham they have created. Cecil is thus reduced to a symbol — he represents appeasement — and Walsingham is his polar opposite. Cecil is the Chamberlain to Walsingham's Churchill.

Instead of conciliation, Elizabeth has chosen a more forceful and darker path, the one represented by Walsingham. His methods are unsavory, but they yield results, and he counsels Elizabeth, "A prince should never shrink from being blamed for acts of ruthlessness required for safeguarding the state and their own person. You must take these things so much to heart that you do not fear to strike even at the very nearest that you have." In light of the historical Elizabeth's almost compulsive aversion to shouldering the blame for merciless acts (e.g., the execution of Mary, Queen of Scots), statements such as these illustrate exactly how far this characterization of Elizabeth diverges. Elizabeth started out as light and innocence, but these are two qualities she rapidly loses in her evolution into effective ruler. With the help of Walsingham's spies, the Duke of Norfolk is entrapped into implicating himself in a conspiracy to kill Elizabeth and place himself (as Mary, Queen of Scots' consort) on the throne of England. The lighting grows dark as the plotting grows even darker. One by one, the conspirators are either arrested or murdered by Walsingham's men. Scenes of the plotters being killed are juxtaposed with that of Elizabeth praying and reading her Bible. The last to be apprehended is the Duke of Norfolk, who seems almost a substitute Mary Stuart himself when he pulls the jurisdiction card, "I must do nothing by your orders. I am Norfolk!" Walsingham replies, "You *were* Norfolk. The dead have no titles. You had not the courage to be loyal, only the conviction of your own vanity." This, again, sounds like Mary Stuart, as does Norfolk when he plays his final card: "Make me a martyr, and they will always remember." Mary Stuart may not appear in this film, but her essence is there.

There is one more implicated in the plot with whom Elizabeth has to deal — Dudley. He sits by the fire, tears in his eyes, numb and bereft. It's never revealed what part he has played in the conspiracy, but he is full of self-pity: "It is no easy thing to be loved by the Queen. It would corrupt the soul of any man." He then begs Elizabeth to kill him, but she refuses. Though Walsingham advises she graciously acquiesce to Dudley's request, Elizabeth states that he shall be kept alive "to always remind me of how close I came to danger." The film's score as she deals with this last, great blow to her innocence is reminiscent of the denouement of a tragic opera, and as it fades out, Elizabeth is shown in a chapel, standing in front of a statue of the Virgin Mary. The film has been moving towards this point all along, the complete identification of Elizabeth with the Holy Virgin — in essence, simply replacing one Virgin with another as an object of veneration for the English people. At the beginning of the film, Mary Tudor begged Elizabeth not to "take away from the people the consolation of the Blessed Virgin, their Holy Mother," and in a way, Elizabeth has not. She has simply reassigned this role to herself; they still have a maternal and virgin figure to worship. Strangely, it is the unreligious Walsingham who reinforces for Elizabeth what she must do, telling her that she must be made of stone "to reign supreme. All men need something greater than themselves to look up to and worship. They must be able to touch the divine, here on earth." The camera continually cuts from the face of the statue to that of Elizabeth, associating the two, as she says, "She held such power over men's hearts. They *died* for her." Walsingham sums it up for the viewer with, "They have found nothing to replace her." The implication is clear: give them another Holy Virgin in the form of their queen, and they will be loyal — even unto death.

From the face of the statue the camera cuts to Elizabeth's face, her stare hollow, almost unearthly in the eerie lighting, as Kat Ashley hacks off her hair. Elizabeth's relationship with Ashley as portrayed in this film, though not examined in any depth, seems to be one of loyalty and friendship. Ashley is characterized as much younger than the historical person, of an age with Elizabeth. Elizabeth looks to her, and unlike most other portrayals of Elizabeth's ladies, though Kat is young and attractive, she is not a rival. Ashley cries over the loss of Elizabeth's hair, and Elizabeth slowly spreads the cut strands on her lap as she relives her filmed life in flashback, lingering over the scene at the beginning of the film where she danced with Dudley, illustrating that this has been the defining point of her life, and one that is now to be lost in her transformation into icon. It's reminiscent of similar scenes in other Elizabeth offerings (e.g., *Elizabeth I* and *Elizabeth I: The Virgin Queen*) where Elizabeth reviews her life in flashback form immediately before dying. Kapur uses it in similar vein to illustrate that Elizabeth the woman is about to die in order to be reborn as Elizabeth the myth. She's allowed one last Fat Tuesday indulgence in sensuality before an everlasting Lent — in her white shift, with her head now shorn, she bears a strong resemblance to the female martyr portrayed at the beginning of the film, bringing things full circle as she says, "Kat, I have become a virgin." Elizabeth is about to martyr herself for her cause: her people. In another one of Kapur's blinding transitions, a backlit Elizabeth emerges before the court. Dressed in silvery white, she has become the icon — she now wears the stark-white make-up, a frizzed red wig, and the elaborate court dress. As the court falls to its knees, Elizabeth pronounces, "Observe, Lord Burghley. I am married ... to England." She proceeds through the crowd, one courtier kissing the hem of her gown in veneration, to her throne, where she turns around and the camera frames her as an iconic portrait, just as it did earlier in the coronation scene. Only now there is no Duke of Norfolk to overshadow her, no power behind the throne. There is only the divine Elizabeth.

The closing titles tell the viewer that Elizabeth reigned another 40 years, with Walsingham remaining her most trusted adviser. She never married. Apparently, she also "never saw Dudley in private again," but on her deathbed "she was said to have whispered his name." The film leaves the viewer with the knowledge that, by the time of her death, "England was the richest and most powerful country in Europe." In keeping with the film's creative aesthetic, with the exception of the fact that Elizabeth never married, not a single word of this pseudo-historical afterword is a literal truth.

Various commentaries on this film have mentioned its episodic, artistic presentation, its "painterly feel,"[36] one even defining it as "filmic pointillism."[37] Kapur's portrait of Elizabeth begins as one thing, finishes as another, and there are glimpses of transitional points in between. She shares this with Michael Corleone, though his transformation was more smoothly marked, and as a result *Elizabeth*'s connections with *The Godfather* (1972) have received significant print space, from comments by those involved with the film to the reviews. In his article, "The Godmother," Richard Alleva posits, "I don't know which historians director Shekhar Kapur and writer Michael Hirst consulted while making *Elizabeth*, but it's quite clear that they must have seen *The Godfather* at least forty-seven times."[38] He goes on to lay out the parallels between Elizabeth and Michael Corleone, and they are myriad: both live in a kind of innocence until they have power thrust upon them and are set about by dangerous enemies; both are unable to trust anyone, including their own friends and relatives; and both ultimately end up relying on those counselors who are the most ruthless to help them completely annihilate their enemies and consolidate their power. Alleva likens Elizabeth's ousting of Burghley in favor of Walsingham to Tom Hagen's dismissal because he is not a "wartime *consigliere*." He also offers Elizabeth's granting of mercy to Dudley as the equivalent of Corleone sparing (at least initially) his burdensome and disloyal brother Fredo. Another parallel Alleva fails to mention is that, when Elizabeth finally strikes, the scenes in the film of her enemies being murdered, juxtaposed as they are with glimpses of Elizabeth praying in her chapel, are strongly reminiscent of the scene of Corleone renouncing Satan in church intercut with those of his mafia minions gunning down his enemies. Alleva draws the line at what both characters finally become: Corleone is a monster, Elizabeth is a martyr. Even though the two characters' journeys leave them at different destinations, both still experience their triumphs (i.e., the realization of their plays for power) as "spiritual catastrophes."

Despite its romantic notions and the religious statements, *Elizabeth* is all about power: those who have it, those who want it, what a ruler must sacrifice to hold on to it. Shekhar Kapur has stated explicitly how his film should be viewed:

> The central focus in Elizabeth was Power. The PLOT conflict was between Elizabeth and her Catholic detractors, in their struggle for Power. The PSYCHOLOGICAL conflict was between Elizabeth's desire be in love and therefore retain innocence, as against the need to have power to survive, and therefore to be ruthless. The MYTHIC conflict was about whether it was possible to be Divine and Human at the same time. Focusing on interpretations of Virginity as a fact, or as a political/mythic statement. Virginity was explored not only as a political need, but as a Mythic idea of Elizabeth's desire to be (perhaps) a representation of the Virgin Mary.[39]

Kapur does manage to answer these questions with what he portrays in the film: it is not possible to "retain innocence" and still have the power to survive; ruthlessness triumphs. It is not possible to be divine and human at the same time; humanity is subsumed beneath the mantle of icon. In the film, Elizabeth's nonexistent virginity is obviously not a fact (as evidenced by the portrayal of her physical relationship with Dudley), but rather a component of a conscious, adopted mythic image constructed to further political goals. In this, as has been noted by various commentaries on the film, Kapur appeals to the current fascination with the makeover — the exploration, as one commentator put it, of "clothing's transformative possibilities and its connections with identity."[40] If one's identity is primarily reactive — defined by the perceptions of others (i.e., "If people treated me differently, I'd *be* different"), and these judgments are based on outward appearance, then by changing the outward appearance, the identity can also be changed, molded into something else. Unlike current makeover shows, Elizabeth's goal with her transformation is not to bring herself more in line with an accepted ideal of beauty, but with an accepted ideal of the divine. Nowhere is this better illustrated than the last scene in this film, where Elizabeth, by cutting her hair and changing her clothes and make-up, literally transforms herself, not into *someone* else, but into *something* else. Her makeover has the desired effect — her people then immediately view her with a sense of awe and reverence, almost worship. The thick make-up also symbolically covers with the mantle of saint what Elizabeth has become on the inside: ruthless and uncompromising in her desire to retain her power. Portraying the historical Elizabeth in this way, however, is extremely deceptive. Elizabeth's iconic image was, in part, a testament to her obsession with clothing and its accompanying perception, but it did not occur overnight, and the motivation behind it was different. The historical Elizabeth was attempting to hide her advancing age; it was not a case of the still-young queen making a conscious decision to put on a Kabuki mask and give her people a virgin to worship.

Since Kapur is of Indian extraction, it comes as no surprise that this film exhibits some almost Bollywood-like elements — chief amongst them its sense of color and motion. Nowhere is this sense of motion more apparent than in Elizabeth herself. This film, as evidenced by the large amount of attention it has drawn, is unique in the Elizabethan canon for a number of reasons, but perhaps never more so than because it's the first film to show an evolving Elizabeth. Regardless of the characterization choices made, in all the films up until this point, Elizabeth does not *change*. She begins as one thing (whether it be the "for God and country" Robson, the glittering husk Davis, or the calculating Jackson) and she remains constant throughout the film. Kapur's Elizabeth exhibits a sense of motion when she moves from the initial point on the characterization continuum, carefree young girl, to her final destination as mythic icon. What makes this even more interesting is that, as will be seen in the sequel, *Elizabeth: The Golden Age*, she may appear to be a finished product at the end of this film, but that static image is anything but, even to the film's director. As is apparent from the first scene of *The Golden Age*, continuity is not an issue that must needs be considered — iconic Elizabeth can very easily be thrown out the window, allowing Kapur to backtrack to a slightly less mythic version and make the trek all over again, though with less sure steps this time.

ELIZABETH: THE GOLDEN AGE (2007)

Elizabeth: The Golden Age does not take up where its predecessor left off (though given the telescoping of events, it is difficult to tell exactly where that was); it begins in 1585, almost 30 years into Elizabeth's reign. The Armada is still three years off, but Philip and his empire are foremost in Elizabethan politics. The film takes a page from *Five Over England*'s book when it announces that "Philip of Spain ... has plunged Europe into Holy War. Only England stands against him," an England ruled by the Protestant Queen, Elizabeth. To show that religion as a representation of the pursuit of power will yet again be a primary theme, scenes of soldiers, cardinals in vibrant red ranged behind Philip, ships on fire, and Elizabeth herself are all framed out as stained glass cathedral windows, and the "t" of Elizabeth's name in the title is a cross. The film is also similar in its portrayal of Catholics as the villains of the piece — like his deceased wife, Mary, in the previous film, Philip's first appearance is in the dark, gloomy, claustrophobic confines of his palace, represented again by Gothic stone rather than period architecture. He stares fixedly at a single sputtering candle, representative of Elizabeth and, by extension, gallant little England, muttering to himself as black-clad monks chant ominously.

Philip, as Elizabeth's brother-in-law turned arch-nemesis, is played by Jordi Molla in an interesting bit of characterization. From the waist up, he has "a handsome authority,"[41] but when the camera pans out, he's revealed to be an odd little man who, despite his mincing walk on bowed stick-legs, still manages to exude menace rather than provoke pity. One reviewer called him "a sniveling poster boy for short man's disease," and another noted how he and the other Spaniards in the film "are presented with a shrouded and sinister gorgeousness, like figures from Velasquez."[42]

Taking a page from Elizabethan authors and poets, this film is chock full of allegory — there is Elizabeth herself, and then there are the multiple representations of Elizabeth that pervade this film. In a way, she is made to be ubiquitous; even when Elizabeth is not present in a scene, her representations almost always are. In various shortened and foreign-language forms, these representations even share Elizabeth's name. The first, and perhaps strangest, of these allegorical Elizabeths is Philip II's daughter, Isabel. Though the historical Infanta Isabella Clara Eugenia was close to 20 years old by 1585, the film's Isabel is a child. Throughout the film she is a silent symbol; she carries a red-headed doll, dressed in royal gowns, yet another version of Elizabeth. To this silent child and her doll, Philip often addresses what would otherwise be internal monologues. In Spanish, he tells her, "England is enslaved to the Devil. We must set her free," before walking with the child out into the blinding sunlight, a transition familiar from *Elizabeth*. When the vista before them fades back in, Philip and his daughter stand on a balcony overlooking a sea of chanting Catholic faces bearing crosses — a silent Elizabeth forced by Philip to quietly take stock of the vastness of her Catholic enemies.

Meanwhile, the real Elizabeth is in council with her advisers, being warned of the familiar threat of Catholic assassins and Mary Stuart. Unlike the previous film, Walsingham now sits at the council table; he's not only a member, but obviously its driving force. He and all the other black-clad councilors make a noticeable contrast to Elizabeth, dressed in vibrant rust-red. This is the single time she appears in this color in the film — its color palette is widely divergent from that of the previous film. Whereas *Elizabeth* focused on whites and reds, innocence and passion/blood/power; *The Golden Age* opts for cooler tones — various shades of blue and purple predominate, with an occasional splash of gold to represent Elizabeth's power.

While Elizabeth was portrayed at the end of the previous film as an icon, a static image fixed in stone, there is no continuity in this film with that portrayal. In the first scene, though she now wears a wig, her make-up is still naturalistic and her clothing the softened "theatrical" style rather than elaborate court dress. She may not be dressed as the icon, but Elizabeth has come into her own as a ruler. She displays confidence before her council; she's much more certain of herself, and they cannot goad or bully her into acting precipitously as did the Duke of Norfolk in the earlier film. She is also merciful, telling them that "fear creates fear ... I will not punish my people for their beliefs, only their deeds." Lines like these set Elizabeth up as a counterpoint to the intolerance of Philip — as in the previous film, Catholics are almost always shown going about their nefarious business in dark corners while Elizabeth is bathed in light. In one instance, she even goes so far as to order the Spanish ambassador back to the darkness of his "rat hole."

Elizabeth takes a boat ride to her chapel, which gives Walsingham a chance to sing Burghley's old refrain about her unmarried state, but also to set up her relationship with another metaphorical Elizabeth — Elizabeth "Bess" Throckmorton. Bess, played by buxom blond Abbie Cornish, can be seen to represent Elizabeth's "body natural" — her womanhood and sensuality, as well as her "feminine weakness" — and in many scenes in the film, she weirdly serves as a surrogate to allow expression for this facet of Elizabeth's personality. As is indicative of this, she and Elizabeth discuss their ideal men, with Elizabeth's defining criterion being honesty. Bess's connection with Elizabeth comes not only through her name and position as favorite, but is also denoted by her costuming. In almost every scene in the film, she wears the same color as her royal mistress, although usually in a slightly lighter, more muted shade. Thus, she is literally a washed-out shadow of the real thing. This Bess Throckmorton is the same character (Beth Throgmorton) which appeared in *The Virgin Queen*, played by Joan Collins. However, the relationship here diverges greatly from that characterization. While Collins's Beth was always a rival, this Bess enjoys friendship and intimacy with the Queen, though she will eventually go the way of almost all other women who surround Elizabeth and dovetail with previous characterizations as a competitor for the attentions of a male love interest.

Since Bess is to be the rival, a man is needed to serve as the object of rivalry. Enter Clive Owen as the testosterone-soaked and innuendo-laden Walter Raleigh. As Elizabeth walks underneath her canopy of state, dressed in vibrant gold with Bess in a slightly lighter yellow shade behind, Raleigh arrives out of nowhere to toss his cloak underneath her feet. Elizabeth is obviously interested, so she sends her surrogate to find out about the man who interests her sensual side while she examines the illustrated list of suitors appropriate for her queenly aspect. Their portraits are paraded in front of her while their praises are sung and the political advantages of each match are propounded. She asks Walsingham how much longer he thinks she can play this game, and he replies that "virginity is an asset that holds its value." As in the previous film, Elizabeth's virginity is not a literal fact but rather a political playing card.

After these cardboard cutout suitors, Raleigh appears before the Queen in all his three-dimensional masculinity. His audience with Elizabeth borders on the unintentionally comedic; Owen does his best to charge the exchange with sexual undertones through his demeanor and line delivery, but the dialogue does not lend itself to double-entendres. Raleigh has just returned from the New World where he "*claimed* the *fertile* coast in your name and called it Virginia," and he produces a potato and insinuates, "You *eat* it. Very *nourishing*. And tobacco, very ... *stimulating*." Modern cigarette commercials notwithstanding, raw tobacco is less than sexy, and there's nothing erotic about a potato. Though still, as one reviewer noted "the potato was good; best performance by a potato I have seen in a long while."[43] Perhaps if Raleigh had produced a large cucumber, the atmosphere might have been different, but as it is, the entire exchange comes off as a bit ridiculous. It does allow the Spanish ambassador a chance to accuse Raleigh of piracy, and this is how his characterization comes across in this film — as a romanticized pirate. Richard Todd's Raleigh was a man's man and a soldier, and Owen's Raleigh follows a similar characterization, although more emphasis is placed upon his status as adventurer and harasser of the Spanish, and he's emphatically rougher around the edges. Raleigh's clothing is a bit unkempt, his five o'clock shadow perpetual, and his love for the sea, discovery, and adventure continually expressed. Sailors are often used to represent the freedom to be found in the roving life of the sea, and Raleigh serves that purpose in this film — he represents romance, adventure, and freedom beyond the confines of the court. As in Todd's characterization, he also represents honesty — a straightforward man willing to tell Elizabeth what he really thinks, a refreshing presence in a court full of simpering flatterers.

Though *Elizabeth* was one of the few films to diverge from this trope, in *The Golden Age* the mirror makes its triumphant return as a representation of encroaching age. As Bess slowly removes her wig to reveal the Elizabethan equivalent of a do-rag, Elizabeth examines herself sadly in the mirror and bemoans, "More lines on my face. Where did they come from?" even though Blanchett still looks young and attractive. At this point in the historical timeline, the real Elizabeth would have been in her fifties, and Blanchett's face simply cannot convince. Elizabeth's concern over her appearance is understandable though, for not only is the dashing Raleigh about, but from her list of suitors, Erik of Sweden has come to call. The historical Erik XIV was born in 1533, so was of an exact age with Elizabeth — both would have been in their early fifties according to the film's timeline. Instead, the film presents a 30-something Elizabeth who is just beginning to notice smile lines, and a teenaged and painfully awkward Erik. His interactions with Elizabeth showcase the formality and artificiality of the royal courtship game, played out on the world stage — like a desperate-to-please child, he continually spouts praises to Elizabeth's beauty and charm in his broken English. She makes several attempts to put him more at ease, engage him on a more personal level, telling him, "I pretend there's a pane of glass between me and them. They can see me but they cannot touch me. You should try it." He has nothing to say in reply to this; with the language barrier, he seems not to even understand. Elizabeth seeks intellectual engagement; she *needs* it, but she cannot find it in this child. Realizing this, she treats him like the boy he is, but kindly, lapsing into his native tongue to basically send him off to bed. She shows her softness by warning Walsingham, "I don't want him hurt by your schemes."

The transformative properties of clothing: Elizabeth (Cate Blanchett) in her queenly persona as divine Madonna in *Elizabeth: The Golden Age.* (Studio Canal/Working Title/The Kobal Collection)

Bess, meanwhile, has been working tirelessly on Elizabeth's behalf; she has questioned Raleigh and decided to help him with the Queen. She tells him the way to win the Queen's favor is to speak as plainly as possible, with no artifice, for "all men flatter the Queen in hope of advancement — pay her the compliment of truth." She shares with him the secret of being Elizabeth's ideal man: honesty. When Raleigh discovers Bess's name, he muses, "A second Elizabeth," cementing her status as surrogate for the real thing.

The historical Elizabeth possessed a vast wardrobe and employed it as a tool — she was known for using her mode of dress to mold herself for different audiences (e.g., dressing in the French style for a meeting with the French ambassador). For this reason, scenes of dressing and undressing often feature in Elizabeth films to denote Elizabeth putting on or taking off certain responsibilities or aspects of her personality. In a single dressing scene, this film melds the importance of clothing as outward expression with the metaphor of multiple Elizabeths. Elizabeth, in only her white corset and chemise, a blank slate, stands in what is presumably her wardrobe — a large stone space, like all the spaces in these two films. She's surrounded by dozens of headless mannequins, all of which wear her dresses and are shrouded by a single layer of transparent gauze. She surveys this silent audience, representative of all the different Elizabeths she can elect to become based on how she chooses to mold her appearance, before pointing at one and commanding, "Blue."

Elizabeth is careful in her dressing for a reason — she has a date; Raleigh is scheduled for an audience with her. By this point, their attraction is unmistakable, and as Raleigh describes discovery of the New World to her, she listens, enthralled. He speaks of "pure, naked, fragile hope" and slowly moves towards her, everything but his face in soft focus and the music building to crescendo as he finishes, "Land, life, adventure, resurrection ... out of the vast unknown, out of the immensity, into new life." If Elizabeth has martyred her sensuality at the end of the previous film, then Raleigh has resurrected it — the entire scene is strongly evocative of aural sex; when a courtier risks *auris interruptus* by attempting to engage Elizabeth's attention, she ferociously dismisses him so the crescendo can finish building. Elizabeth describes Raleigh's oceans as "a kind of eternity," and adds that "such great spaces make us ... small." When Elizabeth intimates that she wishes to reward him, he asks that the mission be rewarded, not the man, for then she leaves him "free to like you in return," what he calls the "simple pleasure" of being liked for herself. At this he hits a nerve, and Elizabeth dismisses him with "now you grow dull."

Elizabeth may "like" Raleigh, but with the exception of Bess, no one at court is happy to see their queen so engaged. Since Raleigh represents freedom, he and Elizabeth are shown in the sunlight of an open field, breathlessly laughing as they ride together at breakneck speed, a trope which is also used in films as a substitute for sex, and certainly appears to this effect in multiple Elizabeth films. They return to a dour group of courtiers, with Walsingham the least pleased of the bunch. The court, clad in drab, stand like statues, silently watching with disapproval as Raleigh helps the Queen down from her horse. The political creature and the feminine one cannot, must not meld.

This film exhibits the same sense of voyeurism as did its predecessor, and it uses the same methods to accomplish it — high-angled God's-eye view shots or shots which start at a distance and pull in closely in roundabout manner, often combined with shooting through stonework or gauzy, transparent draperies. One such scene involves Elizabeth lounging in her huge candlelit bath, all alone except for her ever-present Bess, who stands behind her outside the tub, stroking her hair, her face, her shoulders. The scene is charged with homo-eroticism — Elizabeth wears nothing but a transparent wet chemise as her lady-in-waiting pets her and speaks in soft tones into her ear. As one review put it, "Bess holds the queenly hand, caresses the royal head and keeps the imperial body intimate company, suggesting that Elizabeth abandoned the metaphoric sword but not the chalice."[44] At the same time, however, the scene displays a strong sense of autoeroticism; since Bess represents Elizabeth's sensual side, it is almost as if Elizabeth touches herself. Their topic of discussion is, of course, Raleigh, since he's the cause of this morass of sexual frustration. Elizabeth is slightly unkind and not altogether correct when she warns Bess that "he likes you because he wants my favor. You do realize that?" In the metaphorical realm, Raleigh pursues Elizabeth's body natural in order to gain what he wants from the power her body politic possesses, but his pursuit of Bess is simply literal — he wants her, romantically and physically. In more gentle and wistful tone, Elizabeth goes on to tell Bess that she envies her, for "you are free to have what I cannot have. You're my adventurer."

While Elizabeth has been busy mooning over Raleigh, the ever-present Catholic threat has continued to draw closer. Philip has put in place a group of conspirators, led by "a Jesuit" who is never named in the film. Along with the Jesuit and Sir Anthony Babington, another of the conspirators is none other than Walsingham's brother. This film is not quite so heavy on the intrigue as was its predecessor — with so much going on in the romantic and symbolic realms, the conspiracy itself receives relatively short shrift. While in *Elizabeth* intrigues were fostered in dark palace hallways, close to the seat of power, this sequel chooses a dimly lit dye shop where dead deer hang from the ceiling and white cloth is turned red by dye that drips like blood. Hundreds of miles away yet still at the heart of this conspiracy is Mary Stuart, played with a thick Scottish brogue by Samantha Morton. With her ladies-in-waiting, she wiles away the hours of her house arrest by writing letters and scheming. She's often shown reflected in her mirror, which is partitioned into leaded panes, fracturing Mary's image just as she fractures the English people. Mirrors present a tool for seeing oneself (to Elizabeth they reflect her advancing age), but Mary is more often reflected to the camera in her mirror rather than looking into it to view herself— she does not see herself for what she truly is, though the viewer does. Mary is contemptuous of her royal cousin, asking her jailer, "They call her the Virgin Queen. Why is that, sir? Can it be that no man will have her?" Even after her laundress is caught smuggling out letters and her jailer warns her that everything she does will be monitored, everything she writes will be read *for her own protection*, still she does not learn her lesson.

Elizabeth, on the other hand, has learned — Walsingham has discovered the existence of the Armada and has informed her that there is a plot against her life. Elizabeth rails against the Spanish ambassador, "Tell Philip I fear neither his priests nor his armies!" The ambassador threatens her with a Spanish wind that will wipe England off the map — the Armada — but Elizabeth blasts him with "I, too, can command the wind, sir. I have a hurricane in me that will strip Spain bare if you dare to try me!" She dismisses the entire Spanish retinue from her court, and all that's needed is a single catalyst to set a war in motion. Elizabeth has shown bravado, but she is also afraid — she spends a great deal of this film exhibiting that duality: blustering in public and trembling in private. Raleigh is on hand to see the trembling and his knowledge of her weakness angers Elizabeth; she dismisses him with, "What are you looking at? Lower your eyes! I am the Queen! You are not my equal, sir, and you never will be." He may not be her equal in rank, but there is an intellectual equality between the two that draws her to Raleigh, and in this, at least, the characterization borders on something real.

In Spain, the Armada is almost complete — entire forests have been denuded to produce instead a forest of masts, and Philip and his crucifix-carrying retinue are shown in silhouette behind the sail of his flagship, also tattooed with a huge red cross. When he emerges, mumbling about England's destruction, a vista of ships stretch as far as the eye can see. The metaphorical Elizabeth, Infanta Isabel, is there with her Elizabeth doll to calmly and silently observe this multitude of ships as her father takes her hand and leads her off, just as he wishes to lead Elizabeth and the English people to the Catholic Church.

The real Elizabeth takes a moonlit boat ride through still waters to visit her astrologer, John Dee, to see what he can foretell for the future of her country. He tells her that the planets predict the rise of one great empire and the fall of another, but he cannot say which is which. Elizabeth should be able to guess from the context — at this point, though England had made tentative steps in the New World, it was not a great empire; this description obviously applies only to Spain. Elizabeth is completely uncertain, however, and what's more, in the midst of this crisis for her country, she's just as concerned about her private life and questions Dee about what's in store for her there. Dee looks not to the stars and planets for an answer, but to her face, pronouncing, "Wonderful. Such strength ... but you doubt yourself. Something has weakened you. There are hard days coming." The implication is that Dee's "something" is her love for Raleigh; it has weakened her, making her a less proficient ruler. She will need to control or excise it, for all her strength will be needed for the trials ahead.

Elizabeth finds it impossible to do this — she sits, again looking in her mirror with tears in her eyes, her wigs ranged behind her, her many disguises. Raleigh is slated to sail for the colonies, telling her that "there's nothing to keep me here." Elizabeth goes so far as to say that he's "needed here," before frantically pacing around and summarily making him captain of her personal guard and a knight in one fell, manic swoop. He says nothing, and Elizabeth's expressions are desperately uncertain as she tries to read in his face the emotions he will not express. He refuses to make eye contact, and when her frustration finally gets the better of her she resorts to fishing for flattery: "Am I so hideous you can't even look me in the face?" Raleigh has proved himself to be an honest man, and he will have none of her courtly games. He's even less tactful than Todd's Raleigh when he replies, "Why do you speak like a fool when you're anything but a fool?" Blanchett's Elizabeth is a far cry from Davis's, so instead of being angry, she's resigned, admitting that she's "a vain and foolish woman" and collapsing at the foot of her throne as she says with yearning that it's as if Raleigh comes from a different time and place, and she would follow him there if she could. The implication is that Raleigh is a modern construct — he embodies the freedom and adventure that a woman of Elizabeth's time but, more importantly, position could never hope to experience. She yearns for the postmodern feminist triad of a successful career, equality in love, and self-respect, but it is not possible for her. She knows which of these must be sacrificed.

Regardless of what he feels for the Queen, Raleigh is not averse to unbuckling his swash with her surrogate, Bess. In another instance of Elizabeth as allegory, the real Elizabeth stands naked in front of a floor-length mirror, looking at herself, while in a juxtaposed scene Raleigh slowly undresses her surrogate, Bess, and then makes love to her. Both scenes are firelit — Elizabeth by candlelight and Bess and Raleigh by a roaring fireplace, but Elizabeth's paltry lighting is blue, provoking a feeling of cold, whereas Bess enjoys the warmth of fire and passion. By cutting back and forth between the two scenes, Elizabeth's two sides — the cold loneliness of the ruler and the sensuality of the woman —

are emphasized. It has been noted that this scene also harkens back to the pervasive voyeurism of these two films; close-ups of Elizabeth's staring eyes intercut with scenes of the lovers make it seem almost as if she is watching them, making it "simultaneously sensual and voyeuristic."[45]

This same dynamic traverses even stranger territory in a scene where Elizabeth has Bess taking lessons on how to dance the Volta. Viewers of the previous film are already familiar with this particular dance and the connotations it holds for Elizabeth — she performed it with her lover, Robert Dudley. As Bess attempts the dance with an instructor, Elizabeth looks on, shouting instructions, "Let him throw you 'round. Be bold! You can trust him." Raleigh also looks on, with Elizabeth fawning all over him and flirting desperately but also combatively. His dissatisfaction at being forced to stay at court bubbles to the surface when he tells her, "You like your ladies to jump at your command," and Elizabeth replies, "To tell the truth, I'm very, very tired of always being in control." The control to which she is referring is control of herself— she wishes to let go and express herself physically to Raleigh as Bess has. Raleigh is not in the mood for romance; chafing at Elizabeth's power over him, he tells her pointedly, "Nonsense. You eat and drink control." As if to prove Raleigh's point, Elizabeth then shoves him towards Bess, commanding that the two dance the Volta together. She positions them like two uncomfortable marionettes, and the erotic atmosphere grows even stranger as Elizabeth stands behind Bess, holding her and stroking her, as she tells Raleigh in a sultry tone, "You hold her firmly. I don't want her dropped." She gives Bess a lingering kiss on the cheek, never taking her eyes from Raleigh, then takes to her throne to watch them dance. The camera pans almost 360 degrees, past Elizabeth's symbolically empty bed, as the love theme which represented Elizabeth and Dudley in the first film begins to play. There are juxtapositions of Raleigh dancing with Elizabeth watching and, even more oddly, with scenes of Elizabeth from the first film, but no Dudley. The intercutting of scenes is meant to give a sense of Elizabeth dancing with Raleigh — his face and body are the focus, as a stand-in Bess hardly registers — but the overall effect is discomfiting rather than romantic, and for viewers who have not seen the first film, probably confusing. Elizabeth personifies the film's voyeurism with her almost obsessive observation of Raleigh and Bess, and when Walsingham approaches Elizabeth through a side entrance, she waves him away with, "I want both of them left alone," her intensive focus never leaving the two dancers. Walsingham represents her duty, her body politic, and Elizabeth wants none of him since she's busy indulging her body natural; she enjoys through her surrogate what she cannot have with Raleigh — a chance to be together without interruption and enjoy a physical relationship.

As if to show how this fascination with Raleigh has allowed her femininity to weaken her, the plot immediately switches to the enemies who conspire to bring about her downfall. The Babington Plot has been set in motion; as Elizabeth's protector, Walsingham is the first to be targeted, a mission given to his own brother. The inclusion of Walsingham's brother as a member of the conspiracy is meant to show how the divide over religion has pitted brother against brother. As characterized in the previous film, Walsingham espouses no religion; he's simply a servant of a Protestant ruler. The Walsingham of *The Golden Age*, however, is a different animal from his previous incarnation. From bisexual ruthless assassin he has been transformed into a family man who makes it home in time for dinner with his loving wife and children. He also pursues Burghley's old priority: attempting to get the Queen married. It would be inaccurate to say he's gone soft — he still serves Elizabeth tirelessly and is not averse to torture (he's shown extracting information by use of an Iron Maiden-like device) — but Walsingham has lost his edge. He is older, weaker, and since Burghley does not appear in this film, Walsingham's characterization makes him seem almost a melding of Burghley's role as councilor with his previous role as spymaster. The latter role suffers for the transition. The Walsingham of the first film, who warned Elizabeth she must not be afraid to strike even those closest to her, spares his own brother — a man who participates not only in the conspiracy to kill the Queen, but attempts to kill Walsingham himself. Though he still warns Elizabeth against mercy in one instance, he counsels for it in another, and most tellingly, displays it himself.

Just how much Walsingham is slipping in his old age is shown by the fact that he's unable to prevent the conspirators from achieving their aim. Elizabeth makes her way to chapel, dressed (as she has yet to be previously in this film) like the icon — she wears an elaborate white dress with wired veil and the unnatural make-up. As she prays at the altar, Babington enters the chapel and yells, "Elizabeth! Whore!" She slowly turns to face him and the barrel of the gun he holds pointed at her. As she did at the closing of the previous film, she displays all the trappings of the martyr-saint as she opens her hands, palms upward, and waits for the fatal shot. It comes, and somehow it does not harm her. Perhaps she is divine after all. Babington looks astonished as he's seized. When the news that the Queen is unharmed is brought to Mary Stuart, she attempts to distance herself from her last great mistake: "Me? What has any of this to do with me?" she asks. Her jailor informs her, "That's the trouble with intrigues. So many secrets, you can never be sure who's on whose side until the game ends." As in *Mary of Scotland* and *Mary, Queen of Scots*, again Elizabeth and Mary's relationship is couched in terms of a high-stakes game where the winner takes all and the loser is utterly destroyed. When Mary realizes her letters have been intercepted and she will be tried for high treason, she again takes no responsibility for her actions — she begins screaming about the traitors who have brought her to this.

Mary *has* been betrayed, though she does not understand the true traitors — the plot was never meant to assassinate Elizabeth, only to implicate Mary in an attempt on her life. This is why Babington's gun was not loaded, and this was the Jesuit's charge from Philip all along. In this his plot was successful — with proof of Mary's guilt, Elizabeth has no choice but to execute her, providing Philip with the justification he needs to launch his Armada against England. His gambit has worked perfectly. In Spain, he asks his silent little Isabel how she would like to be Queen of England. Walsingham has been outmaneuvered; he does not foresee the conspiracy's true objective, and only discovers how great his mistake has been when he has already been checkmated. As he admits to Elizabeth, he has failed.

Elizabeth, as is often depicted in films about her life, is distraught at the thought of Mary's execution. She locks herself away, crying, with only Raleigh to observe. She looks to him for strength, but he tells her, "Only you know where your duty lies." This is refreshing, for in various versions of Elizabeth's life as well as every version of her cousin Mary's, male councilors are always on hand to define duty for their female rulers, who cannot see it through their emotional haze. Elizabeth reveals the extent of her fear when she replies, "Was it my father's duty to murder my mother? She was a queen. For a time." Elizabeth admits that she's always afraid, and Raleigh sums it up for the viewer in case the point has failed to come across: "Kill a queen and you make all queens mortal. We mortals have too many weaknesses. Feel too much. Hurt too much. All too soon we die." This is what Kapur's Elizabeth fears — not the wrath of God for murdering an anointed queen or guilt at killing her kin, but fear for her own pain and suffering, her own mortality. She hides behind the icon because stone cannot feel, and the divine cannot die. Raleigh gets even more maudlin when he tells her that despite all the pain, humans, unlike icons, have "the chance of love." Elizabeth asks him blankly, "Do we? I have given England my life. Must she also have my soul?" It must be Rhetorical Question Day. At this point in the film, Elizabeth is neither fully human nor fully divine, but already what is possible for Raleigh is not possible for her. She has no choice; her path is set, and she knows it.

Mary Stuart gets yet another romanticized death in this film — she is calm and sensually beautiful, shot in slow motion as she reveals her martyr's red, looks up from the block to forgive the executioner, readies herself for the blow. The slow motion of this scene is contrasted with juxtaposed scenes of Elizabeth in frantic motion, running through her palace screaming, "I want it stopped!" before she finally ends up collapsing in Raleigh's arms. Later, it is Elizabeth and Raleigh who sit by the fire while he tries to give her the strength she has lost, as well as pass on his "eat, drink and be merry" philosophy: "Why fear tomorrow if today is all we have?" he says to her, in one of many instances illustrating "the facile nature of the dialogue."[46] Elizabeth lets herself go as much as she dares, Raleigh admits he loves her, and they share a lingering kiss before she rests her head in his lap. As Ford and Mitchell note, it's a moment "a virgin queen might treasure,"[47] but the comfort of it is quickly overwhelmed by events that Elizabeth the ruler must confront.

Elizabeth's indulgence in her feminine side has gone far enough; it's time for action. The Armada is on its way, and as Walsingham explains, "We must prepare for the worst." Elizabeth stands on a floor which is a map of the world (a nod to the depiction of Elizabeth in the Ditchley Portrait) upon which golden models of ships and troops are ranged as she discusses the logistics of war with her councilors. As it becomes clear how insurmountable are her odds, she kneels under this heavy weight, clothed in regal purple and framed behind a large golden model of Philip's flagship. Her political life is in shambles; her personal life mirrors it. As Elizabeth starts up from her bed, alone and afraid, Raleigh and Bess repeat their wedding vows in voiceover — Bess is pregnant, and though she asks that Raleigh "do his duty and forget" her (in so doing evoking shades of Ingolby and Cynthia from *Fire Over England*), he chooses to wed her, for the only sacrifices in this film must be made by Elizabeth. Unlike in *Fire Over England*, this is not a case of drumming up patriotic fervor to present a united front and defeat a common enemy — it's all about Elizabeth sacrificing the human to become divine.

To show the irreparable rift this marriage has made in Bess's relationship with Elizabeth, a metaphorical tearing asunder of Elizabeth's personal and political halves, for the first time the two women are shown in different colors. Elizabeth wears her vibrant, regal purple; Bess is in pale, baby-nursery pink. Elizabeth is infuriated: "You dare to keep secrets from me? You ask my permission before you breathe!" and then in a retooling of the lapdog idiom Elizabeth used in both historical context and in other films (e.g., *The*

Virgin Queen; Elizabeth I) with her male courtiers, she screams, "My bitches wear my collars!" Not only is she screaming, but Elizabeth is also physically violent, striking poor, pregnant Bess. Even Walsingham tries to call her to heel, telling her it's time for mercy, but she will have none of it until Raleigh enters. He quietly chastises her with, "This is not the Queen I love and serve." Elizabeth has had more than she can bear; she has lost her friend and her love at once, and her much vaunted self-control as well. She orders Raleigh arrested and Bess banished from court.

Elizabeth has, in essence, banished her feminine side in preparation for meeting the Armada. Or perhaps she has not banished it so much as channeled it into a more useful form — she "sublimated her libidinal energies through court intrigue" in the first film, until in this one she finds "sweet relief by violently bringing the Spanish Empire to its knees."[48] She does order Raleigh's release since he's needed as a military man: "He is forgiven. As I, too, long to be forgiven." It works on a number of levels, whether it's Raleigh's forgiveness or God's for the execution of Mary or Elizabeth's for allowing her body natural to briefly overrule her body politic. Never one to be outshone, Kapur has Elizabeth not just in an armored breastplate for the famous Tilbury speech, but in a full suit of armor, with her hair down, an Amazon on her horse. More than one commentary on the film likened her to Joan d'Arc, but others were less awed, wryly noting that she looked more like C3P0 astride.

The weather threatens and the Spanish's candles to their Catholic statues are almost blown out by the winds of the English sea when Raleigh finally gets a chance to display his swashbuckling by single-handedly sailing his fireship into the Spanish fleet. As the Spanish ships burn, white horses jump overboard and are shown underwater, from below, as they swim away from the Spanish ships, hope abandoning the Spanish cause. Elizabeth watches from a high precipice, clad only in a billowing nightgown. The gale picks up, carrying the fire from ship to ship, and it's as if Elizabeth has commanded the wind — the hurricane with which she earlier threatened the Spanish ambassador has blown in to destroy the Armada. As she watches the ships burn, the scene cuts to Philip, mumbling his prayers in the darkness, lit only by a single candle, which is quickly snuffed by the wind Elizabeth has called to rage. Spanish soldiers and ships' bells sink slowly to the floor of the sea, the power of Spain, followed by the symbols of the Catholic faith: a rosary and a crucifix. Philip's silent little Isabel, holding her Elizabeth doll, stands at the foot of a cathedral altar as the defeated Philip falls at her feet. The metaphorical Elizabeth takes a long moment to look down upon him with disdain and triumph before holding her head high and leaving him where he has collapsed, her doll clasped firmly in her hand. In this way, Elizabeth is allowed almost a face-to-face victory over her enemy. The cardinals, a red sea of robes ranged behind Philip, also turn their back on him. His loss is complete — Elizabeth has crushed him, and God has abandoned him.

In a shot carefully constructed to evoke a three-dimensional image of the Ditchley Portrait, Elizabeth, dressed as icon, stands upon the map of the world painted on her floor, her hands in the same saintly attitude as at the end of the first film and before the assassin's shot, as the camera swings 360 degrees around her and then completes the scene with a blinding-white transition. Elizabeth has come into her own; she is fully divine.

To neatly illustrate that, as divine, she no longer needs protection, it's time for Walsingham to go. Elizabeth is shown at Walsingham's bedside; the old man is dying, and despite all he has been to her, Elizabeth's attitude is more one of detached kindness — the cold Madonna — than any deeper, more personal sentiment. He whispers, "I have served Your Majesty in all things. You won't need me anymore," and Elizabeth simply tells him to rest, though she does bestow upon him the appellation of "friend" before walking out of the room. Even though she is leaving, Elizabeth is still present — the Rainbow Portrait hangs above Walsingham's bed, looking down upon him.

If Elizabeth is the Virgin Madonna, then all she needs is a Christ-child, and it's provided by her surrogate, Bess. In the final scene of the film, Elizabeth visits Raleigh, and to equate Bess with herself, she uses her full name for the first and only time: "Elizabeth has a son." Bess, in a dressing gown and diminished by her childbirth, highlights how Elizabeth's sensual, feminine side has weakened as her mythic side triumphs. Elizabeth presents a perfect Madonna and child tableau as she holds the baby to give her blessing. Light streams in through the window, illuminating the two, as Elizabeth says in voiceover, "I am called the Virgin Queen. Unmarried. I have no master. Childless. I am mother to my people. God give me strength to bear this mighty freedom." Elizabeth has finally found the freedom she sought in Raleigh — her version lies in acceptance of her duty to her people. She looks directly at the camera, her face luminescent, as the voiceover says, "I am your queen. I am myself." She is not just a queen of sixteenth-century England; she has become the viewer's queen as well. Another blinding-white transition leaves the viewer with the final image of Elizabeth the divine icon, her feet planted firmly upon the map of the world she has conquered and the wind she has at her command gracefully billowing her veil out around her.

By and large, *The Golden Age* was not as well received as its predecessor, which is understandable given the journey that film made; *The Golden Age*, though the players and events are different, is essentially the same journey for Elizabeth — from uncertainty and fear to invulnerable icon. In many respects, it rehashes themes and symbolism novel in the first film, but predictable by the second. Kapur himself admitted that *The Golden Age* "ran into difficulty." He has stated that the film is about "absolute power and aspiring to divinity," but as he had already covered these elements in the first film, he had to make the focus of *The Golden Age* the effect of human desires on the divine. This is where, he admits "the film did not reach the expectations the first one had set up."[49]

As one commentary puts it, the film "pauses often to admire its own beauty,"[50] giving it less a sense of forward motion than *Elizabeth*. Period pieces surrounding royalty always face the danger of succumbing to the weight of their royal accouterments, and there is a certain element of this to *The Golden Age*; it focuses more on pageantry and spectacle than its predecessor, and is the worse for it. One review called it "lavish and entertaining in the grand old Hollywood manner ... a beautifully mounted and well-acted soap opera with overripe dialogue that plays fast and loose with history — just like they did in the 30s, 40s, and 50s."[51] This focus on spectacle worked for productions from Hollywood's golden age, but it does not fit well with the pretension and rampant symbolism of Kapur's idiom. Despite the less than enthusiastic reviews of the film itself, Blanchett was again praised for her portrayal of the Virgin Queen. One reviewer stated that Blanchett "throws herself into mature queenliness with an unfiltered passion all the more precious for its fiery sincerity."[52]

It's interesting to note that, while Catholics are the villains of both films, the tenor of these "villains" has changed somewhat. *Elizabeth*, released in 1998, before the destruction of the World Trade Center, features Catholics who play for power, but more for personal reasons rather than ideological ones. Mary is emotionally unstable, and her policies are cruel. But by and large, these are not religious fanatics. Philip II, as he is portrayed in *The Golden Age*, however, certainly warrants this designation. He mumbles constantly about an Elizabeth he equates with the Devil and who is "leading her people to hell"; he croons about how, though Elizabeth is darkness, "I am the light." Elizabeth warns her court that Philip represents a dangerous fundamentalism whose success will result in "no more liberty in England, of conscience or of thought." In this way, the film can seen to be influenced by the rise of Islamic fundamentalism, what one reviewer called flirting suggestively "with the idea that the English or perhaps the English-speaking world is engaged in another holy war against another set of radical fundamentalists."[53] *Fire Over England* spoke to the Nazi threat (and more fluently, it must be noted) faced by its moviegoing audience, and *The Golden Age* does the same for contemporary audiences faced by a different threat — acts of terror by religious fundamentalists.

As has been mentioned, the dialogue in this film is superficial, and more than one commentary dinged screenwriters Michael Hirst and William Nicholson for reducing "this most turbulent and eloquent period of history into a celluloid storybook that seems designed for a child of nine."[54] The bodice-ripping (Hirst) and the bombast (attributed to Nicholson since he had a hand in bringing *Gladiator* to the screen) of certain parts of the film are, in combination, often jarring enough to knock the viewer out of the period. There's also a dose of the historical Elizabeth thrown in via her speeches which, rather than evening things out, simply provides greater contrast. The dialogue is almost incidental, however; given Kapur's viewpoint, it is certainly not his focus: "I love music and visuals in a film and feel that a film needs as minimum [sic] dialogue as possible."[55]

In taking on the character of Elizabeth, Kapur brought what he calls his "mythic sense" to a "film genre that was considered to be much more about Costumes, Royal and Court politics and (most of all) wit." Both of these films, *Elizabeth* and its sequel, *The Golden Age*, require a certain viewpoint in order to succeed as any kind of representation of the Virgin Queen. First and foremost, any reliance on historical fact must be discarded. If either film is approached from this angle, it fails entirely. Kapur notes that his sense of the "mythic" is what "pure historians" call history translated into melodrama, but Kapur chooses to see it more as a difference in cultural expression occasioned by his Eastern (i.e., Indian) point of view.[56] The result is that both of these films are portraits of a time and a person painted with very broad, very modern, almost mystic strokes, the first film with more depth than the second, but there is something to be found in the overall impression each conveys. Kapur is unconcerned with relating facts; his goal is to make an impact, and he uses every visual tool at the filmmaker's disposal to impose his point on the viewer — camera angles and transitions, vivid color palettes, architecture, and symbolism by the ton. When the romanticism is stripped away, what is left is more a sense of Elizabeth's myth than a sense of Elizabeth herself. Taken together, from the beginning of the first film to the end of the second, Elizabeth appears as princess and lover, progresses to uncertain queen, falters through webs of intrigue before finding her footing in ruthlessness, and transforms herself into the glorious virgin. She melts for a time during the second film, but by the end of *The Golden Age*, she has reconstituted herself as the Madonna with England serving simultaneously as her husband and her child — a divine being both benevolent and unassailable who reigns over a golden age.

Given its critical reception and the redundancy *The Golden Age* exhibits in its themes when viewed in light of the previous film, it may seem an odd choice for Kapur to risk more repetition and pursue yet another film focusing on Elizabeth's life. However, from the beginning, Kapur intended his Elizabeth project to be a trilogy. The stated focus of the first film was power and the second divinity, and with the third and final in the trilogy, which will cover the last years of the Queen's life, Kapur plans to explore the theme of Elizabeth's mortality. Doubtless, if this project is realized, it will follow its predecessors in "mythic" tone and visualization. If the end result is Elizabeth's mortality, her death, it may prove a challenge for Kapur to reconcile this with the myth of the divine and immortal being he first fashioned and then perpetuated in the first and second films.

CHAPTER 5

Glimpses of Elizabeth: The Bit Parts

Elizabeth has appeared in so many minor roles, especially in television episodes, that examining them all would entail a separate monograph; the Internet Movie Database[1] lists nearly 100 appearances in film and television of the Tudor monarch, in offerings as varied as *The Wonderful World of Disney* to *Doctor Who*. However small her role with regard to overall screen time, there are certain notable "bit parts" which are unique to informing the understanding of the characterization of Elizabeth in film, and as such, bear examination.

ORLANDO (1992)

Perhaps the award for most unique portrayal of Elizabeth in a motion picture goes to the odd little film *Orlando*, primarily because filmmaker Sally Potter chose to cast a man in the role of the Virgin Queen. Elizabeth is a perennial favorite in the field of gender studies, and to call this film gender-bending would be an understatement of monumental proportions; at times, the androgyny borders on the surreal and certainly the confusing.

Orlando is based on a singular novel by Virginia Woolf, one that critics have called "a wonderful phantasmagoria, in which imagination has all its own way and all matter-of-factness is exorcised from the start; in which ... the writer combines images and historic facts, possibilities, and impossibilities, reflections upon history and manners with scenes from a dream-world."[2] As might be expected from a description such as this, the film based on Woolf's novel is a unique piece of cinema. Set at the end of Elizabeth's reign, it is the story of a young Englishman, Lord Orlando, who seeks companionship, poetry and happiness, and spontaneously changes sex. As if that were not enough, Orlando also does not age. Who has granted him this amazing boon of eternal youth? None other than the Virgin Queen herself, simply by telling him not to grow old, a command he decides he would like to obey. The title character is played by Tilda Swinton, an actress who manages to be convincing as a young man or a woman, and still exhibit a strange, disconcerting beauty as both.

The film opens with Orlando, who dreams of being a poet, seated under a tree, quill and blank paper in hand, and the viewer is told that Orlando is a man, even though his looks tend towards the feminine, presenting this as a trend that was popular in the late sixteenth century. Though Woolf's original Orlando was completely and unequivocally masculine, this is not something Swinton can accomplish, hence the explanatory narration. The viewer is also informed, "It wasn't privilege he sought, but company." As if on cue, Orlando suddenly remembers that company is coming — he rushes back home at break-neck speed; in all his poetic daydreaming he has forgotten that Queen Elizabeth is soon to arrive at his parents' enormous estate.

Much is made in the literature of Elizabeth's masculine side, and *Orlando* provides an interesting take on the issue by using a male to portray her — gay icon Quentin Crisp. It certainly gives a new definition to the epithet "old queen." Crisp was known for his flamboyance, his style, which he called "an idiom arising spontaneously from the personality but deliberately maintained."[3] For Crisp, this meant wearing cosmetics and feminine clothing based on that of the male prostitutes from London's East End, but it is just as easily applied to Elizabeth and her idiom — her style, which became more and more flamboyant as she aged, was distinct, arising from her personality, but deliberately maintained to further her political image. When viewed in this way, it does not seem quite so odd to cast Crisp in the role. Sally Potter, the film's director, certainly did not think so. She has called her decision to solicit Crisp for the role "a divine inspiration" and noted that she was "profoundly proud of this piece of casting."[4]

Elizabeth would doubtless have been horrified at Crisp's portrayal of her in the film, but despite all its strangeness, there are elements of it that succeed. Orlando rushes for home, darkness has fallen, and Elizabeth's state barge makes its way towards his house while torch-bearing servants run out to line the path, lighting up the night. As the barge slowly pulls towards the wharf, a servant (pop singer Jimmy Sommerville) serenades the Queen in falsetto about her beauty: "Blessed be each day and hour where sweet Eliza builds her bower…. Eliza is the fairest Queen, Eliza's eyes are blessed stars," lines actually sung to the historical Elizabeth in the 1590s. The viewer is then treated to his first glimpse of this "fairest Queen." Elizabeth appears in profile, showing the elderly Crisp's hawk-like nose and sagging countenance, a creature almost monstrous underneath its red wig. It is this duality between what is professed by those around the Queen and the reality of what the aged Queen has become that resonates so clearly in this film portrayal of Elizabeth.

The imagery in *Orlando* is particularly powerful; it has been called "a highly visual film,"[5] and it conveys a strong sense of authenticity with regard to the Elizabethan period it attempts to portray. Potter uses Swinton's figure "as anchor — a calm center in a storm of images … [transforming] the screen into a living pop-up book of British history."[6] The costuming in the film was created by Sandy Powell, known for her imaginative style, especially in period pieces (her work also includes the next film examined, *Shakespeare in Love*). One commentator noted, "Sometimes it seems that if you see a movie in the 1990s with bold and inventive costume design, the name on the credit will be Sandy Powell."[7] Powell's work on *Orlando* garnered her an Oscar nomination, and whether it's Queen Elizabeth's rust-red petticoat or the door-defying Robe à la Française Orlando dons upon first becoming a woman, Powell always gives her designs "an extra kick of idiosyncratic color or adornment or style."[8] Powell's designs can be breathtaking, and in *Orlando*, they add to the lush visual palette that gives this film its unique ambiance.

A breathless Orlando makes it out the door just in time to slide to his knees and offer the Queen a bowl of rose water, allowing a leisurely close-up of Elizabeth's hands as she slowly dips them and brushes off the petals which stick to them — large man's hands, with long, none-too-clean fingernails and enormous rings on eight out of ten fingers. From this angle, the camera pans up to the first close-up view of Elizabeth's face, and it looks as if one of Jim Henson's Mystic puppets has donned Tudor drag. The Queen regards the terrified Orlando with bemusement, and the contrast created between the close-ups of Crisp's aged visage and Swinton's unlined young face is practically an allegory in itself. It's especially remarkable in that one could do worse than to cast Swinton as a young Elizabeth — she is pale and red-headed, with unsettling eyes that bear a strong resemblance to those staring out from Elizabeth's coronation portrait. It's almost as if Swinton and Crisp represent, not simply youth and old age, but the youth and old age of a single person, two discreet points on the same chronological continuum.

Orlando's parents have given a banquet in the Queen's honor, and she sits at the high table, looking passively out over the full banqueting hall, holding a delicate flower in her huge, unappealing hands. She says nothing, and Orlando's parents signal that it's time for him to recite to the Queen. The lines of poetry he chooses come from "The Bower of Bliss" in Spenser's *Faerie Queen*, and it would seem a logical choice. The historical Elizabeth's now familiar title of Gloriana originates with Spenser's work — the character of Gloriana in his allegory *is* Elizabeth, and things have come full circle in that the Queen is now called by the name of the character that represented her in a work written to praise her. It also evokes all the glory of the Elizabethan era. As it turns out, however, Orlando has chosen poorly. He begins:

> Ah see the Virgin Rose, how sweetly shee
>   Doth first peepe forth with bashfull modestee,
> That fairer seemes, the lesse ye see her may;
>   Lo, see soone after, how more bold and free
> Her bared bosome she doth broad display;
> Loe, see soone after, how she fades, and falles away.
>
> So passeth…

This is as far as Orlando is allowed to get before Elizabeth interrupts him, the first words she has spoken: "Is this a worthy topic from one so clearly in the bloom of youth to one who would desire it still?" Her tone is not angry, but more ironic, and Crisp's Elizabeth, while being almost grotesque in appearance, is yet sympathetic in her own self-deprecation, not with what she says, but in how she says it. Orlando's father steps in, simpering, and comments on how Elizabeth's "bloom is legendary," then tries to diffuse the situation by offering, "All that is mine is here for your pleasure." The Queen, her tone still ironically amused, replies, "All you call yours is mine already."

The book is more direct about a romantic attachment between the Queen and Orlando, but the film, thankfully, chooses to show more discretion in portraying the evolution of their relationship. Elizabeth is shown lumbering carefully down the garden path on Orlando's arm, her two wolfhounds at her side, and there was seldom a scene of more incongruity. Crisp, broad in his huge skirts, beside the svelte Swinton in her doublet and hose, a man portraying a woman on the arm of a woman portraying a man. The Queen eases herself into a chair and has her attendants place a velvet pillow at her feet, upon which she bids Orlando kneel. She bestows upon him a garter, sliding it up his leg with the pronouncement: "I want you here in England with me. You will be the son of my old age ... my favorite, my mascot." If Orlando is Elizabeth's "mascot," he is a representation of the youth and beauty that Elizabeth wishes to portray as unchanging, the physical manifestation of her body politic, which her body natural no longer mirrors. In Orlando, however, she has designated a surrogate, and if she cannot control her own descent into age and death, then she will command that he not follow the path she has no choice but to take.

The last scene in which Elizabeth appears in the film is somewhat uncomfortable. As Orlando waits outside the door, Elizabeth's ladies-in-waiting are undressing her, luckily only down to her petticoats, at which point they thankfully stop. After hiking her skirts up for her and helping her hoist herself into bed, she dismisses them and calls Orlando to her. As if reeling in a reluctant fish, he stops several feet away. She motions towards the bed. He stands at the side of the bed. She pats the bed next to her. The viewer shares Orlando's frightened uncertainty as he climbs into bed and she has him lay next to her, then put his head in her lap. The Queen has said he will be the son of her old age, but the scene's sexual overtones are unmistakable, and therefore uncomfortable in the extreme. "Ah, this is my victory," Elizabeth breathes, and then kisses Orlando on the forehead. She then demands his "handsome leg," and when he offers it to her, she reaches slowly into her bodice, removing a rolled parchment. She slides her large hand up his leg and slips the deed to the house in the garter she has already bestowed upon him. "For you and your heirs, Orlando, the house. But on one condition. Do not fade. Do not wither," the Queen says, and then, looking away from his young face, "Do not *grow old*." Crisp's portrayal rings true because he imbues it with all the sadness of lost youth — here is a woman who has the world at her command, but she cannot command youth and beauty for herself, the things she most desires. Crisp manages to convey a sense of the acceptance of the inevitably of this, as well as a sense of finality. It is with some relief that the scene switches to Orlando, alone in his bed, looking directly into the camera, and stating, "Very interesting person," of his visit with the Queen. It's Elizabeth's last scene in the film, for though the next scene depicts the snowbound funeral procession of Orlando's father, it is symbolically Elizabeth's funeral as well; the viewer is told that Orlando has lost the Queen and now his father, all in the same year.

Orlando goes on through more than 400 years, in the process spontaneously changing sex to become female, until finally ending up exactly where he (now a she) began — underneath the same tree on her ancestral estate. His interlude with Elizabeth is indicative of the film's ability to visually convey a historical period before becoming unfocused, temporally unmoored, slipping through years to stop at another, equally immersive moment in time. The film has been called "an exquisite spectacle, a cross-dressed costume drama sequined with feminist wit ... an amusing escapade full of arresting images."[9] Filmmakers always face potential criticism from historians, but Potter faced the additional literary criticism for liberties taken with Woolf's original material. Her response to this was that "sometimes when somebody sets out to make an 'entertainment' the more serious issues surface in their own right in a less pedantic or polemic way."[10] This is certainly the case with Crisp's portrayal of Elizabeth. The lush imagery of this film entertains without losing the ability to express something of the historical woman's essence. Her desire for youth and beauty, her loneliness, her absolute power in everything but the ability to command what she most desired for herself, is conveyed through the few minutes Crisp spends onscreen.

SHAKESPEARE IN LOVE (1998)

Shakespeare in Love was released almost simultaneously with Kapur's *Elizabeth*, and the publicity for the two fed off each other in a sort of Elizabethan mania which swept the Oscar nomination pool. The films share roughly the same period and also some of the major players (i.e., Joseph Fiennes and Geoffrey Rush); however, in subject matter, temperament, and tone, these are two completely disparate films. *Elizabeth* is an historical drama/thriller and *Shakespeare in Love* a tongue-in-cheek romantic comedy, but because of the timing of their release and their corresponding periods, a great deal of comparison was made between the two films. It has been noted that, though period movies are always a risk commercially, with these two offerings "something about the era struck a chord, because both films are arthouse hits."[11] These two films do fit the same era, namely Elizabethan, but there are 30-odd years between the two settings, since *Elizabeth* begins before Elizabeth's ascension and *Shakespeare in Love* comes in at the end of her reign. Their production designs are also vastly different — the cold stone medieval interiors of *Elizabeth* are a total contrast to *Shakespeare in Love*'s bustling streets, teaming with human and animal filth.

Shakespeare in Love is a concept film, and the concept is eponymous: how would love inspire the work of the Bard? Young Will Shakespeare (Joseph Fiennes) has a serious case of writer's block, and his apothecary-cum-Freudian psychiatrist manages to divine the reason — when he attempts to ... write, it is like "trying to pick a lock with a wet herring," his "quill is broken," the "proud tower of his genius" has collapsed and he's unable to resurrect it. What this young man needs is a romantic muse, and he finds one in the person of Viola de Lesseps (Gwyneth Paltrow), a beautiful young noblewoman with an overwhelming passion for the theater. In true Shakespearean fashion, she even goes so far as to disguise herself as a boy so she can tread the boards, and she's quickly cast as Romeo in Shakespeare's latest work of literary greatness, *Romeo and Ethel, the Pirate's Daughter*. The play is written and rewritten, evolving as Shakespeare's relationship with Viola progresses.

The story begins in 1593, in the "glory days of Elizabethan Theatre," and before a production at Greenwich, none other than the great Richard Burbage sums up the prevailing tastes which mirror those of England's queen: "The Queen has commanded it — she loves a comedy." Elizabeth (Judi Dench) enters to great fanfare and seats herself, and her expression is, at best, dour. Burbage has spoken true, for when an actor and his canine companion engage in childish slapstick, she bursts into uproarious laughter, and the entire court follows suit. The perennially cash-strapped theater owner Philip Henslowe (Geoffrey Rush), for whom Shakespeare is composing *Romeo and Ethel, the Pirate's Daughter*, remarks to the Bard, "You see? Comedy, love, and a bit with a dog. That's what they want." Elizabeth denotes her approval by commending the actor while tossing a treat to the dog, almost as if both were on the same level. By contrast, when another actor goes on to recite lines of love from *Two Gentlemen of Verona*, the Queen is asleep and snoring within seconds; Elizabeth's tastes are not exactly refined. In the audience is Lady Viola de Lesseps, and she's much more appreciative of Shakespeare's work than is her queen. When the Earl of Wessex (Colin Firth) presents her to the Queen and she's asked what it is that attracts her to the theater, she says (with starry-eyed enthusiasm) "to have stories acted for me by a company of fellows." Elizabeth interrupts her, "They're not acted for you. They're acted for me." She goes on to expound on her views about the stage's portrayal of love: "Playwrights teach us nothing about love. They make it pretty, they make it comical, they make it lust. They cannot make it true." When Viola has the temerity to suggest that there is one who can, the Queen places a wager upon whether or not "a play can show us the very truth and nature of love." The entire exchange sets up a plot point, but it does more than that — in the space of a few short minutes, it illustrates the rapport between Elizabeth and her court. She is a creature both awesome (in the original sense of the word) and feared. She is also a woman apart; she is not shown with any advisers or a favorite. Her characterization is harsh, and her dialogue consists almost entirely of sarcastic quips, belittling and unkind, which elicit laughter from the court. When Lord Wessex makes the mistake of off-handing, "I'll wager my fortune," the Queen replies, "I thought you were here because you had none." Wessex has presented Lady Viola to the Queen in order to pave the way to marry her; as a member (albeit fictional) of the ancient nobility, he requires the Queen's permission to wed. Elizabeth again shows her harshness when she gives him her permission: "Have her then, but you're a fool. She's been plucked since I saw her last and not by you. Takes a woman to know it." The Queen's comments set in motion a series of events that send Wessex after Shakespeare, resulting in a finale where Wessex asks of the Queen, "How is this to end?"

As does Kapur's *Elizabeth*, *Shakespeare in Love* "plays fast and loose with literary and British history,"[12] but the purpose here is different. *Shakespeare in Love* is, at its most elemental, fun. It plays with literary and historical tropes, intentionally mixing them with anachronisms, resulting in an endearing, entertaining, and at times hilarious film. Many of the jokes are inside ones, and the more the viewer knows about the period, about the historical Shakespeare and his contemporaries as well as their work, the more amusing the film. This is also a film that "pairs commercial Elizabethan theater with the contemporary commercial cinema."[13] This is, in effect, a satire on the current state of affairs in the film industry — writers are nobodies, investors pull the strings, there are a great number of producer credits, and actors are promised a share of nonexistent profits. It has been noted that "with most historical films, the viewer scrutinizes in order to cluck at errors,"[14] and *Shakespeare in Love* is an ode to this — the Elizabethan era created by director John Madden is crammed "with the hubbub and bustle and squalor and panoply that history justifies," but he mixes it with farce in order to play games with both history and literature. The very "errors" that "ruin" most films for those familiar with the historical source material are transformed into intentional plot devices which are delightful to seek out and enjoy in *Shakespeare in Love*.

Sandy Powell, the costume designer who also worked on *Orlando*, was tasked with making the actors in this film "look like they were wearing normal clothes," albeit normal for the sixteenth century. In this way, the everyday costuming of Shakespeare and his coterie could be contrasted with that of the court scenes, where Powell was allowed to "have fun and go madly over the top."[15] Her costuming for Dench's Elizabeth certainly reflects this; her gowns, wigs and headgear are lavish and eye-popping, but none of them are "portrait" gowns. The goal here is not to faithfully recreate the iconic image of Elizabeth. Rather, the costuming reflects the role that Elizabeth plays in this film; she's used (just as are the filthy streets, rotting teeth, lusty wenches, and other set dressing) to give a feel for the period, to add "period color."[16] More than this, it's almost as if Elizabeth represents the viewer (she has already said that the performance is for her), for she stands apart from the dirt of Shakespeare's world, and from her higher vantage point, is able to see and understand elements of the plotting that the other characters cannot. She knows, for instance, simply by looking at Viola that she has given herself to Shakespeare, something of which Lord Wessex is unaware. She knows that, though Wessex has every appearance of wealth, he is, in fact, almost penniless. When Shakespeare follows Viola to court dressed as a woman and no one notices, again Elizabeth observes and understands. These are all things the viewer knows, but as a character, Dench's Elizabeth "sees through all artifice and every disguise.... She knows because she is the biggest role player and drag artist of them all."[17] As Elizabeth says herself with regard to Viola's turn on the stage, "I know something of a woman in a man's profession. Yes, by God, I do know about that." In the swirling panorama of this film, which is filled with quotes from the Bard himself, this has been called one of the film's most "serious and resonant" lines,[18] and it is indicative of the significance of Elizabeth's part, however small, in the film.

The role Elizabeth fills in this film has been literarily likened to one of Shakespeare's magician or fool figures — the characters in his work who ultimately "doff the masks and dissolve the fiction."[19] In this way, Elizabeth in *Shakespeare in Love* is almost the alpha and omega — she gives a feel for the period that is named after her, making the fiction immersive, and in the end, it is also she who resolves the plotting, dispersing the illusion. As is fitting, the denouement happens on the stage. Shakespeare and Viola have played the parts of Romeo and Juliet in this great, tragic love story which does not fit the prevailing tastes of the time, yet the audience reaction is astounding, for the masses have overwhelmingly accepted Shakespeare's depiction of romantic love. Elizabeth herself has been portrayed almost as one of the masses, a sort of theatrical vulgarian who prefers slapstick to poetry. Yet she is the arbiter of everything, so when she also is moved and acknowledges that Shakespeare has won the wager — he has captured the truth and nature of love — Shakespeare becomes what the viewer already knows him to be: great. His play has been a resounding success, the theater is saved, and Shakespeare has enough money to be independent. Elizabeth has served as the "dea ex machina."[20] She reveals herself and literally descends from on high, the theater's nose-bleed seats, to resolve the plotting.

However, it has been noted that Dench's Elizabeth is "less powerful" than she seems.[21] Wessex has asked her how the story will end, and her answer is not what one would expect. "As stories must when love's denied," she says, "with tears and a journey. Those whom God has joined in marriage, not even I can put asunder." Interesting words from the daughter of Henry VIII, but the point is that Dench's Elizabeth recognizes the limits of her power — there will be no happy ending for Viola and Shakespeare. He is already married, she is now married, and to Virginia with Lord Wessex she must go. This leaves Elizabeth to demand of Shakespeare something "more cheerful" for the next time, before making her exit. The film takes one more amusing stab at the popular perception of the period as Elizabeth hesitates before a huge mudhole. She rolls her eyes in exasperation at her gaping male courtiers, before trudging through it as they all take off their cloaks and chunk them in the mud just a few seconds too late.

Dench's Elizabeth was universally praised; she has been called the best thing about this movie by some reviewers, who use words such as "astonishing" and "indelible" to describe her performance. She "registers as one of the most fully developed characters, jealous of her power but eager to dispense true justice when it is called for."[22] This is especially significant given the fact that, while other actresses have had multiple hours to craft their portrayals of the Virgin Queen, Dench had to condense hers down to mere minutes. It is a testament to her abilities that she was able to provide such a forceful portrait in less than ten minutes of screen time, and this is something her Academy Award for Best Supporting Actress in this film recognizes. Dench has said that she thought Elizabeth would be "a commanding person, that if she just glanced at you, you'd be pretty dodgy inside." This is how her portrayal of Elizabeth comes across: as a woman whose very presence commands attention and awe, a queen who "dominates every scene."[23]

ALICE IN WONDERLAND (2010)

At first glance, the inclusion of a film adaptation of Lewis Carroll's marvelously imaginative children's story in a work about Elizabeth might seem out of scope. Upon closer inspection, however, it becomes apparent that adaptations of Carroll's heroine have been constantly re-imagined over the years, just as Elizabeth has, and for the same reason, because "like all great literary [or historical] figures, she's always managed to keep up with the times. Alice has changed remarkably over the years, often in ways that reveal as much about the era in which she was re-imagined than about the character herself."[24] The time-lines of these films closely parallel that of Elizabeth's various reincarnations, beginning with an Edwardian silent film, peaking again in the 1930s, the 1950s, a brief stint in the 1970s, and finally the late 1990s and 2000s. Actresses who played Elizabeth have even appeared in these adaptations to again portray a monarch (e.g., Flora Robson as the Queen of Hearts in the 1972 iteration of *Alice in Wonderland*). Mia Wasikowska has remarked, as has more than one actress playing Elizabeth, that her turn portraying Alice required stripping away the "baggage" that comes with depicting an "iconic" character in order to find the real person underneath.[25] Playing six degrees of separation with actresses and timelines keeps boredom at bay, but is not the reason the 2010 *Alice in Wonderland* is examined here. All other considerations aside, the characterization of the Red Queen that appears in this film is an unmistakable representation of the historical Elizabeth. Her very name, Iracebeth, is, like the character to whom it belongs, a distortion of Elizabeth.

Alice in Wonderland is directed by Tim Burton, and it bears his distinctive visual marks. It has been said that, in Burton's view of the world, there "is no true beauty without a touch (or a ton) of decay."[26] Burton's tales and characters reflect this; in his world the macabre mixes with the surreal to provide a unique atmosphere, at once engaging and unsettling. His retelling of the *Alice in Wonderland* story fits this mold, though it is decidedly different in plot and characterization from the original construct created by Carroll. The new Alice is no bored child — she's a young woman faced with the prospect of marriage to a wealthy and socially elite, yet utterly distasteful, young aristocrat. Rather than give him an answer to his proposal (a staged affair in front of a hundred guests at a garden party), she runs off to think, following the White Rabbit, and falls down the rabbit hole. Since this story is more a sequel to the original *Alice*, every familiar character — the perennially unpunctual White Rabbit, Tweedle Dee and Tweedle Dum, the Mad Hatter, the Cheshire Cat — already knows her, for she has met them before, even if she doesn't quite remember it. This new version of Alice's story also exhibits many of the themes that iterations of Elizabeth feature, and especially focuses on one that takes precedence starting in the 1970s — women's independence. The reasons for Alice to marry that are enumerated by those around her and parroted by Alice herself have much in common with those Elizabeth faced: her suitor is a hand-picked member of the nobility; she must provide an heir and avoid the dreaded unmarried state at all costs (a half-crazed maiden aunt is used to depict the terrible consequences of this); and most importantly, her "face won't last." Alice is encouraged by all those around her to take the husband that has been selected for her, but like Elizabeth, she has her own ideas about how she wishes to live her life. In the end, she chooses a vocation over marriage — like a retooled Elizabethan sailor-explorer, she sets sail to new and exciting countries in search of lucrative trade opportunities.

Alice's younger, less girl-power incarnation in Disney's 1951 animated *Alice in Wonderland* faced her greatest challenge in the Queen of Hearts, whose characterization more closely resembled Elizabeth's homicidal sister Mary. In Burton's version, the Queen of Hearts has been re-imagined as the Red Queen (Helena Bonham Carter). The Red Queen is not the historical Elizabeth; instead she is the myth of Elizabeth, especially as perpetuated through film representations, after it has been fed through Burton's distortion field.

In a film full of distorted and strange characters, Iracebeth still stands out, literally and figuratively — her digitally enhanced head is disproportionately large, earning her the adjectives "monstrous"[27] and "suggesting an enormous overdressed infant."[28] Overdressed is certainly applicable, but it's more than simply the sumptuousness of her costuming that evokes the extravagance of the historical Elizabeth. Though Alice left behind a nineteenth-century setting when she tumbled down the rabbit hole and much of the costuming even in Wonderland reflects this (e.g., the White Rabbit with his waistcoat and pocketwatch, the Mad Hatter's ensemble), Iracebeth wears unmistakably Elizabethan period gowns. This impression and the instant association with Queen Elizabeth it provokes is intentional — the Red Queen's look, from costume to make-up, was inspired by

Bette Davis's turn as Elizabeth.[29] Costume designer Colleen Atwood consulted the original illustrations from early editions of Carroll's books, created by John Tenniel and Carroll himself, to inform her costuming, but, as Atwood called it, the route she chose to take with the Red Queen was "tipped to Elizabethan."[30] Bonham Carter was given an enormous red wig weighing three pounds and a prosthetic forehead to push back her hairline, rather than the shaving endured by other actresses portraying the Virgin Queen. The finishing touch to this Elizabethan look was added by make-up artist Valli O'Reilly. O'Reilly faced an especially difficult task, for not only did she have to achieve a certain look, but because Bonham Carter's head was digitally enlarged, the make-up had to stand up to scrutiny under this magnification.[31] The precision required made it necessary for O'Reilly to use stencils for the eyebrows, eyelids, and lips. Like everything else in this film, the make-up provides an essence of the Elizabethan — the stark-white face with flashes of color at the cheeks and lips — but no attempt is made to faithfully recreate Elizabeth's look. Bonham Carter has very defined eyebrows (unlike the historical Elizabeth, who had none), and her wide swathes of electric-blue eyeshadow up to the brow bone would be more at home in a 1980s music video than Elizabethan England. Still, the overwhelming visual impression conveyed is that the character is a caricature of Elizabeth I.

The Red Queen's palace has much in common with the interiors from Kapur's Elizabeth films — light filters through arched stained glass windows, and these are huge, echoing stone spaces, more medieval than Tudor. The court which inhabits these spaces is reflective of the Queen at its center; all the courtiers appear to be as distorted as she, and they, too, are dressed in Elizabethan-cum-Burton fashions. Rather than flatter Iracebeth with words or hollow gestures, they step up the ode to her vanity — if imitation is the sincerest form of flattery, then Iracebeth's courtiers are one earnest bunch. They take her distorted appearance as the aesthetic ideal and follow suit: some have enormous noses or ears, others jowls of which Jabba the Hut would be proud, and one lady-in-waiting sports a bosom so gigantic a steel reinforced infrastructure is required to hold it up — one pities her poor corset. As the Red Queen eventually learns through the machinations of the Mad Hatter, her courtiers' deformities are not real; made up of prosthetics and other disguises, they are a conscious effort to imitate a look of which the Queen will approve — namely her own distorted aesthetic. In this way, there are echoes of the historical Elizabeth where, for a time, the ideal of beauty was based entirely on that adopted and personified by the Queen — stark-white skin, unnatural make-up, and red-gold hair.

The visual look of the Red Queen character is not the only association with Elizabeth. Almost every review noted that Bonham Carter's portrayal of Iracebeth appeared to be channeling Bette Davis's Virgin Queen or Miranda Richardson's Queenie (covered in Chapter Six), or a combination of both. She especially resembles the latter with her constant cry, "Off with his head!," her innate petulance, and her desire to be constantly entertained. Tweedle Dee and Tweedle Dum, her "fat boys," are used to serve this purpose, with the Red Queen summoning them and commanding, "Speak, boys. Amuse us," as if they were trained monkeys. As one reviewer noted, "Iracebeth is as much a spoiled child as an evil monarch."[32]

The list of those she sends to the block includes the Mad Hatter (Johnny Depp), and he plays an interesting role with regard to the Red Queen — that of reluctant courtier.

He mentions that his "clan" has always been "employed at court," and originally he was milliner to the White Queen. Though unwilling, he's forced to fill this role again for the Red Queen, and she displays all of the historical Elizabeth's much-vaunted vanity as she has him fashion every conceivable type of headgear for her and tries them on in front of the mirror. When he displeases her, the scene of his execution is unmistakably Elizabethan in its staging. He mounts the scaffold where the executioner waits with his axe, and a throng of the Red Queen's subjects murmurs as he lays his head on the block. Iracebeth herself, with her inner court circle, watches from an overlooking balcony in a scene that's staging closely mirrors one in HBO's *Elizabeth I* where Helen Mirren's Elizabeth punishes an unfortunate pamphleteer. Iracebeth lisps her favorite phrase, "Off with his head!" and seems immensely pleased with herself, just as Richardson's Queenie does when she calls for the execution of her courtiers. In this way, the popular perception of Elizabeth as a monarch under whose reign executions flourished is perpetuated, and the aspects of capriciousness and vanity in her personality are underlined.

Another facet of Elizabeth's story that filmmakers cannot resist are her romantic relationships, so in this, also, the Red Queen echoes her historical counterpart. While the earlier Disney-animated Queen of Hearts was married, like the historical Mary Tudor whom she more closely resembles, the Red Queen has eschewed the married state — not by a vow of virginity, but through the execution of her husband, whose stated crime was falling in love with another woman (her sister, the White Queen). The Red Queen is given instead a courtier favorite, not a consort, in the person of Lord Stayne, the Knave of Hearts (Crispin Glover). Like his queen, he also is a distorted picture — extremely tall, with stretched, elongated limbs. Iracebeth provokes shades of Bette Davis in *The Virgin Queen* and Cate Blanchett in *The Golden Age* with her desire to keep her favorite constantly beside her at court warring with the need to send him off to accomplish her objectives. Stayne's demeanor with his queen is slickly subservient, and he does Iracebeth's bidding while also paying her romantic attentions, but both are done in service of himself. Stayne's motivation is political advancement through royal favor, another nod to the Elizabethan court system. His duplicity is demonstrated in a scene where he happens upon Alice in a palace corridor and pins her against the wall, attempting to woo her. It's reminiscent of scenes from Kapur's *Elizabeth*, where every corridor hides courtiers either intriguing or engaging each other romantically or both. Alice manages to escape, but they have been observed, and the Red Queen is immediately informed. Her apoplectic reaction echoes almost every portrayal of Elizabeth upon the discovery of a favorite's romantic betrayal. Stayne manages to talk his way out of the predicament and Iracebeth focuses her ire solely on Alice, but it's clear that Stayne serves only his own ambition. After Iracebeth's defeat, when it becomes clear that he can no longer gain anything through the Red Queen's favor, his true feelings are revealed as he begs not to be sent into exile with her and, when denied this, immediately attempts to murder her.

Iracebeth is ultimately defeated (through Alice as champion) by her sister, the White Queen, and in this dynamic of a struggle between two related queens vying for the throne of one kingdom, there are shades of Elizabeth's relationship with both Mary Tudor and Mary Stuart. If there were any doubt left as to the historical personage upon whom Iracebeth is based, Burton even provides a nod to her parentage. As Alice makes her way through the Red Queen's palace, the dormouse throws open a door to reveal a large painting that is immediately familiar — a distorted but unambiguous reproduction of Hans Holbein's portrait of Henry VIII. Alice, as does the viewer, pauses in recognition and then hurries on her way.

The character of Iracebeth in Burton's *Alice in Wonderland* is made up to look like the historical Elizabeth, but her characterization is based not upon the historical woman; instead, it takes as its inspiration film depictions of Elizabeth and her court and then exaggerates them even further. In this way, it is more strongly informed by popular perceptions about Elizabeth than by Elizabeth herself. However distorted she may be, Bonham Carter's Iracebeth clearly demonstrates the near-universal appeal of Elizabeth's image — the myth of Elizabeth is so pervasive that she appears in the most unlikely of places, even in Wonderland.

CHAPTER 6

Serialized Elizabeth: The Miniseries

Film adaptations of Elizabeth's life are often denigrated for being too narrowly focused, especially in the area of Elizabeth's romantic relationships, resulting in a neglect of the Elizabethan political situation. Though usually an artistic choice, this is also a practical one—filmmakers are severely limited by a prescribed amount of screen time for a feature-length film. Even if they were so inclined, they have not world enough and time in two hours to cover all the major events in Elizabeth's life. It is here that the miniseries format holds sway. What Elizabethan miniseries sometimes lack in production value (with their much smaller budgets for much longer runtime, they are hard put to compete with the pageantry of their big-screen counterparts), they make up for in depth of portrayal. In most cases, there is also a stricter adherence to historical timelines, for the need is not as great to telescope events. When granted twice as long (or more; the seminal *Elizabeth R* weighs in at nine hours) to put their point across, miniseries can provide greater insight into Elizabeth's life, and it is to the miniseries that one must look if one is in search of a larger serving of the political to accompany the romantic main course.

ELIZABETH R (1971)

Before she was Elizabeth in *Mary, Queen of Scots*, Glenda Jackson defined the role with her portrayal as the titular monarch in *Elizabeth R*. *Elizabeth R*, a BBC *Masterpiece Theatre* production, was produced as a sort of sequel to the BBC's successful *The Six Wives of Henry VIII* miniseries, which aired in the early 1970s. Taken together, the two provide a continuous Tudor history from Henry VIII's childhood to the ascension of James I. Like its successor, *Elizabeth R* is a series of six interconnected plays—each 90-minute episode was penned by a different screenwriter, and the production teams differ. While some praise the episodes as so seamless that the difference in writers is not evident, there are certain unmistakable inconsistencies which sometimes push their way front and center. This series has an advantage over every other adaptation of Elizabeth's life covered in this work — its nine-hour run time — yet each episode still exhibits a particular, and rather narrow, focus. Due to this, at times there is a certain feeling of incongruity, such as when an episode focuses so tightly on the Babington Conspiracy that Lord Burghley and the Earl of Leicester simply disappear, only to reappear in the next episode as if they had never left the Queen's side. These issues aside, *Elizabeth R*, more than any other adaptation, has the screen time to provide a fuller, more detailed portrait of the life and times of Elizabeth I.

Elizabeth R also displays a greater adherence to historical veracity than perhaps any other adaptation of Elizabeth's life, and as such, in the canon of film Elizabeths, it is the hands-down favorite of historians. The prevailing feeling one has upon watching this series is that the writers took every scrap of historical dialogue they could find and worked it into their screenplays, often fitting the dramatic plotting around the known facts, rather than the other way around. Each episode has a separate title, and the series begins not just before Elizabeth becomes queen, but even before her sister Mary has ascended the throne — with the reign of her half-brother, Edward. "The Lion's Cub" opens with Lord High Admiral Thomas Seymour sneaking into the young king's apartments in an attempt to kidnap him. Alerted by the barking of the King's dog, which Seymour quickly skewers, the Lord Protector, the Duke of Somerset, rushes in to thwart his brother's plans. King Edward is very cold for so young a man — though Seymour has carefully cultivated him, giving him pocket money and playing the dutiful uncle, with no prompting whatsoever, Edward pronounces: "This matter tends to treason," and Seymour is done for. As his brother is dragged away, the Lord Protector mentions that "we shall investigate your dealings with the Princess Elizabeth," and Elizabeth is instantly in danger. In addition to the dramatic tension this creates, audiences also relate well to women in danger — women identify with them and men want to protect them — so introducing Elizabeth in this way assures audience engagement from the very beginning.

The viewer's first glimpse of Elizabeth is as she wakes up — Jackson, like others before her, has shaved back her hairline, and also allowed the BBC to build her "an appropriately Plantagenet nose."[1] As has been mentioned, this series' 1970s BBC production values cannot compete with the larger budgets for film versions of Elizabeth. For *The Six Wives of Henry VIII*, for instance, the costumes were constructed using cheap materials that were later screen printed with paints and resins and/or drawn on with fiber pens and then painted over to achieve a richer look.[2] For *Elizabeth R*, approximately 200 dresses were created for Jackson, and the majority of the production budget was focused on these costumes, which resulted in sets so insubstantially constructed that when courtiers gently close doors, the whole wall waffles and looks set to collapse. The sets may not be sturdy, but they do have the appearance of historicity, as do Jackson's gowns. They were constructed with an eye to historical detail, heavily padded and weighty, and Jackson was tightly cinched and boned into her corsets. The overall effect is convincing, for the most part, but it resulted in Jackson being rubbed raw, unable to bend her arms, and almost incapable of breathing.[3]

Elizabeth starts out in comfort at least — wearing a simple nightgown and cloak. The viewer may understand what's going on when Elizabeth wakes up and finds the house deserted, but Elizabeth is at sea. It helps to show the changeability and confusion of her situation as she winds her way through an empty house, looking for her servants, only to find an agent of the Crown ransacking her personal papers and abruptly questioning her because her beloved Mrs. Ashley and retainer Thomas Parry have been arrested. The conversations between Elizabeth and her interrogators are used to brilliant effect to provide an initial illumination of Elizabeth's character. She has been caught off guard, but she thinks on her feet. She's terrified, but quick — the only evidence she betrays of her fear are her shifting eyes as she furiously tries to think herself out of the situation. Since this depiction is based on historical fact, the tenor of the portrayal of Elizabeth and Seymour's relationship is completely different from that to be found in *Young Bess*. Of Seymour, all Elizabeth will say was that he was her guardian and friend, and she not only vehemently denies he proposed marriage, but states unequivocally, "I will never marry. Never, never, never." This episode sets up the psychological basis for Elizabeth's desire to avoid marriage — if, as her interrogator intimates, she has pursued marriage without consent, it's treason, and "the penalty for a woman is decapitation or burning. Remember your mother, Your Grace." The shadow cast by Anne Boleyn's death is a long one. Unlike Simmons's Elizabeth, if Jackson's princess feels any defensive anger at the way her mother is regarded or the comments made about her fate, she's careful not to show it. If Elizabeth has any feelings for Seymour, this is another area where her circumspection is absolute.

There's what Elizabeth is willing to admit (next to nothing) and then there's the reality of what happened (quite a bit), which the viewer must be shown in order to understand the predicament in which Elizabeth finds herself. This production chooses a rather strange method to accomplish this — a flashback, but shot entirely from the first person (i.e., Elizabeth's) point-of-view: Kat Ashley's face coyly suggesting Seymour wanted Elizabeth more than the Queen Dowager, Seymour's face as he throws back Elizabeth's bed curtains and comes playfully at her, his face again as he woos her, Catherine Parr's feverish last words about Elizabeth and Seymour wishing her death, Seymour's disingenuous bedside denial. Unlike in *Young Bess*, this Seymour is every bit the callous rogue. Insincere and charming, he plays his wife for a fool and Elizabeth as well (she's often heard breathlessly giggling behind the camera) as he pursues her right under his pregnant wife's nose.

All of this and more is confessed by Elizabeth's unhelpful servants, and it is Sir William Cecil who gives Elizabeth the knowledge and advice she needs to combat their foolish revelations and save herself. One of the many strengths of this series is its ability to focus on the minutia, making the bigger picture clearer as a consequence. Cecil arrives to explain the law to Elizabeth and exactly how she must answer her interrogators in order to avoid a charge of treason. Elizabeth has the intelligence, Cecil has the facts she needs to make her decisions — this rapport between the two of them, first illustrated in the series with the Seymour affair, is one which will allow Elizabeth to flourish as a ruler. Elizabeth must first feel Cecil out before she can trust him — mistrust is inherent in her nature as well as the result of her experience. She questions his motives, and Cecil admits that he does all "for the proper order of the realm" rather than for Elizabeth herself. He may be a Protestant, but he can and will serve Mary after Edward's death for this very reason of order, and it is a lesson he teaches Elizabeth. When she asks him, "Will you swallow your conscience with the Mass?" he replies, "I will do what I must: speak softly and wait for better times." Elizabeth spells out her mistrust when she tells him: "I have trusted no man since I was eight, and Catherine Howard went screaming along the galleries to plead with the great Henry. The guards took her, still screaming, and dragged her away. On every hand, men betrayed her. And one before her. First there is trust, then passion, then death." Cecil's reply cements their relationship: "I'm a lawyer. I've told you the law in this matter. Trust *that*." Elizabeth has finally found a man she can rely upon, because their relationship is built on something other than pure emotion, something more enduring than mere feeling — a common goal to pursue what is just for the order of the realm. Above all else, this is Cecil's guiding principle.

The way Elizabeth handles the Seymour affair also demonstrates her character. Once she has the facts she needs, she gives her interrogators nothing while putting on a command performance that saves her life. Her comments about Seymour being "a foolish, strutting man" and "a man of much wit, and very little judgment" are for the benefit of her de facto jailors, who watch her every move. She never shows them a glimpse of her private thoughts. She rhetorically asks one of them who questions her sincerity, "Can you see into my soul?" She knows that they cannot, and as long as she maintains her self-control, she's safe, for they only know what she allows them to know. Jackson herself, through her study of Elizabeth, realized this, stating that Elizabeth had to keep her "central self" hidden since "she couldn't afford to betray herself."[4]

Elizabeth's sister Mary does not trust Cecil — calling him "the most cunning man in the kingdom" — but upon Edward's death she has the sense to heed his advice, and in so doing, is also saved. The fate of Jane Grey is shown as, one by one, cell doors are closed and latched on the Duke of Northumberland, Archbishop Cranmer, Guildford Dudley, and finally, poor Jane herself. With this threat averted, it remains to set up the forces at Mary's court, and the episode manages this adeptly by allowing the viewer to learn as Elizabeth learns. She speaks with the French ambassador, asking, "Must the English Queen choose either Spain or France as a friend? Must it be one or the other?" to which he replies, "It would take a genius to have both, Your Grace." The implication is obvious — Elizabeth herself managed to keep both Spain and France, if not on friendly terms with England, at least from being open enemies for a number of years until circumstances beyond her control overwhelmed her efforts. She may be new to court, but already she understands the politics at play, telling the ambassador that she knows the French have chosen Mary, Queen of Scots as their "friend." Even as early as the first episode of this series, Mary Stuart appears as a threat to Elizabeth.

The other threat to Elizabeth is her own sister. A few other offerings (e.g., Kapur's *Elizabeth* and *Elizabeth I: The Virgin Queen*) choose to treat Elizabeth's problematic relationship with her sister, but none do so in as much depth as *Elizabeth R*. Mary Tudor is a woman past her prime; as portrayed by Daphne Slater, she is pale and wan, looking ill even in the midst of her triumphs. The first scene in which she appears finds her praying before a statue of the Holy Virgin, and she does not immediately inspire sympathy. She praises God for her half-brother's painful death, and her moods are changeable — at first she's warm with Elizabeth, calling herself "your loving sister and queen." Unlike in other adaptations, this version shows the conflict under which Mary suffers, the dichotomy of her relationship with her sister. She and Elizabeth do share a bond; as Mary says to her, "We have been through many perils together." There is a natural tendency towards sympathy with one who has suffered the same trials — both were declared bastards, disinherited, subjected to danger (although Elizabeth's is just beginning), and were disappointments to their great father. Mary speaks of how she loved and befriended Elizabeth as a child and the motherly affection Mary displayed towards her when she was ill. For all this, however, there is still the insurmountable obstacle of Mary's jealousy. When Sir Thomas Wyatt makes the mistake of yelling, "God save Princess Elizabeth!" rather than the for-mulaic "God save the Queen!" Mary's demeanor instantly changes; in private audience with Elizabeth, she's passionately angry, "Why am I hated? The people are glad that I am old enough to die in time for you to become queen." Elizabeth spends her time trying to reassure Mary that she's loved, that Elizabeth is her loyal servant and wants nothing. Elizabeth knows how imperative it is to appear not to be a threat to the unstable Mary, and Jackson executes this tap dance with flair. With regard to the question of religion, Elizabeth first attempts, gently, to stand upon her principles, telling her sister that she was brought up another way: "I beg you to leave the use of my conscience to myself." Elizabeth evinces, even at this early stage, her inclusive philosophy of allowing each man to practice as his conscience dictates, but Mary is not so enlightened. A private man may have the use of his conscience, but the Queen's sister may not — she must be seen to visibly conform, lest others follow her example into heresy. Even in this Mary does not know herself, however; it's not long before even the private citizen cannot exercise his conscience without facing the flames of the heretic's stake. This episode shows Mary's path down the road to fanaticism — she begins as more tolerant because she labors under the delusion that, if given the choice, the people will wish to come back to the "true church." They are merely sheep led astray, and when lovingly shown their error by their royal shepherdess, they will correct it. When it begins to dawn on Mary that this is not the case, she takes away the choice — it's the Catholic Church or death. For Mary, Eliz-abeth's refusal to practice Catholicism is a personal defiance. "You look at me with the eyes of your mother," she says, before launching into a rant that, for the first time, hints at Mary's darker thoughts. She equates Elizabeth with Anne Boleyn's witchcraft, the "foul practices" that Mary believes killed her mother, Catherine of Aragon. At the same time, she takes no pleasure in seeing Elizabeth fearful, so she makes one last attempt to get Elizabeth to Mass. When it's unsuccessful, she sends her away.

Elizabeth may have told her sister she cannot be seen to conform without belief, but she would have been more accurate to say she simply has not yet been threatened effectively enough. When Elizabeth is informed of Mary's upcoming marriage to the Spanish heir to the throne, she realizes the danger of her position, and her turnaround is immediate. It's performance time once again, and she falls to her knees in front of Mary and her ret-inue, claiming to be "deeply penitent" for having been brought up in error. She requests books and teachers to instruct her in the tenets of Catholicism, for she "longs to learn the truth." To the viewer, Elizabeth's performance is near comical, but Mary pontificates happily and buys into her act completely. More than anything, including her principles, Jackson's Elizabeth is a survivor, and if going through the motions will keep her from the scaffold, she's more than willing to make a show of it.

Another strong suit of this episode is its portrayal of the effect of Mary's feelings for Philip II — the personal and political danger of putting emotion before policy. There are two driving factors in Mary's life: her religion and her love for Philip. In keeping with the theme in these films of women being overshadowed by portraits representing male power, Mary is seen almost worshipping a portrait of Philip; she even has her hands clasped in an attitude of prayer as she gazes adoringly at it. It is logical; her religion is all, and Philip represents the furtherance of her religion as well as her personal hopes — the perfect Catholic prince and husband. But it has been brought to her attention that perhaps he's not as perfect as she had initially been led to believe. Mary has been in love with an idea — a dream — and like all dreams, it is painful to watch when the illusion is shattered. Mary tearfully confesses to the Spanish ambassador that the prince of Spain has broken her heart, "He has mistresses. He has bastards. I believed him pure." She is devout and abstemious; she expects no less of her perfect Catholic prince. The ambassador, positioned behind Mary, can barely contain his laughter, and the audience is in on the joke. Astonishment would be the proper reaction only if this were *not* the case — a king is expected to have mistresses, regardless of how devoted he is to his religion. It showcases Mary's naïveté, but it also exemplifies the royal double standard. Philip is allowed, even expected (if not encouraged) to indulge his libido where he will as long as he does his duty and produces legitimate heirs, but Mary must keep herself chaste; a queen is not allowed this freedom. Should she indulge in it, or even *appear* to indulge in it, she would be labeled a whore and her throne would be endangered, as Elizabeth's relationship with Dudley later demonstrates. Mary expects the same of her betrothed as she has always done herself, and there is something pitiable in her expectations, which are bound to be disappointed, despite the lies with which the Spanish ambassador placates her. He also wants Elizabeth out of the way — she has feigned illness to absent herself from Mass, and she's much loved by the people. She is also young. The ambassador uses Mary's love to manipulate her: she longs to have Philip by her side; she must remove Elizabeth or he will not come. Mary does not hesitate, and she's most pitiful as she caresses Philip's portrait, ruing her own lost youth. She moves from the picture of his face to hers — reflected back from the all-too-familiar mirror — which represents Mary's advancing age. Elizabeth is still young, but as Mary herself moans, "Oh God, all my youth is gone." Her time is running out, and it makes her desperate.

Elizabeth is sent away from court, and strongly reminiscent of Vanessa Redgrave's Mary Stuart, as she gallops away, she laughs, "Free, free, free!" She is anything but, however, having failed to recognize the danger. The result is Wyatt's rebellion, and when the soldiers come for Elizabeth, she faints dead away. As the historical Elizabeth was often wont to do in emotionally trying situations, Jackson's Elizabeth becomes ill. The impression is that this is no pretense; Jackson is made up to look truly unwell, pale and listless, and when she sees the heads on pikes as she enters the city of London, she actually vomits. She may retain her mental self-control, but her body is exhibiting what her mind attempts to hide — her fear.

In this series, it is Wyatt's rebellion that truly changes Mary. As Bishop Gardiner says, "Rebellion has quite changed the Queen. Her blood is up." Mary had pardoned poor Jane Grey, but her merciful days are over. Cranmer is burned, Jane and her coterie are sent to the block; Elizabeth knows there is a very real chance she may be next. Several scenes with regard to this affair as well as the earlier Seymour incident are instructive in that they show the ways Elizabethan interrogators used to manipulate prisoners into confession. Prisoners of noble blood could not be tortured into an admittance, so their own fear was used against them. Elizabeth is cajoled to confess, since she is assured that Mary will then offer her a pardon. Elizabeth is smart enough to know that she cannot count on Mary's mercy; Mary has gone down a road from which there is no turning back. Elizabeth wisely chooses to keep her own counsel, refusing to confess, even when confronted with Wyatt, who in this adaptation fully implicates her. These incidents show Elizabeth's ability to manipulate others; she gives a performance on the rainy Tower steps that alternates between wringing sympathy and commanding obedience from her jailors. She faces down the Lord Lieutenant of the Tower, and it is he who backs down under her barrage. Elizabeth emphatically states, "I will survive," and this means using her wits. She will not walk calmly to the gallows and suffer her fate. When told she is to be executed, she has the presence of mind to demand to see the warrant. It has been signed only by the Lord Chancellor; she extracts from the reluctant Lord Lieutenant that the Queen is ill. When Elizabeth asks if he will execute her on such shaky authority when she's heir to the throne of a woman who may die any moment, he can only say that the Chancellor is the head of the council and the "first man" in the kingdom; he cannot be denied. By sheer force of personality, Elizabeth convinces him when she warns, "If you value your life, go not to the first man, but to the first woman in this kingdom." He agrees to get confirmation of the warrant, and Elizabeth has won. She's intelligent enough to understand that she's safe; they have tried to execute her unlawfully because the law will not condemn her, and now that she has seen through their ruse, they are out of options.

Philip finally arrives, and all of Mary's illusions dissipate like wisps of cloud. In a heartrending scene, the happy bride waits for her new husband in a bed strewn with rose petals. To show the passage of time, the candle burns down to nothing as Mary cries and still he does not come. When Philip finally does arrive, he looks none too pleased to do his royal duty. She has waited so long for love and comfort, as well as a political and religious ally, but the reality is that she has procured for herself a husband who finds her repugnant and whose concern is securing England, not supporting his wife.

When things go wrong in one's personal life, there's a tendency to lash out at others as a response to the pain and unhappiness. In Mary's case, this affects the entire country — as things go from bad to worse with Philip, so goes England. Mary has heresy bills passed, and the burnings begin. Her own husband counsels against them, as does the Spanish ambassador, but she's "too devout to hear reason" and seeks a sort of purification by fire. As Mary screams while running through the palace, "I will burn heresy out of this country!" Elizabeth, under house arrest, is under constant scrutiny, and Cecil must go to great pains to bring her the news. It is Cecil who provides Elizabeth with the strength she needs when she has her first true moment of panic. Unwilling to be "shut up til I am old and withered," Elizabeth vows escape. She's completely dejected as she pronounces, "I will never be queen." It seems a very real possibility, with the country in chaos and Mary supposedly pregnant. But Cecil, as always, is the voice of reason and patience. The Queen is old. The Queen is often sick. Her child may be stillborn, or she may die. "Be silent. Be still," he calmly counsels Elizabeth, "You are the hope of the people. If you run like a coward, you will lose their love and kill their hope." Elizabeth has the sense to heed his advice, and she has more than just Cecil for an ally—there's one to be found in the most unlikely of places, her own brother-in-law, the Prince of Spain.

Philip (Peter Jeffrey) is an unlikable man, at once cold and lascivious. He watches his tortured wife's hysteria over her phantom pregnancy and coolly pronounces that he must leave, for "she is old, ugly, and barren and I can neither get the crown matrimonial nor any right to the succession." At first, he's not in favor of a match with Elizabeth ("one of that family is enough for any man"), but all the ambassador has to do is appeal to his prurience, and interest is sparked. Elizabeth is "passionate, mettlesome, ripe for the marriage bed," and the middle-aged Philip falls all over himself to have Mary bring her back to court so, like Seymour before him, he can woo her under his pregnant wife's very nose. He plays the dirty old man, watching Elizabeth dress through a peephole, then demanding that Mary treat her gently if she ever wants to see him again. Mary is pathetic, falling at his feet and begging him not to desert her. She believes she's doomed to repeat the past: Elizabeth's mother bewitched Mary's father away from Catherine of Aragon, and now Elizabeth is bewitching Mary's own husband away from her. There is no comfort for Mary.

The situation is not of Elizabeth's making, however, and she seems as confused as any when Philip has his meeting with her. She's extremely wary, obviously unsure of his intentions and inclined to treat him as a threat. The meeting takes place in Elizabeth's bedchamber, which Philip enters through a secret door, surprising her. He has been watching her through a peephole in the wall as she dresses. One commentary on the film noted that this is the closest *Elizabeth R* comes to the obligatory nude bathing scene which has been a staple in historical films ever since Claudette Colbert's Cleopatra luxuriated in her milk bath. The screenwriters originally wanted Philip to watch through a keyhole as Elizabeth bathed, but in keeping with this series' commitment to historicity, the idea was scrapped when it was pointed out that Elizabeth was only truly bathed without her undergarments twice—when she was baptized and when her body was prepared for burial—and palace doors had no locks, therefore no keyholes.[5] Instead, Philip is only allowed to watch as the final pieces of Elizabeth's elaborate court dress are tied on. During their meeting, he invades Elizabeth's space, touching her as he talks, putting his finger to her lips and kissing her on the cheek. As he speaks of how he wishes to "befriend" her, she never lets down her guard. She carefully weighs each word, each gesture, always suppressing her true feelings. When Philip finally leaves, convinced that Elizabeth will have him, she laughs out loud at her own fear and the irony of the situation.

Events switch into overdrive as Philip leaves for Spain and Mary quickly dies. Cecil arrives to greet Elizabeth, under the oak tree, and give her the ring of state. She holds out her hand for it, and once she has it, she closes it tightly in her fist—this is a queen who will have a strong grip on her power, and none can wrest it from her. The beginning episode is illustrative of the tact taken by the entire series—the focus here is on Elizabeth's "career," not her male love interests. It's one of the few portrayals of Elizabeth to introduce her without some sort of romantic consort. This is no Bette Davis with her Essex, no Blanchett with her Leicester, or even Simmons with her Seymour. Seymour appears only as a catalyst for the situation in which Elizabeth finds herself, a furtherance of the characterization that allows her to show her intelligence, cunning, and resolve in surviving the situation. It is telling that an introduction of any kind of real love interest for Elizabeth does not occur until two hours into the series, with the second episode, "The Marriage Game."

This episode introduces Robert Dudley, and he's meant to be a masculine figure—he's first shown riding boldly over hill and dale—but as played by Robert Hardy, he seems a bad fit for the part, neither overtly masculine nor especially romantic. He and Jackson exhibit little chemistry; her demeanor with him is no different than with her other courtiers. She warns all those gathered around her at Hatfield that she means to be "a monarch for use, not merely for show," and thus they may find "more pains than honor" in serving her. Men like Cecil are not deterred, but Dudley seems less inclined to serve than to flatter in hopes of monetary advancement. He's the very picture of disingenuousness, with Elizabeth admitting, "I never know when you are speaking the truth." Dudley has the audacity to ask, "Does it matter?" and she assures him it does. As they talk of their past together, the other major players discuss Dudley's effect, with the overwhelming sentiment echoing the Earl of Sussex's as he says, "Robert Dudley. I don't like it."

As Elizabeth rides triumphantly into London, the scene is often shot, as were earlier scenes of her interactions with Seymour, from Elizabeth's point-of-view. The viewer is meant to see things through her eyes, from the inside. She takes in the sunny day, pealing bells, and ecstatic subjects cheering from every window, and the overarching effect is that here is a reign with promise. Elizabeth shows that she means to capitalize on this promise by rolling up her sleeves and getting the ball rolling. She puts up her hair for the first time and strides into the council chamber with, "We are minded to join our council today." The council members seem astonished, they even have to rearrange the seating to make room for her, and are especially surprised when she does not sit quietly but sets the agenda. Due to the extra time afforded by the miniseries format, a more in-depth examination can be provided of the day-to-day workings of Elizabeth's government, the political machine of the council with Elizabeth at its head, and the portrayal of this is one of this series' many strong suits. The council discusses the debasement of coinage, appointment of judges, and other issues which show the problems facing the realm. Jackson's Elizabeth evokes a modern-day chairman of the board as she runs the meeting with brusque efficiency, soliciting advice but also acting decisively. That is, of course, until the matter of her marriage is raised, which she effectively tables with, "Leave that aside." Elizabeth is also shown auditing her own household accounts—this is a competent woman, one who's involved in the management of every aspect of government, from official appointments to making sure her accounts balance. She is intelligent and decisive ... unless she can more easily accomplish her goals through studied indecision.

The issue of Elizabeth's marriage may have been tabled in council, but there's no avoiding it, and the marriage suits roll in. Another of this series' strengths is its ability to show the difference between Elizabeth's private knowledge and the public face she puts on it for political effect—her performative aspect. For instance, she's been informed in detail by Cecil that the Spanish mean to propose a marriage with Philip, and her private reaction has been one of snide amusement. But when the Spanish ambassador arrives to propose said marriage, Elizabeth, in front of her entire court, puts on a hilarious show. She gasps, clasps her hands happily to her breast and moons about like a love-struck teenager, simpering, "You must forgive me. I had not expected this." She deftly puts the ambassador off by citing how this unexpected honor must be discussed with her council. Her equivocation and evasion are masterful as she stands in front of her throne and says with what seems regret at not being able to immediately answer in the affirmative, "I am a queen. I may not follow my own desires as an ordinary woman may do."

The actual object of Elizabeth's desire, Dudley, is with his wife, helping her move into her new home, the latest in a line of temporary residences owned by others. In other adaptations, Amy Robsart appears as a sort of saintly figure; though she is much put-upon, this characterization has her play more of the shrew. She does not bear her husband's long absences and attendance upon the Queen with equanimity. She's introduced by Dudley yelling at her, "I tell you it's impossible — the Queen does not like wives at court!" Amy is jealous and extremely unhappy, often melancholy to the point of despondency, and she hates life in the country. For his part, Dudley is cold and manipulative; it's clear he does not love her and considers her more of an impediment than anything else. He explains to her that this is his "chance" and speaks of the advantage to them both of the Queen's relationship with him. He defines his attraction for the Queen by saying that she "never has to pretend with me, and that's more important to her than anything." Amy accuses him of trying to sabotage the Queen's marriage negotiations so he can marry her himself. Instead of denying it, he merely says with disgust, "How could I marry her? I am already married."

Dudley shows exactly how devious he is by doing exactly what his wife has accused him of— sabotaging Elizabeth's marriage prospects by manipulating the major players. He has no qualms about using even his own sister, Mary Sidney, who is one of the Queen's favorite ladies-in-waiting. Dudley shamelessly pumps her for information, using her sweet disposition against her, and then using her even further by feeding her misinformation which undermines the Spanish marriage suit. Dudley's machinations do not go undetected, however. The Duke of Norfolk warns him, "One day someone will plunge a dagger in your heart," to which his poor sister, realizing she has been used, replies angrily, "If he can find it." Even those closest to Dudley are not safe from being used as tools to further his ambitions. This characterization is one of the most unlikable and unfavorable to the historical Dudley to be found in these adaptations, leaving the viewer continuously wondering what Elizabeth sees in this man, for she is smart enough to have taken his measure. Instead, she allows him into her room at all hours, and clad in her nightgown, she kisses him full on the lips, to the astonishment and horror of his sister and her other ladies-in-waiting. Things seem set to go from bad to worse, but Elizabeth is ironically saved by the event that frees Dudley to marry her.

Dudley's wife spends her days in close, dark places — he glibly says to her, "You're always lying in a dark room; no wonder you have sick fancies." Even after she tells him of the lump in her breast, he shows only a moment of placating kindness before becoming all business, directing her about the disposition of his debts and his servants before cheerfully telling her to "see more company." His solution is for his wife to get out more. One cannot help but sympathize with poor Amy, depressed and sick, abandoned by a husband who cares nothing for her. Her depression manifests itself in paranoia as she cries that she's surrounded by "his people" who would kill her "if they thought it would do any good." Dudley seems shocked, not by the implication, but that she would voice it, and hisses, "Amy! Do you want to destroy me?" Dudley goes back to court, the servants are duly sent away by Amy to enjoy the fair. When they come back, all is dark, and they trip over Amy, lying dead at the foot of the stairs. Whether she fell, whether she jumped, or whether she was murdered is left up to the viewer's imagination, though the conclusion of all the courts in Europe is made apparent as the camera immediately cuts to a laughing Mary Stuart who crows, "Fell down the stairs? The Queen of England is going to marry her horsekeeper, and he has killed his wife to make room for her!"

It is supremely ironic that the very event which makes Dudley available to marry Elizabeth, at the same time, puts her forever beyond his reach. Whether he's responsible for Amy's death or not, the public perception, as illustrated by Mary Stuart's comments, is that he has murdered her. A verdict of accidental death is returned, but of course no one believes in the impartiality of the investigation. As Cecil warns his queen, there is "much talk," and if Elizabeth succumbs and marries Dudley, her good name will be lost forever and with it the stability of her reign. Regardless of her personal desires, she must bow to public perception. It's also instructive to have Mary Stuart be the one to voice this public perception, for this is the same queen who would later tumble headfirst into the pitfall Elizabeth manages to avoid with the Robsart incident.

While other adaptations of Elizabeth's life show the court and foreign intrigues that threaten the stability of her reign, *Elizabeth R* is the first offering to demonstrate that intrigue and foreign powers are not the only perils England faces. Elizabeth and her councilors can guard against plots and open aggression, but they cannot guard against the human condition. Elizabeth is young, but in an age where medical care was rudimentary at best, her sudden death from disease or minor injury was a very real possibility and one that no other adaptation up until this point has explored. Elizabeth contracted smallpox in the early 1560s, and *Elizabeth R* uses this to illustrate just how close England constantly remained to the brink of civil war—literally a breath away. As Elizabeth lies almost insensible with fever, the fear is palpable as her council scrambles to come up with a plan for the governance of the realm after her death. She has no heir, and all other contenders seem non-starters. The atmosphere is one of panic, especially when Elizabeth, believing herself to be dying, names Robert Dudley as Lord Protector of the Realm. As Cecil calmly states, "The truth of it is, the Queen is about to die, leaving no bearable successor." Though naturally they all give their word to the dying Elizabeth to recognize Dudley as the de facto ruler of the realm, it's apparent as they feverishly plan in council that none of them will abide by their word. If Elizabeth dies, the possibility of civil war seems set to become a reality. Elizabeth does not die, and thus the danger is temporarily averted, but the situation acts as a catalyst for Parliament and Elizabeth's council to push even harder for her marriage, and oddly enough, for her to push even harder back *not* to marry. Her brush with death seems to have given her an even stronger resolve, one she is no longer afraid of showing in public. She points at each member of the council and the representatives from Parliament before declaring, "I am an *absolute* princess," and assuring them she will marry at no man's bidding.

That includes Dudley. Elizabeth attempts to pawn him off on Mary Stuart, but he secretly writes to the Scottish Queen, denying his suit, which infuriates Elizabeth, especially when Mary marries Darnley. This episode highlights how Elizabeth and Dudley manipulate and play each other — Elizabeth first plans to bestow the Earldom of Leicester on Dudley, then changes her mind at the last minute, humiliating him in front of all who have gathered to see him receive the honor. He plays the jealousy game, pursuing Elizabeth's lady-in-waiting, Lettice Knollys, in order to both punish Elizabeth and manipulate her into marrying him. If there's one main fault in this series, it is its inability to provide a convincing texture for Elizabeth's relationship with her favorite. There's no chemistry between the two, but more than that, Hardy and Jackson often seem not to even *like*, much less love each other. While this dynamic would still seem workable if there were an overwhelming physical attraction, without one, it seems inexplicable. There's little passion to their relationship at all; at best, it seems like cruelty mixed with political power play. As have various other interpretations, this series features an Elizabeth who chooses to couch their relationship in terms of canine imagery; she tells Dudley, "You are like my little dog — when people see you they know I am nearby. I made you what you are. If you try to take more, I will destroy you utterly." This is more than an idle threat made during a lover's spat — it's clear that Elizabeth means it, and the ambitious Dudley should take care. Elizabeth and Dudley have a tug-of-war in their relationship right up until the point where he arranges for her to meet him at St. Paul's churchyard: if she comes, he will marry her; if she does not, she will never see him again. He warns her that he will not wait. He is not, however, strong enough to keep his word. As they walk in the woods, discussing the event, he says, "You came, but too late," to which Elizabeth replies, "You waited, but not long enough." Elizabeth speaks of Catherine Howard, how they dragged her away and cut off her head, her second mention of this event which is clearly meant to underline its importance in the young Elizabeth's life. "I learned then how dangerous life was," she admits. Dudley assures her that "yielding would bring a kind of safety. You would learn that on our wedding night." Elizabeth's pointed reply is, "As my mother did." Her final word on the subject: "As I am now, I owe my life to no man's goodwill." What she relies upon is the goodwill of her subjects, something she has always known how to keep and can be more sure of than the vagaries of romance with Dudley or any other suitor. Dudley finally realizes that Elizabeth will never marry him, and yet still he stays; again, Elizabeth has won. He's no match for the strength of her personality.

Elizabeth does keep other marriage prospects in play, most notably the Duc d'Alençon. As she says to Cecil, no suitor is to be entirely discouraged. The title of this episode, "Shadow in the Sun," is a line taken from a poem written by the historical Elizabeth as a sort of farewell to the man she came closest to marrying. As it does in everything, this series expounds on the details, in this case those surrounding the Alençon marriage suit, which give a deeper understanding of the circumstances that drove Elizabeth's political priorities. The episode opens with Elizabeth and her entire court in mourning. They wear black as a political statement — it is not anyone at the English court who has died, but 6,000 French Protestants, Huguenots, who have been massacred on St. Bartholomew's Eve. The sea of black is a visual cue to display Elizabeth's displeasure to the French ambassador. Elizabeth herself has a realm replete with Catholics, but she shows tolerance, she protects them. What the Huguenot massacre is used to illustrate is that bloodshed of this kind is a very real danger, and one borne of subjects allowed to retaliate against those who differ from the royal religious view. Elizabeth remains calm; the impression is that her priorities are more political than personal, but members of her council are genuinely angry, especially Cecil, Lord Burghley, who calls it the worst crime since the Crucifixion. Dudley, the Earl of Leicester, uses it as he does everything else — to his own advantage, telling the French ambassador that marriage with the Duc d'Alençon is now not to be contemplated. The entire court turn their faces to the wall, literally turning their backs on the French ambassador, as he leaves the court in disgrace. Burghley may be angry, but this also provides him with an opportunity — to again put forth the Catholic threat and its figurehead, Mary Stuart. This is, in his opinion, the perfect opportunity for Elizabeth to "deal with the problem once and for all." This episode also sees the first introduction of Sir Francis Walsingham. Played by Stephen Murray, he's a dour and completely unappealing man; he has his own agenda, which at times does not dovetail with Elizabeth's, but for the time being, even Walsingham can admit the wisdom of Elizabeth's "wait and see" policy. As Lettice Knollys says to Leicester, "The Queen is decidedly indecisive about so many things."

In an attempt to fix the rift with England, the Queen Dowager of France, Catherine de Medici (Margaretta Scott), has decided to offer up one of her lesser sons, the Duc d'Alençon. The historical Catherine de Medici was a powerful force; three of her sons sat on the throne of France, and she's often portrayed in film and fiction as a domineering mother and a cruel mother-in-law to Mary Stuart. This adaptation follows suit — she's deep-voiced and mannish, a strong woman, harsh and unpleasant, but she's also shrewd. The unpleasantness, as well as the prevailing opinion of Elizabeth in foreign courts, is demonstrated by the parody Catherine watches (and directs) with relish — two garishly made-up dwarves, one dressed as Elizabeth and the other as Leicester, play a farce of the Queen and her favorite's relationship while Catherine laughs and encourages their bawdy behavior. The Duc d'Alençon (Michael Williams) and his mother have a rapport that is, at best, antagonistic. In some offerings, Alençon is portrayed as a soft-spoken soulmate for Elizabeth; in others, a cross-dressing buffoon. *Elizabeth R* splits the difference — Alençon has his less-than-admirable traits, and what he puts on for Elizabeth is certainly a façade, but he's no fool; as his mother pointedly says, he is "so sharp you could do yourself an injury." Alençon's stance is, "Why bother when there are plenty of others who wish to do it for me?" For him, Elizabeth represents more than just money and power; he also hopes to find freedom from a overbearing mother and something else he has never experienced — a home. His brother has the throne of France, leaving Alençon with no kingdom of his own. *Elizabeth R* is also adept at depicting the role played by envoys in the process, the concept of courtship by proxy. Alençon's envoy is the handsome, clever and charming Jean de Simier (James Laurenson), and he prepares the road well — Elizabeth is quite taken with him. He also does his best to instruct the boorish Alençon and, when necessary, mitigate the mistakes his royal master has made. Though this marriage has many advantages for Alençon, most notably monetary support he can use to wage war in the Netherlands, he's concerned about escaping one powerful woman only to place himself in thrall to another. When he asks what Elizabeth is like and Simier says, "She is very ... majestical," Alençon looks horrified as he asks, "She's not like my mother, is she?"

From Elizabeth's point of view, Alençon has much in his favor, but one obstacle that may prove insurmountable is his religion. He's obviously not observant (his morality is shown to be flexible at best), and is known not only to be tolerant, but also a champion of the Huguenots; the simple fact remains, however, that he is a Catholic. This adeptly illustrates the political divisions within Elizabeth's own council. Leicester is, as always, out for himself, so he naturally opposes the match. Burghley and Sussex support it, with Christopher Hatton wavering but attempting objectivity. It also shows the dynamic the council has with Elizabeth; none of them dare to gainsay her or be the bearer of bad news, and there's bad news in a big way. Though it's supposedly a secret, all of them know of Leicester's marriage to Lettice Knollys. In fact, everyone at court knows, with the exception of Elizabeth. All agree that the Queen is bound to find out, but none will risk telling her. They fear any advantage in putting down Leicester would not be worth the devastation of the Queen's displeasure with the bearer of such unwelcome news. Hatton wryly remarks that when Elizabeth does find out, "If I were Leicester, I believe I'd spend a year or two circumnavigating the globe."

The fact that she's unaware of Leicester's marriage makes it all the more pitiful when Elizabeth asks him not to be jealous after she marries the Duc. For his part, Leicester shamelessly flirts with her and begs her not to wed. He tells her he loves her, and rather than saying she loves him in return, Elizabeth's reply is telling, that she *depends* on his love. Elizabeth has a public persona, but she also has a private need to be loved; whether she returns that love or not is a non-issue. It is demanded, unequivocally.

The writing of this episode and the way Elizabeth's courtship with the Duc is conducted provides something that, up until this point, has been entirely lacking in this series — humor. He's not a buffoon, but Alençon is a comic character. When he arrives unannounced, causing a wary Simier to draw his sword, Alençon sighs, "Put that damn thing away — it reminds me of mother." The disparity between his behavior with Simier, his true personality, and his exchanges with Elizabeth highlights the absurdity of the whole process, as do Simier's tireless machinations on Alençon's behalf. He writes florid letters supposedly from the Duc while Alençon himself snores in bed, and it's Simier who provides Alençon with the persona he should put forth: "Remember, you're a soldier — a man of deeds — not a courtier." It is also Simier who manages to flirtatiously finagle "personal" gifts from the Queen, such as her garters and nightcap, causing Alençon to dryly remark as he dons the nightcap that soon he'll have her entire wardrobe.

Unlike in other adaptations, both Elizabeth's first meeting with the Duc and his introduction at court go remarkably smoothly. Even Leicester manages to behave himself, and the framing of the scene is indicative of the situation; it's a sort of tug-of-war, with Elizabeth standing in the middle as her two suitors, on either side, insincerely flatter each other. All is surface veneer and politeness. The main theme is one of insincerity — the entire process involves constant pretense and flattery, with no one ever entirely certain where the truth lies. Elizabeth tells one of her ladies that Alençon "will do very well," as well as telling Burghley, "I mean to have him, you understand that?" All appearances are that she is serious. She demonstrates this by walking out on a sermon where the preacher unwisely launches a veiled attack on the French marriage, practically comparing the Duc to the Devil, who also appears in beauteous raiment, bearing gifts. Elizabeth, incensed, threatens to hang the poor cleric.

Elizabeth treats Alençon with condescending affection, and Alençon may be insincere in many ways, but he does seem genuinely impressed by Elizabeth, remarking that she's a "splendid woman" who "plays the game for all it's worth." He makes this statement at a ball Elizabeth has given, and the atmosphere indicates how very much goes on beneath the surface gaiety at court. A panicked Leicester watches Lettice Knollys, his secret wife, making eyes at other courtiers and does his best to quietly get her to leave before Elizabeth senses something is amiss. Alençon languishes in a window seat. Simier watches Elizabeth from the corner, planning, planning, and Elizabeth calls for the Volta. Unlike in other adaptations where this dance is used to demonstrate the unsuitability of Elizabeth's relationship with Leicester and the overwhelming disapproval it fosters, *Elizabeth R* uses it as a matter of course. Elizabeth and Leicester begin the dance, and after one set everyone else happily falls in to follow suit — an entire court dancing to Elizabeth's tune, and perfectly content to do so.

The problem is that Elizabeth's council isn't quite sure in what key they are required to sing. This series, more than any other offering, shows how difficult Elizabeth's councilors found it to decipher what it was their queen truly wanted, the rampant confusion she intentionally caused in them. They realize that the people are not in favor of a marriage with a French Catholic; there is mention of the fear of a massacre occurring in England as it did in the Netherlands. The scenes in council also depict the mind-numbing aspects of governance — everything is not all flash and tension and heated debate as often appears in depictions of the Privy Council. Some councilors are eating, others stretching or yawning, heads down; the entire atmosphere is one of hopeless deadlock, fruitless hours spent as exhaustion threatens, the same point being argued over and over with no progress or solution achieved. Finally Burghley states that he will deliver the news to the Queen, that her council "is divided and irreconcilable, except in loyalty to her." This series also demonstrates how absolutely irrational Elizabeth could be in her dealings — in essence, providing a lose-lose situation for her council by forcing them to guess at her true wishes when her behavior was intentionally equivocal. When Burghley delivers the news, he tries once and for all to pin Elizabeth down. As one commentary has noted, the historical Burghley was often "Elizabeth's mouthpiece. At times, their separate voices are indistinguishable." But on the other hand, Elizabeth sometimes made her wishes indecipherable to the point that she almost drove her poor secretary mad. The diplomatic Burghley even admitted, "Sometimes so, sometimes no, and at all times, uncertain and ready to stays and revocations ... this irresolution doth weary and kill her ministers, destroy her actions, and overcome all good designs and counsels ... [Her Majesty] driveth me to the wall."[6] She has asked, nay *commanded*, the council to give an opinion, and, as Burghley says, they cannot give her one "until they know exactly what you want." It's the quintessential catch-22: the council cannot back Elizabeth's play because they do not know what it is, and Elizabeth will not make a play without their backing. She either expects them to read her mind or, more likely, she expects them to wallow in confusion, buying her time and plausible deniability for any unfavorable consequences regardless of the decision made. Elizabeth pronounces, "I expected a universal and unanimous request from you for me to proceed with the marriage." She actually begins to cry, the first tears Jackson has shed onscreen, as she confesses to Burghley, "You have wives, you have children. You know what it is to love and be loved.

It is your right. It is every man's right. Yet in your wisdom you would make me barren." Her pain seems genuine, her sincerity beyond question. That makes the viewer's astonishment all the more powerful when, shortly thereafter in private conversation with Sussex, the most trenchant supporter of the marriage, she says, "I hate the very idea of marriage. I cannot do it. Every day I am more and more afraid." Elizabeth's body language and placement is revealing: she fidgets with her bed hangings and coverlet, she talks to the sympathetic Sussex from behind the barrier of her bedpost, an outward expression of how she toys nervously with the idea of filling her royal bed. She admits, "I had wanted and not wanted. Made your lives a misery. But I am telling you the truth now, I do not mean to marry. *Ever.*" She admits her earlier prevarication, and again, she *seems* in earnest. Her councilors must choose which they wish to believe and pursue it as policy, for Elizabeth certainly will not tell them. As she irrationally pronounces when they cannot give her an answer, "As you have kept your feelings from me, so shall I keep mine from you."

In other onscreen representations of Elizabeth's marriage suits, the suitors, snide remarks optional, simply disappear into the ether from which they came or, at best, take leave of Elizabeth with both of them going through the courtly motions of being devastated. Alençon chooses the latter, but this series has shown in minute detail exactly how far the marriage negotiations have progressed — almost to the point of no return. As it still does today, in Tudor England financial remuneration could fix a host of problems, unwanted lovers included, and *Elizabeth R* shows exactly how mercenary the marriage market could be. Alençon is not exactly happy to be sent on his merry way. His priorities have always been political; he'd "sooner have Elizabeth's money than body any day," but he does seem genuinely distressed that the marriage has fallen through — he not only cries when he's alone with Simier, but confesses that he has never had a home and hoped to find one in England. There's nothing for it but to pay him off, not so much to force him to leave, but to ensure he keeps up the pretense so that the rest of Europe still considers the marriage a viable possibility. Simier negotiates a settlement with Burghley, and Alençon is on his way. Elizabeth evinces some strong emotions at his departure; as do other miniseries offerings (e.g., *Elizabeth I*), *Elizabeth R* utilizes the poem mentioned earlier and written by the historical Elizabeth describing her feelings at the loss of Alençon, "monsieur" as she calls him.[7] Using voiceover, Jackson recites it as Elizabeth watches Alençon leave and Leicester passes him in the corridor to come back from the exile caused by his marital transgression. Elizabeth's loss has been two-fold, for in another similarity with other screen Elizabeths, she's learned of Leicester's marriage to Lettice Knollys through Simier, a clever ploy to remove this impediment to his master's wedding plans. Leicester's return marks a change — Elizabeth may have him back as a poor substitute for the real lover she would have had in Alençon, but she no longer wants Leicester in this capacity. The change in their dynamic is readily apparent when he attempts to flatter her with talk of love and she informs him that they can no longer speak of such things, for he is married, and adds, "We will deal with each other more honestly from now on."

Leicester disappears from the scene altogether, as does Burghley, along with other major players Sussex and Hatton, in the next episode in the series, "Horrible Conspiracies." Perhaps the most lacking in a feel for continuity, this episode focuses almost entirely on Mary Stuart, the Babington Conspiracy and Elizabeth's relationship with Walsingham.

The depiction of this relationship is drastically different from Kapur's ideological marriage of the minds or later interpretations' near comical reciprocal irritation. Elizabeth greatly dislikes Walsingham, at times seems even to loathe him, and she's often quite cruel to him. For his part, he's overwhelmed with concern for the safety of this woman who treats him abominably and whom he can barely do more than tolerate on a personal level. The driving force in his life is the "constant threat," Mary Stuart. Mary herself gets a great deal more screen time in this offering than in many others (excluding the biopics of her life), and she is less-than-pleasant company — querulous, complaining, and none-too-bright. She spends the majority of her time whining to or quarreling with the man charged with overseeing her house arrest, Sir Amyas Paulet, one of several minor players who add to the depth of this series. One of the more interesting characterizations in this vein is that of Elizabeth's "rackmaster," Richard Topcliff, who seems to be almost a precursor of the celebrity stalker, which in its way reinforces Elizabeth's celebrity status. He's devoted to Elizabeth, to whom he claims, in rather deluded fashion, to be very close, as he tells one of his hapless victims, for he has "seen her bare, above the knee." He's a man who gets an enviable amount of enjoyment and satisfaction out of his professional life — he likes getting up in the morning and going to his "job" — and his entirely creepy portrayal adds a splash of color to an otherwise slow episode.

It's clear from the beginning that Walsingham has the upper hand. Babington is an idiotic fop (Walsingham calls him a "callow youth") who has no idea of the true ramifications of his actions; Father Ballard is the only one in the conspiracy who seems to have average intelligence and a grasp of the situation — he warns Babington, "Let a wise man look where he leap" — but what judgment he has is clouded by his religious ideologies. Walsingham, on the other hand, has the situation well under control; he's the puppetmaster who holds the strings, using his agents, who are suave and convincing, to entrap Mary as well as Babington. Walsingham is also used to illustrate the change in the perception of Mary Stuart that has occurred over time. At this point, she has been incarcerated in England for several years; how she came to such a state is not examined in detail in this series. There's a tendency in these films and miniseries to show certain events as static — Mary is viewed by her Catholic supporters as a martyr from the moment she loses her throne. However, *Elizabeth R* is closer to the truth. As Walsingham tells Elizabeth, Mary is now more dangerous than in times past because the *perception* of her has changed. Her past transgressions (e.g., Darnley's murder and her marriage to Bothwell) garnered her widespread disapproval at the time, even in the Catholic courts of Europe, and ensured that they were less likely to complain of her treatment when she was originally "invited" to be Elizabeth's "guest." Time has softened the public perception of Mary, however; Darnley and Bothwell are a distant memory, and in the 20 years that have passed, Walsingham warns, sentiment about Mary has evolved so much that "some have described her as a martyr."

Since Elizabeth has cruelly ordered that new tortures be devised for these particular conspirators, Babington has the execution to which he can look forward duly described to him by an ecstatic Topcliff. This has the side benefit of informing the viewer of how executions for treason were conducted in Elizabethan England. This is immediately followed by a shot of a crucifix covered in what is meant to be Babington's blood. Mary's trial is not shown, but the viewer is told that the court "heard her case with the proper indifference," and Elizabeth does her tap dance before a Parliament hungry for Mary's blood. Her double-talk is masterful before she leaves them with a gem only the historical Elizabeth could devise: "Take in good part my answer answerless." Despite what she has said, this series chooses to portray an Elizabeth who is most decisive when it comes to the execution of her cousin. A routine stack of papers is brought for her to sign, with Mary's execution warrant filed in amongst them. She signs them with so little hesitation and emotion that the viewer is almost certain she's unaware what she has done, until she says to the clerk, "Davison, you know what has occurred? Does it not affect you in any way?" before demanding to hear no more of the matter until it is quite finished. This version of Elizabeth has no compunction about the actual death of her cousin, only the ramifications for herself—she tells Paulet, Mary's puritanical jailer, that she's very disappointed in him, for he's "found no way to shorten the life of this captive queen." She even intimates that "there is still time to do it privily," but Paulet is a man of principle and refuses. It had never occurred to him that there would be a royal desire for him to murder his charge, and he's astonished, as well as disappointed in Elizabeth. He wants a public execution for Mary, as does Walsingham. Elizabeth does not fear the act; she fears bearing the responsibility for Mary's execution. As she says to Paulet, "Like all great matters, this act is my burden. No one will aid me."

Mary is unrepentant—something all screen Marys have in common. She has reviewed her life and proclaims, "I regret nothing. I know my faults and my virtues. I know that I am a creature of impulse, seldom thinking before I act, driven on by passions, delighting in the unexpected, and bored by sensible caution, disliking all who are not of my humor. This is my alchemy, and I rejoice in it, even though it has brought me much unhappiness. Even though it has led me here, I would not have been created differently." This is just one of this episode's absurdly expository bits of dialogue—Mary describes herself point by point for the viewer, so there's no doubt about her characterization. Mary's execution is duly shown, with its cutaway three strokes of the axe, and Elizabeth is informed that Mary "is quite removed from this earth." Unlike the corresponding scene with this same actress from *Mary, Queen of Scots*, there is no tearfully dejected Elizabeth who looks down to her hands at the relics Mary has left behind—her Bible and rosary. Instead, Paulet assures an unemotional Elizabeth that the block and all of Mary's clothes have been burned, that no trace of blood remains, nothing that the people could use as a saint's relic. Elizabeth has done all she can to accomplish execution without martyrdom, and she certainly feels nothing for Mary on a personal level.

This episode is also the first to depict the evolving dynamic at court. Though contemporaries Leicester and Burghley reappear with later episodes, this episode shows the passage of time, and the faces at court are much younger than Elizabeth, who now not only looks older, but has various health problems, from bad teeth to digestive issues. One commentary noted that, while a "tooth-conscious Hollywood would never tolerate a black smile,"[8] Jackson and the BBC evinced no such scruples, opting for the historical over the attractive, and consequently Jackson's teeth were progressively darkened. Walsingham shares Elizabeth's digestive issues; the one enemy that is truly a match for him is disease—he is obviously unwell. Rather than show sympathy, Elizabeth demonstrates her loathing for him with how horribly she treats him. She exhibits almost sociopathic cruelty, praying to God that the conspirators "die in great agony, their bodies torn apart, and their souls in great torment." She's just as awful to those who loyally serve her; she has described Walsingham to his face as "a piss-bowl of self-righteousness" that "sickens" her, and in an extremely disturbing bit of haranguing, she calls particular attention to his digestive issues, employing metaphors which revolve around excrement, and then goes into graphic detail about what he has to look forward to when it finally consumes him — the joys of worms and decomposition. She leaves him with, "Dying is a fearful process," and bids him remember all the terrible things she's said to him when he lies on his deathbed, which is not far off. She then laughs hysterically.

Elizabeth's relationship with Walsingham as portrayed in this episode is strange — she treats him as badly or worse than she would an enemy, and yet he works for the realm. Walsingham is not a likeable character — he's at once smug and puritanical — but aversion to his personality does not seem a strong enough motivation for her behavior; neither does fear, a fear of her own mortality that causes her to lash out. Her feelings are also much less vehement in the other episodes in which Walsingham appears, manifesting themselves more as dislike than hatred. Accordingly, the characterization of Elizabeth in this episode feels different, out of sync. It is yet another indicator of this episode's lack of continuity, the only episode in this series to display this failing.

It's with a sigh of relief that things return to normal with the next episode, "The Enterprise of England." As the title suggests, it focuses on the Spanish Armada, and opens with Philip II interminably confessing his sins while his young son waits outside, playing with a model ship. This ship is a metaphor for the Armada and everything it represents, but Philip is no eager crusader gleefully planning Elizabeth's demise. He is no fanatic. He has changed since, in thrall to the lusts of the flesh, he sought Elizabeth's hand; his beliefs have strengthened with the passage of time and the aging of his person — every time he is shown, he's either praying, confessing, taking the sacrament, or discussing religious matters — but he's most reluctant to take up the "enterprise of England." As yet another supplicant, an English priest, arrives to convince him to avenge Mary Stuart's "murder" by attacking England, Philip says wearily, "For 20 years men have urged this enterprise on me." His animosity towards Elizabeth is purely religious and political rather than personal; if anything, he admires her, saying that he's envious of her brilliance, and even the Pope "at once praises her and demands I destroy her." Though other offerings present the Spanish threat as one unified and unassailable force, this series shows the truth of the matter: it's a joint effort — Philip is dependent upon the military assistance of the Duke of Parma, and Philip's exchequer cannot handle the expense of outfitting a Spanish naval force of appropriate size. There's a tendency in these films to couch the conflict in terms of David and Goliath — the gallant little English are victorious over the Spanish because they are ingenious and God is on their side (or, in some cases, Elizabeth as His handmaiden, who commands the very wind). This is only partly true; though the Spanish did greatly outnumber the English, *Elizabeth R* shows the cracks in the Spanish façade from the very beginning, long before the fleet ever sets sail. Philip's admiral, Don Alvaro de Santa Cruz, begs him to abandon the enterprise, for Philip's cost-cutting measures have resulted in a fleet that is far too small and not appropriately outfitted. Any employee ever tasked with accomplishing an impossible project by an administration that refuses to allocate appropriate funding sympathizes when Philip commands the poor Santa Cruz to get on with the invasion, "Count me ever your friend, Don Alvaro, but be gentle with my purse." In addition to being miserly, Philip also relies on faulty intelligence: a few disaffected English Catholics have convinced him that *all* English Catholics will rise up in support of him, causing him to mistakenly count one-third of England's population as friendly to his cause. There are some tragicomic scenes as the experienced commander Santa Cruz lies dying, his ships still in harbor, with Philip demanding they depart immediately even though nothing is ready. Santa Cruz wryly tells the messenger to assure Philip he will soon depart, and he immediately does just that by dying. Philip appoints that most inexperienced and reluctant of orange growers, the Duke of Medina-Sedona, as Santa Cruz's totally incompetent successor. The poor man struggles over nautical charts and lists of contradictory and convoluted instructions from Philip, and on his way out, steps on and crushes the model ship — a portent of things to come. Everywhere Philip is warned of failure, but he remains stubbornly and irrationally assured of Spanish victory.

Elizabeth is inclined not to take the Spanish threat seriously. In Burghley's bedchamber, bandying with her sick secretary, who has been laid low by gout, she demands both Burghley and Walsingham's service on her council, and she's very pleased with herself. Elizabeth is in the mood for peace after so much war and has been negotiating with the Duke of Parma in the Netherlands, confident that she's about to be successful. She's very dismissive of the Spanish threat, teasing Burghley that he has been on about it for 20 years and nothing has changed. Something *has* changed, however — Mary Stuart has been executed. While Parma distracts Elizabeth in the Netherlands with his talk of peace, Philip has more time to prepare his attack. Walsingham warns Elizabeth that Parma "plays you for a dupe," but she does not heed him.

This is one thing that the characterization of Elizabeth and Philip are shown to have in common in this episode — both willfully ignore sound advice from competent counselors. Walsingham warns Elizabeth; Sir Francis Drake begs her to be allowed to harry the Spanish ships in their ports; Leicester, back from the fighting in the Netherlands, brings news of Parma's mendacity. Still Elizabeth is unmoved. If he cannot achieve his ends through direct methods, Walsingham is more than happy to employ others — he pays off a few soothsayers to prophesy the fall of empires and circulates rumors that the populace is clamoring for Drake to put to sea. This series, as do other Elizabethan films, also shows the importance of pamphlet propaganda. In an age when there was no such thing as the news media, pamphlets were circulated concerning current events, and they were considered very dangerous indeed, for they could influence public opinion with their unmitigated rhetoric. Offending printers and authors could be imprisoned, lose body parts, or even their lives. When it's brought to Elizabeth's attention that a dangerous pamphlet concerning the Spanish takeover of England is being circulated, she finally springs into a flurry of action, making preparations and sending Drake to sea.

One other thing Elizabeth and Philip have in common is that both their admirals have no experience. Elizabeth appoints Lord Howard of Effingham as admiral of her fleet, but unlike the bumbling Medina-Sedona, Howard is intelligent and a quick learner. He has no experience of his own, but utilizes the experience of Drake and heeds his advice, proving himself an effective commander. The engagements are relayed to Elizabeth through one of Drake's salty sea dogs who reads letters and details battles in annoyingly roundabout pirate speak. Elizabeth's speech at Tilbury is framed so that the camera focuses on her face as she declaims it in the grand theatrical tradition. Since showing a massed force was more than the BBC's budget could manage, audience reaction is displayed through two guards stationed at Elizabeth's tent, who assure the viewer, "God's Death, she breedeth courage in a man" before looped cheers resound.

As is typical for these offerings, the jubilation of the Armada's defeat goes hand in hand with the devastation of Leicester's death. By this point, he and Elizabeth alternate between mild affection and mild irritation — an old couple whose passions have long since been spent. When Elizabeth baits him by remarking on what a pretty youth young Essex is, she gets no response, and at Tilbury, they "sit like two old folks and remember gay times." Elizabeth also plays the mother hen, specifying a particular diet for Leicester to "reduce that sagging flesh" for "God, you look so old. So sick." Ever the flatterer, Leicester assures Elizabeth that she is Gloriana, ageless, but she snorts and bids him, "Look in your glass, my lord. We are mortal." Unlike Kapur's mythic treatment of the Queen, Jackson's Elizabeth has no aspirations for divinity; her goal is to rule as an absolute monarch, but a mortal one.

Leicester's mortality is demonstrated during the festivities marking the Armada's defeat. One scene in particular portrays Elizabeth in an extremely callous light. Lord Howard informs Elizabeth that her loyal sailors have not only not been paid for their great service, but are actually starving in the streets. He begs her for the funds to pay them, feed and clothe them, and Elizabeth refuses, instead telling him to simply dismiss them. Her words are all the more terrible because she turns around and speaks of striking a medal with her image to commemorate the Armada's defeat, wasting money on useless trinkets while the men who laid down their lives for her starve. It's particularly upsetting given Elizabeth's near-constant talk about her care for her people and the love she bears them. She appears almost completely heartless. As if she's invoked instant divine retribution, Burghley enters to inform Elizabeth that the Earl of Leicester is dead. Various portrayals dramatize Elizabeth's handling of this news in different ways, from disbelief to hysterics. Jackson chooses a different route, showing nothing more than bemusement at first. She goes to her desk, takes out a letter, and labels it as his last. The Earl of Essex bounces in like a huge puppy, almost as if to denote that as soon as one favorite is dead, the next steps into his place, and exuberantly cries, "Your court cannot be gay without you!" When Elizabeth learns that he's aware of Leicester's death but is completely unaffected, she shows the first emotion she's exhibited — anger. She throws him out, locks the door behind her, and sinks to the floor as the episode ends.

The introduction of Essex is always the beginning of the end for Elizabeth in film adaptations of her life, and this offering is no different. The last episode, "Sweet England's Pride," revolves around Elizabeth's relationship with Essex, which is made readily apparent from the opening scene. The camera focuses on Elizabeth's wig, the symbol of her advanced age; her makeup has been significantly enhanced to show the aging process, and she looks disturbingly garish, like a white-painted puppet. Despite this, and unlike other adaptations, she still does not seem displeased with what she sees in the mirror that is handed to her, nor the obviously insincere comments about her beauty with which those around her flatter her. Her problem is with Essex: "Lord Essex has imperiled the kingdom ... our proud men lead us to a fall." Essex is not the only one to blame, but he's the catalyst. Elizabeth sums up the situation: "Essex fights Raleigh harder than the Spaniard. They squabble like small boys. I will give them no more toys of war to play with." Elizabeth cannot even trust her own council, who "advise me for their own ends, for their own glory and when they fail it is I who must pay!" Later series, most notably *Elizabeth I: The Virgin Queen*, focus in greater detail on this idea of self-service versus service — a dynamic that has evolved at Elizabeth's court as her old counselors are replaced by younger, more selfish ones, and a feature that marks the downward slide at the end of her reign. Burghley makes his final appearance, old and infirm, at a ball, showing the progression which has occurred. Elizabeth sits with him as they observe the dancing courtiers, all young, and he warns Elizabeth against the "fiery stallions" which now fill her court, proud and ambitious young people she may be too old to harness, to the detriment not only of herself, but also the realm. Elizabeth realizes that now there is no one without "self-interest" in the entire court, and she's tired of their "sweet words." As Francis Bacon puts it, "Each man goes his own way." While other representations tend to show the rivalry between Essex and Robert Cecil as strictly personal, *Elizabeth R* hits it closer to the mark by depicting the conflict as one between a war faction (led by Essex) and those that favored diplomacy (Cecil). There is no personal glory in diplomacy, and this is why Essex wants none of it. He contemptuously bids Cecil to "go fight your paper wars."

The Earl of Essex, as played by Robin Ellis, is certainly tall and handsome enough, and he gets the vain and foolish part right, but his portrayal is affected and most unconvincing when he attempts to convey the extremes of the historical Essex's character. To illustrate how "swiftly changed" he can be, he progresses into absurd territory as he goes from blanket-clad illness to jumping up and down and overturning tables in mad exuberance. Bacon warns him that "the Queen must not be forced into a corner. If you challenge her, she will have the last word. It is not safe to be too proud," but for the moment, Essex remains loyal out of practicality rather than any other consideration — he does not currently have the money to raise a force.

Elizabeth treats Essex with precious little affection, much as she did the Earl of Leicester before him. There is certainly nothing untoward about their physical relationship — if there's any love, or semblance of it, between them it is of the courtly variety. Elizabeth wryly admits, "I stand more from him than any man," but the viewer is left wondering why, for her motivation for this tolerance is never made apparent; it's certainly not affection. The closest Elizabeth gives to explaining her use for Essex is, "I am not Gloriana without the magic of his mirror," and this takes the prevailing mirror theme of these films a step further — Elizabeth finds the glory she has lost through her advancing age reflected in the flashy Essex. On a personal level, he seems more of an irritant to her than anything else, and this series has the time to show the ebb and flow of their relationship, which runs something like this: offense, disfavor, illness, reinstatement. This cycle is repeated several times, until Essex goes off to Ireland. He's ecstatic to go; there's a laughable scene in council where he details the qualities needed in a Lord Protector for Ireland by bragging about himself— courage, military prowess, nobility — then pretends false modesty when Elizabeth says he embodies these qualities and should have the job. Raleigh has been cleverer; he knows that Ireland has claimed the political if not actual lives of many English nobles. Raleigh's rivalry with Essex gets a more in-depth treatment in this series than in any other offering. Raleigh is older, and he's clearly the intellectual superior, though his relationship with Elizabeth is not used to illustrate this. It is confined more to isolated incidents, such as allowing it to be Raleigh who draws his dagger to protect the Queen when Essex draws his sword on her.

After his dismal showing in Ireland, Essex cannot expect a warm welcome at home, where he has been forbidden to go, and yet still he believes all he needs do is tell Elizabeth his side of the story and all will be right. As the Earl of Southampton (a much more suave and worldly courtier than the sniveling sycophant of other adaptations) sardonically warns him, "I would've liked to have seen Tyrone, just once — before I face the gallows." Tyrone himself is a clever and devious fellow, and he reads Essex is an instant and adeptly plays on his weaknesses — when Essex demurs that the Queen might not like a settlement, Tyrone replies, "Who's talkin' about the queen, man? She's as good as dead."

Essex returns home to a semblance of "sweet calm" from Elizabeth, who listens without reproach to his tale of woe — the constant rain, the Irish bogs, the truce — before saying with meaning, "We must consider how to treat your achievement." Elizabeth strips Essex of his offices and effectively bankrupts him. Cecil is smugly satisfied, feeling that without his offices Essex represents no danger, but the prescient Raleigh has sense enough to be worried. When Cecil ignores his warnings, he tries his luck with the Queen, telling her urgently, "If we do not act, we are lost." Her reply is telling: "We, we — who is for *me*?" Elizabeth's young courtiers include their own welfare in the equation, putting it on the same level with, if not a higher one, than their queen's, and Elizabeth longs for the days of her more selfless councilors.

Finally action must be taken, and after his abortive coup attempt, Essex is sent to the Tower where he makes a pitiful showing. Other adaptations allow their Essexes, no matter what their demeanors up until that point, a brave death. *Elizabeth R's* Essex is repugnant in his cowardice — he cries like a child, sobbing that he's frightened. He crawls and begs at Cecil's feet, attempting to blame anyone but himself, naming everyone he can possibly think of, even screaming after the retreating councilors that his own sister was involved and must be taken. He tries to send the proverbial ring to Elizabeth, but the jailor refuses to take it. Emotionally spent, he passes out. He does manage to pull himself together long enough for the stroke of the axe to be met with a modicum of dignity, but his behavior up until that point almost negates this clean ending.

Elizabeth writes the whole thing off with no remorse, only the admittance to Parliament: "I have nourished proud men at the expense of my people." Essex's death is also the death of any rapport between Cecil and Raleigh. Other adaptations show the two as fast comrades, united against Essex; *Elizabeth R* also demonstrates elements of this union against a common foe, which was an understanding between the two for a time. It did not last, however, which is something only *Elizabeth R* hints at when Cecil almost immediately turns on Raleigh by insinuating to Elizabeth that the people fear the honors of Essex will pass directly to Raleigh and the cycle will begin anew.

As Elizabeth admits herself, the fabric of her reign is unraveling, and the time has come for her to die. She takes a good long while to do it, with attempts made to remove the ring of state before she is actually dead. The entire court stands silent, waiting. Raleigh walks through the echoing audience chamber, pausing to look at the empty throne. One can practically read his mind: who will sit here next? Cecil tries to the last to get a straight answer about the succession, asking the Queen to nod if it is to be James Stuart. She nods first up and down, then shakes her head from side to side before dying — equivocating to the very end.

Elizabeth R appeared during the first season of *Masterpiece Theatre*, and as a retrospective published at the 25-year mark of this inauguration stated, "The official image of Queen Elizabeth I passed down to us by historians for centuries and more recently by movie-makers is of a pasty-faced woman with a splendid dressmaker and an indifferent sex life. *Elizabeth R* came along just in time to expand this narrow view of the virgin queen."[9] Jackson was able to accomplish this expansion in part by her acting abilities, although the benefit of having nine hours on screen cannot be overlooked. Jackson is often hailed as the definitive Elizabeth, but her main advantage was being allowed the *time* for a detailed portrayal, as well as the wealth of historical material *Elizabeth R*'s screenwriters' chose to include. Jackson's Elizabeth is more formal than many, a structured rather than nuanced performance, in keeping with Jackson's theatrical training. As there is a tendency to view far-removed historical time periods as a great deal more formal than the present, Jackson's portrayal resonated with audiences. *Elizabeth R* was called an "outstanding production," and hailed as one where "all of the characters have been built as closely as possible around their historical originals."[10]

Like others before her, Jackson did her research — she read extensively about the period as well as about Elizabeth herself. She not only studied the woman's personality, but pursued entirely new skill sets for the part, learning to ride, shoot a bow and arrow, dance, play the virginal, and write in high calligraphic style.[11] There is more than one close-up in the film of Jackson carefully and perfectly reproducing the historical Elizabeth's grandly flourished signature. Gems such as this are a delight to enthusiasts who have studied the historical woman. All of Jackson's research brought her to the conclusion that Elizabeth "was like a chameleon, altering to suit the circumstances and the people she was with, keeping her central self very much to herself."[12] In essence, Elizabeth was an actress, and this is something that Jackson is able to convey; the words Elizabeth may be speaking or, at times, even her body language and outward demeanor cannot be taken at face value, for there is no guarantee they represent what goes on inside — she puts on not one, but several different acts, depending on her audience and what she hopes to elicit from them. It has been noted that Jackson "makes a virtue of Elizabeth's inaccessibility, uniting her contradictions ... into one regal and slowly aging, rouged and hardening, human being."[13] Jackson has elucidated her view of Elizabeth's basic personality, her "central self" as "arrogant, selfish, flamboyant, and thoroughly mean."[14] This perception on Jackson's part comes across in the characterization in this series — Elizabeth is many things, but very seldom kind and overwhelmingly mean and selfish. If she has one absolute goal, it is self-preservation, and she's willing to do whatever she must to achieve it. She is not a likeable woman, but she is a capable one.

One reviewer noted, "In her portrayal of Elizabeth, [Jackson] brings to life the stormy, complex personality of this woman ... with great zest, humor, and insight into the driving ambitions of a power-hungry woman."[15] Jackson herself was less than sanguine about her performance, despite the amount of work she put into it. She felt she "had not made Elizabeth extraordinary enough," and was quoted as saying, "I should have given her a lot more brilliance." Though she received very few truly negative judgments from critics, some did agree that she was "just average" and her acting was, at best, only that to be expected from "an accomplished repertory company actress."[16] Biographers of Jackson have noted, like those of Bette Davis before her, that a demanding and difficult disposition is something the historical Elizabeth and the woman playing her shared, "Elizabeth I, high-handed and autocratic, was very much Glenda's kind of woman."[17] Jackson herself is a politician (she gave up her acting career for a seat in Parliament), and so her portrayal of the political aspect of Elizabeth's life is convincing. Her Elizabeth is a competent administrator, and though she has good people working underneath her, this series is also the first to show Elizabeth as the driving force behind English government. Jackson's portrayal is a reflection of the flourishing of Women's Liberation in the 1970s — Elizabeth is a self-assured career woman who expects to work and play with the boys. In a decade when, for the first time, a significant number of women were entering the workforce in positions where they outranked men, this theme resonates. Unlike in earlier, more romantic adaptations of Elizabeth's life, by the 1970s, Elizabeth's "dedication to her vocation is seen as more admirable than unnatural."[18] In *Elizabeth R*, Mary Stuart is not allowed to grandly accuse Elizabeth of being less than a woman simply because she's committed to her job and good at what she does. A series of contemporary articles in *Vogue* magazine which focused on both Elizabeth offerings of this decade (i.e., *Elizabeth R* and *Mary, Queen of Scots*) is illustrative of the ideology behind film portrayals of female monarchs of the period. "Woman as sovereign, as ruler, as a majestic force and presence has suddenly become the *idée fixe* of the entertainment world ... the resurgence of interest in woman as an historical figure can be attributed almost too easily to the current concerns of Women's Liberation and woman's role as political and social catalyst."[19] Rather than be viewed merely as the tragic royal heroine of a courtly romance, Jackson's Elizabeth was finally and fully realized as a creature who could play a pivotal role in bringing about political change — a woman who could govern a realm, not just a heart.

While emphasizing this role, Jackson's portrayal still manages enough balance to create a portrait of depth, and while it's obviously influenced by Women's Liberation, it is not constrained by it. "To its credit, the series ... does not try to turn Elizabeth into a card-carrying member [of Women's Lib]. Instead, the six plays ... are a scrupulously factual reconstruction ... of Elizabeth's ascendancy to the throne and reign."[20] The reviewer who made these comments concentrates on *Elizabeth R*'s historicity — she hesitates to even call it a dramatization of Elizabeth's life, preferring instead the term "reconstruction." The danger inherent in such adherence to historical fact is the very reason why so many filmmakers eschew it — they want to avoid "textbook dullness." *Elizabeth R* strays very close to this mark in certain sections; it is instructive, but it is not always interesting. As has been mentioned, *Elizabeth R* is given high marks by historians, who tend to be the single-most vocally critical group with regard to films about Elizabeth's life. Tudor biographer Alison Weir has stated that *Elizabeth R* is one of the few films in the Elizabethan canon that "rings true," and is "incredibly accurate." Even in this opinion by an historian, however, it's made clear that this is attributed less to Jackson and more to the screenwriters and the time allowed by the format. This miniseries "delivers what no feature film can. It pulls up the smaller moments of a life, moments that fill in the historical time line."[21] Each episode is used to highlight particular aspects of Elizabeth's personality in detail "while adhering to a chronological sequence of events and a unity of style that is more literary than cinematic."[22] In essence, this is a visual representation that feels more like a written history. As such, it exhibits the strengths of an historical text — accuracy and the ability to be pedagogically instructive. The flip side of this coin is that, in so doing, the entertainment factor is sometimes sacrificed, and in some instances, the series cannot avoid what can only be described as tediousness.

BLACKADDER II (1986)

If *Elizabeth R* is meant to be taken as the closest to literal history a filmed life can be, then the *Blackadder* series is the polar opposite — peopled by characters both fictitious and historical, this comedy series revolves around the hilarious exploits of several generations of the Blackadder dynasty, beginning during England's Middle Ages. *Blackadder II* is set during the Elizabethan Age, and stars Lord Edmund Blackadder (Rowan Atkinson), described by the series blurbs as a ne'er-do-well with "a big head and a small beard" who seeks "grace and favor from the stark raving mad Queen Bess." It has been noted that the scripting for the series, crafted by Richard Curtis and Ben Elton, employs "a broad-brush approach based on the fictional and feature film version of history."[23] The result is a comedic farce centering around the popular perception of history, not history itself, and as such it provides valuable insight into the mythology surrounding Elizabeth. Situational comedy, the category into which *Blackadder* falls, is based on a shared understanding of the situation being exploited for comic effect — in this case, the plight of a courtier in Elizabethan England. Some concepts are universal, but a grasp of the "situation" of Elizabethan England is necessary in order to find amusement in a parody of it, and the way in which Elizabeth and her court are portrayed in *Blackadder II* is indicative of what its creators viewed as the prevailing perception of Elizabethan England when the series was made in the mid–1980s. As one commentary noted, in the *Blackadder* series, "The situational context is a grossly distorted representation of a period of English history which comprises the 'characters' and stereotypes which populate 'commonsense' notions of the past. The show precisely pinpoints the banality of popular conceptions of English history, making the point through frequent anachronism and cliché."[24]

Several popular conceptions about different aspects of life during Elizabethan times appear in the series, from Tudor sanitation practices to the mania surrounding exploration of the New World. Foremost in the series is the portrayal of Elizabeth's court and the courtiers who populate it. Lord Blackadder is handy with a quip, amoral and completely devious, and his tenure at Elizabeth's court is based on a self-described "tissue of whoppers" that he's used to insinuate himself into the royal favor. He's accompanied by his straight-man servant Baldrick, a creature of most questionable hygiene, and the foppish Lord

Percy Percy. Percy is a perfect parody of the effeminate Elizabethan courtier — silly, stupid, and obsessed by the latest fashions, which he's all too keen to display to Blackadder. When he rushes in with the most recent version of the Elizabethan ruff, which has grown to enormous size, Blackadder remarks that he "looks like a bird that has swallowed a plate."

The arbiter of all this fashion, Elizabeth herself, is essentially a one-trick pony — ditzy, vain, and flirtatious, she spends her days playing annoying jokes, the most annoying of which is indulging her penchant for having her friends executed. This unfavorable picture is completed by her high-pitched, lisping voice and a tendency to squeak in near dog-whistle register. Far from being averse to the idea of marriage or attempting to portray herself as an untouchable Virgin Queen, she's constantly on the make. "Everyone seems to get married but me," she sighs, before commanding that the wedding ceremony she's attending hurry up so she can "get squiffy and seduce someone" at the reception. She confesses her "enormous crush" for Lord Flashheart, an overblown and hypersexualized amalgamation of sailor-celebrities such as Sir Francis Drake. Sir Walter "what a big ship I've got" Raleigh has a similar effect on her. Primping before his arrival, she asks, "Do I look absolutely divine and regal and at the same time very pretty and accessible? If he's really gorgeous, I'm thinking of marrying him." As portrayed by Miranda Richardson, Elizabeth appears nothing so much as a spoiled child, and this characterization is only reinforced by the fact that she's accompanied always by her "Nursie," an equally ditzy matron who suffers from an udder fixation and spouts tangential bits of history for comic effect. She reminisces about Elizabeth's birth, stating that everyone shouted, "It's a boy!" until Sir Thomas More pointed out the fact that a boy "without a winkle" was actually a girl, and then "everyone was really disappointed." The circumstances are ridiculous, but the underlying concept — that Elizabeth's birth was a disappointment because a boy was expected and desired — is still effectively conveyed. In the same way, the characterization of Henry VIII as callous and cruel is made apparent when Elizabeth remembers, "He used to laugh at those people with the funny faces and the bells." When Lord Melchett (Stephen Fry) helpfully offers, "Jesters, ma'am," Elizabeth replies, "No ... lepers." Melchett as adviser is a sort of silly William Cecil; wearing the bonnet and carcanet that denote his office, he's constantly at Elizabeth's side, serving as "Lord Chamberlain." Since everything in *Blackadder* highlights the absurd, all his policies have as their ultimate goal either flattering the Queen or amusing her, not promoting the good of the realm. His rivalry with Blackadder, as does Blackadder's reaction when Raleigh arrives in London, demonstrates the dynamics of favor and power play as the men of Elizabeth's court jockey for position.

As has been mentioned, various Elizabethan issues appear in this series, such as the practice of alchemy or the state of medicine in England during the Tudor period. When Blackadder experiences what he's sure is mental illness (he has fallen in love with his new "manservant," whom he does not realize, in true Shakespearean fashion, is a girl dressed as a boy) he visits the local doctor. The Elizabethan concept of disease of the mind or body being an "imbalance of the humors" caused by an excess of black bile which must somehow be extracted is made apparent by the "extraordinary new cure developed for just this kind of sordid problem" which the doctor advises. When Blackadder, who has had leeches prescribed for every possible ailment from headache to digestive issues, asks sarcastically if this cure will involve popping a leech down his codpiece, the doctor looks at him with pleasure and exclaims, "I had no idea you were a medical man!"

In addition to the problem of medical care, the plight of the peasant is also examined through Blackadder's servant, Baldrick (Tony Robinson). Blackadder treats him abominably, assuring him after his dismissal that he need not worry, for "surely you'll be allowed to starve to death in one of the royal parks." When Baldrick asks for permission to attend the festivities celebrating Raleigh's return, Blackadder replies, "Who do you think you are, Wat Tyler? You can have the afternoon off when you die." Commentaries have noted a theme that resonates throughout all the *Blackadder* series, and *Blackadder II* is no exception — that of a focus on a class-based hierarchy. Baldrick, who is "dirty, unkempt, lacking human dignity," represents the working class at the bottom of the pyramid while the characterization of Queen Elizabeth as a "pampered, stupid, infantile ruler" occupies the top.[25] Somewhere in the middle is Blackadder himself, who is frustrated with and contemptuous of both ends of the spectrum.

Another major Elizabethan issue, the question of religion, is addressed in this series in a variety of ways. In one episode, Blackadder has to deal with his fanatical aunt and uncle, who represent Protestantism in its most extreme form — they wear huge crosses about their necks, consider chairs an extravagance, will eat only raw turnips, and are most disapproving of the worldly Blackadder. Religious figures in this series (as is almost always the case in film and television, not to mention literature as far back as Chaucer) are not portrayed favorably. In addition to Blackadder's unpalatable relatives, there's also the grossly overweight and morally repugnant Bishop of Bath and Wells, who baptizes babies and eats them in the vestry afterwards. He also indulges in various other horrific practices, and Blackadder is unfortunate enough to owe him money. The Catholic threat appears in passing when Elizabeth remarks that "there are hundreds of Catholics who desperately want their heads snicked off, and there's no one to organize it," before appointing Blackadder the Minister in Charge of Religious Genocide. In this instance and many others, the series conflates Elizabeth's reign with that of her father, brother, and sister — it ignores her more tolerant religious policies and the relatively few number of executions during her reign (as compared with that of her more homicidal Tudor family members') in order to play up for comic effect perceptions more accurately accorded to other Tudor monarchs.

The main idea this conveys is that Elizabeth was a queen who executed her friends, major personalities of the Tudor period, early and often. The "Book of Death" which Blackadder uses to schedule his executions is enormous, and the first two on the docket are Lord Howard of Effingham and Sir Francis Drake. Percy remarks that scheduling them together should draw a fine crowd given England's many "sailing enthusiasts." Elizabeth is fond of calling for execution warrants, pronouncing "off with his head," and gallows humor, such as the instance where she says she's off to visit her friend Lord Ponsonby "who I believe I'm having killed on Friday." Blackadder himself faces the axe more than once in the series, with Elizabeth telling him at one point, "Sometimes I think about having you executed just to see the expression on your face." When she admits to Blackadder that she's very keen on him, he replies with an examination of her capriciousness, a trait often attributed to the historical Elizabeth, by saying, "Oh yes, ma'am. As you were keen on Essex. Right up until the point at which you had his head cut off." Elizabeth giddily replies that he didn't mind it, and that "his head looked jolly super on its little spike."

Even Elizabeth's chosen "type"—the adventurous sailor-explorer—isn't safe from her homicidal practical jokes. When Sir Walter "what a big ship I've got" Raleigh arrives at court, the mania for exploration of the New World reaches fever pitch; crowds line the streets, and everyone dresses up as pirates. This includes "Queenie," who adopts an eye patch and sailor dialogue so convoluted that Raleigh has no idea what she's attempting to say. The only one immune is Blackadder, due to his intense jealousy of Raleigh, whom he fears will outshine him at court. Much is made of the introduction of the potato; Blackadder explains to Baldrick with contempt, "To you it's a potato, to me it's a potato, but to Sir Walter bloody Raleigh, it's country estates, fine carriages and as many girls as his tongue can cope with. People are smoking them, building houses out of them—they'll be *eating* them next." Raleigh demonstrates the favor his voyages of exploration have brought him by making himself comfortable on Elizabeth's throne while she sits at his feet, raptly listening to his tales of hardship and adventure and making sure to mention that her bedroom is just upstairs. As a man of deeds, Raleigh has nothing but contemptuous barbs for the career courtier Blackadder, remarking, "I can see he is the sort of pasty landlubber I have always despised." In this way, as have other, more serious offerings (e.g., *The Virgin Queen* and *Elizabeth: The Golden Age*), the idea of a contentious dynamic between those at Elizabeth's court who bow to her will and the man's men, such as Raleigh, is yet again put forth. Since this is a farce, Blackadder's solution is not to sabotage Raleigh through court intrigue, but to boldly go where Raleigh has gone before—to set sail for the New World himself and, as Elizabeth commands, discover her a country and bring her back a vegetable. Raleigh predicts failure and indulges in the New World explorer's penchant for exaggeration when he warns that around the cape "the rain beats down so hard it makes your head bleed," to which the nonplussed Blackadder replies, "Then some sort of hat is probably in order." Like *The Virgin Queen* and several other film adaptations of Elizabeth's life, *Blackadder II* also employs canine metaphors to describe Elizabeth's male courtiers. The incomparably mental Captain Redbeard, whom Blackadder hires to take him to the New World, says of him, "Courtiers to the Queen—you're nothing but lapdogs to a slip of a girl." This "slip of a girl" is only interested in the "presents" these explorers bring her back and the fascinating stories they tell. Once these are exhausted, Elizabeth complains, "I'm completely bored with explorers, and if you haven't brought me any presents, I'm going to have you executed." While this is a parody, the underlying concept is there—the historical Elizabeth funded these voyages of exploration not out of altruism but in the hope of a return on her investment; explorers and privateers were expected to bring back plunder or items of lucrative value from their voyages. When they did not, regardless of the fascinating (and often exaggerated) stories of adventure and discovery they could tell, they were in danger of being imprisoned. Elizabeth was always in need of funds, and this was one way in which she could replenish her treasury and avoid the less-than-popular method of asking Parliament for money through taxation increase. *Blackadder II* shows Elizabeth not so much avaricious as absent-minded when it comes to financial matters. She taxes Blackadder 1,000 florins to help fund the navy, and demands his last sixpence to use for betting.

Blackadder has been compared to other British comedy series that displayed historical elements, such as *Monty Python*, but unlike that predecessor, which "handled the past with stunning abandon," *Blackadder* "first carefully digs history's grave, and only then begins to dance on it," regarding history as "a colorful, comic festival."[26] Overall, Richardson's turn as Queenie distills the person of Elizabeth down to two facets of the historical woman's personality: capriciousness and vanity. The court spends the entirety of its time flattering her; like a spoiled child, she expects to be constantly entertained, all her demands instantly met, and she treats her courtiers as playthings. Her expectation to be obeyed is also conveyed in the habit she has of rhetorically asking, "Who's queen?" when courtiers step out of line. This Elizabeth is more a parody of all members of the Tudor dynasty rolled into one than a farcical representation solely depicting Elizabeth. With regard to the high-ranking nobility who surround her, she has Henry VIII's tendency to execute first and ask questions later, and she also displays Mary's penchant for the mass murder of those who differ from the royal religion. She's a self-described "naughty scatterbrain," which is probably the greatest divergence from any aspect of the historical woman's character — Elizabeth possessed a formidable intellect, but Queenie is a ditz. This allows for the sarcastic wit Blackadder to play off her silly insanity. The result is an extremely entertaining caricature of the Elizabethan era which, through the very aspects it exaggerates, distorts, or removes for comic effect, manages to provide a sense of the Tudor period.

ELIZABETH I: THE VIRGIN QUEEN (2005)

Elizabeth I: The Virgin Queen is a miniseries produced by *Masterpiece Theatre* for public television, and as such, it suffers under the constraints of a limited public television budget, as did its predecessor from the 1970s, *Elizabeth R*. Compared to *Elizabeth R*, it looks positively glamorous, though when viewed in light of productions from Hollywood's golden age or the more recent Kapur offerings, it does not fare as well. The settings, though relatively authentic in feel, are not grand; there are no pitched, special effects-laden battles; and though it's well done for television, the costuming will prove a disappointment to those seeking textile porn. What this film lacks in lavish production values, however, it makes up for in its characterization of the Virgin Queen.

If one looks at the artwork accompanying this series, one might form an erroneous opinion of what it is. At least three separate DVD cases were produced, with one a headshot showing Elizabeth as Gloriana against a white background and another with Elizabeth and Dudley nuzzling. It is the third that is most interesting — the DVD case shows the back of a young woman, presumably Elizabeth since she has waist-length red hair, naked except for the drape upon which she sits. To the far right of her, almost out of view, is the English crown. So there it is — sex center stage, politics barely visible stage right. The overall impression is of a tasteful bodice-ripper, perhaps even one with literary pretensions. Looking at two out of these three cases, one would expect this series to be full of romance, lust and heaving bosoms. One's expectations in this regard would be disappointed, and wonderfully so. What this miniseries does offer is a Virgin Queen who seems less anachronistic than some of her other onscreen sisters, and the bodice-ripping is kept to a minimum in favor of historicity. Unlike Kapur's offerings, the concentration is not on symbolism; like Elizabeth's previous *Masterpiece Theatre* incarnation, the focus is historical fact. It also showcases Elizabeth's intellect and, in so doing, with the possible exception of *Elizabeth R*, this particular aspect of the characterization rings truer than any other portrayal of Elizabeth Tudor.

The series opens with Kat Ashley (Tara Fitzgerald) running through darkened halls, past dwarves and monkeys, to warn her royal mistress that the guard has been summoned by her sister Mary. When Kat bursts into the room, the first face the camera focuses upon is that of an attractive and breathlessly frightened young redhead — the perfect romantic heroine. As if to tease viewers who expected an Elizabeth who looks like this, it then pans to Elizabeth herself (Anne-Marie Duff), decidedly less attractive and decidedly more self-controlled. She's poised and certain of herself. The first redhead, who turns out to be Let-tice Knowles (Sienna Guillory), wavers, "God help us!" and Elizabeth replies coolly, "God helps those who help themselves." It might well serve as a mantra for Elizabeth. From the moment of her first appearance onscreen, it's clear that this is an Elizabeth whose independence is innate. Unlike Blanchett's Elizabeth, Duff does not grow into her role, for there's no need — this Elizabeth was born to rule. One commentary noted, "To its credit, *The Virgin Queen* does not submit to the kind of hagiography committed in the 1998 film *Elizabeth*. There, Elizabeth seemed sweet and tremulous during the early years of her reign, unsure how to govern her new kingdom."[27] Duff's Elizabeth, by contrast, feels much closer to the mark for someone with the historical woman's intelligence, political acumen, and love of scholarship. She's clever, quick, and does not falter under pressure. Elizabeth uses the precious moments gained from Kat's advance warning to showcase how every decision she makes considers the political — as her ladies offers her different dresses, she dismisses each with, "Too gaudy. Too red. If I'm to live this night, I must not outshine her." She chooses a simple grey dress with no adornment. This is in keeping with historical fact — the real Elizabeth dressed simply at this point in her life, as befitted an unostenta-tious Protestant princess; from the first, she made a statement through her manner of dress. Though so far her poise has been absolute, the viewer is clued in to Elizabeth's pri-mary weakness by Kat when she cautions her, "Control your temper, no matter what she says." This also demonstrates the role Kat plays in her life — mother surrogate. She tosses Elizabeth the prop she needs, a rosary, and she and her ladies have just enough time to fall to their knees and pretend to have been at prayer when Lord Chancellor Gardiner (Robert Pugh) and the Earl of Sussex (Dexter Fletcher) burst into the room with their soldiers. The scene with which they are presented is a dutiful princess observing the tenets of the Roman Catholic faith, upon which reverential activity they have intruded. Elizabeth is not only the consummate actress, she's also proficient at staging. Mary refuses to see her, but Elizabeth skillfully manipulates her captors into allowing her to write to her sister.

Like its Elizabeth, this series also chooses to be more balanced in the portrayal of its Mary (Joanne Whalley), though no more favorable; there's no attempt at rehabilitation for Bloody Mary. It's clear that she dislikes Elizabeth, distrusts her. Mary is also wary of Elizabeth's formidable intellect, of being manipulated by her. Mary tells her confessor, "She thinks if she buys time she can soften my resolve." It is why she has refused to see her sister, for she knows how convincing Elizabeth can be. At the same time, Mary is fearful of what the consequences may be of her actions towards her sister, asking, "Will God punish me as I am now punishing her?" Though she's shown on her knees at Mass, the incense wafting about her as she takes communion, this is no bloated, hysterical Mary whose abode is a lair of darkness; she tends more towards verisimilitude than caricature, a refreshing divergence from some previous portrayals. Yet still, Mary's reign is one of terror, and this series also chooses to treat the burning of Ridley and Latimer to illustrate that fact, though it does so in a more realistic manner than other offerings. The scene of these Protestant martyrs bravely meeting their fate, included as it is in more than one film about Elizabeth's life, is used as a sort of catch-all to represent all the Protestants burned during Mary's reign, and the public response to these executions.

Elizabeth is taken to the Tower, and she's forced to pass by heads on pikes and washerwomen cleaning the scaffold of blood by the gallon. Still she shows no fear, even when she can barely hear her interrogators' questions for the screaming of Thomas Wyatt, who's being tortured nearby. She remains poised, and Gardiner is clearly no match for her. She maintains her innocence while sarcastically appealing to his ego by denigrating her femininity: "Like most women, I have no head for politics, sir." Sussex has taken her measure, and he holds his peace. As he tells Elizabeth's jailor later, he goes no further in his commission than is absolutely necessary, for he fears he may have to answer for his treatment of her — he knows she's a survivor, and he's smart enough to plan for his future. The Earl of Sussex, described by PBS in its blurbs about this series as "one of the ablest political figures in Tudor England, as witnessed by his ability to hold senior posts under all three monarchs in the latter half of the sixteenth century,"[28] is used to illustrate another of the strong suits of this miniseries. Rather than polarize all Catholics as villains unequivocally against Elizabeth, the series portrays closer to the truth: that some Catholics were first Englishmen (and/or politicians) and were loyal to the Crown, and that Elizabeth did continue to employ some of them in important positions when she came to the throne.

When Elizabeth arrives in her quarters in the Tower (non-threatening apartments rather than the exaggerated dungeons of other portrayals), she wastes no time asking Ashley if she has destroyed Wyatt's letters. The historical record is unclear on exactly what kind of (if any) involvement Elizabeth had in Wyatt's planning process, so in this telling of the story, Elizabeth is guilty — she's saved by her wits, not her innocence. Ashley has burned the incriminating letters with her own hand, and there is no proof of Elizabeth's involvement in Wyatt's intended rebellion for Mary to exploit.

Wyatt goes to his death on the scaffold pronouncing Elizabeth's innocence to all, and as she's released for a meeting with her sister, crowds line the banks cheering for Elizabeth when her boat passes by. In the palace, as she waits for Mary, she finds herself oppressed by that familiar trope of Elizabeth movies — a portrait of Henry VIII. Placed above her on the wall, he looks down upon her. Unlike other representations and illustrative of the strength of Duff's interpretation, Elizabeth stands underneath the portrait and stares right back; she neither cowers nor cries beneath it. It is not a symbol of her defeat or fear, but a challenge. The only influence Henry VIII still has over his daughter's life manifests itself not in portraiture, but in the subconscious world of dreams — she walks a gauntlet of courtiers (who whisper epithets such as "bastard" under their breath) to end up in front of her father on his throne. Her mother stands behind him, a shadowy background figure. When Henry throws back his head and laughs, Elizabeth wakes up terrified. She only allows herself the luxury of fear in the dream world, however; in the real world she banishes it by sheer strength of will. This is not the only emotion which manifests itself in this way — she also uses her dreams as an outlet for another emotion she best not show: lust.

Speaking of lust, it is Philip (Stanley Townsend) who first meets with Elizabeth, not Mary. They speak to each other in smooth Spanish, Elizabeth showcasing her gift for languages as well as her education. Philip is definitely smooth — to the point of being slick. It is he who has intervened with Mary on Elizabeth's behalf, and he has ulterior motives. His interest in the young princess is more than brotherly; he fingers her hair and looks her up and down like a side of beef as he speaks to her. Into this cozy scene strides Mary, understandably perturbed. She wears a metal breastplate for fear of assassination, and she's furious. This Mary has Elizabeth's number — there is no conflict or uncertainty; she's bitter, angry, and hates her half-sister. She only fears divine retribution for acting on her murderous impulses, and she rages that Elizabeth's "charade of purity" offends God. Elizabeth tries to placate her, stating that she was not raised in the Catholic doctrine as Mary was, but that she's trying to learn from her sister's example. Mary is no fool and calls her a hypocrite. Showing the strength of character (and also the dangerous temper) with which Duff imbues this Elizabeth, she stands up to her sister and calls her bluff. Knowing the proof to have been destroyed, Elizabeth taunts Mary that she must prove she has done wrong. Though bitter and angry, Mary does provoke compassion when she wails, "I had hoped my marriage would bring me peace, companionship. But thanks to you, it has imprisoned me." As does *Elizabeth R*, this series is adept at depicting the fact that this is more than just a political struggle for Mary — Elizabeth has ruined her only chance for personal happiness. If it were not for a Protestant princess around which they could rally, the detractors who make Mary's foreign alliance with Philip untenable would be powerless. Mary has waited her life away, only to see her hopes dashed at the moment of their realization because of her half-sister.

To illustrate the recurring theme of a total lack of privacy and echoing similar scenes from *Elizabeth R*, Mary's palace is filled with peepholes through which Philip and his allies, like rats in their holes, watch the goings on, from Mary's "labor" to the waiting Elizabeth. Philip shows exactly how much he values the political over the personal (and his tender feelings towards his wife) when he schemes with his ambassador to marry Elizabeth: "It was England I married. One sister will do as well as another." This attitude is historical, but it also provides justification for Mary's bitter anger — she's surrounded by callousness, has been since she was a small child, and even her own husband betrays her for the Protestant princess who has ruined all her hopes.

One of the other elements this miniseries showcases is not the terror of confinement, but its soul-devouring boredom. Elizabeth is no longer in the Tower, but she's still under house arrest at Woodstock, and for someone of Elizabeth's character, captivity provokes endless frustration that almost rivals the fear of the Tower. Her much put-upon jailor writes letters to Mary about Elizabeth's "ill-temper" while suffering her irritated invectives: "How can I endure this purgatory without stimulation?" Other adaptations may have her pining for a male love interest, but in keeping with its concentration on Elizabeth's intellectuality, this miniseries shows her asking for her books, her tutor, the things she needs to stimulate her mind. It also depicts Elizabeth's passive resistance—she's shown playing the good Catholic, kneeling to take the host, and then coughing it into her handkerchief when the priest turns his back. As did the historical Elizabeth, she whiles away the hours by carving into a window pane the words, "Much suspected of me, nothing proved can be, quoth Elizabeth, prisoner."

Her boredom is finally relieved when Sir William Cecil (Ian Hart) arrives to see her, under the pretext of discussing the accounts from her house at Hatfield. Philip has already remarked of Cecil, "That one says too little, sees too much," and he's certainly had his ear to the ground at court. Unlike in *Elizabeth R*, where a wary Elizabeth must decide whether or not to trust Cecil, this Elizabeth already has a longstanding relationship with him, and their dynamic is all business. Elizabeth is unfazed by his information that Mary is thought to be pregnant; instead she's sarcastic: "A queen, a mother, and a wife—her own holy trinity." Cecil's advice to Elizabeth is invaluable, and she acts upon it: "If you want to survive, you must remain invisible to your allies and your enemies." Elizabeth has been completely engrossed in the political, and only after Cecil has finished filling her in on this does she allow the personal to intrude—she asks after Robert Dudley. Cecil's feelings toward the man are evident as he says, "He knows the trick of survival, if nothing else."

This telling of Elizabeth's glorious ascension comes across as much less dramatic than its big-screen counterparts. Gardiner arrives to tell Elizabeth she must come to court; the Queen is dead. He explains that her "child" was a tumor, and hands Elizabeth the ring of state. The moment feels almost anti-climactic; Elizabeth herself seems uncertain, as if waiting for the other shoe to drop, but she finally accepts and runs out into the grounds, like Jackson's Elizabeth before her, breathless and free. When the members of Mary's Privy Council ride up, she stands underneath the oak tree and spouts her patented line, "This is the work of the Lord, and it is marvelous in our eyes." There is no hesitation and she uses the royal "we" almost instantaneously; she has been preparing for this moment for a long time.

To show that the route from ring of state handover to coronation is not seamless, the palace is shown in chaos with the old being moved out and the new being moved in. Elizabeth sends Mary's Catholic retinue packing, and Mary's icons are removed from the palace, the new religion replacing the old. Elizabeth is joyously reunited with Kat Ashley and Lettice Knowles, and then she looks to John Dee, the astrologer, to set a propitious date for her coronation. She has barely had time to collect herself when her cousin, the Duke of Norfolk (Kevin McKidd), comes calling. He expects to be named Secretary of State, and he's representative of the prevailing mindset with regard to women rulers. His misogynistic attitude towards Elizabeth is as unmistakable as it is irritating, since he obviously has no superiority of understanding. There's no love lost between them, though he's so condescending that at first he seems not to notice. His characterization allows for Elizabeth to again showcase her intellect and education: "I was tutored by the finest scholars in the land. I am fluent in five languages and know the principles of economics, as well as philosophy, ancient and modern. I'm also an expert in music, literature, and poetry. My horsemanship, they say, is unparalleled." This Elizabeth is every bit the Renaissance woman, and it's clear that she neither requires nor will tolerate the advice of arrogant men like Norfolk. She's a competent ruler right out of the gate and entirely on her own merit. It takes a self-effacing man to be an effective political partner for her, and this she has already found in Cecil.

The selection of the men who will surround Elizabeth is shaping up, and it only remains to introduce her relationship with Dudley (Tom Hardy). In her examination of the historical Elizabeth and Dudley's relationship, Sarah Gristwood notes, "Most writers of modern days have seen this lust for the simulacrum of love as a pathology, an expression of a miserably frustrated sexuality. But in terms of courtly love, it was something closer to artistry."[29] *The Virgin Queen*'s characterization does pursue the more modern view — Elizabeth certainly lusts, though not for a simulacrum, but for the real thing. Dudley, also, appears to lust for a physical relationship, though it's difficult to tell if his actions and words represent any real feeling or are simply a pretense used to manipulate Elizabeth. What is unique in this portrayal is Elizabeth's conflict over Dudley's married state. Other portrayals show Elizabeth and Dudley avoiding the subject altogether; until her inconvenient death or a devastating "revelation" of the fact that he's married, it's as if Dudley's wife simply does not exist. The other tact often taken is an Elizabeth who is either angry and jealous or cruelly triumphant. Duff's Elizabeth is, instead, truer to the character of a woman who believes in the tenets of the Protestant faith and the sanctity of marriage. Dudley is careful to point out for modern viewers that his was a marriage arranged by his father rather than his own choice. The implication is that, with his marriage merely an arrangement, there's no love involved, and thus no betrayal inherent in pursuing a romantic relationship with Elizabeth. Elizabeth loves Dudley, but she's also acutely aware of the sin of adultery, and it is she who often reminds him of his duty. She also uses his wife as a sort of defense. When he begins to flatter her or become too physical, she says, "I trust your wife is well." Dudley seems frustrated by his position; he clearly does not share Elizabeth's scruples, and feels his marriage should be no impediment: "Your court is stuffed with married men. Why am I to be the exception?" When he admits that his wife is ill, Elizabeth says to him softly, "If she is unwell, they your duty lies with her." Dudley manages to change the subject and, with suitable application of the boyish charm Hardy brings to the role, ends up sweeping Elizabeth into the saddle so they can go riding together — in slow motion. It is not a case of a woman playing courtly games, Gristwood's "simulacrum"; Elizabeth is in love with a married man, and she experiences all the conflict occasioned by the difference between what her heart wants and what her conscience will allow. For this reason, the greatest physical intimacy permitted between them occurs in her dreams — unlike other portrayals of the Virgin Queen, this Elizabeth never allows Dudley into her bed in the waking realm, and their physical relationship never goes far beyond the closeness occasioned by dancing.

Elizabeth appoints Cecil as her Secretary of State, and in the portrayal of her relationship with this counselor, this adaptation excels, perhaps more so than any other. Rather than an ineffectual grandfather figure, Cecil is presented more as he historically was — much closer to Elizabeth's age and much closer to Elizabeth, period. His appointment is conditional, based on a single point: that he always "give me the counsel I need, no matter what I want to hear," a mandate the historical Elizabeth made to the man she called her

"Spirit." Elizabeth values Cecil's counsel and she often acts upon it, but she also has her own ideas about how the country should be run. Cecil gives her a list of names for her council, but she questions a few and adds one name — Dudley. Cecil is contemptuous of Dudley, calling him the "son of a traitor and a rank opportunist." Elizabeth defends him by saying what might well describe her own behavior under her sister Mary's reign: opportunism is no sin when it is for survival. Cecil shows Elizabeth what she's unwilling to see, however; though it may not have been so in the past, now Dudley does what he does not for survival, but for advancement of his insatiable ambition. Cecil allows himself one barb at Elizabeth's expense, asking, "Will you be inviting his wife to court also?" Elizabeth may be willing to showcase her inner conflict with Dudley himself, but she resents being confronted by others about their relationship, and she snaps, "A wife's place is at home."

While Dudley's wife is in her place at home, Elizabeth is enjoying a little romantic fireplace blaze with her absent husband. As Dudley attempts to woo her, this film displays its concern for the political, often absent or oversimplified in portrayals of Elizabeth's life, by having her expound to him about the body politic and the body natural: "A woman ruler is not as other rulers, is she? Like the coin that bears her image, there are two sides to her. On the one, she embodies the feminine frailty of her sex. On the other, she is the body politic, ordained by God." Dudley admits that he prefers to appeal to the feminine side, but Elizabeth assures him she only listens to the politic, stating the familiar lament, "For how can a woman be sure she is loved for herself, and not her power as queen?" When Dudley unwisely allows his ambition to show by stating, "Cannot a man love them both?" Elizabeth brings out her best defense — his wife. He has had enough, and leaves her alone with, "Your wit is your protection, Bess. But I fear it makes for a lonely bed."

Elizabeth's persistent mentioning of Dudley's wife demonstrates yet another area where *Elizabeth I: The Virgin Queen* explores new territory — the wives left at home. *Elizabeth R* touched on this briefly with its depiction of Amy Robsart, but more to inform Dudley's characterization than as any kind of examination of Amy's situation. Dudley's point about Elizabeth's court being stuffed full of married men is a valid one. The historical Elizabeth was surrounded by married men who played the game of courtly love with her, and Dudley was not the only one whose wife was seldom invited to court — Elizabeth discouraged some of her male courtiers from bringing their spouses, possibly to avoid overcrowding, possibly because she simply did not want the competition. The men all dance attendance upon their Virgin Queen, but where are all their wives? In the case of Dudley's wife, in this series, she's sitting at home, waiting for her husband and quietly dying. As portrayed by Emilia Fox, she presents an intensely tragic and almost saintly figure, and the contrast of her near-pastoral existence with the whirl and action of court life is forceful. Amy is shown resting outside or in bed; Elizabeth is watching her goshawk rip its prey to shreds. Amy does not receive much screen time, but she's an effective counterpoint, and she also reveals the innate disloyalty in her husband's character. The series' Dudley has been described as an ambiguous man, one who is "torn between affection for his wife, his love for Elizabeth, and his own ambition."[30] This is, at best, two-thirds true, and Elizabeth is the one left out of the triumvirate. Dudley implies to Elizabeth that he feels nothing for his wife, that their relationship is strictly one of duty. Regardless of what he may say to his queen, however, when he's shown with Amy, it's clear that Dudley cares for her. He is solicitous and kind, and though he's not altogether forthcoming, he does not lie to her. Avoidance of the issue is his strong suit, and being gentle as she is, Amy does not press him; she's not the paranoid shrew of *Elizabeth R.* Dudley even goes so far as to tell her nurse to be good to her, since "she might well be the best part of me." Amy shows no anger at being forced to languish away in the country, only sadness, loneliness and concern for her husband. She's not unhappy in the country and pining for court, she simply misses the man she loves. She does go so far as to ask if Dudley can stay with her, to which he replies that he must attend the court for the "rewards that come with the Queen's favor." Amy cares not for the Queen's favor, though she is never accusatory towards Elizabeth. Rather, she knows that her husband's ambition may not be the best thing for him. In her letters, she tells him to take care, for regardless of Elizabeth's feelings "such games are about power. It could be your soul you mortgage ... if my life has a purpose, it is to protect you from your vanity and the price you will pay if you fall prey to hers." Amy's counsel to Dudley is strongly reminiscent of the role Francis Bacon plays for the Earl of Essex in Elizabeth films, warning him not to set too much store upon the loves of queens. In neither case is the counsel heeded, though Amy remains loyal regardless.

Amy Robsart is a shadowy historical figure — as Sarah Gristwood has noted, "There are no certain portraits, no contemporary descriptions of Amy herself to be found, and very little correspondence."[31] Certain elements can be pieced together from the historical record, but the characterization of Amy (reflected in *Elizabeth I: The Virgin Queen* as well as other offerings) as gentle, meek and retiring is based more upon Sir Walter Scott's characterization in his fictional work, *Kenilworth*, rather than any historical evidence. Her relationship with her husband is yet another matter of speculation; the best that can be said at this remove is that they were not visibly at odds with one another, given that she visited him when he was in the Tower, and though they did not see much of each other after 1558, there is evidence of occasional visits and gifts were often exchanged between the two. However, "Amy Dudley's name is known not for anything about her life; merely for the manner of her death."[32]

The only thing known for certain is that Amy Robsart, aged 28, was found either dead or dying at the foot of a "pair of stairs" — a flight of stairs separated by a landing — at Cumnor Place after having sent the others in the house out to the fair. Dudley did not attend Robsart's funeral, and in his correspondence directly following the event, he sounds extraordinarily cold to modern ears — his main concern is to find out all the particulars so that he can defend himself "considering what the malicious world will bruit [gossip]." In short, he's worried about what people will say and what they will suspect of him, and how it will affect the Queen's favor. He seeks political spin. Gristwood examines all the known facts (as well as the hypothetical suppositions) and the conclusion she comes to is that suicide is the most likely manner of death, given information from several contemporary sources that, apart from a physical malady (most likely breast cancer), Robsart was described by those closest to her, such as her maid, as being melancholy and depressed. Since suicide was a mortal sin, punishable by unsanctified burial, it's unsurprising that the inquest which reviewed Robsart's death chose not to come to this conclusion, instead citing "misfortune," accidental death. Dudley was right in his foreknowledge that gossip would be rampant, and as recently as 2010, new evidence has been put forth to support a theory of murder. The original coroner's report as well as other contemporary information has been discovered, and authors such as Chris Skidmore have interpreted these new facts in more sinister fashion.[33]

The filmmakers behind *Elizabeth I: The Virgin Queen* choose to go with the less ominous interpretation — the series presents an Amy who is obviously unwell, and they show why. She pulls back the collar of her dressing gown to reveal a large tumor on her neck. Her husband has just written that he will not have time to stop by as he promised, and the despondent Amy drags herself from her bed in order to throw herself over the banister of the stairs. Dudley is guilty of nothing more than being a terrible husband. With the removal of Amy, however, any check on his vanity is gone. His conscience is dead, and he is now ruled entirely by his ambition.

Dudley's ambitions are not so easily realized, for he is far from the Queen's only suitor — both the King of Spain and the Archduke of Austria have thrown their hats into the ring. In a revealing scene, Elizabeth's council, without her present and led by the self-important and offensive Norfolk, chooses a husband for Elizabeth. The council passes around several portraits of potential suitors as if window shopping, while Elizabeth, in her apartments, gazes at a miniature of Dudley — a graphic illustration of the difference between what she wants and what the realm wants for her. Norfolk pronounces with an authority he does not possess that the decision has been made, Elizabeth will marry Archduke Charles, and thus "end this wretched petticoat government." Cecil, with more insight, realizes it may not be that simple. At first, Elizabeth's temper gets the better of her — she rages, furious and screaming, before controlling herself and repeating what will become for her a mantra, "We will consider the suit most carefully." Elizabeth's equivocation has begun. Even the perceptive Cecil does not realize with what he is being confronted, telling the council, "Like others of her sex, the Queen can tend to frivolity and prevarication when faced with a decision. Time will mellow her." What he fails to understand in his dismissal of her feminine weakness is that Elizabeth has found another tool to add to her arsenal, and she's not likely to relinquish it, for it accomplishes her purposes and puts off her marriage most effectively.

As in Kapur's *Elizabeth*, this series also chooses to use the Volta as an illustration of Elizabeth's unacceptable relationship with Dudley. They perform it in front of the court, as well as the Archduke's ambassador, and Kat Ashley, Elizabeth's mother-figure, berates her for it in private. Not yet aware of Robsart's death, she furiously hisses to Elizabeth, "He has a *wife*. You cavort with him as if he were a suitor!" Elizabeth is defensive, but Kat provides her with a solution, to admit her love for Dudley, for only then "can you find the courage to do what you must: discard him." Elizabeth is not willing to discard him, but neither is she willing to have him realize his ambitions. She takes on all comers by settling the matter of her marriage (and, by extension, her relationship with Dudley) in front of Parliament. She pins up her hair so she looks more grown up, waltzes in, and informs the stunned crowd that "it is monstrous that the feet should think to rule the head. You presume I should bend my will to yours on such a subject?" Her strength of will thus asserted, she leaves behind a shocked Dudley and murmuring court as she walks down the hall, laughing loudly.

When Dudley ignores what has just been made apparent and makes the mistake of asking Elizabeth to marry him, he receives what has been described as "an unchecked rant on the sanctity of feminist independence."[34] However, not long afterward, the depth of Elizabeth's feeling for Dudley is shown. Like *Elizabeth R*, the only other offering to explore Elizabeth's potentially devastating contraction of smallpox, the Queen lies dying while the court is in chaos, for Dudley is slated to be Lord Protector if she succumbs. His behavior during this episode shows exactly how deep Dudley's feelings for Elizabeth run — approximately half an inch. While the council scrambles, he takes the opportunity to languidly lower himself onto Elizabeth's throne and caress the wood of the arms in pleased anticipation, practically salivating at the power he can already taste. While sitting in the council chamber, however, he receives the news that Elizabeth will live, and rather than be ecstatic or even relieved at the survival of the woman he supposedly loves, he stares blankly off into space, the life of Elizabeth weighed against his desire for her power and found sadly wanting. If Dudley feels anything for the Queen, it's imperceptible when contrasted with his monumental ambition.

Since she has wisely decided not to marry Dudley herself, all that remains is for Elizabeth to offer him to Mary Stuart. Unlike in other representations where Dudley's reaction ranges from slightly grudging to very willing, in this portrayal, he's completely furious. This scene, along with a few others, showcases the dynamic that Elizabeth and Dudley share in this miniseries; it portrays them as equals — or at least, of equal temper — a role he does not usually occupy in these offerings. Dudley is neither intimidated by Elizabeth nor subservient to her. He starts off by stating that he's a commoner and a Protestant, and as such, Mary will never countenance the match. They go back and forth, him using his "love" for Elizabeth like a weapon, until finally she tells him that there's no greater love than that which manifests itself in sacrifice. But this is not how Dudley's "love" for Elizabeth (if it even warrants that definition) can manifest itself — it is completely self-serving, and as he has yet to give up his own aspirations of marrying an English queen, he's certainly not willing to consider a Scottish one. He sarcastically asks her if it is the frail, feminine side speaking or "the divine virgin." Finally he agrees "for queen and country," but ultimately because he has no choice.

It's already too late, however, for Walsingham informs Elizabeth that the Scottish Queen has wed that "feckless, unstable youth" Darnley against her wishes. Walsingham, as portrayed by Ben Daniels, is sophisticated, severe and single-minded in the pursuit of his purposes, and his purpose is the downfall of that Scottish Queen whose "assurances are as threadbare as her honor." He's sure to make the point that, in the absence of a standing army, his spies are the best protection Elizabeth has. Just how efficient he has been is illustrated when he provides her with proof of Norfolk's treachery — he has been plotting with Mary Stuart. The disaffected Norfolk, unhappy at not being given the premiere position within Elizabeth's government, tries to fragment responsibility and place blame on Dudley, saying "your trust in him is fatally misplaced, and always has been." Elizabeth will have none of his evasions, however, and shows no compunction about sending her own kin to the gallows: "Our royal blood is from birth. How we use it thereafter is our choice. You have made your choice. As I have!" she says, before ordering Walsingham to "dispose" of him. This is one of the few major divergences from the historical record, as Elizabeth found it intensely difficult to order the execution — she changed her mind not less than four times. In the end, Norfolk lost his head as a sort of consolation prize to Parliament, who had been demanding the death of Mary Stuart for the Ridolfi Plot, something Elizabeth was not yet ready to countenance.

Mary Stuart has been imprisoned for ten years at this point, her length of imprisonment and Burghley's title showing the progression of time. Walsingham puts his plan in motion to entrap Mary, while Elizabeth spends her days being courted by the Duke of Anjou, her "frog prince," and seems inclined to marry — so much so that Burghley begs the Earl of Leicester not to undermine the match. Unlike other representations of Elizabeth's relationship with Anjou (e.g., Helen Mirren's *Elizabeth I*), this is no true love match. Anjou's ambassador, Simier, is shown mocking Elizabeth behind her back, as do her own courtiers, and though they put on a good face, neither Simier nor Anjou seems too disappointed when the marriage negotiations fall through, calling the whole thing a "farce" which has wasted enough of their breath. Before they go, the French take a figurative swing at Leicester, informing the Queen that he has married Lettice Knowles. The exchange this provokes between the Queen and her favorite again shows how this Leicester diverges in characterization from others — he does not backpedal, neither is he afraid. He's not even defensive. Instead, what comes across more than anything else is his pride; he seems every bit as angry as Elizabeth, standing with his hands on his hips, not looking at her, as she rails at him, cursing like a sailor. The camera work during these furious exchanges is handheld and jerky, giving a feel for the raging emotions of the characters. Finally, Leicester tells Elizabeth what she already knows, that he offered her marriage countless times, and countless times she refused him. Echoing the phraseology from his dead wife's earlier letter, he says, "I mortgaged my life in the hope that someday we'd be together. I have stood by and watched while others fall at your feet, flattering your vanity." He has not gone unrewarded for this, a fact of which Elizabeth is all too happy to remind him, but Leicester counters with, "It was a poor exchange for an empty bed! This wretched vow of virginity was your choice, not mine." He places the blame for the failure of their relationship squarely upon Elizabeth's shoulders. This miniseries also goes where none other does in that it has Elizabeth asking about the timelines of his romance, hinting that the Earl of Essex might actually have been fathered by Dudley. This gives an added dimension to Elizabeth's relationship with Essex later in the series. Like Blanchett before her, Duff evokes shades of the Godfather as she dismisses Leicester with, "You are dead to me."

Lettice fares much worse. She is Elizabeth's kin (the historical Lettice Knollys and Elizabeth were cousins), and as she appeared in the beginning of the film, she's almost like a romantic double of Elizabeth — superficially more attractive, gaudier, but with none of Elizabeth's substance. She also lacks her intelligence; whereas Elizabeth knew to dress simply so as to not provoke Queen Mary by outshining her, Lettice has no such sense in her encounter with an even more furious queen. She sports a very fashionable bright yellow dress, made of imported silk, which Elizabeth remarks is "too vulgar" a color for her tastes. As was illustrated with the characterization of Amy Robsart, Lettice also provides an exemplar of the plight of the women left at home. Two disparate women, both married to the same man, Elizabeth's favorite, are left alone while he dances attendance on her, and they represent all the Elizabethan courtiers' wives who suffered this fate. Their characters are different, so the ways in which they deal with their situation also differ. Whereas the gentle Amy languished away in the country, selflessly trying to be supportive of her husband while caring nothing for the monetary benefits of the Queen's favor, Lettice is anything but retiring. She is avaricious, dresses richly and flamboyantly, and she has a large house in the city where she entertains lavishly. She revels in the money and influence her husband's position brings with it. Elizabeth remarks on her queenly behavior; Lettice is self-important enough to be confrontational. When Elizabeth denigrates her for this, in essence pegging her as a jet-setting gold-digger, she replies, "I must occupy myself somehow while my husband attends you." This is the wrong tact to take, and Elizabeth strips Dudley of his salary and monopolies, not to punish him, but to bring Lettice down several notches. Elizabeth tells her sarcastically, "You must learn to live within your means," and she threatens her with the Tower if she ever defies her queen again.

Though in *Mary of Scotland* the Scottish Queen claimed the damning letters were forgeries, this series chooses to showcase Walsingham's machinations in actually making them so. Knowing that the Queen requires written proof, he realizes that Babington's letters alone will not be enough to convict the Scottish Queen. Even when he has Mary's reply in hand, it is, as he says "circumspect" with regard to Elizabeth's actual assassination. To guarantee Mary's guilt, Walsingham has his agent add a postscript to the letter, which he himself dictates, making her guilty beyond a shadow of a doubt. He has already paved the way, convincing the Queen to sign the Act of Association, declaring that any who conspire against the crown forfeit the right to the succession, as well as their lives. In effect, is absolves Elizabeth of the need to *act*; condemnation is automatic. Walsingham cites peace of mind for the Queen as his motivation; in a strange bit of dialogue given that this miniseries displays nothing of the kind with regard to Elizabeth's emotions, Walsingham says he knows how upsetting she found it to sign Norfolk's execution warrant. The truth is that, knowing Elizabeth's tendency to vacillate, Walsingham has stacked the deck, and though Elizabeth is suspicious, she does not realize the extent of what he has done until Mary is implicated in the Babington Conspiracy. While other portrayals of Walsingham show him to be Machiavellian, he's usually working in what he perceives to be the Queen's best interests. This portrayal follows its BBC predecessor *Elizabeth R* in that Walsingham has his own agenda — to destroy Mary Stuart — and he manipulates Elizabeth to accomplish it. When she finds out what Walsingham has done, Elizabeth states that she will not make the mistake of underestimating him (read: trusting him) again. He has outwitted his queen to achieve his objective, but it's a dangerous game he plays. This series gives Elizabeth a reason to dislike Walsingham.

In choosing historicity over drama, this series eschews the face-to-face visit between the queens which most filmmakers find irresistible. It does, however, allow for contact via a letter from Mary, read in voiceover, where she claims she would rather shipwreck her soul than seek Elizabeth's death, and that Elizabeth will be held to account for her treatment of the Scottish Queen. When Walsingham presents Elizabeth with the evidence of her cousin's complicity and she states that still "if my wretched cousin confesses her guilt, she shall yet be pardoned," Walsingham reminds her that it is essentially out of her hands due to the Act of Association. "How prescient you were in that legislation, Sir Francis," she replies angrily. Walsingham is the puppetmaster — he has manipulated Elizabeth and the evidence, and he also pulls the strings with regard to Mary's trial. Since he fears she "intends on treating her trial as a theater where she plays the martyr," Walsingham does everything in his power to prevent her having the opportunity. Preparations are shown, the arrangement of the room — Elizabeth's empty throne is placed, and Burghley remarks that if Mary is situated adjacent to it that will make her "an equal." Walsingham indicates a much less prominent position, "She goes there, where we can read her face." Unlike in other films and miniseries where the trial is used for great dramatic effect (e.g., *Mary of Scotland, Elizabeth I*), this series chooses not to show the trial itself at all, almost as if, since its verdict is a foregone conclusion, its inclusion is also irrelevant. Elizabeth is simply informed that her commissioners have found Mary guilty, and Walsingham remarks in Latin, "A dead woman biteth not." This bit of dialogue is interesting in that this aphorism was supposedly whispered to the historical Elizabeth not by Walsingham, but by an emissary sent to Elizabeth's court, supposedly to beg for mercy for Mary Stuart, by none other than Mary's own loving son, James.[35]

As has been mentioned, there is much mirror gazing in Elizabeth films, and there is much standing beneath towering portraits of Henry VIII or Philip II or the Earl of Essex or [ad infinitum]. There are also a plethora of "portrait shots" — shots framed so that the actress playing Elizabeth resembles historical portraiture of the Queen. All of these tropes employ images of Elizabeth to reflect different themes filmmakers wish to convey, usually having to do with power in one form or another. This offering is unique in that, though it is not the first to show Elizabeth having a portrait painted of herself (*Elizabeth R* shows Elizabeth being sketched for one), it's the first to display an Elizabeth literally having her image fashioned to her specifications. Kapur attempted to achieve the same effect with his Elizabeth's abrupt and symbolic self-transformation into virginal icon, but this Elizabeth's image-building is done in a much more plausible manner, the Elizabethan equivalent of a politician directing a photo shoot. Elizabeth tells the silent painter to "let the jewels on my dress be like 1,000 eyes, so that my subjects know I am always watching out for them." By modern standards, a leader who would have herself displayed as always watching has sinister, Big Brother connotations, but Elizabeth's 1,000 eyes denote security for her realm — she sees all, and as such, is prepared to protect her subjects from danger. She also counsels the painter, "Immortal is the look we're after, sir. And virginal. Divinity, if you can so render it ... henceforth, when my people think of their queen, this is the image they must see." Elizabeth foresees that she will age, her body natural will appear weak, and she needs to always be seen as the glorious body politic — a figure of strength, immortal. By regulating her depiction in portraiture, she can mold how her subjects view her, and thus inform public opinion, the love of her people upon which she has built her reign. This offering shows Elizabeth fashioning the very image which the miniseries itself propagates.

This series is also significant in that, in the end, it is not a powerful male such as Henry VIII whose portrait looks down upon Elizabeth — a forbidding father overshadowing his daughter — but rather Elizabeth's own countenance. She stands before her portrait, a representation of her own strength and ability to rule, examining herself,

self-searching. Elizabeth is not the only one who stands before this image of power; Leicester is also with her. To him falls the unenviable task of convincing her to go through with the execution of Mary Stuart. He does this, finally, by appealing to the strength, the body politic, which the portrait symbolizes. Of Mary Stuart, he says, "You and she are both queens, in that you are alike. Is it not in how you discharge that duty the difference lies? She has always let her heart rule her head, passion before politic need. If you shrink before this duty now ... indeed you risk the accusation that you *are* alike. As a woman, you are just not equal to the task." He has shown Elizabeth the path of feminine weakness, and also appealed to her vanity and pride in threatening comparison with a woman she considers inferior. Elizabeth chooses politic need, and Mary's fate is sealed. As with Mary's trial, her execution is also not shown. It begins from Mary's point-of-view, her long walk to the scaffold as Walsingham looks on, but when she lays her head upon the block, it is Elizabeth's face which looks up at the executioner — it has been nothing but another one of Elizabeth's nightmares. She has substituted herself, and no *Die Traumdeutung* need be consulted for the proper interpretation: in Mary's execution, Elizabeth sees her own mortality.

With Mary's execution begins the chain of events which ends with the Armada, and rather than have the Tilbury speech appear extemporaneous, as does almost every other adaptation, this series chooses to show the preparation that goes into Elizabeth's political speechwriting — the Queen is shown carefully crafting it beforehand, copying it out to paper. It also shows the resonance provided by the Elizabethan political machine — the scene starts out with Elizabeth in voiceover reading to herself what she has just written; her voiceover fades to Burghley's voice as he reads out the speech to her council, and ends with Elizabeth's voice again as she actually gives the speech, addressing the troops at Tilbury. In this way, the practice of circulating copies of a speech and its political reach far beyond those few who hear the original version is exemplified. The defeat of the Armada is likewise presented with plausibility — rather than have Elizabeth watching the defeat from a windswept cliff, word simply arrives. Leicester reads to her the details of the Armada's losses from a letter. While this has the practical application of saving the expense of portraying a battle, it is also more realistic and true to historical form. So also is this series' portrayal of Elizabeth's loss of Leicester.

Elizabeth is in her quarters at the palace, exuberant and being prepared by her giggling ladies for the celebrations surrounding the Armada's defeat. Into this atmosphere enters a solemn Burghley, who breaks the news of Leicester's death — he has succumbed while traveling, and Burghley hands Elizabeth his last letter. She collapses, crying, and locks herself in her apartments. She does not eat, and various courtiers yell through the closed door about the victory celebrations, trying to entice her out. Revealing the strength of their relationship, it is Burghley, finally, who is the only one who can bring her out of her solitude, saying, "Your Majesty, enough now. They cannot celebrate without you. My Lord Leicester would never want his passing to eclipse your finest hour." With that, she puts away his letter, her grief with it, and emerges to the court to put duty before the personal once more.

To demonstrate the path that Elizabeth's relationship with her next favorite, the Earl of Essex, will take, she sits on her throne and seems to see the young Leicester from the beginning of the series making his way through the jostling courtiers. When she looks again, it's not Leicester, but the Earl of Essex (Hans Matheson), and Elizabeth breathes, "His son in all but name." She sees this man as the child of her great love, not just figuratively as a stepson, but literally, and it informs their relationship. The timeline flashes forward ten years, and time has not been kind. Burghley, now white-haired, hobbles around on a crutch. Elizabeth is behind the curtains of her bed, swearing because of an abscessed tooth. When she throws back the curtain, the transformation is almost hideous. She's an old woman, her teeth black and her countenance grotesque. Like the previous *Masterpiece Theatre* Elizabeth, there's no fear of making the actress look truly horrible, down to the ravages of rampant tooth decay. This series' make-up artists earned their salaries; Elizabeth's reverse makeover is disturbingly convincing. Duff called the make-up process "Bess's routine," and it took several hours each day, up to 17 hours for one scene of Elizabeth in her bath, where much of her body shows. Duff has stated that she found the make-up to be an important part of "the journey, getting into the look of the character, let alone the insights."[36] She likened it to the routine the real Elizabeth faced each day, and she used it to inform her characterization of the historical woman.

Burghley warns Elizabeth of how the Earl of Essex, on his way back from the Cádiz raid, is not truly responsible for the victory, yet still "every town, every village calls him England's glory. He basks in their praise." Burghley's son, Robert Cecil, is introduced, as is his rivalry with Essex, which Elizabeth says is like "two spitting hawks, and as tiresome." While almost every other film portraying the relationship of Elizabeth and the Earl of Essex chooses to manifest it as both romantic and, in some cases, overwhelmingly physical, *Elizabeth I: The Virgin Queen* again diverges. Elizabeth treats Essex almost exclusively like a son; their dynamic is one of mother and child, rather than two lovers, even of the courtly variety. She reprimands him as would an angry parent, and when she coddles him, she does so in motherly fashion. At one point, he even says to her, "Does not any son rail against the rule of his mother?" Elizabeth has cast herself in the maternal role, and she can be a stern parent. When Essex presents her with the spoils he has captured, she calls them trinkets, demands that they be assessed towards the debt Essex owes, and leaves him with, "I'm not inclined to award incompetence." She does reward the true hero of Cádiz, Walter Raleigh, and there's much more of his rivalry with Essex shown in this adaptation than in any other, save *Elizabeth R.*

The maternal dynamic is not depicted solely with regard to Elizabeth—Essex has two domineering women in his life, and his real mother is the more unpleasant of the two. She schemes tirelessly and incites Essex, denigrating her son while providing him with helpful hints she learned from the Earl of Leicester about how to manipulate the Queen and the rewards to them both if it is successfully accomplished. This, more than anything else, tarnishes Leicester's relationship with the Queen posthumously—that he shared with his wife the things she knows shows the shallowness of his feelings for Elizabeth, and also his duplicitous motives. The Countess of Leicester assures her son that Elizabeth's "heart can be yours again if you play her right." These conversations with her son on how to go about controlling the Queen are conducted underneath a portrait, placed high on the wall, of the deceased Earl of Leicester. He appears haughty and proud, looking down upon his son with what seems disapproval; Essex cannot measure up. He definitely has parental issues, and it's little wonder he acts as he does.

Heeding his mother's advice and attempting to win her approval, Essex sets about to play Elizabeth in earnest; he picks a fight with Sir Charles Blount, Elizabeth's poetical favorite and Essex's antithesis. He makes sure that it's Elizabeth who attends him when he's injured during the duel. She asks if she has not proved her affection by giving him countless opportunities for advancement, and they are reconciled. When his friends congratulate him on manipulating the old woman so well, with tears in his eyes, he blasts them, "You think I am so callous that my words were but a cynical ploy? You know me less well than you think." A half-second later, however, he's laughing uproariously and triumphantly with them. This scene and others like it elucidate Essex's changeable character, which is only fully explained later by his friend, Francis Bacon.

Essex is at times unpalatable, but there are instances where he provokes compassion. He's trapped between the opposing wills of two powerful and domineering women, his mother and his queen, and his position is not an enviable one. The hold his mother has over him and the cruelty she exhibits toward him when he's unsuccessful with Elizabeth makes him an object of pity. She warns him that her love is not unconditional, "You lose her favor again, and you will forever lose mine," and at one point, she even tells him, heartlessly, "The best part of you was left running down my legs when you were born." The Countess of Leicester is not only brutal but also constantly nagging — she wants a place at court, along with everything else that has come to her through her son's association with the Queen. Essex sighs, "She gives me no peace," and it's one of the truest statements he makes.

This does not excuse Essex's behavior, however. To demonstrate his wildness, he's shown drunkenly in flagrante with not one, but two of Elizabeth's ladies-in-waiting, immediately after reading a letter in which his friend Bacon has cautioned him, "Your watchword must be *moderation*." Essex is unwilling, or perhaps incapable, of exercising moderation. He's disinclined to curb his aspirations for military success and glory, though he does seek a place on the council as Bacon suggests, since there will be a power vacuum when Burghley dies, and he hopes to fill it in order to realize his military ambitions.

Like most of the gainfully employed, Burghley would prefer to leave his job through retirement rather than death, but Elizabeth will not allow it. As they totter down the hall leaning on each other, two political allies who have grown old together, she confesses she still needs him: "Gloriana is but a memory. The youngbloods that surround me are governed only by self-interest, by ambition. They care not for the values of service and sacrifice which shaped our generation." Though this is, in a sense, the habitual lament of the old with regard to the generations that come after them, the truth of it is exemplified by Elizabeth's court. Her busty and lusty young ladies-in-waiting cavort with her favorite, rifle through her most private things and cruelly mock her behind her back; her gentlemen serve her only insofar as they can gain monetarily by it. She needs Burghley, who represents a type of courtier she can no longer find: "With you at my side, I am invincible, William. You are the rock upon which I built my reign." Even though Burghley has trained his son to take his place, Robert Cecil is not the man his father is — he exhibits the selfishness of the new generation, not the service of the old. None is as vainglorious as Essex, which he displays in council.

All on Elizabeth's council, even the military man Raleigh, seek an alliance with

Spain — all except Essex. His warmongering is not well received; he wishes to attack Spanish colonies as well as send military forays into Ireland. With prescience, Burghley quotes the Psalms to him: "Bloodthirsty men will not live half their days," but Essex is undeterred. "Boldness is the key," he assures Elizabeth. Her manner is fond but patronizing as she replies, "When you are nearer the end of your life than the beginning, boldness loses its appeal." Things devolve quickly, with Elizabeth striking Essex after he calls her a "relic." He pulls his sword and is summarily dismissed from court. Encouraged by his mother to use his stepfather's old ploy, he pretends to be ill; the Countess indulges her flawless maternal instincts by smearing some ash from the fireplace under his eyes to assist with the illusion. It has the desired effect, and Elizabeth grants his request to go to Ireland.

Elizabeth has not allowed Burghley to retire, so he drops in the traces — a stroke which leaves him bedridden and barely capable of speech. Elizabeth visits him and feeds him soup, and he takes the opportunity to offer her the last advice he can; he whispers for her to recall Essex: "He will take you down with him and England with you. Recall him." Burghley dies soon after, and as Elizabeth gazes down upon him, she paraphrases the historical Elizabeth, saying, "You were my alpha and omega. No prince ever had such a councilor." Though Robert Cecil and even Raleigh (who support each other in the power play against Essex) provide somewhat of an alternative, it's the beginning of the end for Elizabeth. The foundations of her reign are crumbling.

Elizabeth has not acted on Burghley's last advice — in an attempt to give Essex the chance to redeem himself, she orders him not to come home until he has defeated Tyrone. Meanwhile, she seeks insight into his character by asking Bacon about him, and the information he gives her is almost clinical. He describes a personality that is bipolar, manic-depressive: "Either he is filled with melancholy and self-doubt or such reckless hubris there is no restraining him. Given the extremes of his nature, he is not just a danger to himself, but to others." Raleigh, also, at one point, describes him as "delusional." This is the first representation of Essex as suffering from anything more than his own vanity; he is genuinely unstable. Matheson manages to convey this through his portrayal — the sense that perhaps here is someone who is truly mentally ill, and as such, deserves pity and treatment (something he obviously cannot receive in Elizabethan England), not condemnation.

As if to confirm this armchair diagnosis of his mental illness, not only does Essex return unannounced, but he seems unhinged, actually riding his horse directly into the palace, tears in his eyes as he sneaks into Elizabeth's apartments with his sword drawn. He finds only a sagging old woman in the middle of her bath. Evoking the camera angles used to reveal Bette Davis's Elizabeth, from the bottom up, the camera pans from Duff's swollen feet soaking in a basin, past cankles, spider-veined legs and a wet chemise revealing her wrinkled, sagging chest, to her face, topped only by wisps of white hair on a nearly bald head. The camera work makes "cruel play of her physical self-regard,"[37] an ironic comment on the historical Elizabeth's much-vaunted vanity. This is the spectacle it took make-up artists 17 hours to create, and it is truly a sight to behold — the 35-year-old Duff appears every bit of a very rough 70. Elizabeth looks like death warmed over, but she does not exhibit shock at Essex's intrusion, only mild annoyance. Essex attempts to justify his actions in every way possible, and Elizabeth finally says, "As ever, your words take the sting out of your actions." She sends him home to refresh himself, and like a combination of lost little boy and prodigal son, he kisses her hand as he says, "I see now this is where I belong. I was a fool to stray so far from you."

Elizabeth revokes Essex's taxes and monopolies, bankrupting him. Still he forms no serious designs on her, lying numbly in bed in the depths of his depressive state. It's his virago of a mother who provokes his manic upswing by demanding he seize the moment, assuring him that everyone is planning their futures beyond the Queen, and he must as well. As Bacon has described of him, he switches instantly from tearful depression to frenzied energy, hopping from his bed to mount his ill-fated offensive. When the others in his coterie are arrested, Essex manages to make it back home, calling for his mother. The echoing house is empty; the inciter of all this devastation is nowhere to be found, and the suicidal Essex makes as if to jump from the ramparts of the house before finally surrendering to Raleigh. Elizabeth shows absolutely no resistance at his trial and conviction or execution. His mother elbows her way through the crowd just in time to see what her ambitious jealousy has wrought — to watch him die.

In voiceover, Robert Cecil speaks of the Queen's downward slide, while scenes of an old woman losing her mind play before the viewer's eyes. Reminiscent of her sister Mary, she walks the halls in a metal breastplate, slashing unsteadily at invisible enemies with a sword. Cecil's voice says, "Then, for a brief moment, her spirit was restored to us. She was Gloriana once more," and Elizabeth gives her Golden Speech to Parliament, finishing with, "It is my desire now, to reign no longer than for your good." The pervasive atmosphere, echoing that of *Elizabeth R*'s final scenes, is one of waiting; silent courtiers line the halls, biding their time until Elizabeth dies. Finger in her mouth, she stares at a wall where scenes from her life play like projections — her nightmare of being forced to appear before her father, Kat Ashley, Burghley, and finally Leicester as a young man. As Elizabeth collapses to a choir singing hallelujahs, Cecil's voiceover states, "Then, after over 40 years as sovereign, she quietly departed this life." The last glimpse of Elizabeth is of her corpse lying on her bed as the ring of state is removed from her finger. Cecil finishes his letter, and the viewer is suddenly aware to whom he has been writing: "As for the succession, she neither denied nor confirmed you." The letter is for James Stuart, whom the adaptable Cecil assures of his fidelity, and who will take Elizabeth's place on England's throne.

Since Duff's turn as the Virgin Queen was yet another BBC/*Masterpiece Theatre* creation and covers roughly the same timeline for Elizabeth's life, comparison with its predecessor, *Elizabeth R,* is inevitable. Due to the timing of its production, it was also forced to suffer comparison with the fundamentally different *Elizabeth I* by HBO — its release was delayed in the United Kingdom so as to avoid overlap with this other iteration of Elizabeth, examined later in this chapter. The two actresses who play the title character in these films, Anne-Marie Duff and Helen Mirren, have performed in theater together, and Mirren even sent Duff flowers, with a card reading "from one queen to another." Duff realized that comparison was inescapable, and admitted that she found the prospect of playing Elizabeth to be "terrifying" given the other actresses who have shouldered the role, such as Mirren and Glenda Jackson. "It's easy to be intimidated. You have to own it, like playing a classical role," was how Duff described her turn as queen. This is, for the most part, how her portrayal feels — that she took the accepted literary material, the "classical" Elizabeth, and exemplified it to craft her characterization, with no frills added. Duff has stated that, being of Irish extraction, Elizabeth was "not part of my national myth," and she also knew little of the historical woman before she took on this role. In order to prepare, like others before her, she did her research, reading biographies by David Starkey and Elizabeth Jenkins. Using these sources, she "gradually thought her way into the role of the Virgin Queen."[38]

Duff was not the only Elizabeth newbie on this production. Paula Milne, the writer responsible for *Elizabeth I: The Virgin Queen*'s script, has said that she started out with only the knowledge that, as there was currently an Elizabeth II, there must have been an Elizabeth I.[39] This is a rather terrifying statement for a screenwriter of a supposedly historical drama to make (as well as anyone who has graduated high school), but the end result is a script which is, for the most part, sure-footed. Though certain small points of dialogue do grate (e.g., Elizabeth's diminutive for Leicester being "Robbie" rather than "Robin"), overall the writing feels much the same as Duff's characterization — a slightly modernized variation on the same classical theme. As one commentary noted, "It aims for authenticity ... it doesn't get everything right, but it hits the mark enough."[40] If this miniseries' antecedent, *Elizabeth R*, was an almost obsessive historical reconstruction of Elizabeth's life in the formal theatrical tradition, then *Elizabeth I: The Virgin Queen* follows that tradition with less attention to detail, giving Elizabeth a slightly less structured and more dynamic feel. Duff certainly crafts an Elizabeth with equal capability but more intellectual flair than Jackson's, though she's hard put to match the emotional dimensionality of Mirren's portrayal.

One reviewer stated that this series "seems deeply invested in its effort to unravel the mysteries of Elizabeth the woman ... refusing to acknowledge that the 'mysteries' don't require all the keys in a locksmith's arsenal. The production prods and pokes at the young queen, laboring relentlessly, and without much success, to draw some sort of grand conclusion."[41] There are elements of this which are unmistakable, the most significant of which is the ending of the last episode. After Cecil finishes his letter to James, neatly tying up loose ends for the viewer, he examines Elizabeth's ring of state, and finds that a clasp has been added. When he pops it open to reveal a miniature, Raleigh guesses, "Robert Dudley." But Cecil replies, "It is the whore, Anne Boleyn. Her mother," and this is the final word with which the viewer is left. Boleyn has not been mentioned throughout the miniseries, appearing only as a shadowy figure behind the terrifying Henry VIII of Elizabeth's nightmares, so ending the production in this way is meant as a sort of revelation. But a revelation of what? Elizabeth does not take pains in this iteration to identify herself with her father, so it does not turn that notion on its head; neither is she defensively angry about her mother, as in *Young Bess*, nor does she express fear about suffering her fate. Accordingly, this "revelation," presented as it is, does not really offer any kind of insight into Elizabeth's character. Elizabeth's projected replay of her life before she dies has the same effect — these are the personalities the viewer has already witnessed in Elizabeth's life; recapping them at the end to show that they are of significance is something the viewer already knows, and it provides no further clarification. So also the scene where the elderly Elizabeth's young and inconsiderate ladies rifle through the most private possessions in her jewel box—first, one pulls out Dudley's last letter and his miniature, an unsurprising find. Then one discovers a miniature of Kat Ashley, misidentifying it as Anne Boleyn, which elicits a gasp from her companion. Cecil and the other young people of Elizabeth's court search for clues to Elizabeth's inner self, but the result is not elucidation—random pieces never come together to form anything coherent, for them, or for the viewer.

This portrayal of Elizabeth has been called "a hodgepodge treatise on sexual frustration," but with the end result being that "if her sex life, or lack of it, was ... a source of torture for her ... then the consequences for what, in the 16th century, became the most powerful country on earth were close to zero." [42] This may be the entire point. Though one commentary uses the word "unwraps"[43] with regard to Duff's portrayal of Elizabeth, this is not, in fact, the case. She *presents* and viewers must do their own unwrapping, draw their own conclusions, for they are never offered up neatly on a platter. What Duff presents is a straightforward take on the historical woman: her formidable intellect, her impressive education, her strengths as a ruler, and her personal relationships. Elizabeth's feelings and personal life are what they are, the viewer can make of them what he or she will, for Elizabeth does not explicate. But the main point is that Elizabeth is, from the very beginning, a brilliant queen—one whose rule equaled greatness for England. This is the present inside the box; the wrappings are unimportant.

ELIZABETH I (2005)

This miniseries begins in 1579, opening to grand choral music and a background of white and red Tudor roses. The opening titles inform the viewer that Elizabeth (Helen Mirren) has been on the throne for 20 years and has so far refused to marry; because of this and the resulting lack of an heir, there is danger of civil war over the succession. Shades of *Fire Over England* occur when England is described as "a small and vulnerable Protestant country" set about by Catholic powers just waiting "to seize the Heretic Queen's throne." *Elizabeth I* has, perhaps, one of the most interesting introductions of Elizabeth to be found in any film, and certainly a unique one. The Tudor roses reveal themselves to be wallpaper, which provides a backdrop against which a woman stands, her back to the viewer, arms perpendicularly outstretched. In a reverse of the opening of *The Private Lives of Elizabeth and Essex*, Elizabeth is not being dressed, but undressed. Slowly the points of her laces are untied and her sleeves removed, then her bodice, her skirts, her forepart; piece by piece, with the soft whisper of fabrics, Elizabeth is stripped down to her white embroidered chemise. This opening showcases the texture evident throughout this film; it completely engages the senses. From the rustle of fabrics to the play of light, this film exudes a sensual naturalism which completely immerses the viewer.

What makes this opening unique, however, is the reason for which Elizabeth is being undressed. She lies back on her bed, a sheet is draped over her legs and a doctor appears as a silhouette on the other side of it, holding an instrument familiar to any woman who has had to endure an annual pelvic exam. For this is the reason Elizabeth has been undressed, and the first glimpse of her face occurs while she's being examined. Other adaptations feature Elizabeth undergoing a physical exam, but none uses this as the viewer's first introduction to the Queen, her countenance during an uncomfortable and mortifying procedure — literally laying herself open for the good of her country. Her expression is distant; she evinces no emotion as the doctor finishes up and pronounces, "All is as it should be, ma'am."

Illustrating the lack of privacy at court, the doctor immediately reports his findings to Lord Burghley (Ian McDiarmid), waiting in the corridor with Francis Walsingham (Patrick Malahide): the Queen is still capable of having children, and she is "virgo intacta." Burghley's reaction is one of pleased satisfaction, and the dourly pragmatic Walsingham states, "If she were too old to bear children, there would be little sense in her marrying." Marriage is, again, forefront, which is only reinforced when Burghley and Walsingham pass the Earl of Leicester (Jeremy Irons) in the corridor, and greet him with a sort of exasperated resignation. He returns their nods with, "My lords Walsingham and Burghley — married men both and peddlers of the matrimonial state." Leicester goes his way as Burghley and Walsingham argue over the marriage supposedly being peddled — the Duke of Anjou. Walsingham's pronouncement is that "the French make better acquaintances than friends," but Burghley is obviously in favor of the match, and sends Walsingham to inform Anjou he needs only the Queen's permission to start negotiations. The major players have all been introduced in a matter of seconds, and this immediately shows the rapport between the favorite and Elizabeth's chief advisers, as well as between the advisers and Elizabeth herself. Burghley sets plans in action on his own — Elizabeth has clearly not yet given her permission — but he will not act independently of her will. Leicester has his own agenda.

During the course of this conversation, the camera has followed Burghley and Walsingham through one long tracking shot from right outside the Queen's bedchamber all the way down to the royal wharf. The sets constructed for this film are extremely realistic and Byzantine in their layout, providing at once a sense of motion (actors are often filmed running through them) and claustrophobia — like watching a mouse navigate a tightly constructed maze. They have an infinitely more realistic feel than previous offerings (e.g., *The Private Lives of Elizabeth and Essex, Elizabeth*) which utilize large, echoing spaces to dwarf the people contained within them.

Leicester was on his way to visit the Queen, and she's obviously very happy to see him, holding her arms out to him and patting the bed beside her. Leicester expresses his uneasiness about Elizabeth's marriage prospects, and she comforts him with, "Be not afraid. I will not marry." He asks if they still have each other, and she replies, "We have each other always, Robin, since that way our affections tend." He speaks to her of the promises they made when they were young, how time has worn them away, and how he does not trust the Duke of Anjou "to love you as you should be loved. I'm afraid, Bess." What Leicester fears so are the dangers of Elizabeth's bearing a child; he fears to lose her. Evoking the cult of Gloriana, he asks, "What is the world without you in it?" and then, kissing her, "Do not I live in the sun of your favor? And does not the world condemn me for it?"

The rapport that is established in this first scene of Elizabeth and Leicester together is different from that of any other onscreen version of these two historical characters.

Reviews and commentary on this film are keen to continually point out that Mirren is "of a certain age," as is Irons. By this point, Elizabeth and Leicester's relationship has been longstanding. Neither is young anymore, and their romance has matured; though they still share a passion, youthful physical attraction has given way to comfortable and deep affection. Leicester has his own agenda, but he also truly cares for Elizabeth, as she does for him. She shows herself to be dependent on him, and the one element this portrayal showcases is their kindness to each other. In other adaptations, Elizabeth is often shown denigrating the males of her court; she puts them in their places for no other reason than to exert her power, and she seems to take great enjoyment in leashing her lapdogs, including and especially Leicester. She sometimes rewards them, but she is never kind to them. This Elizabeth and her Leicester, however, seem to have more of an equal partnership, a relationship based on mutual respect and affection. Leicester is ambitious, but he knows his boundaries, and though he's not always successful, he does make a concerted effort not to overstep them. He also possesses a sardonic wit which Elizabeth shares — their mutual sarcasm provides this miniseries with a humorous undertone that is as realistic as it is refreshing.

The viewer is treated to a first glimpse of Elizabeth's management style when she's shown in council, with Burghley calmly laying out how they have "implored" her to marry for the past 19 years. Elizabeth rolls her eyes and sighs, giving the impression that she's heard all this before, countless times. But she patiently listens as he outlines the advantages of the Anjou match. Even the layout of the council chamber seems to showcase the calm equilibrium with which this Elizabeth's court operates. In other adaptations, Elizabeth sits at the head of the table with her councilors ranged around her. In this series, she sits at one end and Burghley balances her out at the other, so they face each other down the length of the table, with the other members of the council ranged evenly down the sides.

As is understandable to anyone who has had to endure the torture of too many meetings, Leicester ends up face down on the table, his voice muffled as he says, "Oh, *God.* The Duke of Anjou is still a *Catholic.*" Elizabeth, wryly amused, baits him, "But of the *quiet* kind, my lord ... he'll pray in a corner if you ask him to. He's even had private conversation with Master Walsingham, who *eats* Catholics." Elizabeth then states blithely that she must be off, since "Parliament seeks words with us, and we must *seem* to listen."

To say that Helen Mirren does a masterful job with the characterization of Elizabeth in this film would be an understatement. She manages a portrayal of such naturalism, dimensionality, and subtlety that it is almost completely convincing. More than that, it inspires both admiration and empathy. Her Elizabeth is, in the beginning at least, a more *likeable* Elizabeth, a woman one can easily believe would be able to effectively govern through force of personality. This is a woman who is intelligent and clever, but not calculating. She utilizes her manipulative gifts for defense rather than offense, and she possesses a wit she uses not as a sword to wound, but as a shield to deflect. One of her greatest assets is her sense of humor; she uses it to lubricate the wheels of government and entice her male councilors to warm to her. Mirren's Elizabeth displays her temper, but under circumstances that warrant extremes of emotion, and she's always quick to attempt to subdue it — the viewer can see Elizabeth physically struggling to will her emotions under control. She is a complex and extremely engaging woman.

Mirren is helped in this by the costuming of the series. Though there are glimpses of the icon, for the majority of this series, Elizabeth's costuming, and that of those around her, reflects the pervasive naturalism of *Elizabeth I*. Her clothing is relatively sedate, rich, to be sure, but soft, not overstated, the Elizabethan equivalent of everyday wear — gowns that are beautiful, but that one could actually spend the day in without torturing discomfort. The style of her wigs also reflects this; they curl softly, naturally, and are more of a strawberry blond than the boldly artificial red of other adaptations. Her make-up is also far more naturalistic than what might be expected to represent the stark-white face staring out of Elizabeth's portraits — with the exception of a bit of eyeshadow and lip rouge, she wears almost no cosmetics. The overall impression this gives is of a woman who is aging, but still attractive and vital, a woman that is *real*, not a sparkling, artificial construct. As time passes and events that shape Elizabeth's personality occur, however, the costuming in the film changes. As does Elizabeth herself, the costuming starts out naturalistic, informal, and makes its way towards formal, through semi-iconic, eventually ending up at the iconic gowns and accoutrements familiar from the paintings, but only in the public realm — Elizabeth dresses for her public, but still sports more "casual wear" at "home."

Mirren espouses this approach to the costuming and the characterization it represents, stating that one of the great challenges of playing Elizabeth "is to fight through that iconic image and to find a living, breathing, complex person." For the actress attempting to portray her, Elizabeth's iconic image is a double-edged sword — as Mirren puts it, "The costumes are marvelous because they make the statement for you, but then you have to fight your way out of the costume and make-up. It's both a tool and a liability, because you want to make this a living, breathing person and not just a painting."[44]

Elizabeth is also allowed to speak for herself initially, something many of the other screen queens are denied. Instead of having her counselors, courtiers, subjects, or foreign ambassadors gossip about what type of person she is, thus informing viewer perceptions before Elizabeth herself is ever seen, this adaptation allows the viewer to fashion his or her own opinion. Elizabeth is what she is, and the viewer can use her own words and actions to define her, rather than listening to the other characters in the film pontificate about the Queen from their obviously subjective points-of-view.

So far, the mood of the series has been relatively light, but darkness always lurks, showing the tenuousness of Elizabeth's position behind the easy court banter. The Queen walks peacefully in the garden with Leicester, her courtiers all about, graciously greeting and making small talk. She has just shared her view that "a man may be a good Catholic *and* a good Englishman," when a young Catholic assassin attacks with a knife. It's all over in a second — Leicester shows his value and presence of mind as he effortlessly disarms the attacker and saves Elizabeth, who practically swoons into his arms. Later, in the safety of her apartments, he solicitously inquires after his queen, and she replies that "she sometimes wonders if she's allowed the luxury of feeling anything." Leicester comforts her by taking her mind off her troubles, reminiscing about their first meeting, while they were both imprisoned in the Tower of London. In the lull of relief after intense danger, this showcases the deep intimacy, a product of their years together, which the two share, and the strength Elizabeth derives from it. Leicester is not without his agenda, however, and he subtly attempts to entice Elizabeth to stay the night with him in his apartments. He kisses her insistently and she responds in kind, but as she does throughout this film, Elizabeth denies herself; she draws a line. This is not a cold woman shunning physical contact; Mirren's Elizabeth is an intensely physical and sensual creature — she controls herself through sheer force of will, but the struggle is not an easy one. Though he has not said the word "marriage," she tells Leicester, not with anger but finality, "I could not marry you. I could not raise up a subject so." This is not a case of Elizabeth setting Leicester down; she's simply stating facts. He knows it, and allows her to go with a lingering look.

This offering is exceptional in the canon of Elizabethan film because it manages to focus, almost equally, on Elizabeth's relationship with two of her most notable favorites: Leicester and Essex. It also shows the natural progression of these relationships by introducing Essex as a young boy, under the patronage of Leicester. His father has just been killed in the Queen's service in Ireland, and the Countess of Essex brings the boy to court so that Leicester can introduce him to the Queen. In a foreshadowing of things to come, their first meeting does not go particularly well — Elizabeth says, "We will kiss you," but the boy pulls away from her. She takes it well, smiling absently; she has her mind on other things. After complimenting the Countess on her appearance, she adds, "Perhaps you're in search of new offers of marriage," and looks pointedly at Leicester. On her way out of Leicester's apartments, she stops to look at the portraits he has hung on the wall: "The portraits of your ancestors look well on your walls. Pity so many of them turned out to be traitors." Leicester jokes, "Only my father and grandfather. The present generation is entirely devoid of treason." Elizabeth assures him she's pleased to hear of it, but the tension is unmistakable, and after she has walked out, it's made clear her suspicions have not been unfounded — the Countess of Essex begins straightening Leicester's doublet and whispers, "She knows." Leicester may genuinely care for Elizabeth, but he's not above deceiving her to meet his own needs.

In order to understand the dynamic between Elizabeth and Leicester in these films, it helps to be familiar with Leicester's history. In almost every film adaptation, he's depicted as coming from a long line of traitors, as Elizabeth's reference to Leicester's father and grandfather intimates in *Elizabeth I*. Leicester's grandfather, Edmund Dudley, was a lawyer by vocation and later the Speaker of the House of Commons during the reign of Henry VII. He became a member of the council, and it was his money-grubbing tactics levied against the nobility to provide royal revenues that led to his great unpopularity. These tactics were but the outgrowth of his sovereign's policy, but it is not a wise course of action to show displeasure with the King of England. Instead, Dudley served as a scapegoat for Henry VII's unpopular policies, and in a move calculated to increase his popular support, one of Henry VIII's first acts when he ascended the throne was to bring Dudley to trial for treason and have him beheaded. John Dudley, Leicester's father, was a veteran of the French wars and held a seat in the House of Commons. He was politically very useful to the king, and later garnered a variety of titles for himself, including being raised to the peerage as Viscount Lisle, and later Earl of Warwick and Duke of Northumberland. With the Lord Protector the Duke of Somerset, he became one of the most powerful men at court during the short reign of Henry's successor, the sickly boy-king Edward. When

Edward died, Dudley placed the ill-fated Lady Jane Grey, married to his son and Robert's brother Guildford Dudley, upon the throne of England. Catholic though she was, the people still rallied around Mary, and Dudley, along with his sons, including Robert, ended up in the Tower. John Dudley was sentenced to die as a traitor and quickly executed. Guildford soon followed, and Robert himself was sentenced to death, though his sentence was never carried out — he was allowed to languish in the Tower. Finally he and his two surviving siblings (his elder brother John had been released, only to die of sickness three days later) were given their freedom, though still attainted.[45] To portray the Dudleys as a family of traitors for generations is somewhat unfair — none of them had rebelled against a sovereign they had sworn to serve. Also, the fact that Leicester had been imprisoned in the Tower is usually utilized to further the romantic plotline of his relationship with Elizabeth, as is demonstrated in this film when the two reminisce about their time there together. Though their sentences in the Tower did overlap, it seems extremely unlikely that they ever met there; there's certainly no evidence whatsoever to substantiate such romantic claims. What Dudley's stint in the Tower did mean was that he had common ground with Elizabeth, but what happened to his own family taught him the danger of overreaching. Though an ambitious man, Dudley took that lesson under advisement, and he tempered himself more than some of Elizabeth's other favorites, most notably the Earl of Essex.

Despite Leicester's opposition, Elizabeth assures him that the Duke of Anjou's religion is a private matter, and uses her line about windows and men's souls to illustrate her point. She comforts Leicester by telling him that "the only things that will kiss in this affair will be lawyer's pens and lawyer's papers ... poor England stands alone." It is, of course, poor Elizabeth who stands alone, but this is not a woman selfishly pursuing her own needs. She does not look for nor expect a love match; she searches for security for her beleaguered little country. So she accedes to Burghley's request to start negotiations: "Well, gentlemen, if marriage it must be, then marriage it must be." She's far from enthusiastic at the prospect, though not against it in principle, and willing to do what's best for her country. What she finds is something altogether unexpected.

The Duke of Anjou's party arrives, and it gives Elizabeth a chance to showcase her impressive grasp of languages as she easily converses with them in French. She's surprised to discover that the Duke himself has come in disguise, as one of the party. Unlike Elizabeth's father, Henry VIII, who was fond of "disguising" himself (though the illusion could not have been more transparent) for the pretense of pleased surprised his intended targets (always women) displayed, the Duke of Anjou has good reason to conceal his identity — technically he is not in England; his visit is being made in secret. He also does not, as does the idiotic duke of Kapur's *Elizabeth*, hop out and unveil himself before getting fresh with an anointed sovereign. Elizabeth must choose which of the party she believes is Anjou. The viewer shares Elizabeth's apprehension as she points to first one and then another of his party, asking tentatively, "You?" Given the portrayal of Anjou in other Elizabeth offerings as a buffoon (*Elizabeth*) or physically less than impressive (*Elizabeth R*), the viewer also shares in Elizabeth's relief, which quickly turns to delight, when the Duke (Jérémie Covillault) turns out to be a handsome young man with expressive dark eyes and a very pleasing manner.

Including the courtship paid to Elizabeth by the Duke of Anjou allows this film to show the difficulty inherent in royal matchmaking in deeper vein than other offerings (e.g., *Elizabeth I: The Virgin Queen* and *Elizabeth: The Golden Age*) which scratch the surface, as well as to contrast the artificial atmosphere it creates with the naturalism this film espouses. In the era of *paparazzi* and tabloid journalism, the intense public scrutiny that celebrities undergo — whether they be movie stars, athletes, politicians, or royals — is an accepted fact. Even in today's limelight, however, there still remains the concept of a private life for them, perhaps experienced only in a carefully guarded home setting. Elizabeth's relationship with the Duke of Anjou highlights the fact that they are *never* alone, even in Elizabeth's own "home." They must conduct their romance with everyone watching, constantly judging. The atmosphere it creates is difficult for both of them to overcome, but at the same time, provides a common ground and bond for them. Elizabeth (as she sits outside with the Duke, surrounded by courtiers) tells him that "a man and a woman were never at less risk of being natural." The Duke seems pleased by her perception — as portrayed by Covillault, he comes across as intelligent and, for the most part, sincere. His political considerations are paramount, but it's clear that he *likes* Elizabeth as a person. Despite the age difference, he's also genuinely attracted to her, confiding to Simier that "she is quite pretty." He replies to Elizabeth that, with her, he "has never felt more natural," and she confesses she feels the same. They find something extremely valuable to people in their position — in the middle of the court glare, they discover a sort of shared privacy in each other's company, a small space where understanding flourishes and public persona can be put aside.

To reinforce this, the film also chooses to show them most often in naturalistic, outside settings. Their first meeting occurs on the Thames, rowing in the Royal Barge in the brilliant sunshine. Even when they are shown inside, still the outdoors is evoked — they sit together in a room with no furniture save their seats, the ceiling and walls painted to look like a summer sky with sea and countryside, giving the illusion of a day spent outdoors in beautiful weather. The Duke seems to represent light in Elizabeth's life — when she's shown with him, everything is bright. He makes her both hopeful and happy.

In contrast with this are her advisers, who sit in dark, wood-paneled rooms. The room Burghley uses as his office is an extremely interesting part of this film's set — located very near the council chamber, it's small, claustrophobic, barely big enough for a modest desk. The room is forbidding, giving the impression of a shadowy alcove set off a brighter hallway. Burghley's desk faces out, and the only light comes from candles and a stained glass window behind him which filters it into a weakened, yellow glow. Here Burghley sits, in this muted glow, industriously writing and planning. Burghley is not a sinister character in this series; as portrayed by McDiarmid, he comes across as a clever but wry, grandfatherly type. His only concerns are Elizabeth's security and, by extension, that of the realm. Elizabeth's security, however, often comes at the price of her personal happiness, and Burghley can be seen to represent the bleakness inherent in being always forced to choose duty over desire. Francis Walsingham is also cast in this role with Burghley. His characterization is meant to be dour — he offers to deliver unwelcome information to Elizabeth when no one else will because he "has the right face for bad news" — and he's also puritanical. His characterization, while still not sinister, does have an element of pragmatic menace; he's shown calmly torturing conspirators for information, and he methodically plots Mary Stuart's downfall. Amidst this dourness, he often conveys an irony that could be taken for a sense of humor. Elizabeth does not like him (which is historically authentic; the real Elizabeth also did not care personally for Walsingham), but she needs the services he provides.

The Duke and Elizabeth's feelings are obviously not the only factors at play in the matrimonial game. Leicester tries again and again to forestall the marriage, supposedly out of concern for Elizabeth's feelings (he tells Burghley and Walsingham, "I counsel out of love for her ... *her* heart will be broken. Not yours. Or his."), but almost certainly just as much for fear of losing his position. Elizabeth is hurt by his selfishness: "Cannot you wish me happy, Robin? Would my contentment be such a burden to you? Would you bid me hide a passion when passion's caught me?" she asks. Elizabeth is smitten with Anjou; she has found a love she never thought to — one with an appropriate outlet, and she's hopeful for her prospects of happiness with such a marriage. The entire exchange between Elizabeth and Leicester on the subject occurs without heat. Neither is angry; Leicester is frightened, but Elizabeth treats him with compassion, and both display kindness towards the other. There is no pride or conceit on Elizabeth's part, no attempt to humble Leicester for daring to speak to her on the subject. It's yet another testament to Mirren's acting ability that she manages, by turns, to express all aspects of a single personality: Elizabeth is regal before Parliament, intimate with Leicester and Anjou, and here wistful, calling herself "late fruit of the tree, a breath away from withering." She feels the clock ticking, and she wants this last chance for happiness in the matrimonial state.

Her happiness, unfortunately, is plucked out by the roots before it has had a chance to flower. It soon becomes apparent that the match is not looked upon with favor by the majority of her court. When Elizabeth formally introduces the Duke, he's greeted with stony silence until Burghley starts clapping and the rest of the court unenthusiastically follows. Elizabeth, angry, demands "Louder!" and her frustration is completely understandable; for years she has been put upon to marry and now that she attempts it, she's met with opposition from the entire court, save Burghley. "Is this not what you wanted?" she snaps. "Is this gentleman not to your liking? Must I consult you all before I find out if he is to mine?" As much as it infuriates her, he's not to their liking; they distrust both his Catholicism and the fact that he is French. Until this point, Elizabeth had believed that, in this instance, personal happiness and duty to the realm were one and the same, and this knowledge brought bliss. With this one painful scene, Elizabeth begins to comprehend that yet another choice between desire and duty must be made, and she knows which one always takes priority.

Her feelings for Anjou run deep, however, and for a moment it seems as if Elizabeth may waver. She's in great danger of putting her personal feelings before political necessity. She almost channels Shakespeare's *Merchant of Venice* as she asks him, "Does not a prince feel? Does he not have hands, eyes, a tongue and a disposition to be loved?" Anjou assures her that he does, and "if you do, shall we not dare to risk the displeasure of others?" It seems that Elizabeth will dare it, until a final circumstance forces her to face the futility of her hopes. A pamphlet has been published against the marriage, and when the author is discovered, Elizabeth has his hand cut off in public as punishment for his transgression.

As she, the Duke, Leicester, and others watch from the balcony, the crowd is eerily silent. This film is particularly gory, and the camera focuses mercilessly on the poor pamphleteer as his hand is chopped off; he holds it up, dripping blood, to Elizabeth, and shouts, "The hand of a true Englishman who loves his Queen and his country!" Only then does the crowd roar, and Elizabeth realizes just how deep the public animosity towards the Anjou match runs. She cannot marry him. Leicester, who informed her of the pamphlet in the first place, remarks triumphantly and callously, "It would appear the people have little stomach for this marriage." Elizabeth snaps that she has "little stomach for the people," and turns to go. But it will be a day of hurtful events for Elizabeth for, as in several other offerings, *Elizabeth I* chooses to have Simier loose an arrow that wounds Elizabeth deeply and destroys Leicester — the French courtier asks how Leicester's *wife* does, since he understands she is with child.

This news does not come as a shock to the viewer, only to Elizabeth, and the terrified Leicester. Mirren's emotions run the gamut; first there's stunned disbelief— she is literally speechless. Then anger, "Oh, you son of a whore," she says quietly, on the verge of tears. From there she works herself into a truly hysterical state, screaming, "I never wish to see your face again. Be off before I hang you. I'm minded to hang you now, with my own hands! Get out of my sight!" This is all Elizabeth allows herself before she clamps down on her emotions, willing herself under control. To show that the woman has subjugated herself to the monarch, Elizabeth lapses into the royal plural as she says calmly, "We forbid you access to our presence. You are no longer welcome at our court. Be gone, sir. *Now.*" This is one of several instances where Mirren turns the traditional perception of Elizabeth's rages (and the film portrayals that have sprung from it) on its head. The historical woman was known for her changeability, but Mirren interprets this not as unevenness of temper, but rather as a fight for control. Her Elizabeth feels deeply, at times she's almost carried away by it, but always Mirren clamps down; the viewer can see her physically regaining control of herself, recovering from her emotions. As Elizabeth ages and events affect her, however, she becomes less and less proficient at tamping down her temper. For his part, Leicester has tried to shift blame by mumbling something about having to marry elsewhere since Elizabeth would not have him, but his excuses are contemptible. He has betrayed Elizabeth, not by marrying, but by hiding his association with the Countess of Essex from her, by lying to her while he continued to pursue her. The Queen has lost her hope of marriage to Anjou, and she has also lost her anchor, Leicester, all in one moment.

Though Cate Blanchett's *Elizabeth* chose to portray the Queen as unaware that Dudley was married, this was blatantly untrue, since she was well aware of his marriage to Amy Robsart. Leicester's marriage to Lettice Knollys, the widowed Countess of Essex, however, was quite a different matter. The marriage was a quiet affair, kept from the Queen, and exactly how she found out remains a matter of conjecture — some contend that Leicester told her himself rather than risk her hearing it via the rumor mill. Regardless, she was definitely unaware of it at the time it occurred. Since it is unknown when or by what means she first discovered it, her initial reaction also remains unknown. One thing is certain — she definitely did not banish Leicester from court for a period of years, as Elizabeth does in this series. In her book *Elizabeth and Leicester*, which charts their relationship from beginning to end, Sarah Gristwood posits that Elizabeth, while definitely not thrilled about the prospect, was aware of Leicester's flirtations and amorous pursuits, and that the shock came not from knowing him to be with another woman, but from him publicly tying himself to her through the act of marriage.[46]

Elizabeth knows in her head that she cannot have the Duke of Anjou, but it still remains to reconcile this with her heart. She sits in council, the marriage papers in hand, ready for her to sign, as her councilors, even Burghley, furiously backpedal, distancing themselves from the match. Rather than show the dissolution of the Duke's marriage suit as a mercenary, monetary transaction as do other offerings (e.g., *Elizabeth R*), *Elizabeth I* makes it truly heartrending, and the scene is an exceptional one. In no other adaptation is Elizabeth shown to be so inclined to marry, and to a man her councilors have chosen, only to be heartbroken because public opinion dictates that she cannot follow through with what has been demanded of her for 20 years. The irony is terrible. "Have I not been told by you, and you, and you," she says, pointing an accusing finger at each member of the council in turn, "that I should do as other women do and get me an heir? Do you imagine that I do not have a desire to have a child? Am I so unnatural to you by virtue of my exalted position? Now I have finally found a man who is both royal and to my liking. May I not?..." at this point, Elizabeth breaks down completely, head in her hands, sobbing, "Am I made of stone, gentlemen?" she cries. She's a truly pitiable figure, and this characterization is also the first to show Elizabeth with a desire to be a mother to more than just the English people. An heir is expected, so as a matter of course she wants one, but the inflection Mirren's Elizabeth gives in voicing her desire to have a child connotes much more than just securing the succession. She even goes so far as to use the word "unnatural," applied so often with regard to the historical Elizabeth. This Elizabeth is a most unwilling Virgin Queen; she does not wish to be a cold icon, but her wishes are not taken into account. She's terribly alone, illustrated by the fact that all of her councilors silently file out of the chamber as she sobs into the table. Only Burghley pauses, tentatively reaching out to touch her arm in sympathy. Before his hand makes contact, she starts up, instantly controlling the tears and jerking away. She wants none of his pity, and has exerted her self-control once again.

All that's left is for Elizabeth to control herself one last time as she bids farewell to the Duke and his party. He leaves her with, "Some princes do not deserve their subjects. It is the opposite case with you, madam." Elizabeth allows herself only, "There is no other prince in the world to whom I would rather be bound or with whom I would rather spend the days of my life." She retains a restrained formality throughout their parting; everyone is watching, as always. But she hands him a letter, which is read in voice-over as his boat rows away, and it is, as in *Elizabeth R*, the historical Elizabeth's poetry upon the loss of her "Monsieur." She must hide her grief, her discontent, and pretend that she does not love him, when all she wants is to act on that feeling. As she watches his boat row into the distance, she sighs, "Well, England, the Queen is all yours."

With the dramatic tension of the Leicester/Anjou triangle resolved, something must fill the vacuum, so the series skips forward several years and pulls out the filmmaker's favorite: Mary Stuart. Walsingham has discovered evidence that implicates her in the earlier attempt on Elizabeth's life. Elizabeth is not angry, merely incredulous: "This is our cousin! Is she not confined by us at our command? Do we have proof positive?" Having been in the same position herself during her sister Mary Tudor's reign, Elizabeth refuses to act unless it can be proven that Mary Stuart is not just the focus of such conspiracies, but the "active agent" behind them. Elizabeth has declared herself as belonging to the people, and she's shown out among them, laughing, talking, glad-handing. She's enjoying herself, and they are enjoying her. But Burghley has just received word that Elizabeth has been excommunicated, and all Catholics are called upon to pursue her destruction. The change in atmosphere this news provokes is instantaneous. When Walsingham informs her of the Pope's bull, Elizabeth's demeanor immediately changes — the crowd is no longer her beloved people, but a sinister, dangerous entity, a hundred hands reaching out to deal a fatal blow. Walsingham warns Elizabeth that the Pope may act through Mary, and encourages action. "Strike, strike, and strike again," Elizabeth says to him irritably, and then with finality, "When the occasion calls for it, I will strike."

One of the major strong points of this series is its ability to show Elizabeth's progression from a lively woman in the prime of life to an embittered old queen — to give an emotional background for the construct of what she would become. Other adaptations have attempted this more blatantly and clumsily — witness Kapur's Dudley betrayal and Elizabeth's resulting snap decision to physically transform herself into the Virgin Queen with a pair of scissors and some face paint. Through its portrayal of the Anjou match, as well as her dealings with Mary Stuart and finally the Earl of Essex, the viewer understands how the events of Elizabeth's life have shaped her personality over a course of years. She is not presented as a finished product, but rather a work in progress. And this progression is fascinating, if heartrending, to watch.

The heartache is not over for Elizabeth; years have passed, but she still expresses sadness when Walsingham informs her that the Duke of Anjou has died. "Well," she says desolately, "we are ... sorry to hear of it." This news has more than personal consequences for Elizabeth, however. The French have made peace with Spain, and Philip is building his Armada; once again she is threatened. This entire scene is staged with Elizabeth writing at a small desk, Walsingham standing in the doorway, and it's shot through a model ship which sits in the foreground — literally bringing the Armada to the forefront. With these new dangers, Elizabeth feels more alone than ever, and her anger has cooled over the years. She tells a none-too-pleased Walsingham and Burghley: "These are hard times. And no one to talk to, no one in whom I can confide. We have recalled the Earl of Leicester."

The film reintroduces Leicester in a symbolic manner. Elizabeth watches a group of her courtiers, all young men, dancing as she critiques their steps. She has a host of men dancing to her tune, and it is she who tells them when to jump and how high. The Earl of Leicester has entered in the back of the room, dressed entirely in black, unmoving, seemingly moored. He's a static background to a whirling court; something solid Elizabeth can use as an anchor. Elizabeth is the ship that moves to this harbor; she walks through the group of young men to stand in front of Leicester. He abjectly kisses the hem of her gown, and all has been forgiven. She has her beloved Robin back.

Things are not as they were, however; nor will they ever be again. Elizabeth needs Leicester more than ever, but their relationship has changed. He is somber, dressed in black for a reason. The historical Leicester had no surviving children, and this Leicester is in mourning for his only son. Elizabeth offers her condolences; they have both experienced loss, he of his son and she of Anjou. During the course of their conversation, she asks him to tell her the difference between love and friendship. An older, wiser Leicester tells her that there is none. She even goes so far as to teasingly call him "brother Leicester" to denote the mellowing of their relationship. She no longer seeks a lover; she seeks a friend, confidant, adviser. "You must continue to be my eyes for you see things so clearly," she says to him. In the past, this has been completely untrue — Leicester's vision was clouded by its subjectivity, by the fact that every situation was viewed with an eye to how it would advance his ambitions. But he has changed, though he admits to missing court intrigues. This allows an opening for Elizabeth to use him as a sounding board for her plan to meet with her cousin, the Scottish Queen, "Why should I not reason with her?" With insight, Leicester warns her, "You have the great weakness of the clear-minded — you believe that other people think like you." Mary Stuart is anything but clear-minded, which is demonstrated when Elizabeth meets with her.

As in *Mary, Queen of Scots*, Leicester arranges a meeting between the two queens, this time at a snow-blanketed Fotheringhay. On the way in, Elizabeth remarks cattily that she has heard Mary has grown fat. One commentary on the film noted her "chubbiness," saying it was as if she were being "fattened for decapitating."[47] Indeed, physically this Mary (Barbara Flynn) is nothing like the perfectly angled beauty of Hepburn, the breathlessly lovely Redgrave, or the sensually attractive Morton. Flynn's characterization stresses realism over romanticism: she's overweight, sickly pale, with graying hair that frizzes out from underneath her auburn wig. Her clothing is as drab as her person, a simple grey gown and a simple crucifix. All of this is a believable side-effect of many years' imprisonment with nothing to do but sew, eat, and scheme. She is, in short, now unattractive and completely unassuming — the exact opposite of the often-romanticized characterization of Mary. To look at her, one has no idea how she could have garnered such a reputation for beauty in her youth; there is no superior talk about the men who have loved her. She asks in her slight French accent (another nod to realism few films make with regard to Mary) if Elizabeth has come "to see what you have brought me to?" Elizabeth refuses to be baited, and asks in return, "Was it I who brought you to this, Mary? I'm more your friend than you imagine. I am the only thing that stands between you and destruction." Their entire discussion is conducted in a tone both rational and calm; there's no passionate hatred here, though it's clear that Mary dislikes Elizabeth. She stands upon her pride, and she appeals to Elizabeth's sense of divine royal sisterhood: "Royalty stands with itself, madam. Who else will stand with us or for us?" Elizabeth knows that her authority is based on the love of her people, and as if instructing a slow child, she replies, "We serve the *people*, Mary," to which Mary says she is "a little bored with the people." Throughout the exchange, Elizabeth uses Mary's first name to address her, while Mary stands on her pride, calling Elizabeth "madam" as if she cannot bear the familiarity. Elizabeth is solemn; she has not come for idle argument or to bandy words, but to caution Mary. She earnestly wants to save her, but she warns that if she's given proof of Mary's treason, "I will have no choice but to take the sin of your death, the death of a God-anointed queen, upon my head." This is something Elizabeth fears, and Mary doubts that she has the stomach for it. What she does not understand is that Elizabeth does not exaggerate when she warns she will have no choice; Mary cannot stay in England, alive, to be the focus of Catholic plotting, and as Elizabeth points out, "Who would have you? Scotland? Or your oh-so-grateful son?" At the mention of James, Mary tears up and calls Elizabeth "hard." Elizabeth seems tired as she says, "It is the business of living that has made me so ... we're both prisoners of the time, you and I." It is yet another instance in this series which shows the outside factors, the times, that are continually shaping Elizabeth's personality, changing her into something else, something she does not wish to be. Mary, too, seems tired as she swears to Elizabeth, "I have no intent against you; all I seek is liberty." Elizabeth eyes her, weighing, and in the end it seems she cannot be certain either way. She leaves Mary with, "I pray to God the death of one of us is not the only way to buy the freedom of the other."

The Earl of Essex, who was shown as a boy earlier in the series, is re-introduced as a young man (Hugh Dancy) when he and Leicester ready themselves to fight in the Netherlands. Though Elizabeth has warned Leicester he's a "fireside general," he longs for action, as does the young Essex. Upon his second meeting with Elizabeth, he seems to fare a bit better — he tells her he sees a world in her eyes, that they outshine the stars. Leicester rolls his own eyes and laughs indulgently at Essex's shameless hyperbole, and Elizabeth seems amused as she teases, "It is rare to find such beauty gifted with the power of self-expression." Essex is unaware that he's being gently mocked, and is very pleased with himself indeed as he mounts his horse. He and Leicester are shown side by side, the old favorite and the soon-to-be — again, a natural progression.

Walsingham, meanwhile, has his proof of treason — a letter signed in Mary's own hand urging on the conspiracy to bring about Elizabeth's assassination, the Babington Plot. In a nod to historical verisimilitude, Walsingham's ironic sense of humor has even led him to draw a little gallows on the transcript. Elizabeth, confronted with this evidence, pitches a fit. Mumbling that Mary gave her word, she seems much more betrayed by the lie than by Mary's condoning of her assassination. She knows she will have to make a decision, and she's desperate for the comfort of Leicester and his counsel: "All I have to defend me is you and sad old Burghley. I want Leicester! Bring him home!" she screams at Walsingham. Elizabeth shows herself to be more emotionally unstable than she has been heretofore. For the first time, she exhibits a cruel streak: "Do you think because I'm slow to make war that I'm merciful? Do you think women are kinder than a man, more gentle? We women have forgotten more about cruelty than you men could ever remember! What we do not like is *lies* ... shadows and shadows of shadows." The betrayal of Mary after all warnings combined with the fact that her only emotional support is hundreds of miles away sends Elizabeth into an emotional spiral which she is incapable of controlling. She shrieks at Walsingham to kill the conspirators, "I want them alive when you cut out their hearts, their bowels!" Even Walsingham seems surprised at her vehemence, as she tells him, "I am made of cruel passions. And when the time is right, we'll so act on them as to astonish the world!" Alone and afraid, she lashes out blindly. Her passion finally exhausted, she whispers, "I have love and compassion, too. As I can punish, so can I yearn for those who are true and faithful and love me according to my desserts as their queen." This illustrates Elizabeth's duality, and also how much she yearns for Leicester, for the love and comfort he represents. Without him, she looks blindly about for consolation and seems on the verge of seeking it in the only man nearby to whom she has any kind of emotional attachment: Burghley. She holds onto his shoulders, but when he moves to embrace her, she pulls away. Though they are political soul mates, what she needs emotionally, she cannot obtain from him.

As with the earlier removal of the pamphleteer's hand, this film exhibits its passion for blood with the execution of the conspirators behind the Babington Plot. Though gory, the depiction is not gratuitous; it is more instructive in showing all the horror that accompanied a traitor's death in Elizabethan England. Execution for high treason, as a matter of law, was inflicted by hanging, drawing, and quartering — the malefactor was hung by the neck until almost dead, then taken down, sliced from sternum to groin, the entrails pulled out and burned before the malefactor's face (sometimes this was done with the genitals as well), and finally, the malefactor was beheaded and the head often put on a spike. After this, the body was cut into quarters, which were sometimes displayed in public, sometimes simply discarded. In practice, a conviction for high treason did not necessarily mean all the horrors of a traitor's death; the sentence was often commuted to the more merciful beheading, or the malefactor was killed by hanging before the already dead traitor was mutilated in the prescribed fashion. The fact that Elizabeth not only allows but demands that the conspirators of the Babington Plot suffer the full traitor's death illustrates how ruthless her fear and anger has made her, and the film graphically depicts the human cost of the unbridled expression of her emotions.

Elizabeth has finally decided to allow Mary to be brought to trial, and comparison of the depiction of her trial in *Elizabeth I* and that in *Mary of Scotland* provides a good deal of contrast. This Mary is no innocent, and Elizabeth no tyrant. Rather than providing a high judges' bench to dwarf Mary, the judges, including Burghley and Walsingham, are at her level, sitting at a table. Mary stands before them, just a few feet away. The lighting is suggestive — it streams in through windows behind the judges' table, back-lighting them, but does not quite reach far enough to fully illuminate Mary's face. For her part, Mary stands unrepentant and unafraid before her judges, but this is due to her own recalcitrance, certainly not to the fact that she is innocent or expects Bothwell to save her, since he is mentioned not at all in this series. The portrayal of Mary has evolved as much as that of Elizabeth — she's no longer a trembling woman in need of a white knight to save her; she's capable of facing her fate on her own. In fact, the one thing she does stand upon is that, as an anointed sovereign, the court has no jurisdiction to judge her at all. "I am no subject, and would die a thousand deaths before I acknowledge myself to be one," Mary says haughtily, but tells them to go to it nonetheless, since they are so determined. She claims the letter to be a forgery, but her lies are less than convincing, and she is in due course convicted.

When presented with Mary's death warrant to sign, Elizabeth's anger has obviously cooled, for she says that it goes hard with her. The scene is staged to convey what is literally occurring — all eyes are on Elizabeth, on what she will do. She sits upon her throne, in a gold gown, which stands out against the black background behind her as well as the black attire of all her ladies-in-waiting. Everyone in the room watches her, waiting silently to see what her pronouncement will be. Oddly, Elizabeth addresses herself not to the waiting councilors, the men who stand before her, but to one of her elder ladies-in-waiting,

"For mine own life, I would not touch her." With that, she refuses to sign the warrant, rises from her throne, and walks out. Walsingham's vexation is shared by the viewer as he seethes, "Vacillation, vacillation, vacillation!"

Elizabeth has more than Mary to preoccupy her thoughts; Leicester has finally returned. Elizabeth rushes about like an excited teenager awaiting his arrival, and her clothing is also indicative of her mood — she's dressed in vibrant red, denoting her exhilaration and passion. Though Leicester's campaign in the Netherlands has been an unqualified failure, Elizabeth is so happy to see him it barely seems to matter. In sharp contrast to the demeanor she later displays at the Earl of Essex's military failure in Ireland, there is no anger or recrimination; the worst Leicester receives is a gentle, "What did I tell you?" an I-told-you-so on the subject of him being only a fireside general. Leicester is solemn, but it soon becomes apparent that it's more than his military failure — he's tired and unwell. Leicester's demeanor has changed, he seems resigned, no longer ambitious, perhaps a result of the realization that his death will come sooner rather than later. When Elizabeth asks his opinion on the question of Mary Stuart, he answers, "Bess, I cannot lie to you. The Scottish Queen must die." Leicester often serves this role in Elizabeth films — convincing his sovereign to go through with the execution of her Scottish cousin. It's clearly not what Elizabeth wants to hear (she later calls it a "betrayal"), and the location from which he delivers this pronouncement is significant — he has eased his aching body into the only seat in the room: Elizabeth's throne. Calling for Mary's execution from this seat symbolizes the correct choice as monarch; Elizabeth has allowed her fear to overrule what she knows, as a queen, she must do.

When Elizabeth signs Mary's death warrant, she showcases her vacillation and equivocation to the utmost. After declaring that she wants Mary to be executed in the manner of someone of royal blood, she keeps repeating, "I do not wish to hear of it," but then immediately demands to be given an account of it after it is done. The clerk, not Burghley or Walsingham, as might be expected, is no one of consequence, and this is a calculated move by Elizabeth. Signed warrant in hand, he almost makes it out of the room before Elizabeth stops him, does an about-face, and commands him not to give the warrant to the council until she instructs him to do so; for now, it's as if she never signed it. The clerk does deliver the warrant, and watching Burghley, Walsingham, Leicester, and the rest of the council try to decipher what Elizabeth truly wants behind all her contradictory behavior invokes sympathy. It is not as detailed an examination as that offered in *Elizabeth R* with its examination of the Anjou match, but it is instructive, as the historical Elizabeth's councilors were subjected to the same thing — they cannot be seen to act against the royal will, but due to Elizabeth's vacillation, they are unsure what she truly wants. They cannot ask for clarification, for this is not her modus operandi; she prefers willful blindness in order to allow her the safety net of plausible deniability, and it leaves them with the danger of later being lambasted by Elizabeth for acting against her wishes. In short, by creating as much confusion as possible, Elizabeth shifts responsibility for difficult decisions from herself onto her unfortunate councilors — she practices an early form of fragmentation of responsibility. It's the changed Leicester, now working almost in alliance with his former opponents Walsingham and Burghley, who makes the decision: "She wants the woman dead, but cannot bear to give the order. This was ever her way. Sideways, sideways,

sideways." Burghley agrees, but he foresees the danger they are all in with this fatal decision. He warns the council, "We must all put our hands to this order of execution, or I tell you, we shall all hang." Leicester is the first, with the rest following suit. He even agrees to witness the execution and inform the Queen, the most dangerous task of all.

The execution of Mary, Queen of Scots in this film is as graphic as could be, but again, it evokes more a sense of realism than gratuitous gore. There is no beautiful, romantic young Mary ascending a scaffold to the music of the pipes or a merciful cutaway directly from axe to a broken, weeping Elizabeth as in the earlier depictions of Mary's execution. There is nothing triumphant, reverent, or glorious in Mary's end. Real life is not so romantic, and in the portrayal of Mary's execution, this film adheres to the historical record. Mary presents a pitiful figure on the scaffold — bulging against the tight seams of her red martyr's gown, she kneels to pray in Latin, but she's denied even this last consolation. An Anglican priest takes away her rosary and actually attempts to pray over her Latin with his English, until their raised voices provide an aural embodiment of the contest between the Protestant and Catholic churches. After declaring that she sheds her blood for the "ancient, Catholic religion," she puts her head on the block. The downswing of the axe is almost instantaneous, and with infinite horror, the side angle shows exactly how far the axe has penetrated through Mary's thick neck — less than halfway. Her face contorts in terrible pain; this is no merciful, peaceful death — the crowd winces as well. As a lumberjack would, the executioner braces himself and yanks the axe free, then finally dispatches poor Mary with the second stroke. As terrible as this is, the historical Mary actually suffered three blows of the axe. A tangible sense of relief can be felt, until the executioner holds up Mary's head by what he believes to be her hair; in actuality, it is her wig, so the head falls to the ground, rolling off the scaffold, as he proclaims, "God save the Queen!" Leicester, appalled, whispers, "How can I ever tell the Queen of this?"

He's spared this duty by Walsingham, since he has the face for bad news. In a scene that somehow manages to be almost comedic, Walsingham inches into Elizabeth's apartments. She's seated at her virginal, playing beautifully. She looks up, since she has heard the tolling of the bells that signify Mary's death. "What's that?" she asks, "Is someone married?" Walsingham tentatively replies, "I think someone has died, Your Majesty." When Elizabeth inquires as to whom, Walsingham tells her, "A very great traitor ... Mary of Scotland." Elizabeth's response is both typical and terrifying, for it shows the tact she will take, "Who ordered this?" One cannot help but sympathize with poor Walsingham as he raises his eyebrows and replies, "I rather think you did, Your Majesty." Thus confronted by her own decision and a blatant refusal by Walsingham to shift blame, Elizabeth goes ballistic, clawing at the walls, striking poor Walsingham, and as she's wont to do in her most trying moments, screaming for Leicester, "Why couldn't you have stopped this?" She shrieks that she will hang him, and stumbling through the corridors of her palace, she keeps repeating, "Oh God! Oh God forgive me!" and ends up in her chapel.

Perhaps as part and parcel of portraying a less calculating Elizabeth, she seems genuinely terrified at Mary's execution, not for the consequences it will provide in this mortal vale, but because she fears God will damn her. Her grief is not mere show. Other adaptations depict the political cost of Mary's execution, but this miniseries treats the personal, religious cost to Elizabeth of ordering the execution of a God-anointed queen. As one commentator noted, "The film uses the event [Mary's death] as a way into the emotional labyrinth of Elizabeth's mind."[48] Elizabeth is shown through the screen of her prie-dieu, the only light that from a candle on each side, framing her face. For the first time, even in this soft lighting, she looks old. The walls of the room are done entirely in shades of red, liturgical red like Mary's martyr gown, rust-red like dried blood. Finally Elizabeth calms herself as Leicester enters. He quietly tells her the details of Mary's execution, that she was denied her rosary, that it took two strokes of the axe. At this Elizabeth stops him; it's too much, and she replies, "I must remember who I am and learn humility." That she could face such an end as Mary just has is clear to Elizabeth, and it humbles her. It also impresses upon her the fleeting nature of life, the inescapability of her own mortality. She clings ever closer to her anchor, Leicester. Looking at him she asks sadly, "What is there between you and I? What's a crown when love's voice speaks to us? Since friendship outlasts love and is stronger than love, let us be friends. Always." Her emotional need for Leicester is vast, and the tenderness they show each other in times such as these provokes the viewer's empathy. It also seems a kind of portent — the series has so far dropped subtle traces regarding Leicester's failing health, and Elizabeth will soon be unanchored, drifting alone.

Elizabeth may not realize this, but Leicester certainly does. It's the reason behind his changed demeanor, and it also motivates him to find for Elizabeth a sort of successor for the position he knows he will soon vacate. For this, he puts forth his young stepson, the Earl of Essex. Essex and Leicester do share some similarities, but as is readily apparent, Essex is much less adept at self-governance than his stepfather; he's hot-headed and impulsive, as well as less intelligent. In order to deal with the Queen, Leicester counsels him, "Remember this: her favor changes with her moods. She is a woman. But if you love her, and I say this to you as a father, love her constancy, for it is there."

While Elizabeth and Leicester are portrayed more as equals in this film and few attempts are made by her to humble him since he seldom oversteps his boundaries, it's immediately clear that Essex has no such awareness of his limitations. His relationship with Elizabeth is immediately on the defensive. She makes fun of his bow as he is presented to her, teasing him that he will have to learn more of the ways of the court. While someone of Leicester's disposition could take this kind of teasing easily and return with more joviality, Essex does not enjoy it, and the way is paved for a dynamic that can only result in future, devastating resentment.

With Mary's death, Philip of Spain has cause for his attack, and the Armada is on its way. As Elizabeth readies herself to address the troops massed at Tilbury, it is a clearly unwell Leicester who gives her strength and courage. When Elizabeth expresses uncertainty about how to address them ("unwarlike woman that I am"), it is Leicester who gives her the words of her famous Tilbury speech: "I could swear Your Majesty had the heart and stomach of a king." It is also Leicester who has persuaded Elizabeth to wear an armored breastplate — she's not responsible for either her speechmaking or her image-building, and though this may be unfair to the historical Elizabeth, it's used as a sort of last hurrah for Leicester before removing him from the series to make way for Essex.

Leicester may have given her the words, but Elizabeth's delivery of the Tilbury speech is all her own. As with so much else in this series, Mirren chooses a different approach for the speech — she's completely unafraid and the speech does inspire courage. But its tone is joyous, as if the victory were already won and the triumph celebrated. As she walks among the soldiers, she sounds both passionate and happy, and she's smiling, rather than grimly determined, which is the choice made by almost every other film for the portrayal of this event. The speech is moving, and throughout it all, Leicester stands in the background, nodding encouragement, her anchor in all things.

When it's determined that the day belongs to the English, jubilation breaks out as Elizabeth gazes heavenward. Her attention should be on the ground, however, for that's where Leicester has fallen, finally surrendering to his illness. Though the film never suggests what that illness might be, the historical Leicester most probably succumbed to a bout of malaria, after being weakened by a fever for a few weeks. The film gives Leicester a touching if clichéd death scene, complete with an Elizabeth trying to be brave for his sake, and a chance for him to join her hand to Essex's as his successor. He assures Essex that the Queen "needs looking after. To be strong for so many people is not easy. And I will not be there." The implication is that Elizabeth, like characterizations of Mary Stuart, cannot be effectual without the strength of someone else to buoy her. In this case, however, it is attributed less to the fact that Elizabeth is a woman and more to the reality that her burden of responsibility is an almost impossibly heavy one — too much for a single person, regardless of gender or ability, to bear alone.

The historical truth of Leicester's death is less romantic — Leicester was on his way to Buxton to take the waters when he died, nowhere near Elizabeth. It was not until several weeks after Tilbury that news reached England of the Armada's definitive defeat, and Leicester had returned to London to enjoy the victory before setting out to take the waters. As Gristwood has noted, "Elizabeth was condemned to an extraordinary conjunction of public rejoicing and private agony."[49] She shut herself away while the country celebrated; Elizabeth was alone in her grief, literally and figuratively — most were not sorry to see her favorite go, and some even rejoiced at the prospect, as well as at the defeat of the Armada.

It is significant in this film that, immediately after the death of Leicester, Elizabeth is made to look as much like the iconic image of the Queen as she has up until this point. Momentarily gone is the naturalism which she has displayed, replaced with the white make-up, stiff court dress, and enormous ruff. She appears in the distance, before her massed people, the captured banners of the Spanish behind her. She has, quite literally, put on her public face. She intones that "as we commend his [Leicester's] soul to heaven, we turn ourselves to our only solace, which is our people of England. And let them know they may have yet a greater prince, but they shall never have a more loving one." Elizabeth may have declared herself as belonging entirely to the people when forced to give up marriage with the Duke of Anjou, but it's not until this moment, with Leicester gone, that she can devote the entirety of her being, her "love" to them. She has nothing else. The film chooses to end the episode with this image, effectively parsing Elizabeth's life in two — the first half with Leicester, and the last with Essex.

The second half of the series opens with Elizabeth applying the public face the viewer has last seen. She wears no wig, her hair shorn close, as a lady-in-waiting cakes on her white make-up. Echoing earlier films with mirrors as the representation of encroaching

"We turn ourselves to our only solace, which is our people of England." Elizabeth (Helen Mirren) as the icon mourns Leicester and turns to her people for comfort in *Elizabeth I.* (© HBO Video)

age and death, when an attractive young lady-in-waiting holds a mirror out for Elizabeth to view the finished product, she says wearily, "We have no need of that. The look on your face tells the Queen all she needs to know about hers." She then banishes looking glasses from her palace. If Elizabeth was "of a certain age" at the beginning of the series, now she is officially "old."

Elizabeth's world-weariness, however, gives way to girlish laughter with only the application of a little Earl of Essex; the change he provokes in her takes years away from her countenance. Like Leicester before him, Essex's rise is not met with sanguinity by Burghley and Walsingham, who will thank their lucky stars for Leicester by the time the young Earl of Essex is finished. His flashy personality is showcased through the ways in which he vies for attention — he arrives at a tournament riding an oversized unicorn, complete with fireworks, to celebrate Elizabeth's 30th year on the throne. Burghley remarks wryly, "Perhaps he will follow this by disappearing," but Walsingham, always one for delivering unpleasant news, replies, "He's a rising star, gentlemen; we must learn to live with him." While other Elizabethan films, most notably Davis's *The Virgin Queen* and *Elizabeth: The Golden Age*, focus in depth on Elizabeth's relationship with Walter Raleigh, *Elizabeth I* introduces him only as a foil for her relationship with Essex. He unseats Essex in the tournament and earns the right to wear the Queen's favor. Showing his rashness, Essex calls him a fool, and the result is a duel. Though Burghley makes as if to pacify the two young men, Elizabeth stops him, and is reminiscent of Bette Davis's Elizabeth and her lapdogs as she smirks, "Dogs must have blood somehow." Elizabeth has become more uncaring; gone is the tenderness she shared with Leicester. Now she's amused and flattered by silly young men fighting over her. She shows no concern for Essex or Raleigh's safety as they cross swords over her, telling her ladies blithely, "We are going to watch the Earl of Essex at his favorite pastime, which is trying to kill people."

Elizabeth is not only callous towards her male favorites; her behavior towards her young female courtiers has also grown increasingly catty. Frances Walsingham, pretty young daughter of her spymaster, has been making eyes at Essex, and she faces all Elizabeth's angry pettiness for it. After remarking on the fact that Frances's pretty dress must mean she wants to be the center of attention (and it's clear that Elizabeth will now tolerate no one but herself in that position), as the two young men try to hack each other to bits, she nonchalantly asks Frances if she approves of dueling. When Frances stutters, "It is..." Elizabeth interrupts her with, "It is *forbidden*. As are so many other things," she says pointedly. The handsome young men of Elizabeth's court belong to her, and she has no compunction about staking her territory early and often.

Raleigh bests Essex yet again, giving him a nasty but superficial cut to the leg. Elizabeth is thrilled, laughing, "Good, sir! Pull his great heart down!" Elizabeth's relationship with Essex is more like that she displays towards the male courtiers portrayed in other films — belittling, her condescension occasionally tempered by conditional affection. She informs him, as he stands bleeding, that "men like you must be ruled, as was the Earl of Leicester in the end." Elizabeth has made a serious error in judgment, however, and one that will cost her, for Essex is no Leicester, despite the fact that Elizabeth has taken him as a sort of replacement, even giving him Leicester's old apartments and calling him Robin. As if to demonstrate that Elizabeth's favor does not come without pain, while carefully watching his face, a smiling Elizabeth squeezes lemon juice on Essex's wound before binding it for him. It's apparent that, despite the near-constant comparison with Leicester, the relationship Elizabeth has with Essex is completely different — she simpers and flirts, teasing him that he "looks like a naughty schoolboy." Their interaction puts Elizabeth in the role of cougar, and theirs is no courtly flirtation; Essex kisses her passionately. Elizabeth seems amused at first, looking at him appraisingly: "You seem sincere enough. Great things hang on a kiss, Robin, where princes are involved." He immediately kisses her again, and wastes no time before he has her on her back with his hands roaming insistently. Elizabeth seems surprised by her own passionate reaction, but manages to collect herself enough to push him off and walk through her attendants, obviously unsettled, who line the stairs to Essex's new apartments.

To illustrate the new-found youth Elizabeth feels with Essex, they are shown playing cards into the early morning while Elizabeth's exhausted attendants have fallen asleep where they dropped. Elizabeth seems to take great delight in giving Essex teasing warnings. When he accuses her of cheating, she replies, "Princes do not cheat; they simply have the rules altered to fit their needs." Essex cannot win; Elizabeth is holding all the cards, literally and metaphorically, but he's too immature and self-centered to see it. She taunts him to take them by force, resulting in a flirting chase around the room, but when he catches her, she admonishes, "Not too much force — for you to win would be treason." Essex morosely replies that there's no fun in such a game, and he certainly does not seem to realize how dangerous a game it can be. As he turns to look at her, he's illuminated by the first rays of morning light streaming through the window, a beautiful young man whose appearance leaves Elizabeth breathless. The viewer can understand why he has the effect on Elizabeth that he does. There is little substance underneath, however.

Like everyone else, Burghley has been growing older, and showing the natural progression of things, he secures a seat on the council for his son, Robert. Essex is jealous, and Cecil tells him pointedly, "I have *worked* for it, my lord." The implication, of course, is that Essex has never worked for anything — everything he receives through the Queen's favor is an undeserved gift, born only of an old woman's attraction to him. It also seems that Essex and Cecil have some sort of history; through their veiled references, the viewer gleans that, growing up together in Burghley's household, something went on between the two boys. Essex, casting himself in the role of victim, chooses fatherless little boy as his mantle. "What it must be to have a father," he says to Cecil. Though Essex's real father died when he was young, as a ward to Lord Burghley and with the Earl of Leicester as surrogate father to promote him with the Queen, Essex has received far more advantage than Cecil, so his statement rings rather hollow.

The staging of intimate moments between Elizabeth and Essex reveals the sensuality of their relationship and also the danger. As they lay on the floor together, somehow alone, by a roaring fire, Essex invokes the image of the cougar as he confesses that Elizabeth looks at him as if she were "deciding whether or not to eat me." The two lay on sumptuous fabrics, silky and soft, and the pillows are red, the color of passion and blood. The firelight gives the whole scene a sort of boudoir glow. Essex is less subtle than Leicester, and he blatantly uses Elizabeth's sexuality against her. He wishes to lead an expedition to Lisbon to gain riches, but he couches his wishes in terms of masculinity: "Would you have a spoiled boy by your side or would you not let me prove myself a proper man?" They end up passionately kissing again, and Essex wastes no time making his way under Elizabeth's skirts. It's a dangerous game she plays with herself, this temptation, but she pulls away again, leaving a frustrated Essex by the fire as she walks into darkened corridors that seem like a shower of cold water after the firelight ambiance. Elizabeth shows the difficulty she is in with a sort of monologue to the now out-of-earshot Essex: "The more I try to let you go, the more I have need of you. And it will not go away no matter how much I command it. Do you think the Queen is mistress of her feelings? No, she's a fool for love. A hopeless fool."

Just how out of control Elizabeth's passion has made her becomes apparent when Essex defies her wishes and goes off to Lisbon. She physically attacks poor Walsingham, yet again the bearer of bad news (one wonders that he doesn't invest in some sort of protective headgear), and runs through the palace screaming that she will send them all to the gallows, for they have "let him get away." Finally having exhausted herself, she sits down on the steps to Essex's apartments, and her eldest lady-in-waiting hands her a handkerchief, shushing her in motherly fashion, until she manages a modicum of control. Her courtiers stand a distance away, simply watching her, speechless with astonishment at their queen behaving like a hormone-addled adolescent. Her only comment to them is, "One word of this, and you die."

Unlike Essex's Cádiz's homecoming in *The Private Lives of Elizabeth and Essex*, this Elizabeth has nothing but joy at his return, despite the unprofitability of the venture. Elizabeth proclaims him the "champion of liberty, our marvelous boy!" Though Essex, for his part, still displays "every appearance of sincerity," he falls all over himself to know "what I shall have" as a reward from Elizabeth. This gives her only a moment's pause; she's too caught up in her rushing emotions, and when Essex asks for a seat on the council, she acquiesces, after warning him, "Matters of state require the drudgery of being both honest and accommodating." Essex, the fatherless little boy, replies as he would to a parent, "I will make you proud." As in *Elizabeth I: The Virgin Queen*, Essex is shown as a character with parental issues. Luckily for him, his virago of a mother does not appear in the same role she played in *The Virgin Queen*, but Essex still evinces a need for parental guidance of some kind. He's a boy attempting to play the part of a man; the adult nature of his physical relationship with Elizabeth belies the emotional immaturity underneath.

Just how little of the art of statecraft Essex knows becomes immediately clear when, in an attempt to assert his importance, he announces to the council that Elizabeth's doctor has attempted to poison her. Everyone on the council is incredulous; Elizabeth's doctor of many years is trusted and respected, and no one but Essex believes the charges. Though in actuality it's the entire council against Essex, Elizabeth pretends as if there are not two voices in agreement as she says, "How may I act when all present me with their partial arguments?" She ends up siding with Essex against the rest of her council and her own better judgment, and the unfortunate doctor is tried and executed, while Essex's friends mock his cries on the scaffold. It's soon revealed that the doctor was innocent, Essex's only evidence obtained by torture, and Elizabeth is devastated. Walsingham is disgusted: "You breathe war, slaughter, and blood." Elizabeth sends her council away in order to deal with Essex alone, to show him the ruinous consequences of his rash acts, to instruct him as she would a child. "This was a man's *life*, Robin ... you act without thinking. That is not service." The lesson is lost on the impetuous Essex, who replies, "If thought inhibit action, then I will not think again. For I would act for you, and you alone." Again, Essex seems sincere, but his veneer of sincerity is slowly peeling away to reveal the selfishness underneath. Elizabeth immediately forgives him, and as soon as she does, he turns off the contrition as one would a faucet and immediately demands a position for his friend Francis Bacon. Elizabeth, astounded, wonders aloud, "What am I going to do with you?"

Essex's brainless self-aggrandizing has won him few friends, and Cecil, though discrete and circumspect, does his best to undermine Essex with Elizabeth. Essex has done himself more damage than Cecil possibly could, as the Queen is about to learn. Walsingham enters to deliver the news that his daughter is pregnant by the Earl of Essex, and he wishes to know what the Earl's intentions are. Elizabeth's reaction is revealing — it far surpasses her response even when she discovered the Earl of Leicester had married. Elizabeth physically attacks Essex, slapping him until he huddles on the floor. She then runs through the corridors screaming like a madwoman. Yet even after this, Elizabeth is quick to forgive. Essex has himself drawn before her on a catafalque, costumed as if dead, his mourners behind him, and Elizabeth says with amusement, "He's in mourning for the loss of our favor." There's a more sinister element to the amusement as one of her councilors adds, "He looks well dead, does he not?" Still Elizabeth forgives Essex, and quickly. It seems she can deny him nothing, and this casts her in the role of the ridiculous — an aging woman in thrall to a much younger man.

Essex may have been forgiven, but not everything will go his way. Elizabeth sarcastically informs him that he will marry Frances and be happy. For "we must all marry, or so I'm told. But such a thing was not in prospect where you and I were concerned, was it?" Elizabeth laughs at him as she taunts, "Did you think to be king?" Essex mumbles that "you know the secrets of my heart," but Elizabeth declares, "I'm damned if I do, sir." Elizabeth has finally realized that his appearance of sincerity is just that — a façade with nothing of substance underneath. She knows they cannot have the type of love match her raging emotions sought; things have cooled for her. "At the end," she tells him, "Leicester and I were friends. I would hold you close in friendship." Essex declares that when love is changed to kindliness, he will have none of it. At last Elizabeth comprehends what the viewer has long before understood. She sighs, "The same name, but not the same." She will never have her Leicester back, and she has been searching for him in the wrong place.

With this knowledge, Elizabeth can give Essex leave to go; it is now easy for her to bear the separation. After taking Cádiz, Essex returns to an adoring crowd, and there are shades of *The Private Lives of Elizabeth and Essex* as his popularity with the people begins to smart. Essex even foolishly states, "I'm in danger of outshining the Queen's Majesty." His friends, most notably the Earl of Southampton, do not help matters by further inflating his ego.

There's obviously no love lost between Cecil and Essex, and their machinations, as depicted in other films, reach their denouement in the council chamber. Unlike Flynn's Essex, Dancy's Essex does have enough sense not to want to be appointed Lord Deputy of Ireland. Instead, he tries to manipulate Elizabeth into sending Cecil, who has already refused the position. Essex ignores Elizabeth's pleasantly warning tone and blindly pursues his course until she slaps him in the back of the head for his insolence, as one would a disobedient child. To the astonishment of everyone in the room, he draws his sword on the Queen. He sputters that he would not have endured an insult of that nature from a man, and "you a woman to think you could do so! I tell you I would not have suffered it from your father's hands!" After Essex has been escorted out, Burghley looks as if the excitement might provoke a heart attack, but Elizabeth shows no grief, no regret over Essex's departure, only amusement as she says wryly, "Well, I think we've found the right man for Ireland," and lapses again into familiar canine imagery as she adds, "When deprived of our favor for long enough, he will soon come to heel. My dogs wear my collars, sirs." Essex is about to find out what happens when a dog defies its master's authority.

This is a time of great loss for Elizabeth. It's apparent that she and Essex are no longer in lust, and though she drew no strength from him, she has also lost two of her stalwarts — Walsingham has died, as well as Burghley. Essex has been in Ireland six months, and Elizabeth begins to doubt his loyalty, for so far he has managed to accomplish nothing. Elizabeth is shown in her wet shift, fresh out of the bath, when Essex is heard bellowing down the hall. Elizabeth's panicked ladies-in-waiting rush to dress her as a filthy, unshaven Essex bursts into the room. He informs her of the truce he has signed with Tyrone. He's distraught with self-pity, and Elizabeth's demeanor is completely unexpected — she seems soft and compliant. She comforts him, assigns one of her ladies-in-waiting to help clean him up and see that he's put to bed to rest well. As soon as he's out of her sight, Elizabeth shows a duplicity never seen before, and it illustrates how far the evolution of her characterization has progressed. She walks immediately in to see Cecil, explaining that Essex has deserted his post, and they consult together about a course of action to put him down.

The next morning, a confident Essex enters Elizabeth's audience chamber only to be astounded by the fact that charges have been brought against him. One cannot help put pity Essex as he asks with genuine confusion, "Is this a trial? Have I done something to offend Your Majesty?" Elizabeth informs him, "You have sought to touch the scepter of a prince, which is a thing not commendable in you." As Essex is being hauled away under guard, Elizabeth says to him, "Love alters when it alteration finds" before yelling for him, as she did at Leicester so many years before, to be gone from her sight. On its surface, Elizabeth is simply accusing the Earl of allowing his love for her to change, thus justifying the death of her own for him when she finds him changed. The line is jarring, however, paraphrasing as it does a Shakespearean sonnet, Number 116,[50] which reads, "Love is not love, Which alters when it alteration finds." It's debatable as to whether or not this sonnet even existed in 1601, and it seems odd spouted from Elizabeth's mouth at the Earl of Essex at such a moment. Unless irony is intended, the sonnet itself, an ode to the steadfastness of love, seems completely inappropriate as applied to this rendering of Elizabeth and Essex's relationship. The original of the line she paraphrases neatly sums it up — what Elizabeth and Essex have shared cannot have *been* love, since it has altered; Elizabeth's affections have been conditional, and now Essex has lost them. The love of which the sonnet speaks is a "marriage of true minds," a far cry from accurately describing Elizabeth and Essex. It is also "not Time's fool, though rosy lips and cheeks, Within his bending sickle's compass come" — Elizabeth has pursued a relationship with Essex specifically because he's young and beautiful, and she seeks her lost youth through him. Theirs was not a love that "looks on tempests and is never shaken"; the storms borne of politics and ambition have quickly and easily torn it apart. For Elizabeth to couch their feelings for each other in such terms only emphasizes how hollow their relationship has been. This is but one of several bits of dialogue in the film that grate. One commentary noted that the tone of the writing "wanders all over the place ... some lines sound 21st century; others sound pseudo–Shakespearean,"[51] or in this case, misquoted Shakespeare. The temporal instability is worse even than this, however, for in another jarring bit of dialogue, the Earl of Southampton tells Essex, "We must hang together or we will hang separately, for the people are not with us," an adaptation of a statement made by Benjamin Franklin during the American Revolution.[52]

It only remains for Elizabeth to give Essex enough rope to hang himself. She has him placed under house arrest, knowing that his desire to act will soon be more than he can control. Elizabeth also illustrates the depth of her duplicity, how much she has evolved since the beginning of the film, when the Countess of Essex (nee Frances Walsingham) comes to beg Elizabeth to forgive her husband. Elizabeth feigns concern for Essex while cleverly playing Frances, eliciting information from her. Essex has been secretly corresponding with James VI of Scotland; she can now bring him to trial with the letters she knows he has. When she sends Francis Bacon at the head of a contingent to bring him to the Tower, Essex finally breaks. He tells Bacon, "Her conditions are as crooked as her carcass," and has Bacon and his men held hostage. Essex and his supporters take to the streets, expecting the citizens of London to rally to their cause, which they state to be the removal of Elizabeth's treacherous advisers (i.e., Cecil), rather than any design against Elizabeth herself. Essex has, for a final time, miscalculated — the people shut their doors to him, "an appealing young man who has seriously overestimated his appeal."[53]

Elizabeth shows no fear, only anger and contempt, as she assures Essex, "It is I who rule." The trial provides a chance for Essex and Cecil to finally confront each other out in the open. Cecil accuses him of having "a wolf's head in sheep's clothing," and even Bacon rebuts Essex's attempts to defend himself with, "You remind me of the Athenian who cut himself and then cried murder." All that has transpired is consequently laid at Essex's feet, the result of his own ambitions. Southampton, also on trial, breaks down in a contemptible manner, abandoning the friend he had been loudest in encouraging on this destructive course. His crying and begging for mercy provide a contrast with the behavior of Essex, who stands emotionally bereft but dignified, and refuses to beg for the Queen's clemency.

Essex's death scene does provide him with a brave end; in this, at least, he acquits himself well. He admits, "The Queen cannot be safe while I live," and then, as was a matter of rote during executions of the time, he admits his crimes and humbly asks her pardon for "this great and infectious sin of mine — rebellion against her whom I swear I did always love with all my heart." Essex's execution seems to drain the Queen of all her ire, and with it, her vitality. She sits staring out the window, and she looks old, haggard, numbly sad. She spares the distasteful Earl of Southampton with a quiet, "No more blood. Please God, no more blood."

Her life may seem bereft, but the business of government must still go on. When she asks why there are so many glum faces, Cecil replies to her that "money is all, ma'am." This issue with Parliament gives Elizabeth a chance for a sort of last hurrah, the Golden Speech. She stands before them, and in moving tone tells them that she values their love above all, that it is esteemed more than any treasure or riches. "Though God hath raised me high, yet this I count the glory of my crown, that I have reigned with your loves." It's essentially her epitaph, and as the formerly surly Parliament breaks out in loud and adoring applause, she shoots a wry look at Cecil — she has made her last performance, and it has been an impressive one.

For no apparent reason, Elizabeth's health, more mental than physical, fails. Cecil is sent for because she has been lying on pillows on the floor, unspeaking, for hours. When he arrives, as did Jackson's and Duff's renderings based on historical accounts, Mirren's Elizabeth has her finger in her mouth, like a child. Her thoughts are disjointed; she asks to be brought a mirror, and says, "There was a man once ... the hardest thing to govern is the heart." Neither Cecil nor the viewer can be sure which man Elizabeth is referring to — Leicester or Essex, or perhaps even Anjou, and the lighting throws half her face into shadow, illustrating her journey into night. When she sees herself for the last time in the mirror, she laughs, nodding, as if it's exactly what she had expected to see, and it amuses her. Her ladies raise her up so she can stand in front of the window, and she remains that way for hours, haloed in light, until night falls. Cecil returns, having been informed that the Queen has not moved or spoken for 15 hours. The ambiance is eerie. The room is dark, bathed only in blue moonlight, and Elizabeth herself is macabre and strange, standing frozen like a statue, like the icon she has become. The moonlight on her face casts shadows and gives it a pallor which makes her seem already dead. As if she were a zombie, she walks slowly down the corridor for the last time, alone, to her bedroom. Gone are all her attendants, save one, who stands near the wall, in shadow, watching. The only sound is that of Elizabeth's raspy breathing as she says, "That man, whoever he was...." She lies down on the bed, deliberately, and says irritably, "Fetch me a priest, girl. I'm minded to die," and closes her eyes.

The shaping of this unique portrayal of Elizabeth and her court is due in large part to Helen Mirren, who certainly has enough experience playing queens — she's portrayed Cleopatra, Queen Charlotte, and Queen Elizabeth II. Aside from her acting choices, Mirren also shaped the film's plotting. Like *The Private Lives of Elizabeth and Essex, Elizabeth I* was originally to be the story of only Elizabeth and Essex. Mirren felt that this romantic storyline was too shallow; there simply was not enough meat to do justice to the story of the historical woman, and she wanted the addition of more politics. This led back to the reintroduction of Leicester, since he could be used to further so much of that political plotting. Hugh Dancy, who plays the Earl of Essex, has noted how "politics of the time was defined by individual relationships"; clearly his characterization emphasizes this, for the individual relationship his Essex has with Elizabeth is narrowly structured — his romantic association with the Queen is the tool he uses to pursue political gain. Mirren takes this idea a step further to describe Elizabeth's story as being about "how the personal and political come together and split apart." In this vein, the director's stated vision was to create a film where one "cannot distinguish between the personal and the political."[54] If this was the goal, then this miniseries is an unqualified success. In every way, the political and the personal, the vocational and the domestic, meld until the lines are blurred beyond recognition. Elizabeth's romantic relationships certainly manifest themselves in this way, and the portrayal of the Anjou suit is a prime example — her motivation is originally political, but she falls in love, as does he; the feelings are genuine, inextricably linking sentiment with political need. Thus, with the removal of the political, it truly is a splitting apart — it breaks Elizabeth's already much put-upon heart.

There are also elements of this in the characterization Irons gives to Leicester. Unlike any other before him (with the possible exception of Joseph Fiennes, though the difference in depth of portrayal makes comparison almost impossible), Irons manages to transcend the picture of Leicester as a man solely ruled by his political ambitions — he also *feels*. He is deceitful, certainly, and ambitious, undeniably, but he genuinely cares for Elizabeth, even to the point of putting her before his own political gain, especially as he ages. One commentator noted, "His Leicester is a man who has spent his life in an emotional fencing match with the woman he loves and has often felt the sting of her vanity. Yet his devotion and love are heartbreaking and real."[55] Irons described his characterization in this way: "Elizabeth and he are like an old married couple. Leicester provides somebody who will speak the truth as he sees it. Elizabeth valued him for that apart from the physical attraction which they had."[56] While other portrayals, such as that in *Elizabeth R*, also display this "old married couple" dynamic, that couple is one which has simply put up with each other, and they remain together out of habit and longstanding, not affection. *Elizabeth I*'s dynamic is different; it's a passion that has cooled into perhaps the purest form of love, and it's the main element that makes this version of Elizabeth's life so engaging to watch.

Critics almost universally praised Mirren's turn as the Virgin Queen, even while noting that the series itself has some "underlying issues,"[57] such as inept dialogue, plodding exposition, and a certain unevenness between the first and second parts. Mirren's Elizabeth has been called "the most credibly human"[58] and "the defining portrait of the capricious but formidable monarch."[59] Giving Mirren the lion's share of praise in this adaptation is appropriate; somehow, she manages to breathe new life into what could have been one tired piece of cinema, especially given how close the release of her Elizabeth and Duff's were timed. Mirren is helped along considerably by Irons's Leicester; without the dynamic they share, her portrayal would have been less convincing, and just how large an impact he has on this series is illustrated when he no longer appears in it. The first half is much stronger than the second, despite Dancy's respectable turn as the physically adorable but emotionally stunted Essex. The other actors who populate this film in major supporting roles, most notably Ian McDiarmid and Patrick Malahide as Burghley and Walsingham, also give exceptional performances, adding a texture and dimensionality to the series that many other Elizabeth offerings, as vehicles only for the actress playing the Queen, lack. One critic called them "a pair of ministerial worms whose insinuations of advice are shrewd if heartless."[60] This is an unfair appraisal. Mirren has noted of the historical Elizabeth's rapport with her councilors that "she had the intelligence to listen," and in this series, both men, but especially McDiarmid, flesh out the edges, providing an appropriate background against which Mirren can flourish. They are certainly not heartless — Burghley, especially, is portrayed not just as a servant of Elizabeth the Queen, but as someone who cares for Elizabeth the woman. McDiarmid notes of Burghley and Elizabeth that "each needs the other in the beautiful framework that was Elizabethan England." The care for Elizabeth with which he imbues his portrayal of Burghley is evident in the times when he watches her, helpless, as she begins to drown emotionally. That he has an earnest desire to ameliorate her suffering is clear in the way he often reaches for her but never completes the motion — he wants to offer comfort, but he simply does not know how.

As has been mentioned, the overall impression of this series is one of pervasive naturalism, from the costuming to the sets to the characterizations. It also, at times, has a rather cozy, domestic feel, which is not something any other adaptation of Elizabeth's life manages. The focus in most of these adaptations is on pageantry, on the glitter of the court, but *Elizabeth I* shows Elizabeth "at home" as well as "at work." She sits in comfortable silence, either reading or sewing, with her women ranged around her. As the series progresses, her ladies are often shown wearing black, a conscious costuming choice which allows Elizabeth's more colorful gown to stand out against the dark background. As the costume designer of the film has noted, Elizabeth "arranged her own personal and public space so she was always the focus of attention," and he has tried to further this in the costuming of Elizabeth's ladies-in-waiting as a reflection of that personal space. In this way, Elizabeth's ladies serve as background while ensuring that the viewer's focus, like their own, is always on the Queen. When Elizabeth needs privacy, she has no need to direct them; they are so in tune that they stand in unison at a look from her and head for the door. As with its costuming and the background actors, the sets in this film also add to the sense of intimacy. Unlike Elizabethan films from the golden age of Hollywood or Kapur's later offerings, these are not grand, soaring sets with ceilings that stretch to infinity. The spaces are small, intimate, with warm paneling or idiosyncratic and unique decoration; one room even has seashells stuccoed into the walls. They add an impression of authenticity — these are spaces that make sense as dwelling places — and they also further the naturalistic feel of the entire production. All of this fits in with the portrayal of Elizabeth in this series. Mirren's is a more natural and less formal Elizabeth, and as such, she's a more approachable queen. Elizabeth is portrayed in a myriad of ways in these different adaptations of her life; she's many things, but seldom charming and likeable. This is what *Elizabeth I* offers — an engaging queen, one with a sense of humor and vulnerability, and one that feels real. For this reason alone Mirren deserves praise for her performance. One wonders, however, if she's not a bit *too* sympathetic and likeable. Mirren certainly provides a "living, breathing portrait,"[61] but is that portrait a likeness of Elizabeth? Are any of these?

CHAPTER 7

Semper Eadem:
The Evolving Elizabeth

One of Elizabeth's favorite mottos was *semper eadem*—always the same. For Elizabeth's contemporary "audience," the subjects who lived out their lives under her rule, this portrayal of their monarch as unchanging must have provided a reassuring sense of stability and security. As the saying goes, times change, however, and representations of Elizabeth in film have changed with them. When viewed over a chronological continuum, film portrayals of her vary so widely that it sometimes seems astounding they are all based upon the same person. Elizabeth is not the only royal to undergo this evolution; as mentioned in earlier chapters, the portrayal of Mary, Queen of Scots has received similar treatment, as has Elizabeth's father, Henry VIII (witness Charles Laughton's Henry VIII versus Jonathan Rhys Meyers's). As one entertainment article on "rex appeal" noted, "Every era gets a movie-screen monarch to suit the times."[1] A BBC commentator put it more eloquently, "The past is and was static, but interpretations of the past are fluid."[2] Where, in all this fluid evolution, is the tangible—the definitive portrayal of Elizabeth?

This is a question which requires a completely subjective answer. It all depends upon the parameters the viewer uses to define Elizabeth herself—the point-of-view of the person watching the film. For historians or those with a penchant for history, the standard is often an adherence to historicity, and this brings with it a certain set of strictures. Historian Eric Josef Carlson has produced a fascinating article about his experiences using filmed versions of Elizabeth Tudor to teach historical thinking in the classroom. He utilizes historical films in his course on Elizabeth to demonstrate the way historical interpretations of individuals change based on the context in which they are produced, acknowledging that "we [historians] tend as a group to be fairly hostile to this genre of films" and that nothing agitates historians more than watching a film supposedly based on historical figures or historical events. This is attributed to the effect these films have on viewers' constructs of history, an effect much greater than scholarly writings. Carlson is not alone in recognizing this. As far back as 1935, Britain's Historical Association passed a resolution stating that it was "gravely concerned at the effect on children and adults of films purporting to represent historical personages," and even went so far as to suggest that steps be taken to assist viewers with determining the historical accuracy of what they were watching. However, as do the filmmakers who produce these versions of historical lives, Carlson argues, and his point cannot be denied, that these films "are not historical texts; they are works of art. Addressing them only as bad representations of historical reality overcompensates and denies students the right and pleasure of encountering them as creative expressions."[3] Though some come close, none of the versions of Elizabeth's life examined in this book is a perfect dramatized biography of Queen Elizabeth, but all are eminently watchable and, though not without defects, enjoyable. Lavish costuming, impressive sets, and interesting (if not always convincing) acting choices combine to make for good entertainment. In addition to being pleasurable to watch, which is ultimately what a viewer seeks in any film, Carlson feels that they also have value in that they can be used to stimulate critical historical thinking and teach one overarching principle: that representations reflect the concerns of the times in which they were made, not the times they depict, and should be viewed critically as such.

Another commentator, after providing a grocery list of the historical inaccuracies in *Elizabeth: The Golden Age*, went on to echo Carlson's conclusion that historical veracity is not necessarily the yardstick by which these film versions of Gloriana should be measured. His reasoning for espousing this stance is different from Carlson's, however: history is a "literary discipline," the precepts of which simply do not apply to the visual medium. The flipside of the "truth is stranger than fiction" coin is that strict adherence to historical veracity can be boring. It's the reason why historical novels rarely (if ever) manage no deviation from historical events, and historical films even more so. The author points out that "of course these things are riddled with errors, conflations, dodgy chronology and invented scenes.... Historical accuracy inevitably has to be sacrificed, for reasons of drama, simplicity, and narrative drive. What matters is the general thrust and ambience of any history film."[4] This provides an alternate rubric for judging Elizabethan films, one that allows more for the vagaries of creativity, as long as the overall *impression* of the historical person emerges with a prescribed lucidity. A feel for the period, a feel for the person — this a historical film can still convey, even if some (or most) of its facts are "wrong." It's the filmic equivalent of the technical precision of a Holbein portrait versus the sensual delight of a Renoir — which is a "better" likeness all depends upon the tastes of the viewer.

Yet another factor that must be considered with each new actress stepping into the role of Queen Elizabeth are the ones who have come before her (or him). In much the same way filmmakers find the incomparably complex character of Elizabeth to be irresistible fodder for their projects, so, too, do the actresses who portray her. A multifaceted character study of Elizabeth's proportions is not something that often presents itself, and actresses realize the opportunity she provides for crafting a truly exceptional performance. They face a challenge, however: not only does every portrayal risk comparison with the historical woman, but also with each other — the measuring stick includes Elizabeth herself *and* previous film Elizabeths. As one reviewer carelessly but devastatingly mentioned after praising a particular performance, "One thinks, though, of Elizabeths past."[5] With the ghosts of Elizabeths past including names such as Bette Davis and Sarah Bernhardt, as well as a present filled with such talent as dames Judi Dench and Helen Mirren, future

Elizabeths may be hard put to measure up to these great names, as well as the performances they represent.

In 2006, after the advent of Helen Mirren's turn as the Virgin Queen, *The Times* decided to look back over the panorama of film Elizabeths to offer the tongue-in-cheek Gloriana Awards for Outstanding Performances in Multiple Layers of Costume and Make-Up, illustrating that each of these portrayals is notable (or notorious) in some way. The Weak and Feeble Woman Award for Best Surprise Casting went, surprisingly, to Cate Blanchett (especially considering that Quentin Crisp was in the running). Even more surprising, perhaps, was the fact that Blanchett did *not* win the First Pressing, Extra Virgin Award for the Sexiest Elizabeth. That went to Glenda Jackson, "Britain's socialist-feminist sex bomb—irresistible for those who like their mistresses stern." Though Jackson was nominated for the Gloriana Award for Best Overall Performance, one most often awarded to her by historians, *The Times* granted it instead to Helen Mirren, since her performance was "a revelation—a magical blend of wisdom, caprice, tenderness, sensuality and ruthless authority."[6]

In order to see how representations of Elizabeth have evolved historically, it helps to view them not in a mish-mash, and not simply in chronological context, but in chronological order. For that, one must start with *Les Amours de la Reine Élizabeth*, and end up at the miniseries and *Elizabeth: The Golden Age*. One needs two points to plot a line; with these two chronological points given, what is the route taken and, more importantly, the destination reached?

True to the rampant romanticism of the Victorian and Edwardian eras, Elizabeth begins simply as a woman in love. She may be a queen, but the circumference of her world is her love for her favorite. Once betrayed by him, Bernhardt's Elizabeth is not so vengeful (or strong) that she is unwilling to show mercy; when circumstances prevent it, she's not so much remorseful as tragic. Death is her only option, for her world does not extend beyond her love for Essex; she has nothing else, and he is gone. Fast-forward to Eldridge's Elizabeth, a backlash response to the newly liberated woman who emerged from the Jazz Age—she's unnatural in her power, vain and calculating. Elizabeth is a spider, waiting to trap the unsuspecting, domestic Mary Stuart in her web. Elizabeth is a villainess; as such, she cannot be allowed to win. Even her victory is a defeat—still, still Mary wins, for her progeny will sit on the childless Elizabeth's throne. From villainess, Elizabeth is transformed, with the threat of World War II, into patriotic heroine. She may still exhibit the "feminine" weakness of vanity, but she's a strong leader, a rallying point for duty; one can respect Robson and the gallant little England she represents—light in the darkness of a threatening world. By these standards, Bette Davis's first turn as Elizabeth seems almost a throwback. She hearkens more to Bernhardt's portrayal than Eldridge's or Robson's. Her personality is different, she spits and rages rather than swoons and cries, but Essex is again the circumference of her world; without him, she's an empty, glittering husk. She does not die immediately, but she might as well, for she has nothing else to live for, a woman without the man who defines her. *Young Bess* provides a never-before-seen Elizabeth—Elizabeth before the throne. In this, she parallels the romanticism that attended her namesake, Elizabeth II's, coronation—a bright new star to revitalize the monarchy. Yet still, Simmons is all about love; only the name of the man has changed. In swaggers

Davis's second turn as Elizabeth, more assured, more a caricature, but this time, she has to share the stage; this is as much Raleigh's story as it is hers. She may attempt to force her will upon him, but in the end, it's Elizabeth who gives way. She may not be the little wife — she's given the business of state to go on with after Raleigh is gone — but it's Raleigh who will go out into the world to make his way and bring home the proverbial bacon (with a side of potato). It's only with the advent of the 1970s that Elizabeth makes a true sea-change. This time she undergoes a revolution more than an evolution — the self-assured and capable monarch finally emerges, an independent woman and political creature. It's not love or family that holds sway, but vocation. Glenda Jackson epitomizes this in her real-life political career and also in her portrayal of Elizabeth. This is not enough, however. Sex sells, so like everything else in Western culture, Elizabeth is getting sexier — it began with Jackson, but Blanchett personified it in the sensuality of both her portrayals, as well as the addition of the "have it all" philosophy. Blanchett evinces a modern expectation to have a not only a career, but love as well (with or without accompanying family, as preferences tend), and if denied this on either front, the only option is the make-over. The viewer is finally brought full circle — Blanchett has imparted iconicity, Duff provides Elizabeth with intellectuality, and Mirren gives Elizabeth back her humanity, making, together, a comprehensive portrait. There have been revisionist divergences (Crisp), backtracks (Davis), and parodies (Richardson, Bonham Carter) along the way, but in the end, Elizabeth evolves from one dimension into three, finally a fully realized woman and monarch.

A portrait amalgamated in this way may satisfy the search for a representation of the historical woman, but it does not answer the question of which of the portrayals that were blended to make it is the definitive film Elizabeth. If one must choose, the choice is not an easy one. Aspects of several different portrayals ring true, and by the same token, each portrayal is missing something. In his study, Carlson was surprised to discover that, of all the representations several years' worth of his students viewed (which ran the gamut from *Fire Over England* to the *Blackadder II* miniseries), it was Flora Robson with whom they were "most satisfied" as an accurate interpretation of the historical Elizabeth. This was not a random decision as to which they "liked," but rather an opinion formed through comparison of the film portrayals with what they had read of the historical woman in the primary and scholarly sources required for the course. How they felt about other representations is also revealing. As has been mentioned, though historians, by and large, prefer Glenda Jackson's Elizabeth, the students in Carlson's course found her "too tough and professional" and "not enough of a woman." Carlson attributed this to the change in perception since the generation before, which favored the 1970s career woman borne of the Women's Liberation movement; however, the students proved none too comfortable with representations from their own generation. They disliked the overabundance of "girl power" to be found in Cate Blanchett's Elizabeth, though this author feels there was precious little "power" and far too much "girl" in Blanchett's 1998 portrayal. Almost unanimously, the students considered Flora Robson's queen to have the "dignity, purposefulness, and people skills" of the original Elizabeth.[7]

Carlson's study and original course does not include several of the portrayals examined in this work, and one wonders how (or if) the results and rankings of the students would change with portrayals such as that by Anne-Marie Duff or Helen Mirren added into the mix. They certainly have affected the opinions of this author. Helen Mirren's portrayal gives Elizabeth something that none other has been able to so successfully accomplish: pervasive humanity. It has always been Elizabeth the tragic romantic heroine, Elizabeth the iconic ruler, Elizabeth the myth —*never* Elizabeth the human being. Somehow, through a thousand subtle little nuances, Mirren manages this, and it makes her portrayal a joy to watch, for here is a monarch who transcends symbol to feel deeply real. Yet for all this, it is almost *too* pervasive — the balance is tipped slightly too far towards the human to be convincing for a woman with the character ascribed to the historical Elizabeth by her contemporaries and exhibited through her own writings and speeches. Being a student of history, one has a desire to choose Glenda Jackson's Elizabeth as a sort of reward for the almost obsessive technical adherence to historicity that *Elizabeth R* displays — a return on the investment in historical veracity which this miniseries painstakingly makes. But it simply is not possible. Jackson's strength of technical precision is also the same element that makes her portrayal less than engaging.

Though the films in which she appears are far from worshipping at the altar of historical truth, Carlson's students hit on something with their choice of Flora Robson. As has been mentioned, because actresses with strong personalities and established reputations as stars have often chosen to take on the role of Elizabeth, the character of the monarch is habitually subsumed beneath the persona of the actress playing her. Of Flora Robson, it has been said that she "has always kept the faculty, comparatively rare in film stars, of losing her own identity in the role she is playing. For this reason, she may never be a great star, in the ordinary sense. But her characterizations will live in your memory long after those of the more conventional type of screen star have been forgotten."[8] This is certainly the case with her turn as Elizabeth. Robson viewed the Queen as "provocative, aggressive, possessive and perhaps a bit temperamental," but most essentially as "a woman of action, and that is just the kind of women I like best to portray." Robson preferred a focus on women, whether actual historical personages or not, whose lives and work were more important than their romances; this is how she characterizes Elizabeth, and this is what comes to life onscreen in her interpretation. Despite the lack of historical veracity in the films in which she appears, Robson's portrayal still *feels* true to the historical woman, and it resonates in a way that Glenda Jackson's harsher Elizabeth does not, and never could. Robson has the proper formality, but still retains elements of humanity. It's difficult to strictly define, but it has something to do with Robson's combination of gravitas and charm. She is strong, she is commanding, she is intelligent, she is determined — yet her portrayal is also that of a woman who could elicit admiration and affection, something the historical Elizabeth *had* to be able to accomplish in order to have reached the status she retains to this day. Robson manages, in a word, balance. So, if a choice has to be made, Flora Robson it is.

One thing is absolutely certain: Elizabeth will continue to be a significant figure, and it's inevitable that there will be more interpretations in film which explore her life. As Tom Hooper, director of *Elizabeth I* has said, "It's a piece of history that everyone knows something about, but no one knows *everything* about."[9] This is demonstrated by these films about Elizabeth's life — there are so many of them, but no two are exactly alike.

They all share similar elements, but each brings something new, a new piece for the puzzle, a new addition to the evolving portrait of this queen. Elizabeth has proven that she can and does remain continually relevant in the collective imagination. Perceptions change, but the last 400 years have borne out the enduring fascination Elizabeth holds as a woman and as a queen. This fascination began with Elizabeth herself, continued through the literature written about her, and has made its way into the outgrowth of that literature — the medium of modern film. These films accomplish more than just an entertaining attempt at depicting a life. They are part of the cycle which perpetuates Elizabeth's appeal — the life of Queen Elizabeth I continues to be of interest, in great part, because of the films that have been made about her. "Films raised Elizabeth's image and myth, and her myth inspired more films."[10] In essence, the films themselves are self-perpetuating.

The Queen is dead, long live the screen Queen.

Chapter Notes

Chapter 1

1. Betteridge, 2003, p. 248.
2. Higson, 2003, p. 195.
3. E.g., *The Tudors*, starring Jonathan Rhys Meyers as Henry VIII; *The Other Boleyn Girl* with Natalie Portman and Scarlett Johansson as the Boleyn sisters; as well as an upcoming film about Mary Stuart, tentatively slated for production with Scarlett Johansson in the title role.
4. Keegan, 2007, p. 64.
5. For a contemporary examination and comparison of Mary and Elizabeth, see Montrose, L.A. (2006). "The Tudor Sisterhood." In L.A. Montrose (ed.). *The Subject of Elizabeth: Authority, Gender Representation.* Chicago: University of Chicago Press.
6. A few readable popular biographies readers may wish to consult: Weir, A. (1998). *The Life of Elizabeth I.* New York: Ballantine; Starkey, D. (2001). *Elizabeth: The Struggle for the Throne.* New York: HarperCollins; Erickson, C. (1983). *The First Elizabeth.* New York: Summit.
7. Weir, 1998, p. xi.
8. Hollinger and Winterhalter, 2001, pp. 237–257.
9. Toplin, 1996, p. vii.
10. Chapman, 1999, pp. 14–23.
11. Doran, 1998, pp. 30–59.
12. Betteridge, 2003, p. 244.
13. Stevens, 2007.

14. For a detailed inventory with helpful illustrative matter, see Arnold, J. (1988). *Queen Elizabeth's Wardrobe Unlock'd: The Inventories of the Wardrobe of Robes Prepared in July 1600.* Leeds: Maney.
15. See, among others, Budiansky, S. (2005). *Her Majesty's Spymaster.* New York: Viking and Wilson, D. (2007). *Sir Francis Walsingham: A Courtier in an Age of Terror.* New York: Carroll & Graf.
16. Marcus, Mueller, and Rose, 2000, p. xiv.

Chapter 2

1. The film is also alternately titled *La Reine Élisabeth* (French); *Elisabeth, Reine d'Angleterre* (French); *Queen Elizabeth* (English); and *The Queen's Favorite* (English re-release).
2. Shipman, 1984, pp. 17–19.
3. Klepper, 1999, p. 47.
4. Mast, 1971, p. 59.
5. Menefee, 2003, p. 8.
6. Harriss, 2001, p. 68.
7. Bernhardt, 1969, p. 98.
8. Horville, 1984, p. 35.
9. Bernhardt, 1969, pp. 98–100.
10. Menefee, 2003, p. 2.
11. *Literary Digest*, 1912, pp. 190–191.
12. Moreau is also sometimes credited as Amiel Moreau.
13. Klepper, 1999, p. 48.
14. Williams, 1992, p. 80.

15. Norden, 1994, p. 49.
16. Williams, 1992, p. 80.
17. Menefee, 2003, p. 110.
18. Bernhardt, 1969, p. 50.
19. Menefee, 2003, p. 112.
20. Ibid., pp. 28–34.
21. Norden, 1994, p. 49.
22. Weir, 1998, p. 466.
23. Ibid.
24. *Literary Digest*, 1912, p. 191.
25. *Encyclopedia of World Biography 5*, 1998.
26. Wilmeth and Bigsby, 1998, p. 162.
27. Mast, 1971, p. 60.
28. Bowser, 1990 pp. 92–93.
29. Bush, 1912, pp. 428–429.
30. Menefee, 2003, p. 115.
31. *Moving Picture World*, 1912, p. 239.
32. Horville, 1984, p. 42.
33. *London Times*, 1912, p. 11.
34. Bernhardt, 1969, p. 189.
35. Shipman, 1984, pp. 145, 187.
36. *Contemporary Authors*, 2007.
37. Worthstone, 2005, p. 53.
38. Trimble, 1985, p. 11.
39. *Dictionary of American Biography*, 1973.
40. Trimble, 1985, p. 105.
41. Cooper, 1958, pp. 236–237.
42. Trimble, 1985, pp. 104–105.
43. *Encyclopædia Britannica*, 2007.
44. Low and Manvell, 1973, p. 126.
45. Trimble, 1985, p. 126.

46. Ibid., p. 135.
47. Low and Manvell, 1973, p. 126.
48. Slide, 2005, p. 27.
49. Cooper, 1958, p. 237.

Chapter 3

1. Shipman, 1984, p. 233.
2. Burnside, 2008, p. Featuresl.
3. See Dunn, J. (2004). *Elizabeth and Mary: Cousins, Rivals, Queens.* New York: Alfred A. Knopf, and Muhlstein, A. (2007). *Elizabeth I and Mary Stuart: The Perils of Marriage.* London: Haus.
4. His name is sometimes anglicized to Riccio.
5. *Encyclopedia of World Biography 7,* 1998.
6. Guy, 2004, pp. 62–63.
7. *Encyclopedia of World Biography 7,* 1998.
8. Cameron, 2008, p. 122.
9. Ford and Mitchell, 2009, p. 131.
10. Edwards, 1985, pp. 147–148.
11. Ford and Mitchell, 2009, p. 134.
12. Knox, 1950, vol. 1, p. viii.
13. Tasende, 2007, p. 75.
14. Ibid.
15. *Encyclopedia of World Biography,* 2nd ed., 2007.
16. Dickens, 1971, p. 11.
17. Ford and Mitchell, 2009, p. 139.
18. See Borman, T. (2009). *Elizabeth's Women: The Hidden Story of the Virgin Queen.* London: Jonathan Cape.
19. Dickens, 1971, p. 79.
20. McBride, 2001, p. 229.
21. Tasende, 2007, p. 76.
22. *Newsweek,* 1936, p. 22.
23. Quirk, 1990, p. 29.
24. Dickens, 1971, pp. 77–78.
25. Ibid.
26. Ford and Mitchell, 2009, p. 135.
27. Tasende, 2007, p. 76
28. Dickens, 1971, p. 76.
29. Walker, 2001, pp. 9–15.
30. Ibid.
31. *Newsweek,* 1937, p. 22.
32. Wakeman, 1987.
33. Everson, 2003, p. 300.
34. Also appears in some sources as Ingoldsby.

35. Olivier, 1982, pp. 99–100.
36. Barker, 1953, pp. 137–139.
37. Ibid., p. 139–140.
38. Holden, 1988, p. 109.
39. Olivier, 1986, p. 355.
40. Johns, 1974, p. 104.
41. Dunbar, 1960, p. 188.
42. Barrow, 1981, p. 102.
43. Ibid., p. 103.
44. Dunbar, 1960, pp. 188–199.
45. Barrow, 1981, p. 104.
46. Vidal, 1992, p. 48.
47. Betteridge, 2003, p. 248.
48. Reisz, 2006.
49. Magill, 1980, p. 536.
50. Rostron, 2002, pp. 85–96.
51. Vidal, 1992, p. 32.
52. Rostron, 2002, pp. 85–96.
53. Government Printing Office, 2009.
54. Betteridge, 2003, p. 249.
55. Vermilye, 1992, pp. 79–82.
56. Nugent, 1937, p. L16.
57. Greene and Parkinson, 1994, pp. 181–182.
58. *New York Times,* 1937.
59. *Newsweek,* 1937, p. 22.
60. Ford and Mitchell, 2009, p. 229.
61. Betteridge, 2003, p. 250.
62. Stine and Davis, 1974, p. 121.
63. Ford and Mitchell, 2009, p. 230.
64. Ibid.
65. Basinger, 2007, p. 241.
66. Higham, 1981, p. 125.
67. Ibid.
68. Stine and Davis, 1974, p. 121.
69. Flynn, 1969, p. 222.
70. Hartung, 1939, p. 97.
71. Basinger, 2007, p. 241.
72. Higham, 1981, p. 127.
73. Ibid., p. 125.
74. Stine and Davis, 1974, p. 121.
75. Hartung, 1939, p. 97.
76. Ford and Mitchell, 2009, p. 235.
77. Higham, 1981, p. 125.
78. Stine and Davis, 1974, p. 122.
79. Ibid.
80. Flynn, 1969, p. 223.
81. Ibid., p. 226.
82. Kehoe, 2001, pp. 75–77, 102–104.
83. Stine and Davis, 1974, p. 123.

84. Ford and Mitchell, 2009, p. 237.
85. Betteridge, 2003, p. 246.
86. Ibid., p. 252.
87. Hartung, 1939, p. 97.
88. Ford and Mitchell, 2009, p. 237.
89. *Time,* 1939, pp. 80–81.
90. Ibid.
91. Carlson, 2007, pp. 419–428.
92. Higham, 1981, p. 126.
93. Basinger, 2007, p. 241.
94. Shingler, 2008, pp. 269–280.
95. *Time,* 1939, p. 80–81.
96. Higham, 1981, p. 128.
97. Dunbar, 1960, p. 211.
98. Belhmer, 1982, p. 12.
99. See Strachey, L. (1928). *Elizabeth and Essex: A Tragic History.* New York: Harcourt, Brace.
100. Belhmer, 1982, p. 16.
101. Dunbar, 1960, pp. 129–130.
102. Thomas, 1969, p. 93.
103. Belhmer, 1982, p. 29.
104. Dunbar, 1960, p. 130.
105. Ibid.
106. Ibid., p. 131.
107. Thomas, 1969, p. 96.
108. Hartung, 1940, p. 371.
109. Dunbar, 1960, p. 133.
110. Muhlstein, 2007, p. 25.
111. Carlson, 2007, pp. 419–428.
112. Walker, 1998, p. 26.
113. Shiach, 2005, p. 98.
114. Ibid.
115. Ibid., p. 131.
116. Thames, 2010.
117. Shiach, 2005, p. 140.
118. Ibid.
119. Kerr and Martin, 1954, pp. 17–19, 121–125.
120. Levin and Carney, 2003, p. 228.
121. Ibid., p. 230.
122. Ibid.
123. Shiach, 2005, p. 141.
124. Thames, 2010.
125. Shiach, 2005, p. 142.
126. *Newsweek,* 1953, p. 84.
127. *Variety* staff, 1953.
128. Shiach, 2005, p. 140–141.
129. Carlson, 2007, pp. 419–428.
130. Ibid.
131. *America,* 1953, p. 257.
132. Hartung, 1953, p. 249.

133. Brackett, 2008.
134. Sometimes credited as Mindred or Mildred Lord.
135. Stine and Davis, 1974, p. 256.
136. *Encyclopædia Britannica*, 2010.
137. Higham, 1981, p. 237.
138. Ibid., p. 238.
139. Brackett, 2008.
140. Hyman, 1985, p. 29.
141. Ford and Mitchell, 2009, p. 250.
142. *Historic World Leaders*, 1994.
143. Lawson-Peebles, 1998, pp. 17–24.
144. *Historic World Leaders*, 1994.
145. Brackett, 2008.
146. Ford and Mitchell, 2009, p. 253.
147. Lawson-Peebles, 1998, pp. 17–24.
148. Higham, 1981, p. 238.
149. Ford and Mitchell, 2009, pp. 252–253.
150. Collins, 2008, p.12.
151. Stine and Davis, 1974, p. 258.
152. Ibid.
153. Brackett, 2008.
154. Ford and Mitchell, 2009, pp. 252–253.
155. Stine and Davis, 1974, p. 258.

Chapter 4

1. Mast, 1971, p. 334.
2. Schwartzbaum, 1999, p. 56.
3. *International Dictionary of Films and Filmmakers*, 2000.
4. Ebert, 1972.
5. Guy, 2004, pp. 62–63.
6. Ford and Mitchell, 2009, p. 155.
7. Ebert, 1972.
8. Canby, 1972, Film section.
9. Woodward, 1985, p. 82.
10. Bryant, 1999, p. 105.
11. *Variety* staff, 1972.
12. Ford and Mitchell, 2009, p. 150.
13. Burnside, 2008, p. Featuresl.
14. Ebert, 1972.
15. *Variety* staff, 1972.
16. Woodward, 1985, p. 82.
17. Ibid.

18. *International Dictionary of Films and Filmmakers*, 2000.
19. Betteridge, 2003, p. 247.
20. Filmofilia, 2008.
21. Hessey, 1998, p. 9.
22. Sauter, 1999, pp. 108–109.
23. Higson, 2003, pp. 194–195.
24. Combs, 1999, pp. 33–35.
25. Alleva, 1998, pp. 14–15.
26. *Encyclopaedia Britannica*, 2010.
27. Kapur, 2009.
28. Ford and Mitchell, 2009, p. 208.
29. Delamoir, 1999, pp. 46–53.
30. Betteridge, 2003, pp. 254–258.
31. Ford and Mitchell, 2009, p. 281.
32. Beckerman, 1998, Film section.
33. Hirst, 2007, p. 11.
34. Calhoun, 1999, pp. 89–90.
35. Kapur, 2009.
36. Higson, 2003, p. 221.
37. Betteridge, 2003, p. 256.
38. Alleva, 1998, pp. 14–15.
39. Kapur, 2009.
40. Delamoir, 1999, pp. 46–53.
41. Noh, 2007, p. 119.
42. Craven, 2007, Film section.
43. Ross, 2007, p. 88.
44. Dargis, 2007.
45. Ford and Mitchell, 2009, p. 219.
46. Ross, 2007, p. 88.
47. Ford and Mitchell, 2009, p. 292.
48. Dargis, 2007.
49. Kapur, 2007.
50. Schwartzbaum, 2007.
51. Lumenick, 2007.
52. Schwartzbaum, 2007.
53. Dargis, 2007.
54. Craven, 2007.
55. Kapur, 2007.
56. Ibid.

Chapter 5

1. Internet Movie Database, 2010.
2. Woolf, 2006, p. xl.
3. *Gay and Lesbian Biography*, 1997.
4. Ehrenstein, 1993, pp. 2–3.
5. Ibid.
6. Ibid.
7. Calhoun, 1999, Fall, pp. 22–23.

8. Ibid.
9. Johnson, 1993, p. 43.
10. Ehrenstein, 1993, pp. 2–3.
11. Calhoun, 1999, March, pp. 89–90.
12. *Entertainment Weekly*, 1999.
13. Combs, 1999, pp. 33–35.
14. *The New Republic*, 1999, pp. 26–27.
15. Calhoun, 1999, March, pp. 89–90.
16. Ibid.
17. Combs, 1999, pp. 33–35.
18. Shargel, 1999, pp. 20–21.
19. Combs, 1999, pp. 33–35.
20. *The New Republic*, 1999, pp 26–27.
21. Burt, 2003, p. 274.
22. Shargel, 1999, pp. 20–21.
23. *Entertainment Weekly*, 1999.
24. Setoodeh, 2010, pp. 50–51.
25. Zanuck, 2010.
26. *New Yorker*, 2010, pp. 58–59.
27. Verniere, 2010.
28. Setoodeh, 2010, pp. 50–51.
29. Brown, 2010, p. 8.
30. Fitzsimmons, 2010, p. 3.
31. Brown, 2010, p. 8.
32. Corliss, 2010, p. 51.

Chapter 6

1. Woodward, 1985, p. 79.
2. O'Flaherty and Sharpe, 1996, p. 25.
3. Ibid., p. 30–31.
4. Ibid., p. 28.
5. Ibid., p. 29.
6. Skidmore, 2010, p. 73.
7. On Monsieur's Departure by Elizabeth I, Queen of England
I grieve and dare not show my discontent;
I love, and yet am forced to seem to hate;
I do, yet dare not say I ever meant;
I seem stark mute, but inwardly do prate.
I am, and not; I freeze and yet am burned,
Since from myself another self I turned.
My care is like my shadow in the sun —
Follows me flying, flies when I pursue it,
Stands, and lies by me, doth what I have done;

His too familiar care doth
make me rue it.
No means I find to rid him
from my breast,
Till by the end of things it
be supprest.
Some gentler passion slide
into my mind,
For I am soft, and made of
melting snow;
Or be more cruel, Love, and
so be kind.
Let me or float or sink, be
high or low;
Or let me live with some
more sweet content,
Or die, and so forget what
love e'er meant.
Marcus, Mueller, and Rose, 2000,
pp. 302–303.

8. O'Flaherty and Sharpe, 1996, p. 31.

9. Ibid., 26.

10. Hudson, 1972, p. 23.

11. Woodward, 1985, p. 80.

12. O'Flaherty and Sharpe, 1996, p. 28.

13. Haskell, 1972, pp. 12–13.

14. Woodward, 1985, p. 79.

15. *Senior Scholastic*, 1972, p. 18.

16. Woodward, 1985, p. 80.

17. Ibid.

18. Doran and Freeman, 2003, p. 13.

19. Gruen, 1972, p. 64–65.

20. Haskell, 1972, pp. 12–13.

21. Ford and Mitchell, 2009, p. 258

22. Haskell, 1972, pp. 12–13.

23. Roberts, Taylor, and Pronay, 2001, p. 118.

24. Neale and Krutnik, 1990, p. 246.

25. Ibid.

26. Schine, 1990, p. 208.

27. Bellafante, 2005, p. B11.

28. Public Broadcasting Station, 2005.

29. Gristwood, 2007, p. 131.

30. Ford and Mitchell, 2009, p. 269.

31. Gristwood, 2007, p. 100.

32. Ibid., p. 104.

33. See Skidmore, C. (2010). *Death and the Virgin: Elizabeth, Dudley and the Mysterious Fate of Amy Robsart*. London: Weidenfeld & Nicolson.

34. Bellafante, 2005, p. B11.

35. Dunn, 2004, pp. 403–404.

36. Collard, 2006, p. 22.

37. Bellafante, 2005, p. B11.

38. Collard, 2006, p. 22.

39. Ibid.

40. Ford and Mitchell, 2009, p. 268.

41. Bellafante, 2005, p. B11.

42. Ibid.

43. Ford and Mitchell, 2009, p. 270.

44. Reisz, 2006.

45. Gristwood, 2007, pp. 25–68.

46. Ibid., p. 124.

47. Leonard, 2006, pp. 74–75.

48. Wiegand, 2006, p. E1.

49. Gristwood, 2007, p. 334.

50. The full text of the sonnet reads:
Let me not to the marriage of
true minds
Admit impediments. Love is
not love
Which alters when it alteration finds,
Or bends with the remover to
remove:
O no! it is an ever-fixed mark
That looks on tempests and is
never shaken;
It is the star to every wandering bark,
Whose worth's unknown, although his height be taken.
Love's not Time's fool, though
rosy lips and cheeks
Within his bending sickle's
compass come:
Love alters not with his brief
hours and weeks,
But bears it out even to the
edge of doom.
If this be error and upon
me proved,
I never writ, nor no man
ever loved.
Shakespeare, 1974, p. 1221.

51. McCollum, 2006, Features section.

52. The Franklin quote is: "We must all hang together, or assuredly we shall all hang separately."

53. Bianco, 2006, p.1E.

54. Reisz, 2006.

55. Wiegand, 2006, p. E1.

56. Reisz, 2006.

57. McCollum, 2006, Features section.

58. Gliatto, 2006, p. 39.

59. McCollum, 2006, Features section.

60. Leonard, 2006, pp. 74–75.

61. Ford and Mitchell, 2009, p. 276.

Chapter 7

1. Schwartzbaum, 1999, p. 56.

2. British Broadcasting Corp., 2007.

3. Carlson, 2007, p. 420.

4. Morrogh, 2008, pp. 46–49.

5. Leonard, 2006, pp. 74–75.

6. Hoggart, 2006, p. 42.

7. Carlson, 2007, p. 427.

8. LoBianco, 2010

9. Reisz, 2006.

10. British Broadcasting Corp., 2007.

Bibliography

Print Sources

Alleva, R. (1998, December 18). "Screen: The Godmother." *The Commonweal*, pp. 14–15.

America (1953, May 30). "Films: 'Young Bess,'" pp. 94, 257.

Anderson, M. (1930). *Elizabeth the Queen: A Play in Three Acts*. London: Longmans Green.

_____. (1934). *Mary of Scotland: A Play in Three Acts*. Garden City, NY: Doubleday.

Arnold, J. (1988). *Queen Elizabeth's Wardrobe Unlock'd: The Inventories of the Wardrobe of Robes Prepared in July 1600*. Leeds: Maney.

Barker, F. (1953). *The Oliviers*. Philadelphia: J.B. Lippincott.

Barrow, K. (1981). *Flora: An Appreciation of the Life and Work of Dame Flora Robson*. London: Heinemann.

Basinger, J. (2007). *The Star Machine*. New York: Alfred A. Knopf.

Beckerman, J. (1998, November 4). "*Shine* Actor True to Form in *Elizabeth*." *The Record*, (Hackensack, NJ), p.Y1.

Belhmer, R., ed. (1982). *The Sea Hawk*. Madison: University of Wisconsin Press.

Bellafante, G. (2005, November 12). "Such an Unhappy Sex Life? But Such a Glorious Reign." *New York Times*, p. B11.

Bernhardt, S. (1969). *The Art of the Theatre*. Freeport, NY: Books for Libraries.

Betteridge, T. (2003). "A Queen for All Seasons." In S. Doran and T. S. Freeman (eds.). *The Myth of Elizabeth*. New York: Palgrave MacMillan.

Bianco, R. (2006, April 21). "Mirren Puts Crowning Touch on 'Elizabeth I.'" *USA Today*, p. 1E.

Borman, T. (2009). *Elizabeth's Women: The Hidden Story of the Virgin Queen*. London: Jonathan Cape.

Bowser, E. (1990). *The Transformation of Cinema, 1907–1915*. New York: Maxwell Macmillan International.

Brackett, C. (Producer) and H. Koster (Director). (2008). *Virgin Territory: Making of* The Virgin Queen. *The Virgin Queen* [motion picture]. United States: 20th Century–Fox Home Entertainment.

British Broadcasting Corp. (2007, August 8). "Historical and Historiographical Implications of Filmic Treatments of Elizabeth I." BBC website. Retrieved from *http://www.bbc.co.uk/dna/h2g2/A25645331*.

Brown, R. (2010, March 1). "Makeup in Wonderland." *WWD*, *199*(53), p. 8.

Bryant, C. (1999). *Glenda Jackson: The Biography*. New York: HarperCollins.

Budiansky, S. (2005). *Her Majesty's Spymaster*. New York: Viking.

Burnside, A. (2008, February 24). "Something About Mary." *Sunday Times*, p. F1.

Burt, R. (2003). "Doing the Queen: Gender, Sexuality, and the Censorship of Elizabeth I's Royal Image in Twentieth-Century Mass Media." In K. Farrell and K. M. Swain (eds.). *The Mysteries of Elizabeth I: Selections from English Literary Renaissance*. Amherst: University of Massachusetts Press.

Bush, W. S. (1912, August 3). "Review of *Queen Elizabeth*." *Moving Picture World*, pp. 428–429.

Calhoun, J. (1999, March). "Tudor City." *Interiors*, *158*(3), pp. 89–90.

_____. (1999, fall). "From the Bard to Bowie, Sandy Powell Dresses Up Three New Releases." *Entertainment Design*, *33*(2), pp. 22–23.

Cameron, R. (2008). "The Limits of Emancipation: Changing Approaches to Feminism in Early Twentieth-Century British Women's Drama." *Women's Studies*, pp. 37, 122.

Canby, V. (1972, February 4). "A Costume Drama:

Mary, 'Queen of Scots' Opens at Music Hall." *New York Times*, Drama and Film section.

Carlson, E. J. (2007). "Teaching Elizabeth Tudor with Movies: Film, Historical Thinking, and the Classroom." *Sixteenth Century Journal, XXXVIII*(2), pp. 419–428.

Chapman, J. (1999). "Elizabeth I in Film." *Bulletin of the Society for Renaissance Studies, 17*, pp. 14–23.

Collard, J. (2006, January 14). "Girl Power." *The Times* (UK), p. 22.

Collins, J. (2008, March 27). "Bette, I Owe It All to You." *The Times* (UK), p. 12.

Combs, R. (1999, May/June). "Shakespeare." *Film Comment, 35*(3), pp. 33–35.

Contemporary Authors. (2007). "Evelyn Waugh." Farmington Hills, MI: Thomson Gale. Retrieved from *http://galenet.galegroup.com.lib-proxy.jsu.edu/servlet/BioRC.*

Cooper, D. (1958). *The Rainbow Comes and Goes.* Cambridge, MA: Riverside.

Corliss, R. (2010, March 15). "Tim Burton, Wonder Boy." *Time, 175*(10), p. 51.

Craven, P. (2007, December 1). "On Good Queen Bland." *The Australian,* Film section.

Dargis, M. (2007, October 15). "Now, Warrior." *New York Times.* Retrieved from *http://movies.nytimes.com/2007/10/12/movies/12gold.html.*

Delamoir, J. (1999). "Elizabeth's Costumes: The Power of Spectacle, or Spectacles of Power?" *Metro Magazine,* (141), pp. 46–53.

Dickens, H. (1971). *The Films of Katharine Hepburn.* New York: Citadel.

Dictionary of American Biography, Supplement 3: 1941–1945. (1973). "James Stuart Blackton." New York: American Council of Learned Societies. Reproduced in *Biography Resource Center.* Farmington Hills, MI: Thomson Gale. Retrieved from *http://galenet.galegroup.com.lib-proxy.jsu.edu/servlet/BioRC.*

Doran, S. (1998). "Why Did Elizabeth Not Marry?" In J.M. Walker (ed.). *Dissing Elizabeth: Negative Representations of Gloriana.* Durham: Duke University Press.

_____, and T. S. Freeman, eds. (2003). *The Myth of Elizabeth.* New York: Palgrave MacMillan.

Dunbar, J. (1960). *Flora Robson.* London: George G. Harrap.

Dunn, J. (2004). *Elizabeth and Mary: Cousins, Rivals, Queens.* New York: Alfred A. Knopf.

Ebert, R. (1972, March 7). "Mary, Queen of Scots." *Chicago Sun Times.* Retrieved from http://roger ebert.suntimes.com/apps/pbcs.dll/article?AID =/19720307/REVIEWS/20307030.

Edwards, A. (1985). *A Remarkable Woman: A Biography of Katharine Hepburn.* New York: William Morrow.

Ehrenstein, D. (1993, Fall). "Out of the Wilderness: An Interview with Sally Potter." *Film Quarterly, 47*(1), pp. 2–3.

Encyclopædia Britannica. (2007). "Motion-Picture Technology." Reproduced in *EBSCO host.* Retrieved from http://search.eg.com/eb/article-52184.

Encyclopædia Britannica. (2010). "CinemaScope." Reproduced in *EBSCO host.* Retrieved from *http://search.eb.com/eb/article-9082667.*

Encyclopædia Britannica. (2010). "Nicolas Ridley." Reproduced in *EBSCO host.* Retrieved from *http://search.eb.com/eb/article-9063633.*

Encyclopedia of World Biography (Vol. 5). (1998). "Second Earl of Essex." Reproduced in *Biography Resource Center.* Farmington Hills, MI: Gale Research. Retrieved from *http://galenet. galegroup.com.lib-proxy.jsu.edu/servlet/Bio RC.*

Encyclopedia of World Biography (Vol. 7). (1998). "Mary, Queen of Scots." Reproduced in *Biography Resource Center.* Farmington Hills, MI: Gale Research. Retrieved from *http://galenet. galegroup.com.lib-proxy.jsu.edu/servlet/BioRC.*

Encyclopedia of World Biography (2nd ed.). (2007). "Katharine Hepburn." Reproduced in *Biography Resource Center.* Farmington Hills, MI: Gale Research. Retrieved from *http://galenet. galegroup.com.lib-proxy.jsu.edu/servlet/BioRC.*

Entertainment Weekly (1999, March 1). "Best Supporting Actress: Judi Dench." (474). Retrieved from *http://www.ew.com/ew/inside/issue/0,,ew Tax:474,00.html.*

Entertainment Weekly. (1999, March 1). "Shakespeare in Love: Oscar Fell Head Over Heels for this Witty Tale of the Lovestruck Bard." (474). Retrieved from *http://www.ew.com/ew/inside/ issue/0,,ewTax:474,00.html.*

Erickson, C. (1983). *The First Elizabeth.* New York: Summit.

Everson, W. K. (2003, July). "Fire Over England" (movie review). *Film History, 15*(3), p. 300.

Filmofilia website. (2008, March 1). "Scarlett Johansson as Mary, Queen of Scots." Retrieved from *http://www.filmofilia.com/2008/03/01-/scarlett-johansson-as-mary-queen-of-scots.*

Fitzsimmons, A. (2010, March 4). "Designing Costumes for Tim Burton's 'Alice in Wonderland.'" *WWD, 199*(54), p. 3.

Flynn, E. (1969). *My Wicked, Wicked Ways.* Heinemann: London.

Ford, E. and D. C. Mitchell (2009). *Royal Portraits in Hollywood: Filming the Lives of Queens.* Lexington: University Press of Kentucky.

Gay and Lesbian Biography. (1997). "Quentin Crisp." Reproduced in *Biography Resource Center.* Farmington Hills, MI: Gale Research. Retrieved from *http://galenet.galegroup.com.lib-proxy.jsu.edu/servlet/BioRC.*

Gliatto, T. (2006, May 1). "Picks and Pans: 'Elizabeth I.'" *People, 65*(17), p. 39.

Government Printing Office. (2009). *Citizen's Briefing Book: To President Barack Obama from the American People.* Washington, D.C.: U.S. Government Printing Office. Retrieved from *http://www.whitehouse.gov/assets/documents/ Citizens_Briefing_Book_Final.pdf.*

Greene, G. and Parkinson, D. (1994). *The Graham Greene Film Reader: Reviews, Essays, Interviews and Film Stories.* New York: Applause Theatre.

Gristwood, S. (2007). *Elizabeth and Leicester.* New York: Viking.

Gruen, J. (1972, February 15). "Liberating the Queen in Every Woman." *Vogue, 159*, pp. 64–65.

Guy, J. (2004). "Prying Open the Casket." *History Today, 54*(1), pp. 62–63.

Harriss, J.A. (2001, August). "The Divine Sarah." *Smithsonian, 32*(5), p. 68.

Hartung, P.T. (1939, November 17). "A Man Must Stand Up." *The Commonweal*, p. 97.

_____. (1940, August 2). "The Screen." *The Commonweal*, p. 371.

_____. (1953, June 12). "The Screen: A Buss for Bess." *The Commonweal*, p. 249.

Haskell, M. (1972, February 15). "That Woman in Every Woman." *Vogue, 159*, pp. 12–13.

Hessey, R. (1998, October 23). "Like a Virgin." *Sydney Morning Herald*, Metro section, p. 9.

Higham, C. (1981). *Bette: The Life of Bette Davis.* New York: Macmillan.

Higson, A. (2003). *English Heritage, English Cinema: Costume Drama Since 1980.* Oxford: Oxford University Press.

Hirst, M. (2007). *Elizabeth I: A Film by Shekhar Kapur.* London: Polygram.

Historic World Leaders. (1994). "Walter Raleigh." Reproduced in *Biography Resource Center.* Farmington Hills, MI: Gale Research. Retrieved from *http://galenet.galegroup.com/serv let/BioRC.*

Hoggart, P. (2006, January 21). "And Ye Winner Is..." *The Times.* (UK), p. 42.

Holden, A. (1988). *Laurence Olivier.* New York: Athenaeum.

Hollinger, K. and Winterhalter, T. (2001). "Orlando's Sister, or Sally Potter Does Virginia Woolf in a Voice of Her Own." *Style, 35*(2), pp. 237–257.

Horville, R. (1984). "The Stage Techniques of Sarah Bernhardt." In E. Salmon (ed.).*Bernhardt and the Theatre of Her Time.* Westport, CT: Greenwood.

Hudson, P. (1972, March 6). "The Lively Arts: Multi-Media Queensmanship." *Senior Scholastic*, p. 23.

Hyman, B. D. (1985). *My Mother's Keeper.* New York: William Morrow.

International Dictionary of Films and Filmmakers, Vol. 3: Actors and Actresses (4th ed.) (2000). "Glenda Jackson." Reproduced in *Biography Resource Center.* Farmington Hills, MI: Gale Research. Retrieved from *http://galenet.gale group.com/servlet/BioRC.*

Internet Movie Database. (2010). "Elizabeth I." Retrieved from *http://www.imdb.com.*

Irwin, M. (1945). *Young Bess.* New York: Harcourt, Brace.

Johns, E. (1974). *Dames of the Theatre.* New Rochelle, NY: Arlington House.

Johnson, B. D. (1993, July 19). "Orlando: Gender Blender." *Maclean's, 107*(29), p. 43.

Kapur, S. (2007, November 24). "The Golden Age: Divinity, History, Desire." Retrieved from *http://shekharkapur.com/blog/2007/11/golden- agedivinityhistorydesire.*

_____. (2009, 7 July). "Film Design and Narrative: Elizabeth." Retrieved from *http://shekhark apur.com/blog/category/elizabeth.*

Keegan, R.W. (2007, March 22). "When Royals Became Rock Stars." *Time*, pp. 63–65.

Kehoe, J. (2001, November). "Legends: Errol Flynn." *Biography Magazine*, pp. 75–77, 102–104.

Kerr, D. and P. Martin (1954, June). "What Hollywood Did to Me." *Saturday Evening Post*, pp. 17–19, 121–125.

Klepper, R. K. (1999). *Silent Films, 1877–1996: A Critical Guide to 646 Movies.* Jefferson, NC: McFarland.

Knox, J. (1950). *History of the Reformation in Scotland, Vol.1.* W. C. Dickinson (ed.). New York: Philosophical Library.

Lawson-Peebles, R. (1998, March). "The Many Faces of Sir Walter Raleigh." *History Today*, pp. 17–24.

Leonard, J. (2006, April 24). "Virgin Territory." *New York Magazine, 39*(14), pp. 74–75.

Levin, C. and J. E. Carney (2003). "Young Elizabeth in Peril: From Seventeenth-Century Drama to Modern Movies." In C. Levin, J. E. Carney, and D. Barrett-Graves (eds.). *Elizabeth I: Always Her Own Free Woman.* Burlington, VT: Ashgate.

The Literary Digest. (1912, August 3). "Bernhardt in Motion Pictures." *45*(5), pp. 190–191.

LoBianco, Lorraine. (2010). "Flora Robson Profile." TCM website. Retrieved from *http://www. tcm.com/thismonth/article/?cid=276321.*

London Times. (1912, October 23) "Sarah Bernhardt," p. 11.Low, R. and R. Manvell (1973). *The History of the British Film: 1906–1914.* London: Allen and Unwin.

Lumenick, L. (2007, October 12). "Nobody Beats the Liz." *New York Post.* Retrieved from http:// www.nypost.com/p/entertainment/movies/ item_mXpIr6n2VWQxPbYdBj8LCL.

Magill, F.N. (ed.). (1980). *Magill's Survey of Cinema: English Language Films* (1st series, Vol. II). Englewood Cliffs, NJ: Salem.

Marcus, L.S., J. Mueller and M. B. Rose (eds.). (2000). *Elizabeth I: Collected Works.* Chicago: University of Chicago Press.

Mast, G. (1971). *A Short History of the Movies.* New York: Pegasus.

McBride, J. (2001). *Searching for John Ford: A life.* New York: St. Martin's.

McCollum, C. (2006, April 20). "McCollum: The Definitive portrayal of the 'Virgin Queen.'" *San Jose Mercury News* (CA), Features section.

Menefee, D.W. (2003). *Sarah Bernhardt in the Theatre of Films and Sound Recordings.* Jefferson, NC: McFarland.

Montrose, L.A. (2006). "The Tudor Sisterhood." In L.A. Montrose (ed.). *The Subject of Elizabeth: Authority, Gender, Representation.* Chicago: University of Chicago Press.

Morrogh, M. (2008, September). "Hollywood Blockbusters and Historical Reality." *History Review*, pp. 46–49.

Muhlstein, A. (2007). *Elizabeth I and Mary Stuart: The Perils of Marriage.* London: Haus.

Neale, S. and F. Krutnik (1990). *Popular Film and Television Comedy.* London: Routledge.

New Republic (1999, January 4). "Shakespeare in Love." *220*(1–2), pp. 26–27.

New York Times. (1937, February 21). "Fire Over England" (movie review).Amusements section.

New Yorker (2010, March 8). "Welcome to the Fun House." *43*(7), pp. 58–59.

Newsweek. (1936, August 1). "SCREEN: Hepburn Still Hepburn as a Queen Who Lost Her Head," pp. 9, 22.

Newsweek. (1937, February 27). "Entertainment: Studio Reconstructs Elizabethan Nose and History," pp. 10, 22.

Newsweek (1953, June 1). "New films: 'Young Bess,'" *32*, p. 84.

Noh, D. (2007, November). "'Elizabeth: The Golden Age'" (movie review). *Film Journal International. 110*(11), p. 119.

Norden, M.F. (1994). *The Cinema of Isolation: a History of Physical Disability in the Movies.* New Brunswick, NJ: Rutgers University Press.

Nugent, F. S. (1937, March 5). "'Fire Over England'" (movie review). *New York Times*, p. L16.

O'Flaherty, T. and K. Sharpe (1996). *Masterpiece Theatre: A Celebration of 25 years of Outstanding Television.* San Francisco: KQED Books.

Olivier, L. (1982). *Confessions of an Actor: An Autobiography.* New York: Simon and Schuster.

_____. (1986). *On Acting.* New York: Simon and Schuster.

Public Broadcasting Station (2005). "Who's Who in 'The Virgin Queen. Elizabeth I.'" *The Virgin Queen* website. Retrieved from *http://www.pbs.org/wgbh/masterpiece/virginqueen/whos_who.html.*

Quirk, L. J. (1990). *The Films of Frederic March.* New York: The Citadel.

Reisz, B. (Producer), and Hooper, T. (Director). (2006). *The Making of* Elizabeth I (featurette). *Elizabeth I* [television series]. New York: HBO Video.

Roberts, G., P. M. Taylor and N. Pronay (2001). *The Historian, Television, and Television History: A Collection.* Luton: University of Luton Press.

Ross, D. (2007, November 3). "Poor Cate." *Spectator, 305*(9351), p. 88.

Rostron, A. (2002). "No War, No Hate, No propaganda: Promoting Films About European War and Fascism During the Period of American Isolationism." *Journal of Popular Film and Television, 30*(2), pp. 85–96.

Sabatini, R. (1924). *The Sea-Hawk.* New York: Grosset and Dunlap.

Sauter, M. (1999, June). "Elizabeth." *Biography Magazine*, pp. 108–109.

Schine, C. (1990, February). "Television: Blackadder Turns History into a Colorful Comic Festival." *Vogue 180*, p. 208.

Schwartzbaum, L. (1999, March 1). "Rex Appeal." *Entertainment Weekly* (474), p. 56.

_____. (2007, October 10). "'Elizabeth: The Golden Age'" (movie review).*Entertainment Weekly.* Retrieved from *http://www.ew.com/ew/article/0,,20151593,00.html.*

Senior Scholastic. (1972, February 7). "Television: The Bold, Bald Queen of England," p. 18.

Setoodeh, R. (2010, March 8). "Rabbit Redux." *Newsweek, 155*(10), pp. 50–51.

Shakespeare, W. (1974). "Sonnet 116." In G.B. Evans (ed.). *The Riverside Shakespeare.* Boston: Houghton Mifflin.

Shargel, R. (1999, March 8). "Shakespeare in Love." *The New Leader, 82*(3), pp. 20–21.

Shiach, D. (2005). *Stewart Granger: The Last of the Swashbucklers.* London: Aurum.

Shingler, M. (2008). "Bette Davis Made Over in Wartime: The Feminisation of an Androgynous Star in *Now, Voyager* (1942)." *Film History, 20*(3), pp. 269–280.

Shipman, D. (1984). *The Story of Cinema: A Complete Narrative History from the Beginnings to the Present.* New York: St. Martin's.

Skidmore, C. (2010). *Death and the Virgin: Elizabeth, Dudley and the Mysterious Fate of Amy Robsart.* London: Weidenfeld and Nicolson.

Slide, A. (2005). *Silent Topics: Essays on Undocumented areas of Silent Film.* Lanham, MD: Scarecrow.

Starkey, D. (2001). *Elizabeth: The Struggle for the Throne.* New York: HarperCollins.

Stevens, D. (2007, October 11). "Movies: 'Elizabeth: The Golden Age.'" *Slate.* Retrieved from *http://www.slate.com/toolbar.aspx?action=print andid=2175718.*

Stine, W. and B. Davis (1974). *Mother Goddam.* New York: Hawthorn.

Strachey, L. (1928). *Elizabeth and Essex: A Tragic History.* New York: Harcourt, Brace.

Tasende, J.M. (2007). *Action! Memoirs of a Spectator: The Films of John Ford.* Barcelona, Spain: Ediciones Poligrafa.

Thames, S. (2010). "Young Bess." Turner Classic Movies website. Retrieved from *http://www.tcm.com/thismonth/article.jsp?cid=21411and mainArticleId=208724.*

Thomas, T., R. Behlmer and C. McCarty (1969). *The Films of Errol Flynn.* New York: The Citadel.

Time. (1939, November 13). "Cinema," *XXXIV* (20), pp. 80–81.

Toplin, R.B. (1996). *History by Hollywood: The Use and Abuse of the American Past.* Chicago: University of Illinois Press.

Trimble, M. B. (1985). *J. Stuart Blackton: A Personal Biography by his Daughter.* Mentuchen, NJ: Scarecrow.

Variety staff (1953, January 1). "Young Bess" (movie review). *Variety.* Retrieved from *http://www.variety.com/review/VE1117796542.html?category id=3landcs=1.*

Variety staff (1972, January 1). "Mary, Queen of Scots" (movie review). *Variety.* Retrieved from *http://variety.com/index.asp?layout=print_review andreviewid=VE1117793006.*

Vermilye, J. (1992). *The Complete Films of Laurence Olivier.* New York: Citadel.

Verniere, J. (2010, March 6). "Burton Directs 'Alice' down 3-D Rabbit Hole." *Boston Herald.* Retrieved from *http://news.bostonherald.com/ entertainment/movies/reviews/view/20100305 alice-inwonderland.*

Vidal, G. (1992). *Screening History.* Cambridge, MA: Harvard University Press.

Wakeman. J. (ed.). (1987). "Alexander Korda." *World Film Directors, Vol. 1.* New York: H. W. Wilson Company.

Walker, G. (2001). "The Private Life of Henry VIII." *History Today,* 51(9), pp. 9–15.

Walker, J.M. (1998). *Dissing Elizabeth: Negative Representations of Gloriana.* Durham, NC: Duke University Press.

Weir, A. (1998). *The Life of Elizabeth I.* New York: Ballantine.

Wiegand, D. (2006, April 21). "Bloody Good Drama as Helen Mirren Stirs Up Passions in 'Elizabeth I' Film." *San Francisco Chronicle,* p. E1.

Williams, A. (1992). *Republic of Images: A History of French Filmmaking.* Cambridge, MA: Harvard University Press.

Wilmeth, D.B. and C. Bigsby (eds.). (1998). *The Cambridge History of American Theatre, Vol. II (1870–1945).* Cambridge: Cambridge University Press.

Wilson, D. (2007). *Sir Francis Walsingham: A Courtier in an Age of Terror.* New York: Carroll and Graf.

Woodward, I. (1985). *Glenda Jackson: A Study in Fire and Ice.* New York: St. Martin's.

Woolf, V. (2006). *Orlando: A Biography.* M. Hussey (ed.). New York: Harvest.

World Photographic Publication Co. (1912, October 19). "Queen Elizabeth" (movie review). *Moving Picture World.* New York: World Photographic, pp. 239.

Worthstone, P. (2005, October 24). "Private Affairs." *New Statesman,* 53.

Zanuck, R.D. (Producer), and T. Burton (Director). (2010). "Finding Alice." DVD special features. *Alice in Wonderland* [Motion picture]. United States: Walt Disney Pictures Home Entertainment.

Film and Television

Berman, P.S. (Producer), and J. Ford (Director). (1936) (2006). *Mary of Scotland* [motion picture]. United States: Warner Home Video.

Bevan, T. (Producer), and S. Kapur (Director). (2007) (2008). *Elizabeth: the Golden Age* [motion picture]. United States: Universal Pictures Company, distributed by Universal Studios Home Entertainment.

Blackton, J.S. (Producer). (1922). *The Virgin Queen* [motion picture]. Survival status unknown, no distribution available.

Brackett, C. (Producer), and H. Koster (Director). (1955) (2008). *The Virgin Queen* [motion picture]. United States: 20th Century–Fox Home Entertainment.

Franklin, S. (Producer), and Sidney, G. (Director). (1953) (1994). *Young Bess* [motion picture]. United States: MGM/UA Home Video.

Graham, R. (Producer), and C. Whatham, et al. (Directors). (1971) (2001). *Elizabeth R* [television series]. London, England: BBC Video, distributed by Warner Home Video.

Korda, A. and E. Pommer (Producers) and W. K. Howard (Director). (1937) (2003). *Fire Over England* [motion picture]. United States: Genius Entertainment.

Lloyd, J. (Producer) and M. Fletcher (Director). (1986) (2001). *Blackadder II* [television series]. London, England: BBC Video, distributed by Warner Home Video.

Owen, A., E. Fellner and T. Bevan (Producers) and S. Kapur (Director). (1998) (2003).*Elizabeth* [motion picture]. United States: Universal Pictures Company.

Parfitt, D., et al. (Producers) and J. Madden (Director). (1998). *Shakespeare in Love* [motion picture]. United States: Miramax Home Entertainment, distributed by Buena Vista Home Entertainment.

Reisz, B. (Producer), and T. Hooper (Director). (2006). *Elizabeth I* [television series].New York: HBO Video.

Rutman, P. (Producer) and C. Giedroyc (Director). (2005). *Elizabeth I: The Virgin Queen* [television series]. Boston: Power BBC and WGBH Boston Video, distributed by WGBH Boston Video.

Sheppard, C. (Producer) and S. Potter (Director). (1992) (1999). *Orlando* [motion picture]. United States: Columbia TriStar Home Video.

Wallis, H. (Producer) and M. Curtiz (Director). (1940) (2005). *The Sea Hawk* [motion picture]. United States: Turner Entertainment Company, distributed by Warner Home Video.

Wallis, H.B. (Producer) and C. Jarrott (Director). (1972) (2007). *Mary, Queen of Scots* [motion picture]. United States: Universal Studios Home Entertainment.

Warner, J. L. (Producer) and M. Curtiz (Director). (1939) (2005). *The Privates Lives of Elizabeth and Essex* [motion picture]. United States: Turner Entertainment Company, distributed by Warner Home Video.

Zanuck, R.D. (Producer), and Burton, T. (Director). (2010). *Alice in Wonderland* [motion picture]. United States: Walt Disney Pictures Home Entertainment.

Zukor, A. (Producer), and Mercanton, L. (Director). (1912) (1995). *Les Amours de la Reine Élisabeth* [motion picture]. United States: Grapevine Video.

Index